# Left Politics and the Literary Profession

The Social Foundations of Aesthetic Forms

**The Social Foundations of Aesthetic Forms**

A series of Columbia University Press

*Critical Genealogies: Historical Situations for Postmodern Literary Studies,*
Jonathan Arac

*Advertising Fictions: Literature, Advertisement, and Social Reading,*
Jennifer Wicke

*Masks of Conquest: Literary Study and British Rule in India,*
Gauri Viswanathan

# LEFT POLITICS AND THE
# LITERARY PROFESSION

**EDITED BY**
## Lennard J. Davis and M. Bella Mirabella

COLUMBIA UNIVERSITY PRESS   New York

**COLUMBIA UNIVERSITY PRESS**   New York

COLUMBIA UNIVERSITY PRESS
New York   Oxford
Copyright © 1990 Columbia University Press
All rights reserved

Library of Congress Cataloging-in-Publication Data
Left politics and the literary profession / edited by Lennard J. Davis
and M. Bella Mirabella.
    p.   cm.—(The Social foundations of aesthetic forms series)
    Includes bibliographical references.
    ISBN 0-231-06566-3
    1. Criticism—United States—History—20th century.  2. American
literature—20th century—History and criticism—Theory, etc.
3. Literature—Study and teaching—Political aspects—United States—
History—20th century.  4. Politics and literature—United States—
History—20th century.  5. Right and left (Political science) in
literature.  6. Radicalism—United States—History—20th century.
I. Davis, Lennard J., 1949–   .  II. Mirabella, M. Bella.
III. Series.
PS78.L35   1990
801'.95'097309045—dc20        89-71265
                              CIP

Casebound editions of Columbia University Press books are Smyth-sewn
and printed on permanent and durable acid-free paper

Book design by Charles B. Hames
Printed in the United States of America
c 10 9 8 7 6 5 4 3 2 1

*This book is dedicated to the Radical Teacher Editorial Collective, whose continued work and involvement has been an inspiration and education to us over the past fifteen years.*

*We also dedicate the book to Peter Mirabella (1913–1986), whose kindness and love as a father still sustains us.*

# Contents

# Contributors

JULIE ABRAHAM, an assistant professor in English and Women's Studies at Emory University, is completing a study of narrative strategies in modern lesbian writing.

HÉCTOR CALDERÓN is associate professor of Hispanic studies and Chicano literature at Scripps College in Claremont, California. He is the author of *Conciencia y lenguaje en el "Quixote" y "El obsceno pajaro de la noche*. He has written numerous articles on Latin American and Chicano literature, co-edited *Chicano Literary Criticism: New Essays in Cultural Studies and Ideology,* and is currently completing *Contemporary Chicano Narrative: A Tradition and Its Forms.*

CONSTANCE COINER is assistant professor of English at the State University of New York, Binghamton. She is contributing editor to the *Heath Anthology of American Literature.* Her essay on Le Sueur and Olsen is part of a book to be published by Oxford University Press about women writers at the intersection of feminism and the Old Left.

LENNARD J. DAVIS is the author of *Factual Fictions: The Origins of the English Novel* and *Resisting Novels: Fiction and Ideology.* He is currently visiting associate professor of English at the University of Pennsylvania. His next book, to be published by Basil Blackwell, is entitled *From Performance to Text: Revolutions in Culture 1650–1850.*

KATE ELLIS is associate professor of English at Rutgers University, New Brunswick, N.J. She is the author of *The Contested Castle: Gothic*

*Novels and the Subversion of Domestic Ideology.* Professor Ellis is currently at work on a novel about the 1960s.

GERALD GRAFF is John C. Sheffer professor of English and humanities, author of *Professing Literature: An Institutional History,* and co-editor, with Michael Warner, of *The Origins of Literary Studies in America.*

BARBARA HARLOW is associate professor of English at the University of Texas at Austin. She is the author of *Resistance Literature* and *Barred: Women, Writing and Political Detention* as well as numerous articles on Third World literature.

LOUIS KAMPF is professor of humanities at Massachusetts Institute of Technology. A longtime activist in leftist political causes, he serves on the editorial collective of *Radical Teacher.* He has written books, articles, and reviews about politics, culture, literature, and sports.

PAUL LAUTER was co-editor of the first *Politics of Literature* and is currently coordinating editor of the new Reconstructing American Literature/D. C. Heath anthology. He is Smith professor of English at Trinity College, Hartford, Connecticut.

NELLIE Y. MCKAY teaches Afro-American literature at the University of Wisconsin, Madison. She is the author of *Jean Toomer, Artist: A Study of His Literary Life and Work* and the editor of *Critical Essays on Toni Morrison.* Her work in progress includes a study of twentieth-century Afro-American women's autobiography.

M. BELLA MIRABELLA is adjunct associate professor of English and humanities at the Gallatin Division of New York University. She is a member of the *Radical Teacher* collective and is working on a book on dance in English drama from 1550 to 1720.

RICHARD OHMANN is professor of English at Wesleyan University. He directs the Center for the Humanities and helps edit *Radical Teacher.* His recent book is *Politics of Letters.*

SUSAN GUSHEE O'MALLEY is an associate professor at CUNY-Kingsborough and chair of the *Radical Teacher* editorial collective. She edited *The Courageous Turk* and is currently working on editions of pamphlets by and about women written in England from 1560 to 1640.

LILLIAN S. ROBINSON is the author of *Sex, Class, and Culture* and *Monstrous Regiment,* and co-author of *Feminist Scholarship.* She has been awarded an ACLS Fellowship to study the aesthetics and politics of the literary canon. She is 1989–90 Citizen's professor of English at the University of Hawaii. Since 1989 she has been an Affiliated Scholar at Stanford University's Institute for Research on Women and Gender. She holds no regular academic position.

RICHARD RICH is the pseudonym of a teacher at a large western university.

ROBERT C. ROSEN teaches at William Paterson College in New Jersey; he is the author of *John Dos Passos: Politics and the Writer* and co-author of the forthcoming text *Literature and Society.*

PANCHO SAVERY is associate professor of English and American studies at the University of Massachusetts, Boston. His poems have appeared in several magazines, and he has published essays on Ezra Pound, Robert Creeley, Adrienne Rich, and John Berger. Recent publications include *Approaches to Teaching Ellison's Invisible Man,* an introduction to a new edition of Sauders Redding's *Stranger and Alone,* and an essay on Redding's *No Day of Triumph.* He is also writer and host of *Bridge to Writer,* seen on public access television throughout Massachusetts. He is manuscript editor of *Radical Teacher.*

CATHARINE R. STIMPSON is professor of English, dean of the graduate school, and vice-provost for graduate education at Rutgers University in New Brunswick, N.J. She is currently the editor of a book series for the University of Chicago Press and was the founding editor of *Signs: Journal of Women in Culture and Society.* A selection of her essays is entitled *Where the Meanings Are.* She is currently writing a book on Gertrude Stein for the University of Chicago Press.

# Introduction

The crisis on American campuses has no parallel in this history of the nation. This crisis has roots in divisions of American society as deep as any since the Civil War. The divisions are reflected in violent acts and harsh rhetoric, and in the enmity of those Americans who see themselves as occupying opposing camps. Campus unrest reflects and increases a more profound crisis in the nation as a whole. . . . We fear new violence and growing enmity. . . . If this trend continues, if this crisis of understanding endures, the very survival of the nation will be threatened.

—The President's Commission on Campus Unrest,
September 1970

The President's Commission on Campus Unrest, not exactly a revolutionary organization, had fairly dire predictions for the nation and the academic community in the fall of 1970. In a mere twenty years America, among other countries, has gone from a time of involvement and commitment in which the very fabric of state power was unraveling to an era in which the state has consolidated its strength, manufactured consensus, defused dissent, and raised high the ability of ideology to neutralize action and opposition.

For many of the readers and most of the authors of this anthology, the palpable political accomplishments of the 1960s remain as constant reminders of the way in which large numbers of people came together for political action with high hopes for a future that would be progressive, humanitarian, and just. No doubt there was a degree of naiveté to that mass involvement, but the political work done then has promoted a vision of equality and social responsibility that remains, even during the conservative swing that we are currently experiencing.

There are competing visions of the 1960s now. Many of our students long for the mass activism and widespread rebelliousness that they now can only imagine. At the same time, conservatives work at enforcing visions of that time as one of decadence, lawlessness, and ineffectuality. How we think about our past will also determine how we think about our future. The aim of this anthology is to assess the politics of literature as it has evolved over the past twenty years as the function of a particular time and place. We want to get a sense of where we have been and where we are going.

This anthology is born out of the gap between expectation and desire, between then and now. We have taken our impetus from Louis Kampf and Paul Lauter's collection of political writings, *The Politics of Literature: Dissenting Essays on the Teaching of English*,[1] published roughly twenty years ago. That was an anthology produced by the events of the 1960s. It was, as many of us remember, the first American book to try to consolidate the political insights of the New Left into the practice of literary criticism. Now such an attempt to combine politics and literature seems normal if not expected. Indeed, the chair of the National Endowment for the Humanities recently observed ruefully that "viewing humanities texts as though they were primarily political documents is the most noticeable trend in academic study of the humanities today. Truth and beauty and excellence are regarded as irrelevant."[2] Things have changed considerably when a certain practice of literary theory or of photography, in the case of Robert Maplethorpe, is seen, correctly or not, as a threat to the cultural apparatus of the state, while the kind of opposition cited by the 1970 President's Commission on Campus Unrest has been, to a certain extent, neutralized and marginalized.

The material conditions that brought about the original anthology are worth mentioning because they stress the difference between then and now. It was December of 1968. The prehistory constitutes an almost mythical chronology: the student sit-ins of 1960s and the organization by the Student Non-Violent Coordinating Committee (SNCC) of the Mississippi Freedom Summer, 1964; Berkeley 1965; and the Columbia strike of spring 1968. Kampf, Lauter, Florence Howe, and others informally decided to turn the December meeting of the Modern Language Association into an occasion for radical politics. One of the issues at hand was a move to ban future conventions from Chicago, the site of the repressive Democratic convention. Another was a demand that the MLA take a stand against the Vietnam War and against the repression of Eldridge Cleaver and Octavio Paz. It was in the middle of all this that Louis Kampf and two others, while putting up posters at the Americana Hotel in New York, were confronted by hotel officials and then actually arrested for the illegal posting of notices. If history repeats itself as farce, this reenactment of Luther's posting of the Ninety-Five Theses turned fantastically farcical as the MLA, galvanized into action, proceeded to elect Kampf as second vice-president. The "demands" all passed—except one to cut the American Author series, which was seen as an attack on scholarship itself. Out of that convention and other events came the impetus for a political movement in literary studies—and Kampf and Lauter's anthology was conceptualized along with the Radical Caucus of the MLA.

In the introduction to that anthology, the editors describe the state of the English profession in 1968 as one rife with bad feelings. English professors were defensive and apologetic about their profession and contemptuous of their students. Teachers experienced burnout and in general were filled with a sense of uselessness. One of the issues raised about this malaise was how the teaching of literature could be translated into political practice. How could English professors make their teaching politically relevant? But the main concern of radical teachers at that moment was not pedagogy but political activism. Teach-ins against the war, racism, and inequality were high on the agenda; reconceptualizing the teaching of literature and culture was not. Emotions were charged during those days. People seemed to know quite clearly what the issues were, where they stood, and what to do. There was an integration of emotion, intellect, and action directed toward an issue in which many profoundly believed.

Today that degree of involvement has lessened. There are certainly many issues around which university communities can and do rally: such as Central American, Middle East issues, nuclear weapons, the homeless, apartheid, the elderly, equal rights, gay rights, abortion and women's rights—few of which were major rallying points in the 1960s. Many active political groups from the 1960s and 1970s still survive. Groups like RESIST, NACLA, CISPES, Mobilization, Citizen Soldier, and others are active and provide rallying points for particular movements. Groups like this link local politics to worldwide struggles in keeping with New Left traditions. But the fact is that none of these groups or issues provides a single point to focus us and bring large groups of people together. Mass politics, for the most part, has moved back within party politics, back to community organizing and local issues—and so, for example, the Jesse Jackson campaign of 1988 was the major focus of mass progressive aspirations. But the election results show the limitations of leaving things to party politics.

Under the Reagan administration, some of the major progressive advances of the 1960s eroded, although many remain. We are watching the concerted efforts of the Right to repeal a range of progressive legislation, from women's rights to affirmative action to abortion. Social welfare programs have been radically cut back. Federal funds for housing, welfare, food supplements, and the enforcement of equal rights laws have been cut drastically. A new de facto censorship has appeared in government funding for the arts. While the American public, according to opinion polls, seems to remain consistently more liberal than its political leaders, it nevertheless supports conservative Republicans in high office. Conservative voices have become stronger and more effective, especially in the realm of education. The campuses themselves have been relatively quiescent politically. The issue of apartheid spurred campus activity and in some cases led not only to divestment but also the establishment of black studies programs. But by and large the American campus has seen a decrease in the number of black and Hispanic students over the past twenty years. And in many universities black studies programs are increasingly being cut or underfunded. Feminist activities are one of the few shining lights in campus politics. The activity that began, in many ways, on campus has continued there while making inroads in joining the campus to the community. Clinics for battered women and rape crisis centers have kept a lifeline going between academics and nonacademics.

These twenty years have been challenging for radical teachers. The period has been characterized by an increasing political ennui and apathy—and some students reflect this apathy while others are spurred to challenge it. Many of us have seen our students over the past fifteen years turn from the humanities, social sciences, teaching, and art to a seeming hardhearted and calculating dedication to professionalism. Many undergraduate literature majors are going into law and business, sometimes choosing the promise of wealth over social values. In recent years fewer and fewer law graduates are entering the public sector. Currently 61 percent of graduating lawyers enter private practice, as opposed to 50 percent ten years ago, according to the National Association for Law Placement. Of course, students' choices are influenced by material conditions; huge student loans make it difficult to choose lower-paying but more idealistic professions. Yet these choices seem to grow too out of a political and moral climate of conservatism and apoliticalism. Most notably missing is a sense of involvement in current affairs, a knowledge of history, and a feeling that citizens can do anything collectively to affect the state.

Although things may appear grim, there is hope. This anthology, while not expressly about student and teacher activism, addresses the concrete achievements of the radical Left in academia. There has been a substantial body of political scholarship assembled over the past twenty years that is available to the intellectual community. It is now possible to teach courses on gender, race, class, and ideology that would have been unthinkable twenty years ago. While educational criteria vary from the elite institutions to the community and two-year colleges, a radical perspective is not only possible but often expected as part of a curriculum. These are some positive accomplishments, but there is obviously a long way to go. Although institutions may permit a greater diversity in curricula reform, the tenure process still operates to guarantee that nonstandard thinkers will have a difficult time leaping through the institutional hoop of legitimation. Many recent examples indicate that leftists continue to be discriminated against on ideological grounds when tenure issues arise. However, it must be added that there is now a large feminist and Marxist presence on the campus, which is a legacy of the sixties. It is possible now for a leftist to be fired from one university and hired at another.

Intellectuals, however, have not generally succeeded in extending their work outside of the university community. There is a core of activists who organize to bring together theory and praxis. But much of what we see practiced in classes, writings, and conferences as Marxist or cultural criticism tends to focus on relatively abstract issues of language, power, and philosophy. The work of people like Jacques Derrida, Jacques Lacan, Louis Althusser, Luce Irigaray, Gilles Deleuze, Hélène Cixous, and Michel Foucault has been used to break down hierarchical notions of truth and meaning, to attack conceptions of a unified self that is outside of culture, and to combat the rigidity of disciplines and discourses. The insights of these thinkers have largely been gained by applying to various spheres of knowledge the revelations of post-Saussurian linguistics, or opposing those revelations. The work of Jürgen Habermas focuses not so much on language but on communication. Nevertheless, all of these writers claim that their work can help to destabilize categories of knowledge and overthrow hierarchies of knowledge, and so destabilize the power relations of hierarchical societies. But the question remains, for leftist literary criticism, how to bring the insights of that work into the hands of larger numbers of people—if such a project is even remotely feasible.

In putting a division in this way between language-centered theory and political activity, we do not want to create an artificial and simplistic separation between theory and praxis. Nor do we want to encourage "theory bashing." In fact when we, the editors of this work, circulated early drafts of this introduction, we found that our position was attacked on both sides—for being anti-intellectual, by our colleagues who did theory, and as justifying "Lacan-speak," by our comrades who centered their work on activism and radical pedagogy. A question we asked ourselves was: does this double-edged response mean the literary Left has become so polarized that an attempt to assert positively that theory and praxis have a place in contemporary education is doomed to occupy an insidious middle ground?

In fact, education will have only achieved its goal when theory and praxis are integrated again, as they were, to an extent, in the late 1960s and early 1970s. This anthology is perhaps a very modest nod in that direction. We have combined in these pages the writings of both those who regard language-based theories as central and those who think such theories are moving us away from a politics of praxis. Anthologizing makes strange bedfellows, and this convergence is perhaps only forged by the glue that holds the pages of this book together. Yet the achievements of radical scholarship are laid out here for examination. Black, Hispanic, Palestinian, feminist and cultural studies, do constitute a praxis. One of the areas over which some of our contributors would differ is the impact and significance of what has come to be called *theory* in the study of literature. The original *Politics of Literature* paid scant if any attention to this kind of theory. What was floating around in the early 1970s as theory in America was mainly structuralist methodology along with the beginnings of a poststructuralist approach characterized by the early translations of Derrida. As Kampf and Lauter say clearly in their introduction:

> This book has no domestic samples of the latest Marxist, structural, and Freudian modes so popular in French intellectual circles; it has no philological research on left-wing authors of the 1930s; there is no ideological analysis of an Odets play; nor do we include a survey of the political content of contemporary literature.[3]

Less than twenty years later, this anthology contains articles that do all of those things—more or less. What interested the original editors was the space they carved out as "the specific social effects of literature.'"[4] For them, at the time, the social effects of literature did not require any fancy French intellectual idea juggling.

Kampf and Lauter rejected theory as something that could keep people from realizing these social effects or engaging in political activity. It would not be accurate to say that the New Left had no predisposition to theory. The Port Huron statement of SDS was in some ways a theoretical document. The notion of a preordained theory that would be applied to a political problem was itself an issue questioned by the New Left. The work of Mao particularly emphasized that theory would have to evolve from praxis. And praxis was revolutionary political activity in a specific place at a specific time. The New Left read and used the works of Lenin, Marx, Che Guevara, and others who saw an evolution to the theoretical from the concrete—not the other way around.

What then constituted the New Left's agenda? George Katsiaficas, in *The Imagination of the New Left: A Global Analysis of 1968*, lists five "primary defining characteristics of the global New Left"[5] which, while arbitrary, might give us a way of summarizing the political position of groups that loosely fit under the general rubric of the times. These are:

1. Opposition to racial, political, and patriarchal domination, as well as to economic exploitation achieved through a decentralized, nonhierarchical movement.
2. The development of a concept of cultural freedom, not merely freedom from material deprivation. This involves personal liberation and also the freedom to create new human beings—a cultural freedom.
3. The extension of the democratic process and the rights of the individual.
4. An enlarged base for revolution including the middle class, students, and the *Lumpenproletariat*.
5. An emphasis on direct action.

If we apply these criteria to academic politics today, we can see that much of what has transpired is part of the legacy of the New Left, but it is instructive to see which criteria no longer apply. The notion of extending the Marxist critique from sheer economic analysis to racial, political, and patriarchal issues is clearly central to the political agenda of the 1980s. Linked to this is an emphasis on culture, not in the sense of a development of new cultural paradigms (rock music, be-ins, "alternative" life-styles) but rather on uncovering the radical tradition of bypassed cultures—that of women, slaves, the folk, and so on. While cultural criticism is based on a notion that extends the democratic process and the rights of individuals, its mission has centered on extending consciousness through education, and not on direct action for, say, voters' rights, collective bargaining, the redistribution of benefits, and so on. The last two of Katsiaficas' categories—revolution and direct action—have hardly been the priority of literary theory.

What we can say in general is that theory has mainly engaged itself with the refractions of consciousness and power—largely using language-centered paradigms as explanatory modes. Much of structuralist, deconstructionist, ideological, and postmodernist thought has centered first on Saussure's work, then on the complications of subjecting that work to the lens of philosophy, as in the work of Foucault, Althusser, Lacan, and Derrida, and then on the use of communication theory in the work of Habermas and his followers. These innovations have been popularized by Terry Eagleton and Fredric Jameson, among others, who also linked up British pragmatic thought, in the form of Raymond Williams' work, with that of the Frankfurt school and deconstructionist methodology. This core of language-centered thought was then used, reacted against, incorporated, or discarded by emerging groups like women, blacks, Third World peoples, and so on. Revolution in language theory is rarely seen now as a viable option for shaping theory, and direct action has often been put on the shelf in favor of intellectual action in the form of analysis.

Of course, the current moment in America can hardly be seen as revolutionary. It is difficult to imagine how theory could emerge from revolutionary activity now. The very same questions now not only require but demand that "the specific social effects of literature" be conducted, at least in part, in the realm of theoretical discussion. The work of Raymond Williams, Terry Eagleton, and others has provided a set of arguments and a rationale for the study of the social effects of literature. As the recent decade of discussion about ideology indicates, there has been a wide dissemination of the idea that literature as well as popular culture have profound social effects; at the same time, the difficulties of assigning those effects, of arguing for the philosophical and epistemological assumptions surrounding the terrain of ideology, threaten perhaps to make that area almost impossible to translate into action.

The attitude of the radical literary academics of the 1960s was defined by their activism. As Kampf and Lauter note, the scholars whose essays are in their anthology cut their teeth on the bars of jail cells and not on the rigid covers of books out of France.

Nearly all the contributors to this volume are people who have themselves been deeply transformed by the events of the past ten years: most of them have spent short periods in jail; nearly all have committed acts of civil disobedience in protest against the war and domestic oppressions; some participated in the Columbia and Harvard strikes; several have been fired for political reasons, and at least two cannot currently obtain teaching work; another is under suspension and facing academic trial. Some worked in the civil rights movement in Mississippi, teaching black grammar-school children; others in community organizing projects, working with high school kids, in draft resistance, Students for a Democratic Society (SDS), the New University Conference (NUC), women's liberation, the Revolutionary Union, and so forth.[6]

This description is meant to convey an activist set of degrees. The gap between then and now is obvious. Rather than being thrown in jail these days, some leading feminists and Marxists find themselves rewarded with high-paying jobs at prestigious institutions, while others are fired from universities for espousing the same politics.

The insights of Kampf and Lauter might now be seen as the beginnings of ideological theory—although they eschew the term. They suggested that the tradition from Matthew Arnold to New Criticism amounted to a "domestication of literature for the middle classes by institutionalizing the critical function as part of the school curriculum".[7] Terry Eagleton develops this point in his book *The Function of Criticism*. But Lauter and Kampf restrict all criticism to the legitimizing function of "certifying college and university teachers".[8]

Clearly, when we look at the literary criticism of the early 1960s we can see, at least within the American university, a set of limits defined by a blend of New Criticism and humanistic aesthetics. That blend may be seen as a legacy of the cold war years. Typical of critical apparatuses in that period was perhaps the *Twentieth Century Views* series edited by Maynard Mack of Yale University made up of one anthology of essays for each of the major canonical texts or authors in English literature. This series embodied the ultimate function of criticism—the critical apparatus as adjunct to the university education system. The books were designed exclusively for undergraduate English majors and doctoral candidates as a *viaticum* through the underworld of the literary profession. The notion behind these books was that they helped in the writing of papers—a sort of intel-

lectual *Cliff Notes*. The essays basically fit into New Critical modes—
analysis of voice, ambiguities, plot structure, and so on. The ways in
which the politically conservative bias of New Critics ended up in-
forming their own methodology with its emphasis on individual readings and atomized analyses of texts is now widely understood. The
essays in Mack's series deal almost exclusively with the works of white,
Protestant males; where female authors are considered, the essayists
themselves are still primarily white males. Virtually absent and un-
considered are historical circumstances, the social function of literature, the role of women, and the political consequences of such works
and of their tradition. For instance, the *Twentieth Century Views of
Joseph Conrad*, published in 1966, includes essays on the originality
of Conrad, on narrative voice in *Nigger of the Narcissus*, on Conrad's
style, and so on. The one essay on political issues, written by Jocelyn
Baines, entitled "*Nostromo*: Politics, Fiction, and the Uneasy Expa-
triate," dwells mainly on Conrad's hopelessness about political solutions to any problem. Nowhere are issues of colonialism and power
evident. After all, the aim of this series was to help readers appreciate
the greatness of these canonical works and to demonstrate the un-
relenting complexity and sheer brilliance of the authors. If that was
the state of American criticism, then when issues of relevance came
up in the 1960s, it was obvious that such criticism was profoundly
irrelevant.

Criticism has been redefined since then. Although it is possible to
see criticism as still primarily confined to the analysis of specific texts,
the subject has been radicalized by the very features that Kampf,
Lauter, and others brought forward. The inadequacy of the purely
formal New Criticism, particularly when set against the radical politics of the 1960s, led to the development of a more formally elaborated set of questions about the nature of the relationship between
literature and politics. The ideological nature of the seemingly neutral and scientific New Criticism became an area of scrutiny, and the
role of that kind of activity, along with the biographical and the literary-historical, came under criticism.

What has happened since then is a complex set of affairs which
one can only suggest, and perhaps which we all know intuitively. As
Gerald Graff's paper in this anthology points out, theory has come to
be the area in which we can in fact talk about all those issues that
radicals had thought should be discussed in the university in the interests of relevance.

It is significant that the current emphasis on theory came to us not so much from some pipe-smoking dons in tweeds but from a source that emerged during the 1960s: "women's liberation." The action-oriented thrust of the women's movement's first wave, described in this anthology by Kate Ellis, gave way to a phase that needed a theoretical foothold beyond the simple assertion that women were equal to men and should be treated as such. For better or worse, the structural and theoretical concerns from France gave a form and a function to the feminist intellectual struggle. The legacy of that association is seen in the theoretical spine of women's theory today—the writings of Kristeva, Irigaray, Gallup, Spivak, and others. Whether such a poaching from the French was wise or not is largely irrelevant to the fact that for one to be a feminist in the university orbit one must now be at least familiar with such arguments. Ellis' discussion, while contending with the Lacanization of feminism, is still forced to circle around the theoretical concerns raised by Lacan and his American interpreters, detractors, and synthesizers.

One of the issues central to the radical critique of the 1960s continues now in full force, and that is the reconstruction of the canon. Paul Lauter's essay in this anthology is devoted to his analysis of how far this work has proceeded and some of the political problems inherent in revising the canon. It is in this area that the diverse concerns of the Left have come together. Like Jesse Jackson's grandmother's patchwork quilt, feminist, gay and lesbian, black, Hispanic, Marxist, Third World, and other emergent groups come together and agree on the need to reform—or abolish (if that is possible)—the canon. But the issue raised in the 1960s of modifying the canon has now become an area that needs the assistance of theoretical speculation. The problem now is that since so many groups are deemed part of a new tradition, how can we avoid thinking of the canon as a kind of special interest wish-list. To truly reform our tradition we first must decide what our tradition is, and such a decision is perforce bound up with changing the notion of tradition. It may turn out, as Gerald Graff suggests here, that the university, in the name of a common tradition and curriculum, prevents us from engaging in the truly meaningful intellectual struggles that would be involved in wrestling with the political agenda behind any idea of a curriculum or a tradition.

As part of a synthesis of theory and praxis, activists from various excluded groups now can and do turn to theory for orientation and support—although what they get may be support of a wobbly kind. Theory has become a quasi-location in the public sphere where radical questions about knowledge and power can be asked. Terry Eagleton's definition of criticism as essentially asking the question "How do I find my way around here?" is a good one. While the forms of criticism attacked by Kampf and Lauter would answer by handing you a map to the continent of canonical, dominant culture, contemporary theoretical approaches might only spin you around a few times and let you find your way. Thus, Eagleton would see criticism as a process of questioning dominant ideals and overturning at least intellectual hierarchies.

Obviously, there are problems with this nonprescriptive theory. It is not unified. It raises more questions than it answers. It is geared to questions of epistemology and interpretation, demystification and analysis rather than to a programmatic vision of who to attack and how to do so. As a location in the public sphere, it is a back room in a fairly exclusive supper club. Discussion is not open to all, even if all want to get in. And all do not want to get in.

Criticism is no longer the monolithic entity that it once was. Theory and criticism are now plural. There are theories; there are criticisms. This very fact may infuriate some, because it implies that the centrality of a consensual notion of what constituted Marxism is no longer possible. If there are many theories, then perhaps there are none—since there is no regnant paradigm by which one can galvanize direct action. Yet it is the very emphasis that the New Left put on decentralizing and breaking down hierarchical party politics that may in part have led to this pluralization of theory. This movement away from dogmatic centralism seems to be the political legacy of the New Left as it is working its way through contemporary global politics. In socialist and leftist governments throughout the world from Nicaragua to Eastern Europe and West Germany we are seeing experimentations in the spirit if not the letter of the Marxist tradition.

This anthology has had to reflect, much more than did the Kampf/Lauter edition, the diversity in criticism that exists today. There is now feminist criticism, black and Third World readings of literature, now Marxist, Marxist-structuralist, Marxist-structuralist-feminist, lesbian and gay, reader response, Lacanian, deconstructionist, poststructuralist, and postmodernist criticisms. Of course, there was diversity before, but the academy has now at least putatively opened its doors to many more emergent groups, and each of these groups feels the need for a theoretical justification. Of course, the very fact of theories as opposed to theory is ultimately part of the contemporary problem. We do lack a central analysis, but to bemoan this fact is to deny contemporary reality. We may wish that there were a universal drumbeat to which we might all march, but for now the long march is made up of a series of short, interconnected ones.

It may well be that this efflorescence of criticism and theory corresponds to the decline of activism in America—that as theory becomes less dangerous its best-known practitioners start to rank among the highly paid elites of the university. Is it possible that the culture at large really wants to pay its greatest enemies? Or is it some fluke of liberal humanism's respect for the ideology of free speech that is responsible for the ensconcing of radical thinkers in the university? Or again, theory may be the great escape valve that keeps radicals off the streets.

The reality is that leftist theorists are only marginally dangerous to society. If they were more so, we would see greater repression. The denial of NEH grants, nontenurings, and so on only show us that the homeostatic system is functioning well as a self-regulating set of checks and balances. Yet it cannot be denied that the scholarly work of last twenty years has had some effect in shoring up one aspect of leftist political struggle. There have been very few modern political movements that did not have in some central way a theoretical articulation. Of course, there is some distance between literary criticism and political theory. Yet during the last twenty years of cultural criticism it has seemed less and less important to make distinctions between the literary, the cultural, and the political. Rather, the important activity has been to trace their interconnections. Of course, it is possible to see the growth of criticism as mere wheel spinning and professionalization, which to a degree it no doubt is; at the same time, however, theory is also the articulation of political problems, the debate and counterdebate, the raising of issues, and the politicization of the academic and art world—all of which has had a central role in clarifying and accenting the problems of living in administered and capitalist societies. Intellectuals in capitalist, Socialist, and Communist countries are all using contemporary theory to articulate an international vision of the role of art and culture.

At the same time, the danger to us all is that criticism will become an increasingly rarefied discourse, separated from all of lived experience—that only students of criticism will understand it, that it will become simply a highly encoded professional language like the language of doctors or plumbers. We may well ask whether this kind of criticism is part of a viable attack on inequality and injustice, or whether it is only an escape valve that allows intellectuals and college students to mouth off and then go about their business.

The answer to such questions will ultimately be based on the uses of theory, since theory is finally a tool and space for discussion, not an object in any sense. Part of the confusion surrounding theory comes from its reification. As an activity within a consumer culture, criticism risks, as do all activities, becoming commodified. That is, relations between people get turned into objects under capitalism, and theory has suffered to a certain extent by being turned from a process between people into an object. Even the word *theory* constitutes part of this process of objectification. There is no object called *theory* but rather a set of social relations. Those social relations must always be included in the analysis to be truly dialectical.

The fact remains that over the past twenty years there has been a huge amount of intellectual stockpiling. Consider the collective intellectual data that has been amassed during this period in libraries in the interests of a radical perspective. It is true, as some of the personal statements at the end of this anthology testify, that many radicals have found sanctuary in the university. Their raw activism has been translated into bodies of knowledge that provide the framework for political debates and for establishing criteria of judgment. It is probable that very few relevant radical studies are being done in Russian or Chinese universities at this time. European and American universities centrally provide the historical, sociological, and cultural analyses and data that facilitate progressive ways of thinking about the world and its problems.

In editing this new anthology, we have been inspired by some of the same concerns as those of the Kampf/Lauter anthology—notably feminist issues and the revision of the canon. But the past twenty years have produced different issues. In addition to theory, we have paid more attention to the issues of blacks and minorities, particularly black women writers, non-Western literary criticism, and so on. Indeed, it is the very diversity of critical interests, the opening up of the university and the canon to those who have been left out, that has created the contemporary state of the politics of literature. That state is, at its best, diverse, multilithic, and nonhierarchical. This characteristic of the literary scene is shared in the fields of history, architecture, art history, and sociology. A recent article in the *New York Times* concerning the annual meeting of the American Sociological Association pointed out this very dilemma. "Some proclaim this [diversity] as a new richness and openness for a field that attempts to explain how society functions. Others see it as an aimless drift, a kind of special interest sociology created by the generation that came of age in the 1960's and is still trying to get its political point of view across."[9]

The individual authors of the essays in this anthology do not constitute a roundup of the usual suspects. Whenever a conference about politics and literature is organized, we tend to see the same names. Here too a canon is forming in the area of leftist scholarship. We have attempted to include essays that are of value to readers, without stressing the "star" factor. And the aim of this work is not simply to contribute to the ongoing debate over literary theory but to assess what is happening in the practice, teaching, and study of literature. In this sense, our goal in putting together this anthology was to focus on the link between the radical politics of the 1960s and the intellectual activities of radicals who study literature in the 1990s and into the coming century.

We have tried to be sensitive to the multilithic nature of the political moment. Thus we have leftist, feminist, lesbian, Palestinian, Chicano, and black literary criticisms as examples of the pluralization of the study of literature. Obviously, there are more and more varied examples of such diversity, and we had to leave out—by necessity—many of these. We could have included Judaic, Native American, Chinese- and Japanese-American, and other criticisms. Absence here is not a reflection of lack of importance but of logistics and happenstance.

So, when added up, these essays are ones that mainly focus on issues of feminism, canonicity, and theory; they assess the past and look toward the future. They ground themselves in the radical political movements of the last three decades, but they push up from these roots toward a flowering of intellectual accomplishments. The apparent consolidation of conservative political power that has been characteristic of the 1980s provides us with a specific object that demands opposition. However much the objective conditions resist opposition, the presence of a viable intellectual Left on campus offers one facet of a hope for an extension of rights and power in the coming century.

### Endnotes

1. Louis Kampf and Paul Lauter, *The Politics of Literature: Dissenting Essays on the Teaching of English* (New York: Random House, 1971).
2. *New York Times*, September 13, 1988, p. 15.
3. Kampf and Lauter, p. 8.

4. *Ibid.*
5. George Katsiaficas, *The Imagination of the New Left: A Global Analysis* (Boston: South End Press, 1987), p. 22.
6. Kampf and Lauter, p. 9.
7. Kampf and Lauter, p. 17.
8. Kampf and Lauter, p. 19.
9. *New York Times,* August 30, 1988, p. B1.

# ONE

## THEORETICAL CONSIDERATIONS

*The two essays in this section deal not with the issues at the heart of the language-centered literary theory, a theory that makes up the major practice of criticism in our time, but with theoretical discussions of the practice of teaching, university policy, and the consequences of literary studies. The decision not to include examples of Foucaultian, Althusserian, Habermasian, Deleuzian, or Jamesonian criticism was made not so much to exclude a particular mode of leftist criticism but because examples of that kind of work abound in many other excellent anthologies and journals. The aim here was to focus on the institutional and practical aspects of the politics of literature. This area is a relatively underrepresented one for leftist theory in higher education. A few works, like David Livingstone's anthology Critical Pedagogy and Cultural Power,[1] open the subject, but much leftist analyses of education are done on the kindergarten through twelfth grade levels. This section, however brief, allows Gerald Graff to deal with questions of university pedagogy. Richard Ohmann subjects to scrutiny the project of literary criticism as practiced in the university.*

### Endnote

1. David Livingstone, ed., *Critical Pedagogy and Cultural Power* (South Hadley, Mass.: Bergin and Garvey, 1987).

# 1

# Why Theory?

## Gerald Graff

*Gerald Graff tries to situate theory in a political context by placing it squarely in the center of a debate about university curriculum. That debate arises from the interventions of Allan Bloom, William Bennett, and other conservatives who maintain the sanctity of teaching the greatness of Western civilization. Graff begins with a practical notion of theory as "what breaks out when the rationale for the community's practices is no longer taken for granted." This notion of theory as tied to community, communication, and consensus strikes an activist note. Graff then goes on to show how resistance to theory is really a derriere-garde move to uphold a false consensus of community values and norms. The stress on diversity in the university curriculum then becomes a kind of "vapid pluralism" that mimics the liberal model of "diversity." This pluralism holds universities and departments together with a false bond that works because of the enforced absence of debate. The ultimate goal is the transmission of a hoped-for unified culture, which in reality is becoming less and less tenable.*

Let's start with a typical case. A colleague says that a certain poem is better than some other poem. You disagree, and the two of you start to debate the matter. Once the debate reaches a certain point, you will find that in order to make headway on the question of which is the better poem, you have to get into a dispute about another kind of question; what concepts of poetry the two of you are working with and whether you mean the same thing by "good"—the chances being fairly strong that you do not. The more the two of you pursue your debate the more you are likely to find your attention diverted from the poems themselves to the question of what you mean by "poetry" and poetic value.

More than likely, too, in pursuing your disagreement over the value of the poems you will find yourselves disagreeing about what they mean. Just as you were diverted from the poems themselves to the concepts of poetry and poetic value, discussing the poems' meanings will force you to discuss what you mean by poetic meaning and how interpreters can determine it. Again, you will have been diverted from the poems and their meanings to questions about how poems mean and about how we talk about how poems mean, and perhaps eventually to questions about how we talk about how we talk about how poems mean, and so on.

Finally, let us suppose that your dispute carries over into such questions as the respective qualifications of the two poems to be included in the literary canon and taught in high schools and colleges. Should either poem be taught, and if so how should it be taught, emphasizing what aspects and why? What are the poems' relations to literary history? How are they related to past or present culture? What, if anything, do they "mean to us today"? Clearly such questions will have taken you even further from the poems themselves and into issues of educational, cultural, and social theory, into history and sociology and philosophy.

There are numerous ways to describe what has happened here, but one way would be to say that "theory" has broken out. Starting out wishing to debate the value of two particular poems, you found yourselves uncertain about what premises you shared, and your uncertainty about common premises caused you to shift your attention from the poems themselves to the theory of poetry and to theories of value, interpretation, education, canonicity, and culture. The fact that you could not take for granted any consensus on first principles made it impossible to discuss particular literary works without being drawn into matters of theory. Does this, then, mean that discussion of the poems themselves is forever put on hold? No, but it means that the terms of that discussion will reflect the disputed nature of the conversation about poetry in our time.

I have constructed this hypothetical anecdote in order to illustrate what seems to me to have been happening lately in the criticism and teaching of literature. A state of affairs arose in which those who think of themselves as members of a literary culture found that they disagreed radically on first principles. This climate of disagreement generated a theoretical metadiscourse that has shifted attention from works of literature themselves to questions about the nature of literature and its conditions of creation, reception, and cultural dissemination, or that has made it more necessary, when speaking of works of literature themselves, to take into account the cultural and philosophical conditions of the discussion. As this theoretical metadiscourse has developed, it has generated its own internal disputes, which have come to seem increasingly more "meta." Not surprisingly, this trend provokes the complaint that there is too much talk about theory and not enough about literature.

The complaint is understandable, yet notice what tends to result from it. Does it return us to the poems themselves? On the contrary, the outcry against theory only adds to the theoretical controversy. For the outcry against theory is itself a kind of theory, and only adds to the sort of metadiscourse about assumptions, values, and principles that it wants to avoid. All of which gives confirmation to one of the central contentions of recent theorists, that as teachers, critics, and readers we are always theorists, whether we acknowledge it or not, for we cannot talk about literature or culture (or anything) without making theoretical choices. As Fredric Jameson puts it, "every form of practice, including the literary-critical kind, implies and presupposes a form of theory; that empiricism, the mirage of an utterly nontheoretical practice, is a contradiction in terms; that even the most formalizing kinds of literary or textual analysis carry a theoretical charge whose denial unmasks it as ideological. Unfortunately, such a position . . . must always be reargued and refought."[1] In other words, opposition to theory, whether in the name of tradition or of the concreteness of literature itself, is one theoretical choice among others. The belief that theory is optional, that you can decide either to take it or leave it alone, is just a way of refusing accountability to theoretical disagreement.

I am using the word theory here to denote any discourse about the presuppositions and principles that underlie our practices. For example, if one says, "Please pass the salt," one is not in most circumstances talking theoretical discourse, as one normally is if one asks, "What kind of speech act is 'Please pass the salt'?" or "What are the conditions that enable 'Please pass the salt' to have meaning?" (I say "in most circumstances" and "normally," because whether any statement is classed as theoretical or nontheoretical depends not on the properties of the statement itself, but on how it functions in a context, whether reflexively or nonreflexively. One could imagine contexts in which an utterance like "Please pass the salt" functioned to "defamiliarize" the discussion in which it appeared; for example, imagine a Beckett or Pinter character saying it with deflating or ironizing effect in the middle of a windy philosophical dialogue. Nor are such contextual determinations—does this count as "theory" or doesn't it—clear-cut or undebatable, but I pass over this problem here.)

By this definition, whereby "theory" denotes any examination of the assumptions underlying practice, theory encompasses Aristotle, Sidney, Johnson, Arnold, Trilling, Wilson, and Leavis as much as Umberto Eco, Julia Kristeva, and Jacques Derrida. In other words, we have always had theory, and with it a certain jargon that sets itself at a reflexive distance from common-sense practice. Those who attack current theory for its jargon never bother to ask whether Aristotle's *Poetics* is freer of jargon and more intelligible to lay readers than *Of Grammatology*. This is not to say that there is no fundamental difference between the theoretical climate of Aristotle and of the present, only that we do not want so to reify this difference that traditionalists remain permitted to think that traditionalism is not itself a theory.

Such a definition of theory, as a discourse that formulates and debates the assumptions underlying practices, is itself controversial to an extent that I can't take into account here, except to make two points. First, it goes against an established, but I think currently fading, tendency to think of "theory" as a foundational discourse that produces the necessary and sufficient rules on which practices are grounded. In this definition, in other words, which is the one assumed by many of those who currently attack theory, the word *theory* means something like *system*. It is understood as a set of a priori principles that formulate the essential nature of "art," "literature," "interpretation," "language," and other practices. In this uppercase conception of theory, as we might call it, Theory is seen as a medium not just for describing and mediating what is at stake in disputes, but for definitively settling them. It is not just a way of posing questions; it is also a set of answers to them.

It was this "foundationalist" view of theory that dominated the Anglo-American New Criticism, Russian Formalism, and early structuralism, and that has unevenly persisted into the present period. This helps explain why this foundationalist view of theory is the target of current critics of theory, whether they be traditionalists like Frederick Crews, pragmatists like Walter Benn Michaels and Steven Knapp, or deconstructionists like Paul de Man.[2] But this foundationalist concept of theory has increasingly given way to a less prescriptive, low-ercase concept in which "theory" denotes any second-order reflection on practices, without foundationalist claims.

Secondly, even to speak of theory in a "lowercase" sense as I do here ignores the enormously heterogeneous activity that currently goes under the name "theory" as well as the internal antagonisms among current schools of theory, antagonisms that are often every bit as intense as those between theorists and antitheorists. In fact, it is possible that it is only the external hostility to theory from the Right, and the consequent need to close ranks against a common enemy, that has given theorists the feeling of belonging to a "movement." If this hostility were to cease, the world of theory would probably splinter into the myriad warring factions which, on another level, it already has.

I am bypassing these complications that are internal to the world of theory because they do not seem to me to discredit the larger point I am trying to make in this essay, which is that the current eruption of theory is an understandable outcome of a climate of radical disagreement. If this is correct, that the recent eruption of theory grows out of structural features of the dissensual culture we inhabit, then that trend is not likely to be a passing fad, as so many of the critics of theory think or hope.

To put it another way, "theory" is what breaks out when the rationale for the community's practices is no longer taken for granted, so that what could formerly "go without saying" becomes an object of dispute, a dispute, moreover, that may lead to no final resolution. Once consensus breaks down, assumptions that could previously be taken for granted become one set of theories among others, ideas that you have to *argue for* rather than presuppose as given.

If what I have been saying is correct, then it is useless and counterproductive to complain about the displacement of literature by literary theory. For such a complaint is finally a complaint about the existence of disagreement. And nothing is more useless than complaining about the existence of disagreement—unless it is invidiously characterizing that disagreement as a symptom of nihilism, relativism, and the collapse of cultural standards. These complaints today represent a refusal to recognize that the consensus to which literary and intellectual culture could once appeal has been irreparably lost.

Take the current conflict between those who argue that reading and teaching literature should remain a primarily literary activity and those who argue that the very category of the "literary" is already necessarily political, that the very distinction between literature and ideology is itself deeply ideological, functioning as it has to the advantage and disadvantage of particular social groups. It is this conflict that underlies the controversy over the canon and the great books, where what is at stake is not simply which books students should read, but how they should read them. Here is but one instance of the deep division that has destroyed the once tacit agreement about what the study and teaching of literature is all about. What educational institutions should do about such a division is a problem, but merely condemning it as symptom of nihilism, relativism, or disintegrating standards is not a useful response to the situation.

This is not to deny that there are powerfully relativistic and nihilistic currents in recent literary and cultural theory. I believe that the relativism of much current advanced thought *is* a serious problem — it is a serious problem even though Allan Bloom says that it is a serious problem.[3] But is not necessarily relativism to recognize the existence of disagreements. A more familiar, less invidious word for this recognition is *democracy*. Presumably, a democratic culture is one in which questions about how we should think about major issues are always potentially up for grabs, negotiable among competing groups and viewpoints and not foreclosed by authority. Implicit in the idea of a democratic culture, in other words, is that *thought is an inherently political and contested activity*. This does not do away with the authority of professional expertise, but it means that the terms of expert authority are always open to challenge. This I take to be the message of current theory at its most democratic — that culture and the forms of argument and interpretation that take place about and in culture are inherently contested domains.

It is here that we touch on the sense in which the current situation is unprecedented, and in which it is finally misleading to say that earlier periods had their forms of "theory" just like ours, as if Aristotle, Johnson, and Leavis were continuous with Derrida and Jameson. To leave matters at that would fail to acknowledge what is unprecedented about the present moment, which I take it is not the emergence of theories, however, but the more deeply conflictual relation between theories, the lesser degree of unspoken common ground between them, and the "radical" force these theories attempt to have in relation to the assumed common sense of the general community.

Much of the current hostility toward theory — and the attendant outrage at revisions in the canon and new methods of interpretation — seems to me to express a refusal to accept this democratized situation, in which procedures, definitions, and categories that used to be the unquestioned province of those of a certain background have suddenly become open to negotiation and debate. Here, I am afraid, is what is making so many commentators angry about the changes that have been taking place in humanistic education: whereas these critics could formerly assume that their ideas about the study of literature would be the official ideas, they suddenly find themselves in a situation in which they have to *fight* for their ideas just like everybody else. The determination of what books are to be taught, and how, has ceased to belong by default to a relatively homogenous group and has been opened to a diversity of voices approximating the diversity of American culture.

This unprecedented situation can be traced to two concurrent developments since World War II: first, there has been a widely noted explosion of new forms of knowledge, which has so diversified the ways of thinking about intellectual inquiry that once agreed upon definitions of the academic and intellectual fields have been called into question. Second, education has undergone profound demographic changes since the aftermath of the war, as the democratization of American universities has reached truly mass proportions for the first time. Groups that before the war had been excluded or only marginally represented—women, Jews, blacks, and various immigrant subcultures—were then absorbed into the university in large numbers. (It is a fair guess that without this development at least three-fourths of those reading this essay—and certainly the writer of it—would not have attended a university, much less taught in it.) Of course it was not just a matter of raw demographics: it took the 1960s to provoke ethnic, racial, and sexual minorities to begin seeing their experience in specifically political terms.

The collapse of consensus on the ends and methods of the humanities (including the question of whether "the humanities" should be a privileged term), and the consequent theory explosion, have coincided exactly with these postwar changes. Consensus has collapsed and theory has emerged as the shape of the disciplines has been opened to dispute, and as previously marginal groups have reached the point where they could expect to have a say in how terms like "literature," "culture," and "cultural heritage" would be defined. Despite the many new dilemmas that have resulted, the collapse of the old consensus has been all to the good, for it was never more than a pseudo-consensus at best. The sooner our educators and public officials recognize that this condition is here to stay and stop wishing that theory and its explicit politicization of the humanities would just go away, the sooner we will be in a position to act productively.

But how? How should universities react to the openly conflictual social and political situation of literary studies? So far, they have reacted both admirably and ineptly at the same time. Universities have reacted admirably (with some disturbing exceptions) in defending the principle of ideological inclusiveness—often against severe counterpressures—and extending that principle to heretofore unrepresented groups, methodologies, and viewpoints. But universities have acted ineptly in failing to take advantage of the unprecedented state of increased dissonance that has resulted from this increased diversity. As both the Right and the Left complain, the university's only response to its conflicts tends to be a vapid pluralism which satisfies nobody very much.

Much of the problem lies in the university's traditions, which not only ill prepare it to deal with ideological conflict, but encourage it to view such conflict as an embarrassment instead of an opportunity. Traditionally, the university has thought of itself as the transmitter of a unified culture. Inherited wisdom says that the university must either stand for a consensus on what is most worth knowing and teaching or else it is intellectually bankrupt. For presumably it is only if the university represents a consensus that it can hope to transmit culture effectively. If educators cannot agree among themselves on the primary values and objectives of education, or so the traditional logic runs, how can they hope to represent themselves effectively to their already skeptical constituents? The more vulnerable the educators feel in the face of the public, the more inclined they are to think that their welfare depends on presenting a united front to the world. This reasoning may be understandable, but it becomes disastrous when the "united front" is unachievable except in undemocratic terms.

When the modern, professional university first emerged in the late nineteenth century, it was faced with a conflict between old humanistic traditions and new professional expertise. I have shown elsewhere (in *Professing Literature: An Institutional History*) that the modern academic humanities were founded on a marriage between traditionalism and professionalism, between the literary humanism of Matthew Arnold and John Ruskin and German philological science.[4] But this marriage was strained from the outset, a fact that can be seen in the antagonism that erupted right away between specialized research and humane appreciation—and thus between research and teaching—and that would later be repeated in the antagonisms between "scholars" and "critics" in the 1940s and theorists and humanists today. But this strained marriage could be held together as long as the social bonds between those who taught (and studied) literature were stronger than their disparities of taste and methodology.

The genteel man of letters (he was usually male) and the positivist research scholar may have disliked one another's ways of dealing with literature, but the two shared an unspoken sense of common loyalties that made them view each other as much the same kind of person. As much as each disliked the other's way of treating literature, early academic men of letters and early research professionals saw one another as civilized gentlemen, each fighting in his own way to uphold common spiritual values against a vulgar materialist society. The more the two recognized their common ends against the dominant American philistinism, the less it mattered that they differed about the ways in which these ends should be accomplished.

It is just this common background of unspoken goals and assumptions that no longer exists today, or is often on the defensive where it does exist. To take just one example, consider that most radical feminist critics differentiate themselves from traditional humanists not just in their methods of approaching literature, but in their whole conception of their social and institutional role. When it is suggested to such feminists that they share a common culture with their traditionalist colleagues, they point out, accurately enough, that "common culture" has usually meant a culture defined in male terms. The tacit social and cultural bonds that formerly prevented professional conflicts from assuming a radical character can no longer be appealed to in good conscience. (Which is why the genial nudge in the ribs, as if to say, "Come on, now, we're all in this together," no longer goes over.)

Here, then, is the impasse. The university has been increasingly forced to confront the fact that the unified, consensual culture it supposed it existed to transmit is no longer unified and consensual, and never really was. What does the university do? Unfortunately, the only response it is able to imagine is to hope that a new consensus can somehow be created. It is this hope that leads to the proliferation of official humanities committees and blue-ribbon panels, which are commissioned in order to redefine the knowledge most worth knowing and teaching. But here a familiar cycle of frustration sets in. If the panel is representative of the full range of ideological factions in the humanities, its conclusions only end up dramatizing all the more poignantly the divisions that the panel was formed to reconcile. Either it reaches no agreement on the ends of the humanities, or it reaches an agreement whose terms are so platitudinous ("excellence," etc.) as to be intellectually worthless, although not ideologically ineffective.

If, on the other hand, the panel is not representative of existing factions, whatever agreement it arrives at is instantly discounted by the
excluded parties as the ideology of a particular faction. The more intense the search for consensus becomes, the more clearly it illustrates
its futility.

Finding it impossible to resolve the university's conflicts, administrators instinctively feel that they have no choice but to try to neutralize conflicting factions by keeping them from coming into contact
with each other. Hence the great appeal of a privatized pluralism (often
as much to the Left as to the Right), which avoids confronting hard
choices by the simple device of appeasing conflicting parties and en-
couraging them each to go seperate ways. The assumed goal of
"administration" comes to be that of keeping faculty members isolated from one another lest an argument break out—this being something that nobody has ever figured out how to deal with. And one can
hardly blame such thinking as long as the university has no bureaucratic means of making productive use of its conflicts.

I have discussed elsewhere how the need to avoid conflict at all
costs is systematized in the "field coverage" model by which academic departments are organized.[5] In fact, the organization of universities and departments into "fields" was a crucial step in making
possible the shotgun wedding of traditionalism and professionalism
just described. By satisfying their conflicting demands, the field coverage mode of organization permitted those otherwise incompatible
partners to share the same household. It satisfied the research professional, since it organized the department in accordance with the most
up-to-date and efficient division of labor. But it also satisfied the humanist, who, although he still might gripe about overspecialization,
could feel that the sum total of a department's array of fields represented the cultural tradition.

The conflict of traditionalists and professionals was only one of
numerous conflicts of ideology and method that departments and
universities did not have to confront. As long as the business of a
department was to cover a series of fields by its research and teaching, the faculty was relieved of the need to air its methodological and
ideological differences, or even to be very much aware that the differences existed. By a mechanism strikingly reminiscent of the pro-
verbial invisible hand of laissez-faire economy, whatever was at stake
in the clash of approaches, values, and ideologies could be left to take
care of itself. In this respect—although the point cannot be pursued
here—the organization of the university only mirrored the larger

structures of conflict avoidance in American culture, where we still tend to think of "ideology" as a foreign word.

But the crucial feature of the field coverage model was the way it enabled new and even radically subversive fields to be added to the university without the need for the established fields to alter their outlook and behavior. Gary Waller has called it the "park-bench principle of curriculum change: when a powerful newcomer shows up, everyone on the bench shuffles over just a little to make room for the latest arrival. Occasionally, if things get a little crowded, the one at the end falls off—Anglo-Saxon, perhaps, or philology."[6] The beauty of the principle was that it enabled the department to be progressively "innovative" without changing its overall shape. New critical approaches—and new literatures for study—could be overlaid on the traditional approaches and literatures without the need to confront the resulting contradictions of ideology, much less make them an issue for students and other outsiders to be aware of.

In consequence literature departments became free to be as aggressively trendy as they pleased without jeopardizing their reputation as guardians of tradition! Deep polarizations formed, but since there was no structural necessity to confront them these polarizations never had to be noticed—except when hiring and tenure decisions rudely forced them into view. At that point, long repressed conflicts tended to erupt in open rage and antagonism, with their aftermath of backbiting and gossip. This failure to debate conflicts productively was then attributed to *innate* features of the professorial temperament rather than to institutional arrangements that might be changed. What would be the point of proposing structural changes, it was felt, when everyone knows that professors could never interact differently than they always have?

It should now be possible to see what all of this has to do with theory. Under the field coverage model questions of theory, which, as I suggested earlier, are forced into being by disagreement, have not had to be confronted and negotiated out in the open where students might find out about them. The avoidance of conflict has kept questions of theory from emerging into view, or has channeled those questions into the specialized theory courses which have now been established in order to cover the new field.

The conflict avoidance pattern that structures the relations of the faculty is reproduced in the curriculum and passed on to the students, who cover a sampling of research fields without being expected to be aware of the struggles that created those field divisions to begin with. The official fiction prevails that exposure to a representative number of fields adds up in the students' mind to humanism, or an appreciation of the cultural tradition. Nobody really believes that that happens in more than a minority of cases, but the fiction supports the pretense that a unified humanistic tradition is still intact. And reinforcing this pretense is the unspoken assumption that students should be exposed only to the *results* of the faculty's conflicts, not to the conflicts themselves. In effect, students are treated as children who must be protected from seeing their parents quarreling.

This is why, even today, when the conflicts of the humanities have reached a point of unprecedented polarization, it is only a small minority of students (mostly graduates) who are aware of their existence, and an even smaller minority who could give an account of what is at issue in them. Students encounter representatives of the conflicting positions all the time, but since they encounter them only separately they are prevented from recognizing that there is a conflict.

These practices can be defended on the ground that most students would only be bored by exposure to faculty conflicts, which are supposedly merely esoteric, technical, and professional. But this argument underrates the potential of students to be interested in academic intellectual culture, were they ever to experience it as a coherent text rather than the largely unreadable one that is now presented to them. For one might argue that in keeping its central conflicts from view, the university makes intellectual culture both less interesting and more confusing to students than it might otherwise be. The justly deplored incoherence of the humanities curriculum is usually blamed on the absence of consensus, but it would be more properly and usefully blamed on the absence of visible debate, which obscures the relations and differences among fields, positions, and methods and thus renders academic culture incomprehensible to outsiders.

The courses being taught at any given moment in a university form a potentially interesting and instructive conversation, but one that is never actualized in front of the students. This is because it is assumed that the left hand in a university faculty will naturally have no way of knowing what the right hand is doing, and is probably better off not knowing, lest differences emerge out in the open that no one party will be able to control. So the opportunity is missed to make constructive use of faculty differences—as opposed to merely laying them out as a series of discrete options for students to sample.

As an example, consider a recent article that reviews the past and present state of Columbia's Humanities A or "Lit Hum" course, one of the prototype courses in American General Education since its creation just after World War I, and a model for subsequent general education courses everywhere. Predictably enough, as the article brings out, questions have recently arisen about how the great books tradition of the course should be reconciled with the new ideas about the canon favored by the younger teaching staff.

Here, as reported in the article, was the outcome of the staff's debates:

> Some [faculty] maintained that everything depended on how the works were taught, not on which books were chosen for the syllabus, and enlightened teaching, however desirable, could never be legislated as long as the autonomy of the individual teacher and the sanctity of his or her classroom are assumed. Others insisted that only works written by women would satisfy the need that had been identified. Still others argued that the criterion ought to be not the sex of the author but the value and teachability of the work itself. . . . In a real sense, the somewhat revisionary syllabus for 1986–87, which is now being given a two-year trial, is a compromise solution that reflects the various pedagogical, political, and ideological concerns generated by the staff's internal and beneficial critique of the books we teach.[7]

No doubt the "compromise solution" described here has been successful at a certain level. But what if the "Lit Hum" staff had tried a different tack: what if, instead of seeking a compromise between its competing "pedagogical, political, and ideological concerns," the staff had looked for ways to put these very differences at the center of what the course is about?

In other words, instead of assuming that it had to submerge its ideological differences—as if they were obstructions to be got out of the way in order to teach the books, the Lit Hum staff might have viewed those ideological differences as a means of making the books more interesting and intelligible to students. No doubt individual members of the staff already do just this in their own sections of the course. But few teachers can fully represent ideological conflicts to their students by themselves alone. If ideological positions are formed in a larger conversation, then they depend on the presence of the countervoices to make themselves intelligible.

It is not mentioned in the article, but it would not be surprising if one of the questions of concern to the junior faculty of Lit Hum were what should be made of the fact that this prototype for all subsequent Western Culture courses was originally invented as a propaganda device for the American war effort in World War I. Specifically, it started out in the late years of the war as a course entitled "War Issues," whose explicit purpose, as Carol S. Gruber and Cyrus Veeser have pointed out, was to "inoculate young people against Bolshevism and other subversive doctrines," to quiet what one Columbia dean called "the destructive element in our society" and produce students "who shall be safe for democracy."[8] When Secretary Bennett and others today defend the basic Western Civilization course as an expression of universal values transcending politics, they conveniently forget (or perhaps do not know) that this course owes its origin to a wartime crusade, and that its originators never pretended that it should have nothing to do with politics.

Does this mean, then, that present-day Western Civilization courses like Lit Hum cannot help perpetuating nationalist and imperialist ideology? This is precisely the sort of question that is at issue in controversies over the canon such as those at Stanford (and presumably in the Columbia Lit Hum staff meeting described in the article). Whatever response one makes to this issue, my point is that it is the kind of issue that ought to be put in the forefront of courses like Lit Hum rather than buried in staff discussions out of student view. The controversy over the extent to which Western culture is a universal inheritance or the extent to which its universalist claims have masked class, race, and gender oppression is one of the central issues today in American culture, not to mention academic culture. Why shouldn't this controversy be used to give coherence to literary study?

Here would be a practical solution to the "great books debate" now raging across the land: teach the debate. The solution to the problem is to teach the problem.[9] The point would be to go beyond merely exposing students to a variety of different theories and interpretations, by initiating them into the ways in which an intellectual culture negotiates, transacts, and fights out such differences—which would sometimes but not always be antagonistic. One could imagine drawing students into the current canon debate, for example, by seeing it played out by different instructors, not as a discussion set apart from their reading of canonical and noncanonical texts, but as a context in which they would read both kinds of texts.

The aim would be to give coherence to the curriculum not by conforming it to a preestablished grand synthesis, but by drawing on the coherence already latent at a given moment in the unfolding professional and cultural conversation. Coherence would be created by coordinating and clarifying what faculties already do rather than by superimposing a model from the top and desperately hoping that everyone will conform to it.

Several departments have already begun to put these principles into practice, although their efforts are still in the planning and experimental stage, and the outcome remains to be seen. At Carnegie Mellon University, where both the English major and Ph.D. programs are oriented toward "Literature and Cultural Studies" (with strong ties to rhetoric), the starting point, according to chairman Gary Waller, is the recognition that in standard programs, despite the presence of "dedicated teachers, demanding courses, and thorough examinations," what students are not given "is the possibility of systematically problematizing their studies. . . . [They are given] little or no acknowledgement that the contents and structures of the discipline were not given categories but culturally produced, always under debate, always sites of complex struggle." The goal at Carnegie Mellon is "to bring into debate a host of epistemologies, distinctive methodologies, issues, problems, and challenges." Instead of "a polite pluralism" the department aims at "an acknowledged clash of paradigms, frameworks, languages, and methodologies, with an understanding that . . . some will not survive the battle or that we will find ourselves led into conversations we didn't expect."[10]

At Syracuse University, where the literature curriculum is in the process of being restructured around the rubrics of Composition and Cultural Rhetoric, Creative Writing, and English and Textual Studies, the department, according to a joint statement, starts from the recognition that in standard programs "faculty may disagree profoundly," but

> even though students may find out about those disagreements by chance as they move from course to course, the curricular structure implies that it is more important to master certain predesignated works organized by genres, periods, and authors, than to inquire into the grounds of such categories or into the ends and means of reading. Ideally a new curriculum would shift this emphasis without simply reifying a fashionable methodology or settling for a vapid pluralism as a way of defusing disagreements. At Syracuse, we have tried to construct such a curriculum, one that foregrounds differences among modes of critical practice, acknowledges its own provisionality, and looks to its own future transformation.

Given the diverse orientations within the department—humanist, Marxist, feminist, new historicist, semiotic, rhetorical, psychoanalytic, deconstructive—the Syracuse department sees it as its task "to place these various stances in some productive relation to one another without simply writing off traditional positions, and to accomplish this in a situation in which even key terms like 'contestation' were subject to radically different understandings."[11]

Two things should be obvious from these descriptions. First, to move in this new direction means frankly accepting the inevitability of a "politicized" university, but in the sense not of a university that is an instrument of a single political faction, but of a university that recognizes that it is inevitably a site of ideological conflict and that, instead of shrinking from this fact, uses it as a structuring principle. Second, although the new direction takes much of its inspiration from the 1960s, its spirit is fundamentally different from the touchy-feely permissiveness that trivialized the educational thinking of that decade. The point is not to relax rigor and standards but to make education *more* rigorous, by asking students to take an active part in an intellectual conversation that we do not really expect them to participate in now.

In all of this I have so far merely assumed that the university could be changed without a concurrent change in the society that it reflects. But one might ask whether it is realistic to think that we could change the structures of conflict avoidance in the university while more pervasive structures of conflict avoidance in American culture at large remain intact. My only response is that it is easier to imagine changing the structure of the university than to imagine changing the structure of American culture, although changes in the university along the lines proposed here would figure to have an impact on American society as a whole. If we have to wait for a social revolution in order to improve the quality of higher education, we are likely to be in for a long wait.

Unlike many of the proposals being heard on the current scene, mine doesn't figure to make any one faction completely happy. But it does suggest some terms under which we could begin to fight out in a more educationally productive way the very different and contradictory interpretations of who is making us unhappy. Literature teachers might end up educating a few people in the process, including themselves.

## Endnotes

1. Fredric Jameson, *The Political Unconscious: Narrative as a Socially Symbolic Act* (Ithaca, N. Y.: Cornell University Press), p. 58.

2. See, respectively, Frederick Crews, "The Grand Academy of Theory," *Skeptical Engagements* (New York: Oxford University Press, 1987), pp. 159–78; Walter Benn Michaels and Steven Knapp, *Against Theory: Literary Studies and the New Pragmatism*, W. J. T. Mitchell, ed. (Chicago, Ill.: University of Chicago Press, 1985); Paul de Man, *The Resistance to Theory* (Minneapolis: University of Minnesota Press, 1987), pp. 3–20.

3. Allan Bloom, *The Closing of the American Mind: How Higher Education Has Failed Democracy and Impoverished the Souls of Today's Students* (New York: Simon and Schuster, 1987).

4. Gerald Graff, *Professing Literature: An Institutional History* (Chicago, Ill.: University of Chicago Press, 1988), pp. 1–118 *passim*.

5. Graff, *Professing Literature*, pp. 6–9 and *passim*.

6. Gary Waller, "A Powerful Silence: 'Theory' in the English Major," *ADE Bulletin* (winter 1986), 85:33.

7. James V. Mirollo, "Happy Birthday, Humanities A," *Columbia* (April 1987), p. 37.

8. Cyrus Veeser, letter to New York Times (June 23, 1988); see Carol S. Gruber, *Mars and Minerva: World War I and the Uses of Higher Education* (Baton Rouge: Louisiana State University Press, 1975).

9. For suggestions on how these recommendations could be effected, see Graff: "Conflicts Over the Curriculum Are Here To Stay: They Should Be Made Educationally Productive," *"Chronicle of Higher Education"* (February 17, 1988), 34(23):A48; "What Should We Be Teaching—When There's No We'?" *Yale Journal of Criticism* (1987), 1(2):189–211); "Teach the Debate About What Books Are In or Out," *Christian Science Monitor*, Education Pullout Section, April 22, 1988, pp. B6–B7; see also *Professing Literature*, pp. 258ff;

10. Gary Waller, "Polylogue: Reading, Writing, and the Structure of Doctoral Study in English," unpublished essay. Although Waller is speaking of doctoral study, the principles he states are similar to those that guide Carnegie-Mellon's thinking about undergraduate study. The belief that exposure to theoretical and methodological disputes should be reserved for graduate (or advanced) students is part of the pathology that needs to be combated—although, of course, suitable adjustments have to be made for different educational levels.

11. Steven Mailloux et al., "Not a Good Idea: The New Curriculum at Syracuse," unpublished internal draft, Syracuse University.

# 2

## The Function of English at the Present Time

**Richard Ohmann**

*Richard Ohmann presents in his essay a critique of the actual function of literary criticism within the profession and surveys its direct relationship to education. As one of the founding members of the Radical Teacher collective, Ohmann reflects on the differences between criticism, as practiced then and now, from a theoretical perspective. He notes the tremendous shift in leftist literary criticism over the past twenty years and finds that it has become "less intense, less immediate and more somber." But he points to a clarification and maturation of political organizations and practices, and generally expresses a "muted optimism" based on the presence on campus, which would have been unimaginable in the past, of leftists, feminists, and other previously repressed groups.*

I adapt my title from Matthew Arnold's, in part because this essay does include a vest-pocket account of how English and humanistic criticism fit into the broad movement of North American history, an account that responds to Arnold's questions, although not with his high hopes for literary culture. But the title also leads into one of two anecdotes with which I want to begin.

Several years ago there was a conference on the humanities at

This article, which originally appeared in a different form, is reprinted by permission from *The Politics of Letters* (Middletown: Wesleyan University Press, 1987).

Wesleyan University, where I teach. I agreed to respond to a lecture by one of the most respected critics of our time. She chose to use Arnold's title without change: "The Function of Criticism at the Present Time." She spoke of criticism's inherent value and of its value to the general society. It was a high-minded talk; and as is customary with high-minded talks by practitioners, it made no mention of the circumstances within which practitioners actually work, or of the functions that their practice might have *for them*. I thought that Arnold's title called for inclusion of such matters, more so now than in his time, since criticism has become so thoroughly institutionalized. As a shortcut to making that point, I mentioned the function that criticism had had in advancing the speaker's own career—and, old hand though I am at making rude remarks, I can't remember giving such offense, before or since. It was as if I had responded to a theological argument by questioning the theologian's habits of personal cleanliness, so impertinent did our speaker think matters of advancement and reputation to a discussion of the functioning of criticism in this society.

Second anecdote; another conference on the humanities, this one at a leading midwestern university. We have spent two days mulling over precisely the institutional questions that the speaker at Wesleyan thought irrelevant. It is the closing session, and I am on a panel that will try to sum up our debates and discussions. Chairing the panel is the vice-president of the university, himself a humanistic scholar of distinction, who, however, has the disadvantage of having missed the conference he is summarizing. He expresses much concern about the insecurity of humanistic values in our society and the daunting task before us humanists. He finishes, however, on an upbeat note, with a rhapsody on the great works of which we are the custodians, and the great power they exert for sweetness and light. I demur—politely, since the man *has* missed our deliberations. But then, to my surprise, a voice from the audience echoes the vice-president's credo, then another, and another. I thought we had discounted that article of faith at the outset of the conference. Reduced to thoughts of one syllable, I say something like this:

> Imagine a seventh-grade classroom in New York in about 1912. The children of immigrants are studying *Macbeth*. A neatly dressed girl in the third row is learning that the play is great, and that it is about good and evil. She is also learning that she can give answers the teacher likes, that she can get good grades on tests, that the culture of school, though realized via the En-

glish language, is not so different from that of her relatively well-educated parents, that she has a future using her mind—that she might become a teacher herself. Next to her, a boy in shabbier clothes is learning that the play is great, and that it is about good and evil, although he cannot understand its lines. He is also learning once again, from the study of *Macbeth* this time, what he has learned each year in school: that his answers are always wrong, that his way of talking makes other kids snicker, that teachers see him as a nuisance, that school is an alien place, that he will be a laborer like his father and older brother, and that this future is what he deserves because he is dumb.

Does my homely example register with the believers in redemptive Literature? Do they think that such examples have a place in talk about the functions of the humanities?

I think that it belongs there, if the talk is to be consequential and not only contribute to the discourse of professional justification and morale boosting. I did not always think so, socialized as I was into the high and disinterested cultural mission of humanities professors during the halcyon postwar years. Without the stimulus of the civil rights struggles and the antiwar movement, I doubt that my thinking about criticism and the humanities would have veered toward political and institutional questions about culture, questions about the negotiation of inequality from one generation to the next, about professional interests and careers, about seventh-grade classrooms. The events of the 1960s were hard on complacency; they provoked self-scrutiny, and an effort to connect the large with the small, the abstract with the concrete. The effort rose out of activism, which drove many intellectuals to ask what relations there were or should be between our academic work and our political commitments. We formed organizations, we thought and wrote in collaboration, we took on projects like the original *Politics of Literature*. It is good to remember the excitement of that moment, when the pressure of events fused our energies into a ruthless critique of all things, as Marx put it.

One essay in *The Politics of Literature*—"Free, Classless, and Urbane?"[1]—took its title from a phrase of Northrop Frye's and challenged the idea that the culture we ministered to could in fact be classless. Like many of my colleagues, I began cocking a more skeptical eye at the humanities. Why, in spite of much good will and intelligence on our part, and in spite of the great works lined up in marching formation on our bookshelves, did the humanities as we practiced them often fail to humanize, or succeed in humanizing a few at the expense of many? Was that so different from asking why the corporate practices of mainly well-trained and well-intentioned doctors do not spread health throughout our society? Or why the work of lawyers does not always make for justice? The answer to all of these questions—and how could I have been so dim as not to have known it all along?—is that bodies of knowledge and the people (professionals) who mediate them work through institutions designed to serve in part the self-interest of the practitioners, and that these institutions and practices must respond in part to the power and needs of dominant groups in the society at large.

In a book published ten years ago, I worked this proposition out in some detail, with reference to my own profession. Let me quote one passage that expresses the idea in a way I still endorse:

> When George Steiner cites the evidence of cultivated Nazis to prove that the humanities do not necessarily make people humane, or when the more cautious Herbert J. Muller confesses that he does not know whether they do or not, I can only say that the question has been wrongly put. No one should imagine that the humanities always do the same thing simply because their content remains more or less the same. What they do, what literature does, depends on who is doing it. The humanities are not an agent but an instrument. Nazis will make different uses of Goethe and Beethoven than will liberal American professors, and "the" function of literature is almost certain to change within any given society from one century to the next: human values may be eternal, but cultural systems are not. There is just no sense in pondering the function of literature without relating it to the actual society that uses it, to the centers of power within that society, and to the institutions that mediate between literature and people.[2]

Whatever was or is of use in that book to our thinking about what we do derived from the strategy of discounting two common angles of vision, and privileging a third. I rejected the view from the timeless and Olympian heights of *The* Humanities, of disembodied texts and values, without human agents who make criticism and literature function for contingent ends, including careers. I included but tried to broaden the view from the trenches, bearing in mind that the seventh-grade teacher of *Macbeth*, taking pleasure in the bright spirit of one child and despairing at the dullness or intransigence of another, does not *mean* to be reproducing and accrediting a hurtful class structure. The angle of vision I favored, and still do, is one from the long perspective of history and the whole social process, one that tries to discern alignments of power and fields of force within it. Class, gender, and race come into definition, while The Humanities begin to look like a granfalloon.[3]

This outlook also brought into definition the staying power of what we used vaguely to call "the system" or "the establishment." Patriarchy, white supremacy, and bourgeois society were not about to melt in the heat of our movement. The Reagan years enforced the point. Since we wrote *The Politics of Literature* it has become clearer that we are in for a long and uneven march through institutions. I imagine that most of the essays in this sequel volume will be less intense, less immediate, more somber. Yet our side has gained in solidity, too, since 1972. Organizations and practices are more mature, intermediate goals clearer. In the universities, at least, there is a feminist and leftist presence unimaginable twenty-five years ago, and a base for both resistance and new building. So as I spell out, briefly and schematically, the way I now understand the functions of literature and criticism at the present time, I write with the muted optimism of the long view, even though what I describe is grim enough.

I situate English and the humanities within the long, historical crisis of capitalism. By the 1930s capitalism's productive power in the United States had outgrown the capacity of the society, structured as it was and unaided by nonmarket forces, to use power fully. Intervention by the state has made up the difference, along with three wars and a rapid expansion of American capital into other countries. Subtract the "public" sector from our economy, and unemployment would today stand at least at the 25 percent level it reached in 1933; some analysts hold that military production alone makes that much difference. But even the combination of Keynesian measures, imperial expansion, the welfare state, and military spending seems inadequate now. The real income of American workers leveled off more than fifteen years ago. Inflation and unemployment no longer move in a neat reciprocal relationship; both have generally remained higher than in 1967. Credit and debt have ceased to promote expansion, and instead hang like a great albatross around our necks. There is a so-called capital shortage, really a capital strike: growth, the sine qua non of capitalism, is halting, and is often of no human value, as when Ted Turner tries to buy CBS, or T. Boone Pickens an oil company. The system seems unable to keep on doing what—as even its enemies allow—it did so splendidly for 150 years: expand the material basis of our lives.

Meanwhile, its more vicious characteristics show remarkable persistence, in spite of a thousand liberal remedies. Inequality is as great in 1985 as in 1945. A black movement and a women's movement have led to the passage of laws and to some changes of heart, but have had little effect on the relative economic position of these groups; and the New Right assaults what gains there were, in the name of freedom and morality. Our educational system, on which we counted so heavily, has not even created equality of opportunity, much less equality itself. We notice again what it was polite to ignore for forty years: that we have a class system. Most people feel and are powerless. They are bored with their work, distrustful of our major institutions, contemptuous of politics as a means of redress and renewal, except perhaps when it appears as TV spectacle, as in the recent Contragate hearings. And the main irrationality of capitalism—that socially produced wealth is privately allocated, and so allocated by the sole criterion of profitability—has produced energy crises, environmental crises, widespread starvation, and so on. The capitalist countries also find, increasingly, that they must either support bloody dictatorships in the third world and perhaps be willing to destroy societies like those of Southeast Asia and Central America, or watch defection after defection from the system they rule. In support of this imperial house of cards, they have created a military machine that can and may destroy human social life altogether.[4]

Few teachers of the humanities welcome these developments, and a small but increasing number of us have concluded that our liberal values—equality, democracy, civility, the full development of each person—cannot be realized in liberal, capitalist society. For I do think that liberal politics and liberal education have more in common than the accident of a common adjective. The same contradiction that permeates our whole political system also permeates our institutions of liberal education; liberal values are necessary to the maintenance of advanced capitalism, yet advanced capitalism prevents their fulfillment.

Marx and Engels believed that such contradictions would create a revolutionary working class in the industrialized nations, bring down capitalism, and lead to the building of a humanistic socialism. It's been a long time since 1847, and nowhere has this happened according to script. Marxists must ask why the scenario has so often gone wrong in socialist countries, and, as urgently, what in this most advanced capitalist country has held together so unjust and irrational a social order. A repressive state is not the main answer to the second question, although we can have no illusions, after the McCarthy period and after the revelations of the last fifteen years about CIA and FBI politics, that the state has been or will be a neutral bystander to the formation of a powerful socialist movement. Capitalism owes its durability, I believe, first to its immense productive power, however weakened in recent years; second to the extension of its domain beyond our borders, so that the worst immiseration of workers is put out of sight and out of our political arena; and third to welfare-warfare state measures.

Still, I cannot believe that even such a combination of remedies would suffice for long, in itself. Something more is needed to conceal the real workings of the society from those most hurt by it, to make it seem inevitable and right, to close off alternatives from view. Marx and Engels provided the fundamental explanation in their notion of a superstructure—laws, institutions, culture, beliefs, values, customs—that rises from the economic base, rationalizes it, and protects its relations. In this century, Antonio Gramsci elaborated this idea through his account of the hegemony of the dominant class: a whole way of life including culture and ideas, and supported by ideological institutions, which effectively enlists almost everyone in the "party" of the ruling class, sets limits to debate and consciousness, and in general serves as a means of rule—that is, of preserving and reproducing class structure—far more subtle and effective than naked force.

The humanities, like the schools and universities within which they are practiced, have contributed through the hundred years of our profession's existence to this hegemonic process. English teachers have helped train the kind of work force capitalists need in a productive system that relies less and less on purely manual labor. More, we have helped to inculcate the discipline—punctuality, good verbal manners, submission to authority, attention to problem-solving assignments set by somebody else, long hours spent in one place—that is necessary to perform the alienated labor that will be the lot of most. And more important still, by helping to sort out those who will succeed in school from those who will not, we have generally confirmed the class origins of our students, while making it possible for a few to rise (and others to sink). The effect—unintended of course—is to sustain the *illusion* of equal opportunity and convince the majority that their failure to play a significant and rewarding role in society is a personal failure rather than a systemic one.

What about the Arnoldian claims for literacy and literature and criticism: their civilizing effect, their preservation of the best values from our history, their offer of a vantage point from which we may cast a disinterested eye on our society and on the strident factional jostling of classes within it? I do not wish to put aside this hope with a cynical gesture. Most of us have experienced in ourselves and seen in at least some of our students the widening of sympathies, the release from parochial blindness, the refinement of thought and feeling, the keener awareness of cant, that literature and criticism *can* nourish.

But the Arnoldians among us—including (strange bedfellows) those Arnoldian Marxists who make up the Frankfurt school—err by placing faith in the critical force of history, art, literature, and philosophy apart from the institutions within which they are discussed and taught at a particular historical moment. Our own profession, as it has increasingly colonized the experience of literature for American young people, has pretty successfully abstracted it from any but literary history, muted its social resonance and given it a primary reference point in the individual consciousness, striven to anchor it in supposedly timeless values and ideas of human nature, and lately surrounded it with specialist techniques of interpretation and quarrels about theory—New Criticism, myth criticism, Chicago criticism, structuralist criticism, psychoanalytic criticism, phenomenological criticism, linguistic criticism, feminist criticism, Marxist criticism, reader-centered criticism, deconstruction, poststructuralism, and no doubt post–every-ism on this list—that sometimes enlighten and sometimes do little more than advance careers and stake out territories. Oddly, it might seem, the evolution of theory has generated this efflorescence of species just as the old base of our prosperity, laid by the postwar boom, is crumbling. But maybe that's not so odd.

Let me work back to this subject by considering for a while the situation that underlies the often noted crisis in the humanities, demographics aside. The stagnation of the capitalist economy seems permanent. There is (as yet) no new Vietnam to keep it artificially booming, and the chips have been called in on the Vietnam extravaganza itself, with economic results that are familiar. The job market is fairly well choked with highly educated workers. As the subdivision and degradation of labor that has characterized monopoly capital since its beginning goes forward, and as the percentage of Americans doing at least some college study increases (it is close to 60 percent now), a gap widens between the unalienated work and good life that college used to promise and what most college students can actually expect. I think that at some level of awareness students know this. Hence their strategy of going for those subjects and techniques that seem to offer the best chance of a decent first job—however disappointed most will be with where that initial job leads twenty years from now.

We know what that has meant for us. Majors in English and allied fields are down 50 percent or more in two decades. Departments have shrunk. Recent estimates suggest that from 15 to 40 percent of job seekers in our field find permanent employment there. And the students still in our classrooms are mostly studying composition, which accounted for 40 percent of English enrollments in the late 1960s; it accounts for 60 percent now, and for twice the number of literature enrollments.

I see no evidence that students derive less benefit from the study of literature, or are less attracted to that study, now than in 1965. Rather, it seems to me that the statistics tell a simple story: students will pursue an inherently pleasant and humane activity when there is no penalty for doing so, as in the 1960s when there was a shortage of educated workers and every B.A. got a job; but not so many of them will do so when jobs are short, when there is a premium on marketable skills, and when educational authorities set a course toward vocational training rather than liberal arts. These circumstances underscore the folly of discussing our profession in an historical vacuum. The market determines the use of our work by a calculus of exchange value that need not correspond to our own use values, and right now we—or I should say, our students and younger colleagues—are experiencing one of the irrationalities, a minor but painful one, of the market system.

You may detect a contradiction between what I have just said and my earlier remarks about the uses of our work to capitalists in helping to reproduce the class system and the ideology that supports it. The contradiction dissolves if we remember that the meaning of our work as *we* understand it is not the same as its structural valence within the society, and that from the social perspective various parts of that work—especially those connected to literature—are more or less interchangeable with tasks of legitimation and class reproduction performed by others: by teachers of accounting or dry cleaning; by television and the other media; by employers themselves. Any agency that has and uses the authority to grade and rank young people helps, willy nilly, to present a class system as a meritocracy.

If true, this observation suggests that there is not much hope of regaining the position we held two decades ago merely by determining more accurately what our society, as presently constituted, wants of us. In fact, in English we know that well enough: it wants less liberal arts, more grammar, more vocationally useful skills, more emphasis on basic literacy, "higher" standards, generally lowered expectations for our students, a finer and more rigorous sorting out of those who will *have* from those who will *have not*. But acceding to these demands in a servile and unimaginative way can do little, if my analysis is right, to serve even a narrow vision of self-interest, and nothing at all to answer a broader one consistent with the values of civility and democratic culture that most of us hold.

Now, so far I have spoken of the gradually deepening crisis in our economic system and in the humanities as if all of us and all of our students were in the same pickle. This is clearly not true. Worse, it violates one of my own cardinal rules of ideological wariness: whenever you hear someone say "we" or "society" as if we were a homogeneous and conflict-free unity, watch out for a con game. And finally, the picture I have sketched does not include some salient features of English (and the humanities) in the United States in 1990: for instance, the efflorescence of theory that I mentioned a while back, and those voices that are exhorting us, not to move toward basic skills and vocationalism, but to reassert our dedication to the great books and to a core curriculum based on them. In the remainder of this essay I turn to these two matters, trying to suggest how the analysis of culture I have put forward may aid in the understanding of current debates and conflicts.

First, allow me to unpack that bogus "we" by mentioning the single example of my own college, to which little of what I have said about the present moment applies. Wesleyan is one of the dozen most selective schools in the country: applicants jostle and beg for admission, although annual costs for those who pay their own way have passed $15,000. At Wesleyan (and I suppose at Princeton, at Amherst, etc.) there has been no decline in humanities enrollments. The English major—a fairly traditional one—is overcrowded in spite of my department's efforts to stiffen the requirements in recent years. About one-sixth of Wesleyan students major in English. We put enrollment limits on almost all of our courses, and even when the limit is sixty or eighty or one-hundred, the computer usually turns students away. Furthermore, these figures do not reflect a shift in our offering toward composition, although our students would certainly like more of it than we offer. Only about 12 to 15 percent of our enrollments each year are in writing courses. The rest are in literature and in what I would call cultural studies.

Why? I think the answer is easy. For Wesleyan students (and for those at Yale, Stanford, Wellesley and so on) there is *still* no penalty for pursuing the humane and pleasant activity of reading good books and trying to understand the world. They have a reserved place waiting for them in either the professional-managerial class or the ruling class, some by virtue of having made it into an elite college, most by birth and nurture. They will land on their feet, even if they think they are risking downward mobility by studying Shakespeare instead of biochemistry. The class system, I suggest, is becoming more finely etched as the crisis works its way out. This holds true for higher education as for the whole society; and the Reagan administration did what it could to egg the process along, with its tax and student loan measures.

Meanwhile, in the elite colleges our students' privilege frees their teachers to pursue the activities that attract us, rather than turning our minds and energies to technical writing and the like. Some of us at Wesleyan do traditional scholarship and criticism. There are a couple of poststructuralists, a myth critic, a psychoanalytic critic, and people who ground their research and teaching in feminism, black studies, Marxism, and cultural studies. We, too, can try to understand the world in our various ways and (yes) try to advance our careers by emulating the leaders in this very heterogeneous field.

I am suggesting that centrifugal tendencies in theory and method over the past fifteen years have a lot to do with a deepening class division in the academy, which parallels that outside of it. Teachers of English in the more expensive private institutions and in some of the most prestigious public ones feel less pressure than before from students' vocational needs and anxieties, whatever the polls say about these matters. And many feel less professional solidarity with those who teach mainly composition to middle-class and working-class students. That division expresses itself not only in recent angry proposals by writing teachers to secede from the uneasy alliance of the English department, but in the freedom of the more privileged academic group to pursue theories and approaches not very directly related to classroom exigencies or to guild traditions. I can't prove any of this, but I ask you to entertain it as at least a plausible explanation, one rooted in class.

One of the ironies here deserves special mention in passing: that Marxism has shared this kind of class privilege with other—sometimes incompatible—theories. We have our conferences and our journals, but are not ghettoized in these; we also give papers at meetings of established professional groups, and prestigious journals are open to our work, even solicit it. Leftist books stream from the presses. Perhaps the number of us getting tenure for our efforts has even exceeded the number being fired for them. More to the point, we have persuasively reinterpreted wide areas of experience, and in some academic fields have so established the power of historical materialism that it must at least be attacked, rather than simply ignored, as it was in the intellectual darkness of the early 1960s.

The danger I see in our present situation, after such a long string of gains, is a *new* kind of isolation. Acceptance in the academy came to us just as the movements that had fueled our thinking were breaking up, losing steam, or changing direction. So our respectability—precarious and partial, of course—coincides with our greater distance from vital popular movements; cynics might say that the latter explains the former. Trustees and administrators can congratulate themselves on harboring critical thinkers, so long as they produce scholarly articles and an enhanced reputation for the university rather than strikes and sit-ins. I am concerned that our Marxism may become attenuated and abstract, one theory among many, a new Marxology.

Having registered this caveat, I turn now to the other current issue mentioned earlier, the voices calling for "excellence," cultural literacy, great books, a core curriculum in the humanities. Here I will allude mainly to two influentials, very differently positioned in our society, and speaking from very different political orientations, yet speaking in much the same vein. One is William Bennett, whom I dislike, and fear even more than before, since his elevation to a cabinet post. The other is E. D. Hirsch, whom I like and admire, and whose current position strikes me as a sad apostasy, although a tempting one to many liberal humanists.

About the egregious Bennett: probably few readers of this anthology find his position in "To Reclaim a Legacy"[5] congenial; so I will not spend time opposing the list of great books he recommends for all our students, whatever their circumstances and goals. (I will note in passing, though, that since most of us *also* think it would be a fine world if everyone had thoughtfully read Montaigne and Melville, Bennett's recommendations have a kind of utopian seductiveness that we must strain to resist: Montaigne and Melville as requirements for all will change nothing, unless for the worse.) What I mainly wish to note is the absurdity of his premises about society and history. Their plausibility dissolves as soon as one looks twice at the stirring phrases. (Where is this discourse coming from? Why is anyone listening?)

Bennett begins by asserting that few students get "an adequate education in the culture and civilization of which they are members." If they don't, one might ask, in what sense are they "members" of it? Is a culture something hidden in mysteries? Is it not the practices and beliefs of a people? No, for Bennett it is the knowledge and practices of some people. Immediately we see that he has set culture over and against society, in a way that has very specific historical origins, those traced by Raymond Williams many years ago in *Culture and Society*.[6] Bennett seems unaware of them. Otherwise, he might ask why the culture critique to which he subscribes has generally served to set intellectuals off against the millions on whose behalf we have claimed to speak, and why things should be otherwise in the Reagan epoch.

Perhaps because Bennett's initial position is plainly contradictory, he quickly undertakes a maneuver that projects a unified humanistic culture back into the past. The humanities—"history, literature, philosophy, and the ideals and practices of the past," have "shaped the society" that our students enter, and to be ignorant of them is to be culturally disenfranchised. Again, he writes that "our society was founded upon such principles as justice, liberty, government with the consent of the governed, and equality under the law is the result of ideas descended directly from great epochs of Western civilization." Never mind, for now, how well you think Mr. Bennett's society is doing to guarantee equality before the law in Harlem and Wall Street, or to grant government the consent of the governed in Nicaragua. I am concerned to point out, rather, that Bennett seems to think that our society has been shaped by "the best that has been said, thought, written," etc.—in short, by the Arnoldian humanities. As a materialist, I believe that ideas have a secondary role in shaping this or any other society; but if one does subscribe to idealist history, surely the shaping ideas of our society are rendered more accurately in such immortal words from the past as "The business of America is business" and "What's good for General Motors is good for the country."

So if Bennett-culture is not constitutive of our society, either now or as a legacy from the past, what makes the humanities an essential study? His other main rationale, as he slides around the difficulties I have mentioned, is that the humanities well taught can *make* students "become participants in a common culture," not the one they actually have, but one "rooted in civilization's lasting vision, its highest shared ideals and aspirations. . . ." In other words, we are to sift out the best (by whose standards?) from the past, and *create* a "sense of community" around that high culture.

But is this not precisely what the professors and schoolmen set out to do in the 1890s and have been spasmodically trying to do ever since? And has a good dose of Milton or Goldsmith generally made the farm youth or the Italian immigrant or the recent black arrival in Chicago feel part of a common culture? Or has it more often made her/him feel, precisely, *excluded* from the culture that counts—at best angry about that, and at worst convinced that she or he deserves, because of invincible ignorance, the station of laundress or parking attendant? For the decoded message of Bennett's report is that some-one—educational leaders? John Silber? us?—should tell everyone else what the cultural prerequisites are for entry into capitalist elites, that most will fail the test, and that most of these will blame themselves. Either Bennett is a more wicked man than even I think, and under-stands all or this; or, more likely, he is himself invincibly ignorant about culture, history, and power, and has produced this vacuous re-port out of his own profoundest cogitations, buoyed by the mean-spirited crassness of the Reagan administration—upon whose poli-cies of triage it lays a veneer of resonant cliches.

Briefly, now, E. D. Hirsch, whom Bennett approvingly cites—I hope to Hirsch's therapeutic discomfort. In two articles in *The American Scholar*[7] which have apparently influenced not only Bennett but the California educators working toward a core reading list for the state's high schools, Hirsch reports the latest discoveries of his long, groping tour through the dark realms of composition and literacy theory. He has now determined that national languages and national cultures are in fact nationalistic. So far so good. But instead of interrogating nationalism as an educational purpose, Hirsch goes on to lament the decline in *our* common culture, as measured by such instruments as the verbal SAT. After working through the implications of the con-tent-neutral theory he developed in his book on composition,[8] he dis-covered that literacy is *not* after all content neutral, and that com-munication works better when both parties know what the discourse is about. Ergo, we must promote "cultural literacy," and shared knowledge; then when we test students on what they know, literacy scores will rise in a most gratifying way—if one finds tautological results gratifying.

Hirsch says that "a certain extent of shared, canonical knowledge is inherently necessary to a literate democracy." This, I believe, is true, and has nothing to do whatsoever with his argument about con-tent and literacy tests. But of course it brings him immediately face to face with what he calls the "political decision of choosing the con-tents of cultural literacy"—that is, of dictating the terms of literate democracy. Hirsch, unlike Bennett, recognizes this as a problem, and he wonders who the "we" might be that could make such a decision. But like Bennett, he neglects to wonder how one might legislate de-mocracy in the spheres of culture and education when there is no democracy, no equality, no empowerment for the many, outside those spheres.[9]

Interestingly, both Hirsch and Bennett mention along the way an area in which this society does possess a common culture: television Hirsch: "Television is perhaps our only national curriculum." Bennett: "Even television and the comics can give us" a national culture. But both theorists drop that subject instantly. That is a mistake. If we already have a cultural center of shared knowledge, why not base the SATs on that, and watch scores shoot up? And if, as most students of the media agree, television expresses broadly shared and historically grounded values and myths, why not accept it as canonical? It would be interesting to hear Hirsch and Bennett on the subject. I imagine that they would both say, in different ways, that this truly national culture is shallow and crude. Hirsch might even answer, as would I, that it is undemocratic. But then we would all have to talk together about how this society came to have such a mass culture in the first place. (My answer: it is inseparable from the ways in which monopoly capital has in just a hundred years reshaped human life.) And that would in turn carry us back into the political arena where Bennett (but not Hirsch, to his credit) scorns to tread.

But to put it in that way is of course to expose the absurdity of such claims. Bennett made the case for the political disinterestedness of culture, in "To Reclaim a Legacy," from his political post at the National Endowment for the Humanities. In preparation for his report he assembled a conference of right-wing educators whose ideas have gained credence only within the ambience of the Reagan administration, and gain further legitimacy from their association with Bennett's report. The power of those ideas grows with his political appointment as secretary of education, from which position he can exercise a more direct influence in federal legislation and on state bodies that control public schools. His agenda for the humanities is deeply etched with the new right's design for our future. All of this would be too obvious to put into words, except for the mesmeric power still carried by the idea that criticism, or English, or the great books, or the humanities, or culture can somehow stand off from the clash of purposes and interests, and serve some higher purpose of its own in a politically neutral way.

The move to reassert the centrality of the traditional canon, seen from the perspective of this essay, contributes to a much broader social strategy. In the economic arena, that strategy calls for freeing up capital to accumulate more or less as it did 125 years ago: in the pockets of the rich, who will presumably invest it in a way such as to stoke up the weary engine of production again. (Never mind for now the anachronisms entailed by this idea.) Toward that end, the strategy openly demands unraveling the welfare state. Less openly, it authorizes the further enrichment and empowerment of the bourgeoisie, the consolidation of the professional-managerial class, and a wider spread between these and the working class, with a hopeless underclass—here and abroad—permanently isolated and forgotten. I say "less openly," but this tendency is fairly evident in the tax "reform" and fiscal policy that looks likely as I write, and in many other acts of the Reagan administration.

In the cultural arena, the strategy calls for the reestablishment of "traditional" values that link religion and patriarchy to the free market. Mr. Bennett's project is a minor skirmish in this battle. Were it to succeed, it would join a kind of cultural authority to the power that schooling must exercise in reproducing class inequality.[10] And of course it would defeat or redirect the more democratic educational movements that arose twenty years ago, in particular those that addressed racism through a multicultural idea.

Here the question of intent arises. I do not believe that Bennett sees his plan for the humanities in this way. (No more does Senator Bradley understand his tax "reform" efforts as fostering an even nastier distribution of wealth and power.) Certainly neither E. D. Hirsch nor the many humanists drawn to his idea of cultural literacy and a core curriculum see ideological support for inequality as their cause. Of course I may be wrong in my analysis. But if not, the convergence of such different projects and such politically diverse agents in this attempt to reground English and the humanities nicely instances the process of hegemony in a particular moment of capitalist crisis. Ideas from the front lines of capital seep through devious channels back to the ivory towers, joining with and giving momentum to certain ideas that originate there—ideas often motivated initially in quite other ways.

This argument should in no way be understood as identifying the classics or the humanities with domination, transhistorically. If human beings ever achieve a decent world order, I hope that classics from many cultures will have a place of honor in its memory and in its legacy to the young. For now, however, we—and here I mean all of those whose allegiance is to equality and justice—should reject the dangerous calls for a spurious common culture handed down from above. In recent years those calls have most often expressed, even if unintentionally, the deepening crisis of our social system, and have represented efforts to patch it up by hardening class lines, calling the result fair, and enlisting us in its behalf under the name of culture.

## Endnotes

1. Barbara Bailey Kessel, "Free Classless, and Urbane?" in Louis Kampf and Paul Lauter, eds., *The Politics of Literature: Dissenting Essays on the Teaching of English* (New York: Pantheon, 1972), pp. 177–93.

2. Richard Ohmann, *English in America: A Radical View of the Profession* (New York: Oxford University Press, 1976), p. 303.

3. Kurt Vonnegut coined this useful term: "A *granfalloon* is a proud and meaningless association of human beings." Kurt Vonnegut, *Wampeters, Foma, and Granfalloons: Opinions of Kurt Vonnegut, Jr.* (New York: Delacourte Press, 1974), p. xv.

4. What about the Soviet Union? someone asks. That is not the subject of this essay, but I am aware that the USSR is not a pacifist regime.

5. William Bennett, "To Reclaim a Legacy," report of the National Endowment for the Humanities' Study Group on the State of Learning in the Humanities in Higher Education. I quote from the reprint in *The Chronicle of Higher Education*, November 28, 1984.

6. Raymond Williams, *Culture and Society: 1780–1950* (New York: Harper Torch Books, 1958).

7. E. D. Hirsch, Jr., "Cultural Literacy," *American Scholar* (1983), 52:159–69, and "English" and the Perils of Formalism," *American Scholar* (1984), 53:369–79.

8. E. D. Hirsch, *The Philosophy of Composition* (Chicago: Chicago University Press, 1981).

9. Since I wrote this, Hirsch's *Cultural Literacy: What Every American Needs to Know* (Boston, Mass.: Houghton Mifflin, 1987) appeared, and made its way straight to the *New York Times* best-seller list. In this book Hirsch adapts (from Orlando Patterson) a more satisfying idea of culture, addresses some of the issues raised in this essay, and makes it clear that in proposing specific elements of cultural literacy he is posing a political challenge (p. 145). His positioning of literacy in wider social structures and processes remains naive.

10. For instance, in 1986 Bennett was pressing the colleges to become cops in the fight against drugs. A university official commented, "I don't think we are here to tell students how to behave." Bennett replied, "Well, then, what *are* they there for?" (National Public Radio, July 8, 1986). Apparently the secretary saw no line between education and law enforcement.

# TWO

## FEMINISM THEN AND NOW: ANALYSIS AND EVALUATION

*We asked three feminist scholars to look back over the past twenty years and critique the women's movement from various angles. We have taken this specific focus because the women's movement, of all the political movements generated from the 1960s, is the one that has most successfully become part of the academic scene and has most successfully jumped the wall that separates town and gown. The 1989 pro-choice demonstration in Washington D.C. was a graphic and moving reminder of the efficacy and continuing strength of the women's movement and a testimony to its ability to unite disparate groups of the American public.*

*Because feminism and feminist scholarship has consistently gained ground, developed theory, and consolidated its advances through academic positions, political organizations, and access to various media, it represents a model for other struggles. By looking realistically at the achievements and problems inherent in the women's movement, we can perhaps learn more about praxis in the academy.*

*The three scholars whose essays are included in this section represent various points of view on the movement. Catharine Stimpson reflects on the accomplishments of women's studies as a discipline in the university. However, women's studies has been criticized because it is largely a white, middle-class, reformist movement. Nellie McKay, a black feminist, offers a vision of the marginalized scholar whose needs were only half-met by the women's movement. Another critique of that movement is offered by Kate Ellis, who takes on the influence of French feminist thought on the literary study of gender.*

# 3

# What Am I Doing When I Do Women's Studies in 1990?

## Catharine R. Stimpson

*The intention of Catharine Stimpson's article is to examine what it means to teach women's studies today and to assess what changes have occurred in this field over the past twenty years. In doing this, Stimpson identifies what have been three major aims for women's studies: seeking an "ethic"; trying to encourage institutions to recognize this ethic; and finally raising consciousness. With these three themes as a backdrop, Stimpson goes on to evaluate many of the current and prominent trends in women's studies within institutions, programs, and literary theory, including what she calls the "minimalist" and "maximalist" controversy over attitudes toward sexual difference.*

*While recognizing many of the positive changes in women's studies over the past twenty years in the academy—changes such as the increased number of doctorates for women—Stimpson is careful to point out that it is still mainly men who hold tenured positions while women increasingly are filling the ranks of new nontenured positions.*

In Amsterdam, Holland there is a postcard company. It has an ironically Utopian name: Art Unlimited. Among its productions is a 1982 photomontage, entitled "Untitled." The artist is Tobias Raymond. A shiny, metal, old-fashioned manual typewriter rests on a slatelike surface. Unknown hands have rolled a piece of paper around the typewriter's platen. However, the paper is not blank. Rather, it is a photograph of part of the head of a fair-skinned, dark-haired woman. If the keys were to strike, they would hit the naked lobe of her ear. Some ear/ring.

In part, the photomontage is a formal exercise, a study of shapes and surfaces. In part, it is a surrealistic blurring of conventional categories, of machine and person, of paper and picture. Finally, in part, the card presents a challenge. What are we to do with its representation of Woman? On the one hand, the card seems to recirculate old Western images. First, a woman's cheek waits, passively, to be written on, to be struck. Next, the cheek is white. Woman is racially marked. Next, the card obscures the connections between women and menial labor, which a typewriter can signify, by transforming them into an elegant surface. On the other hand, the typewriter is waiting for a typist. If the typist is a woman, she might begin to write on and with the body of woman. Man or woman, the typist might roll out the picture and begin again.

In brief, this postcard sends a mixed message. For me, that mixed message provides a double metaphor for doing women's studies in 1990. First, women's studies exists in a culture in which conflicting interpretations of "woman" now fight for dominance. Often it feels like a struggle unto death. Women's studies participates, passionately, in that conflict. Next, women's studies is itself richly divided. It is opening up problem zone after problem zone. However, our rifts are splitting open a terrain that is still firm enough, spacious enough, to provide a common ground. Women's studies has been sturdy enough to develop hospitable settlement after hospitable settlement. What do I do when I do women's studies in 1990? I skirt both rifts and clearings. Here, now, is my map.

The contemporary study of women and gender is a vast endeavor. To borrow from Adrienne Rich, it has been at once wild and patient: wild in its ambitions, patient in the way it has sought to realize those ambitions. Briefly defined, this study is a transdisciplinary, and interdisciplinary, intellectual and educational movement that is irrevocably altering what we know, what we think we know, and how we think. Two decades ago, this movement was the tiniest of annexes in the citadels of education. In the United States alone, in 1969–1970, less than twenty women's studies courses existed. If the growth of the study of women and gender had been measured as if it were a developing economy, that growth would be called a "miracle." I am American enough to cheer growth—at least in some industries. For today, the study of women and gender claims nearly 30,000 courses, over 500 degree-granting programs, and at least 50 research centers. The founding of journals has given way to the creation of book series about women and gender. Between 1969 and 1978, the number of articles about women in *Sociological Abstracts* rose from less than 50 to more than 450. The number about men, as a group, increased from less than 50 to about 300.[1]

### The Necessity of Opposition

The antecedents of women's studies go much further back than the 1960s. Perhaps they exist in the first voices that stated that the experience of women was an appropriate object of serious regard and, moreover, that the perspective of women was an appropriate perspective from which to regard the world seriously. In the West, a founder was Christine de Pisan (1364–1430?). A vigorous participant in that rancorous debate about women, the *querelle des femmes*, she defended her sex's right to be literate, learned, and cultured, and her sex's capacity for literacy, learning, and culture.[2]

Like that of Christine, the discourse of women's studies begins in opposition. Before generating its own ideas and facts, it must first negate dominant theories and practices, ideologies and instruments. So doing, women's studies rebukes the prevailing character of knowledge: its ethos, institutions, and paradigms. Necessarily, any challenge to a prevailing paradigm entails two mutually reinforcing activities. The first demystifies the paradigm itself; the second demonstrates how much of the reality that the paradigm has promised to explain exists outside of the borders of the paradigm itself. In the study of women and religion, for example, scholars both questioned the adequacy of early Christian history and revealed the presence of material, such as the figure of a Mother God, that the history of early Christianity had rubbed out.[3] In the middle and late twentieth century in the United States, challenging the structures of knowledge has meant being suspicious of almost everything—of traditional psychoanalysis and behaviorialism; of Marxism and functionalism; of a humanism that subsumes everyone under the universal rubric of a white, male "he"; and of the claims of objectivity of the gaze of that white, male "he."

### From Opposition to Recreation

Some discourses are content to oppose. Others desire to replace the ideologies and structures they expose. Such has been the case with women's studies. Since 1969, it has persistently, insistently, said that change was necessary, desirable, and possible.[4] The calls for change have never had the chordal discipline of the chorale, nor the close harmonies of the barbershop quartet. Rather, they have been a series of improvisations and set pieces—for both solo voices and ensemble groups. Unifying them have been at least three dominant themes.

*First,* women's studies has sought a particular ethic. (*Sought* is a verb form that combines the words *see* and *ought,* vision and moral imperative.) This ethic values the freedom, the self-empowerment, and the moral equality of all of those who seek education and those who offer it. Women's studies has promised that such an ethic will enhance education, not smash it to pieces.[5] In general, women's studies has always had ethical concerns, even ethical passions. The fact that one child in four in the United States now lives in poverty seems, to most women's studies practioners, not simply a fact, but an immoral fact.

Implicit in the ethic of freedom, self-empowerment, and moral equality, with its liberal faith in the individual, is a further belief: that each of us can be the first witness to our own experience. As we construct a mature sense of reality, we begin with our own perceptions and histories. We are active participants in the process of the construction of a mature sense of reality, not passive recipients of higher truths from higher orders. Such a process ensures us our due.

*Second,* women's studies has sought to alter institutions so that they embody such an ethic. We have asked them to act affirmatively. This means, for example, increasing the number of women in academic life and treating them as all academic workers ought to be treated—with fairness and dignity. More and more women are earning higher-education degrees. In 1986, United States colleges and universities awarded 1,383,953 bachelor's, master's, doctoral, and first-professional degrees. (Unfortunately, the move to remove invidious gender markings from English has not yet touched academic degrees.) Women got 50.8 percent of the bachelor's degrees, 50.3 percent of the master's degrees. Men may have earned 49,261 first-professional degrees, but women earned 24,649 of them. More and more women are earning their doctorates, their credentials for admissions to a faculty. Between 1974 and 1984, the number of women getting a doctorate did jump 65 percent, from 6,453 to 10,660. In 1986, women received 11,834 doctorates. Let me offer an exemplary dream—from an associate professor of classics in a private southern university. After nearly a decade of work she finished her book on Vergil. To understand that Latin epic, she used a philosophical text: *The Human Condition.* One night, after she put her children to bed and went to sleep, she had a dream. She was shopping. She saw a designer dress, on sale, for $46.52. The designer was neither Klein nor Kamali nor Kenzo, but Hannah Arendt.[6]

However, I do not wish to warble optimistically foolish songs about bluebirds and blue skies. In the late 1970s, I spoke of the "galvanizing marginality" of women in higher education. Though electrifyingly energetic, they were not yet central. I have not yet abandoned the phrase. The transformation of a doctorate into a tenured faculty position remains arduous: 71 percent of men are tenured; 49 percent of women are. In 1987 the American Association of University Professors regretfully reported that non–tenure track positions are increasing, and women are more apt to be in them than men. Eighty-one percent of faculty women are on tenure track appointments; 93 percent of men are. In general, women still lack power within the academy. Today, only one land grant university, and no Ivy League university, has a woman president. Women still suffer from an acute lack of child care facilities, uneven parental leave policies, and sexual harassment. Women doing women's studies probably suffer even more acutely than women in "conventional subjects" in terms of job discrimination, although less acutely than they once did. A sociologist, Nancy Shaw, had to sue the University of California at Santa Cruz. A scholar in religious studies, Diana Paul, had to sue Stanford. So did the historian Estelle Freedman.[7]

Simultaneously, we have assumed that we can best work for change if we have our own institutions that make women's interests their first interest. Such institutions can be "freestanding," like women's colleges or battered women's shelters. Such institutions can also be spaces within larger structures, like women's studies programs. The new scholarship about women has fortified this conviction, for research seems to suggest that some women's institutions, of some sort, are imperative if history is to march, slither, and struggle toward gender equity. In brief, women's studies has needed both the educational equivalent of a fission process, in which it has created its own settings, *and* of a fusion process, in which it has become a part of other settings. The two processes have complementary, not competing, virtues.

*Third*, women's studies has sought to change consciousness—that of individuals and that of institutions. This has meant more than occasionally referring to a specific woman—to a Queen Elizabeth I or an Abigail Adams. This has meant more than occasionally referring to women as a group—to elite women or to our Founding Mothers. It has meant a constant, serious, deepening awareness of sets of problems and ideas about women.

Today these ideas play themselves out in three major patterns. The study of women and gender has developed three models of presence, ways of existing within our institutions of consciousness. The first is a women's studies program itself, self-consciously interdisciplinary in theory and practice. These programs have a variety of names, each with its own connotations: feminist studies, female studies, sex role studies, and, more and more often, gender studies. However, "women's studies" is the common rubric.

The second model of presence, more focused, takes up the subject of women and gender within a specific academic discipline. It might, for example, explore women in German history or black women novelists, both subjects of enormous interest. Given the reward structure of higher education, which disciplines control, this second model has probably flourished more easily than interdisciplinary "women's studies" itself. This second model is also healthiest in the arenas of postgraduate and undergraduate work. Graduate school is too important a gatekeeper to the academic professions to yield its treasures up easily to impetuous feminist scholars.

The third model of presence is "mainstreaming," a problematic metaphor for a vital activity begun in the mid-1970s. "Mainstreaming" calls for the integration of the new scholarship about women and gender into the ordinary curriculum on all levels. Surely, Zora Neale Hurston belongs in Afro-American studies programs, in women's studies programs, and in American literature courses. In the past decade, "mainstreaming" efforts have found their greatest welcome in the humanities and social sciences; in large, introductory courses, such as "Western Civilization"; in conjunction with other redemptive curricular programs, like those committed to people of color; and in institutions with strong leadership that supports systematic faculty development efforts.[8]

By 1987, at least six major sets of problems and ideas about women and gender had entered contemporary thinking. Once blasphemies, they had become banalities. Permit me to list them:

1. The need to distinguish sex, a biological condition, from gender, a social construction. Woman, like man, is made, not born. However, postmodern theory warns us against thinking in terms of binary oppositions, against the custom of dividing a complicated world into the polarized duality of "sex" and "gender," equivalent to "nature" and "culture."

2. The pernicious existence of gender stratification and discrimination, which economics, among other disciplines, has documented. However, this generalization must be modified. First, not all women

have been wholly powerless. Indeed, individual women, like Hedda Nussbaum in her "relationship" with Joel Steinberg, and entire groups of women have often been simultaneously powerful and powerless, victimizers and victims, dominant and dominated. White women did own, and maltreat, black slaves. As Claudia Koonz shows in *Mothers in the Fatherland* (1987), Nazi women maneuvered, swaggered, and murdered. Next, some societies, like some Native American tribes, seem to believe in gender differences and in gender equivalence at the same time. They seem to perceive men and women as different. However, each sex has equally valuable powers and capacities.

3. The fact that sexual stratification and discrimination have helped to create distorted, distorting representations of men, women, and gender. In 1970, Kate Millett's *Sexual Politics* brought this insight to wide public attention. Though women have been a part of the process of ideological warping, women are more likely than men to see the gap between representations and realities. In general, the strong are blinder than the weak to the wrongs of ideology. Despite being misrepresented, women have created their own cultural traditions, be they the novel or the quilt, in which they often seek to represent their experiences for themselves.

4. The importance of seeing the dynamic connections between public and domestic worlds, productive and reproductive spheres, reason and feeling, relationships that Marxist feminist thought has scrupulously traced.

5. The complexity of the causes, nature, and extent of sexual difference.

6. The profound differences among women themselves. My maternal grandmother, for example, was a servant in a farm family when she was twelve. I, obviously, was not. I was a bike-riding, book-reading, Hollywood-mad seventh-grader. Today, in the United States, the study of differences has focused on those that race, class, and gender create.[9] However, the study of differences can, and must, be even larger than that. For nationality and tribe, age and religion, the experiences of colonization and neocolonization, also create differences among women that we must understand and, sometimes, seek to erase.

For a number of reasons, including the sheer difficulty of the task, women's studies does not yet know how to come to terms with the social differences among women or, on the little landscape of the self, the differences between self and many others, some more powerful, some less powerful. My own responses to the Baby M case, my initial suspicions of Mary Beth Whitehead, taught me, again, how hobbled I am as I move out of my class.

Nevertheless, I believe that we can so inhabit the problem of the study of differences among women that our in-dwellings and out-dwellings can become a way of studying differences among all peoples. Indeed, "herterogeneity" is the name I have given to the use of women's studies as a way of grasping and living with human differences. Women's studies represents a "herterogeneous" vision, analysis, and practice. Recognizing diversity, and abhorring the error that erases it, are necessary in and of themselves. In addition, they are nurturing a virtue that all of United States education must imitate. As everyone ought to know, United States students are themselves becoming more and more diverse. By 1990, the groups we label "minorities" will represent 30 percent of the youth cohort nationwide. They will be 45 percent of the public high school graduates in Texas and California; 32 percent in New York; and 28 percent in New Jersey. They will deserve an education that gives them the survival skills we all must have today; a grasp of the realities of their own culture; and a sense of the realities of all of the many cultures that will people United States society.

What if research and teaching about women were to be among the first genuinely to embody the experiences of all of us? What if research and teaching about women could bring together the tense realities of an entire people? All colors? All classes? All sexualities? All powers? Both genders? What if women's studies were to show what a conceptual democracy really might be like? What if women's studies were to serve as a laboratory for thinking through the complexities of community? What if herterogeneity were to school us in heterogeneity? It would be wonderful, but, of course, it will not be without studies of women of color; without women of color. One of the most vital developments in the past decade has been the powerful emergence of academic communities of women of color.

Increasing the herterogeneity of women's studies is the fact that several generations of scholars have now joined those crazed pioneers who, in the 1960s, took women as a subject "in a material and local world."[10] Actually, the 1960s had two groups of "crazed pioneers." To abuse a now mealy metaphor, one group consisted of "the mothers." Among them were Jessie Bernard, Eleanor Flexner, Mirra Komarovsky, Gerda Lerner, Ellen Moers, and Ann Firor Scott. During the 1950s and 1960s, they often worked in isolation. In contrast, the second group, "Millett's sisters," had a sense of moving comradeship. Graduate students or young writers in the late 1960s, we enjoyed the self-conscious bonds of sisterhood. As Carroll Smith-Rosenberg, a founder of women's history, has recently written: "it is easy to forget the spirit of those early years. Nor have younger scholars just becoming aware of women's history any way of knowing the fervor we brought to our task or with what elation and camaraderie we turned to each other."[11] Many of the formulations of "the mothers" and "Millett's sisters" have deservedly become commonplaces. Think of "the female world of love and ritual," "gynocritics," "the madwoman in the attic," "the female experience," "double jeopardy," "our bodies, ourselves," or "sexual politics" itself.

Gazing back at this lot, I feel enormous pride and the occasional bout of intellectual embarrassment. For some of our ideas and analyses had their sweet and sour simplicities. Given our position, and our perception of writing many things *for the first time*, this was inevitable. That perception, of course, was part of our elation. Gazing across at the newer generations, I feel enormous relief that they are there. For who wants to say something, *as if it were new*, and then have it disappear before it has a chance to get old? Moreover, women's studies began as a revisionary act. So doing, it provided a model of thought as persistent revision, consistent correction. In brief, women's studies demonstrated that thought was thinking. It would be, at best, ironic if the growth of women's studies meant betraying that model.

One crucial development in the 1970s was a sophisticated query into the theory and practice of science. Evelyn Fox Keller, for example, began to publish her influential essays in the late 1970s. Significantly, Keller used some of the tools of revisionary psychoanalysis. For a second expansion in the 1970s was the alliance of various schools of revisionary psychoanalysis and feminism. Think of the difference between two equally important texts: *Women and Madness* (1972) and *The Reproduction of Mothering* (1978). In turn, revisionary psychoanalysis joined with the postmodern concern with ideology, the production of meaning, systems of signification, interpretation, and the reliability of our representational codes. This wonderful ferment, feminist postmodernism, boldly announced itself in 1979 at the Barnard College Scholar and the Feminism Conference. Women's studies is still swimming in the shock waves.[12]

Let me cite three examples of these changes:

1. Many of our smartest literary critics are supplementing the concept of "gynocritics," i.e., the study of the traditions of women writers as women writers, with that of "gynesis," i.e., the study of what the "feminine" and "woman" mean in the symbolic contracts, the accepted sign systems, of various cultures.[13] Both men and women can utter "the feminine."

2. Anthropologists and historians are debating the pervasive practice of separating social reality into two empirical spheres: one his, one hers. Studies of labor, in particular, have consistently investigated "the sex-ordered division of labor" and contended that such a division of labor has been a source of gender inequities.[14] This analysis still very much matters. However, some scholars are now asking for less emphasis on what women seem to do and more emphasis on the interpretations of those activities. In 1980 the late Michelle Zimbalist Rosaldo, a founder of the contemporary anthropology of women, said: "It now appears to me that woman's place in human social life is not in any direct sense a product of the things she does (or even less a function of what, biologically, she is) but of the meanings her activities acquire through concrete social interactions."[15]

3. Some philosophers of science are shifting from a "reformist" to a "revolutionary" position. In an interesting book, Sandra Harding speaks of moving from the "Woman Question in Science" to the "Science Question in Feminism." Inquiry has evolved from "analyses that offered the possibility of improving the science we have, to calls for a transformation in the very foundations both of science and of the cultures that accord it value."[16] Such a transformation would create a culture "uncomfortable with domination."

The presence of several generations is also one sign of the decreasing fragility and the increasing strength of women's studies. At least three widely dispersed, general metaphors for power are now common: the *circle*, or *field*, in which the powerful are in the center, and the less powerful scattered toward the edges; the *ladder*, in which the powerful occupy the top rung, and the less powerful the lower ones; and, finally, the *car*, in which the powerful are in the driver's seat, and the less powerful in the passenger seats, in the trunk, or on the running boards and bumpers. Women's studies is closer to the center, to the top, and to the steering wheel than it was in 1969, or 1974. One of our tasks, then, is to maintain the security of the powers we have gained so arduously. Powerlessness is no fun. Who, after all, would not prefer winning tenure to losing it? Who would not prefer having a budget line to not having one? Who would not prefer being published to being silently garreted? Who would not prefer having a research center in a house rather than an attic? An attic to no shelter at all?

Yet women's studies cannot afford to lose the insights that marginality and alienation offer as rueful compensation for their pain. In *A Room of One's Own*, in a taut meditation about consciousness, Virginia Woolf thinks about being a woman, walking down Whitehall, at the center of what was once an imperial power. "One is often surprised," she writes, ". . . by a sudden splitting off of consciousness . . . when from being the natural inheritor of that civilisation, she becomes, on the contrary, outside of it, alien and critical."[17]

But how does one maintain some power and retain the acute perspectives of the outsider? How *does* one do *this* balancing act? Surely one way is to be wary of the sneaky suzerainty of the unconscious. Such a wariness reminds us that our conscious ideas and actions have their hidden motives and disguised compulsions, which personal circumstance and ideology form. As Sandra Harding writes, "it is the tensions we long to repress, to hide, to ignore that are the dangerous ones."[18] Fortunately, both "gynesis" and other postmodern feminist theoreticians insist on the power of the unconscious, over men and women alike. Another way, in the domain of consciousness, is to guarantee that new voices resound through women's studies. Crucially, women's studies in one country can connect even more systematically with women's studies outside of its borders—whether or not those efforts call themselves "women's studies." In the mid-1970s, the Wellesley Center's Conference on Women and National Development, like the United Nations conferences during the Decade of Women, helped to initiate this process.

Obviously, women's studies outside of the United States has more to do than to teach women's studies to the United States. If we adopt the role of dependent student, we will be lazy and self-pitying. Nevertheless, if we are willing to learn, women's studies outside of the United States has much to teach us. It can challenge our affluent, but tacky, provincialism. It can offer approaches that the United States has not yet tried to such policy questions as child care; to such social and political questions as the best forms of women's collective action; and to such methodological questions as the most useful ways of doing research about women. Especially in the developing countries, where poverty is so vast and vile, women's studies must investigate literacy as well as higher education; rice-milling technologies as well as household appliances; water supplies as well as information retrieval and data banks. As a result, most projects bind research to social action even more closely than the United States does.

Finally, women's studies outside of the United States can repudiate loftier United States generalizations about women as a globally common group. Of course, women's lives do mirror each other. In country after country, women are victims of rape and of domestic brutality; sexual viciousness and control; illiteracy; labor exploitation; and the growing pauperization of women. In country after country, they are also responsible for basic survival needs—for preparing food, water, milk. Women are responsible for offering the breast, the back, and the knee. Perhaps if one question can bring researchers about all women together, it is that of basic survival. How are we to free ourselves of hunger, thirst, sapping illness, ignorance, violence, and the threat of nuclear death?

Yet as women within one country differ among themselves—by race, class, political convictions, religion, region, sexual preference, and temperament—so, too, do women around the world differ from each other. Women's studies must understand these differences, *this* herterogeneity. For example, women's studies outside of the United States can remind United States women that they may suffer from sexism. Nevertheless, many United States women also have privileges as comparatively free citizens of a country that takes such an armored interest in international relations. The process of mapping those privileges is one reason, although only one reason, why United States women's studies has had to revise and roughen its pictures of women as victims.

## Women's Studies as a Contested Intellectual Zone

In the collaboration and collision of women's studies in the United States and abroad, women's studies will become even more of an intellectually contested zone. I will not generate an encyclopedic list of themes, of subjects, that will flourish in this zone. However, some entries are now more nagging than others. To outsiders, the first may seem arcane, but it asks nothing less than what the subject of women's studies is. Is "it" women, or is "it" gender? A recent editorial in *Signs* put the matter more reluctantly: "should women's studies yield to gender studies?"[19] That verb, *yield*, represents women's studies as both a road sign and a pliant maiden. And what, the feminist postmodernist would ask more forcefully, is the meaning of "women" and of "gender"?

Obviously, *some say*, we should first understand women: their histories, culture, labor, and habits.[20] That vantage point can then help us to see the rest of history and society. However, our first responsibility is to women. *No*, others say. We must first understand gender: the economic, social, familial, and psychological architecture of femininity and masculinity. We must connect the lives of men and women and graph the formation of sexual identities. We must decipher the patterns of behavior that men and women, *as men and women*, learn, act out and act on. That vantage point can then help us fit gender into other social structures—like those of race and class—that organize culture and society. In 1981 Myra Jehlen, in a famous article, lamented the "isolation" of women's studies. She called for an "alternative definition" that would make women's studies "the investigation, from women's viewpoint, of everything, thereby finding a way to engage the dominant intellectual systems directly and organically."[21] So reasoning, in 1986 the Center for Research on Women at Stanford University changed its name to the Institute for Research on Women and Gender. In 1987, the University of Texas Press announced that it would publish a new journal in 1988 entitled *Genders*. An initial advertisement promised it to be "the first journal in the arts and humanities to make issues of gender its principal concern. . . . The significance of sexuality and gender in relation to particular historical periods or cultures will be explored as well as the representation of gender in the words of specific artists, critics or historians."

This dialogue between women's studies and gender may seem to be pointing to a distinction without a difference; to be more nutty academic nit-picking. However, this dialogue points to far more than a distinction without a difference. A case in point: the study of teenage pregnancy matters enormously in itself, as a basis for social policy, and as a way of helping young adults to understand their own behavior. However, whom should we study? Young mothers, or, simultaneously, young mothers and the fathers of their children? Indeed, as women's studies has become more panoramic, as the study of a sex has become the study of a system, something else has come into clearer focus: the other sex, men; the other sign, "man." In 1987, men's studies had new vigor. Doing women's studies, I spy two schools of men's studies. The first seeks to combine the study of men with women's studies. Sensitive to gays and lesbians, in debt to feminism, it is wary of using the study of men to reconstitute a liberal chauvinism. The second seeks to combine the study of men with a suspicion of women's studies. It seems not to mind using the study of men to reconstitute some of the hectoring moods of patriarchy.[22]

Several years ago, women's studies discharged a great deal of energy on the question of the relationship of separate women's studies programs to mainstreaming activities. Would mainstreaming permit institutions to erase, not only women's studies, but independent women, especially women of color and lesbians? The process of answering this question showed that separate programs and mainstreaming could and should coexist. They were interdependent. Today, the question of whether we are studying "women" or "gender" is equally demanding. Shooting through our debates is a fear similar to the one our earlier debate provoked. That is, are we erasing women and the women's movement? Are we diluting, even sacrificing, our passions and pain? I believe that once again the process of answering our own question will show the weakness of the question itself. For the study of women and that of gender are not mutually exclusive. They, too, are interdependent, as mingled as the verb and the sentence.

Both the study of women and the study of gender struggle with the meaning of sexual difference. Inexorably, definitions of "woman" entail contrasting definitions of "man." Just as inexorably, sexual differences mesh with, if they are synonymous with, gender markings. I have often isolated two major attitudes toward sex differences. Many call the quarrel between them "sameness" versus "difference." In law, it becomes "equal treatment" versus "special treatment." I refer to the two groups as "minimalists" and "maximalists." The "minimalists" are more pervasive. They realize that men and women have had dissimilar bodies, work, life spans, speech patterns, and powers. However, minimalists go on, historical forces, and processes of socialization, have largely determined those dissimilarities. Neither cosmic spirits nor hormones have mattered as much. If we were but to change historical conditions, and conditioning, most sex differences would become obsolete. We would see them for what they very well might be: a concept, a construct, a cultural fiction. In science fiction, Ursula LeGuin's novel, *The Left-Hand of Darkness* (1969) explores this vision; in literary criticism, Carolyn Heilbrun's *Towards a Recognition of Androgyny* (1973) does so. Not surprisingly, a sociologist, Cynthia Fuchs Epstein, most recently stated the "minimalist view":

> On the basis of current research, the biological differences between men and women have little or no relevance to their behavior and capacities apart from their sexual and reproductive roles; even the effects of early gender socialization may be reversed by adult experiences. A growing body of knowledge indicates that, under the same conditions, men and women show similar competence, talent, ambition, and desire in activities that range from running races to doing scientific research. That conditions vary so regularly and decisively for men and women has more to do with divisions of power in society than with innate sex differences."[23]

The second attitude is that of the "maximalists." They propose that deep, transcultural forces create many sex differences; that the link between sex, a biological condition, and gender, a social creation, is far more profound than the easygoing "minimalists" believe. Traditionally, the belief in sex differences has joined with and ratified a commitment to hierarchies of power within the family, community, and state. Think of St. Paul and Charles Darwin. However, the "maximalists" are also feminists. Their politics unites a theory of sexual difference to a commitment to gender equity within family, community, and state. To oversimplify, a "minimalist" stresses sexual similarities, the sexual sameness, between men and women as a theoretical basis for gender equity. A "maximalist" stresses the novel possibility of using sexual dissimilarities as a theoretical basis for a double task: recognizing what might be "special" about women and simultaneously claiming that they ought to have the opportunities and rights of men.[24] How this latter position might embed itself in law (through regulating pregnancy, for example) and everyday life (pregnancy itself, for example) is still murky, unsettled, controversial, and messy.

Speaking up for the "maximalist" position are some unusual allies: American social science; French gender theory, which revisionary psychoanalysis has influenced; and American radical feminism and lesbian theory. More and more outspoken, the "maximalists" divide against each other. In the 1970s, at least four "maximal" positions began to emerge. As they did so, "female" characteristics have assumed more and more grandeur. This development, too, both paralleled and influenced the growing suspicion of too active and complete an adherence to the theory of women as passive prey; too flattened a picture of Woman, be she Total Woman or not, as Total Victim.

The *first* position claims that differences between men and women exist. The cause is unclear. Because female characteristics have value, we tamper with sex differences gingerly. I think, for example, of Carol Gilligan's famously famous work on moral reasoning. In part, Gilligan's work is appealing because it is correct. Earlier pictures of moral development did erase women. In part, Gilligan's work is appealing because it is eloquent and humane. Finally, it dares to talk about morality, about value, in ways that validate the difference of women's experience without casting women as a radically separate species.[25] I think, too, of Alice Walker's lyrical definition of "womanist." The womanist is first a "black feminist or feminist of color," but she is also "a woman who loves other women, sexually and/or nonsexually. Appreciates and prefers women's culture, women's emotional flexibility . . . and women's strength. Sometimes loves individual men, sexually and/or nonsexually. Committed to survival and wholeness of entire people, male *and* female. Not a separatist, except periodically, for health."[26]

Interestingly, some "socially conservative" women (that group that women's studies tends to ignore) also believe in strong sex differences, in deep gender markings. They often fear gender change because they assume that men will then evade their "male" responsibilities, while women will lose their "female" role without any acceptable alternatives. To them, feminism destroys the reliabilities of gender, and then, heedlessly and headlessly, passes on.[27] Sex and gender as usual mean security.

A *second* position claims that differences between men and women exist. The cause is evolution. As our species developed, its survival depended on each sex having certain capacities. Because the cause is so immense, we tamper with sex differences gingerly. I think, for example, of Alice Rossi's theories. First appearing in the 1970s, they partially elect the body as a legislator of social relations.[28] Though far more disdainful of positivism than Rossi, radical cultural feminists who work on peace issues also claim that women, because they are women, have a special relationship to survival issues.

A *third* position claims that differences between men and women exist. The cause lies in the psychological, linguistic, and somatic relationships among mother, father, and child. However, these maximalists differ violently among themselves. *Some* work with Freudian and revisionary Freudian theory. They tend to focus on the triangle of father, mother, and son, and the son's entrance into the father's culture during the Oedipal period. Indeed, the male, the phallic, signifies culture itself. *Others* work with lesbian feminist theory. They tend to focus on the relationship of father, mother, and daughter. When the daughter enters the father's culture, she must relinquish the deepest of bonds, those between mother and child, in order to seal herself into a patriarchal cell, a submission that law, money, religion, government, and male physical power demand. *Still others*, largely in France, work with a volatile compound of psychoanalytic, lesbian feminist, and deconstructive theories. They often praise a specifically female and/or feminine language, "écriture féminine," that will flow forth from women's flesh and from our pulsating engagements with that flesh when women permit their flesh and bones to speak.[29]

A *fourth* position claims that differences between men and women have existed in history. The cause is reproductive capacities. However, history is severing the link, first for men, now for women, between biological, reproductive self and social roles. The scholar ought to be a maximalist in examining the past, a minimalist in examining the present. I think, for example, of Mary Hartman's ideas about the development of gender roles in the West.[30]

Frankly, I am an unregenerate minimalist who learns from the maximalists. However, I am wary, in the late 1980s, of too excessive an infatuation with this particular debate. I have at least three reasons for my suspicion. *First,* when we talk about sex differences, we are talking about statistical differences, about averages. We tend to forget the overlap between the sexes; the fact that some men may be very good at "female" tasks and some women very good at "male" tasks. *Next,* when we talk about sex differences, we often try to say that "nature" is responsible for so much, "nurture" responsible for so much. However, the relationship between nature and nurture, biology and culture, is too complex, subtle, and dynamic to admit of any precise and final measurement. To define that relationship is like weighing air with broken balloons. *Finally,* to speculate too much about sexual difference, about what is "female" and what is "male," is to recapitulate that old error of thought: dualizing the world, dividing it into rigid sets of binary oppositions, and then insisting that these sets stamp out our identities. Surely one of our great challenges is to rethink the world—not as a monolithic blob, not as a set of dualities, divided, for example, between an Evil Empire and The City On a Hill, but as a multiplicity of heterogeneous identities and groups, as a dazzling display of individual complexities, of others, and of othernesses. Only such a perception will organize the politics that the late twentieth-century so desperately needs: a politics that accepts differences and rejects dominations.

Despite my doubts, the debate about sexual differences goes on and on. Its lack of resolution is intellectually and politically significant. Many people apparently hope that the discovery of deep differences between men and women, lying beneath the seas of history like tectonic plates, will explain why and how the experiences of men and women have been so different as they have ridden through those waters. Moreover, the analysis of those deep differences may justify one set of social and legal policies, or another.

Let me offer two recent examples of the intersection of controversial research about sex differences and policy. The first is a recent article in the *New York Times Magazine,* that journalistic bridge between ideas and influential publics. In it Richard J. Herrnstein and James Q. Wilson argue that both biological and sociological factors help to create criminals. Moreover, they go on, men, especially young men, are far more apt to be criminal than young women, *because they are young men.* To support this assertion, they cite the work of Eleanor Maccoby and Carol Nagy Jacklin about possible sex differences in aggression.[31]

My second example is a courtroom in Chicago in June 1985. This official site has now become liquid fuel for the rocket engines of contemporary notoriety. A judge is trying a great anti–sex discrimination case, which the EEOC had filed, in 1979, against Sears Roebuck. It is the last of the class action suits against major companies. Two feminist historians are among the witnesses. One, Rosalind Rosenberg, supports Sears Roebuck. The lessons of history, she asserts, teach us that a female culture has created women who have values other than those of a masculinized, competitive marketplace. They choose to take less well paid and less competitive jobs. Rosenberg also testifies that statistical evidence is no evidence of discrimination.

The second feminist historian, Alice Kessler-Harris, supports the EEOC (Nearly every other feminist historian I know, but not every other one, thinks Kessler-Harris the more accurate witness.) The lessons of history, she asserts, teach us that the structure, ideology, and practice of the marketplace discriminate against women. Give women opportunities, she goes on, and they will choose to go after well-paid and competitive jobs. In February 1986 the judge, a Republican appointee, ruled Sears not guilty. He explicitly cited Rosenberg's testimony as one reason for his ruling. The vapor trails of this case are still traveling through women's studies and women's history, in part because the media construe it as an intellectual drama, or, more vulgarly, as a "catfight between two feminists." However, the case asks severe questions, not only about women's history, but about the broad relationship of scholarship to action and about the more specific relationship of scholarly to legal discourse. Finally, it shows that women's studies has lost an absolute moral consensus about what its practice ought to mean.[32]

In the next decade, the practitioners of women's studies must decide if they will rebuild a consensus or live, consciously, with sects and schools. Simultaneously, these practitioners must confront even more intellectual mysteries, both old and new, that demand their attention. In more sober terms, women's studies has a research agenda. Linking theory and practice, each item on this agenda ultimately concerns the ways in which women will lead their various lives and in which societies will manage gender. My questions begin with the body and become more and more expansive until they touch "the spirit" itself. They start at a physical point and then move outward in four widening circles.

Let me chalk in these circles.

First, among the most obvious differences that *we perceive, that we believe we see*, between men and women today are those of the body as a sexual agent. Indeed, some powerful feminist intellectuals believe sexuality—"its social determination, daily construction, birth to death expression, and . . . male control"—to be their central issue.[33] However, sexuality means several things. *On the one hand, sexuality can mean eros, desire.* What is the nature of female sexuality? Is it the construct of an exploitative male culture, or is it a source of a rebellious female pleasure? If it is a source of a rebellious female pleasure, what provokes and gratifies that pleasure? Can it include a self-chosen sadism or masochism? A delight in pornography?[34] The fierce divisions among feminists about the legal control of pornography are as much a quarrel about the nature of female sexuality as they are about the importance of the First Amendment or about the wisdom of coalitions between feminism and right-wing political groups.

*On the other hand, sexuality can also mean motherhood, reproduction.* Physically, what are the appropriate forms of family planning and maternal health? Psychologically, what does it matter, as Nancy Chodorow and others have asked, that mothers mother? Psychologically and socially, who else but women can mother? Who are the new fathers? The new caretakers? Socially and economically, what are we to think of the new technologies of birth? Who will devise and profit from them? Socially and politically, who will control women's bodies—their sexuality? their maternity?

Next, our body is only part of our identity, of the self. Indeed, our identity, both psychic and cultural, probably shapes our sense of the body. How are femininity and masculinity designed, built, and kept going? How, in other words, is "gender identity" generated? If we believe that a sense of autonomy is a good for both sexes, not just for men, how do we create such a sense of autonomy in more women without, at the same time, breeding monsters of selfishness and self-regard? But, postmodernist feminists are asking, what does that term, "the self," really mean? Women's studies has tended to believe in the Cartesian ego; in an autonomous, unified, and substantive self. It has wanted women to claim the potencies of this ego. However, what if such a concept of the self were an illusion? What if our interrogations showed "the self" to be the consequence of the discourse of a particular culture, not a universal metaphysical entity? What new narratives of "the self" might we then wish to write? Might we, for example, wish to describe ourselves as an incessantly evolving and uncertain, but valuable, series of fragments? Of several simultaneous, often conflicting, identities? Split, as Adrienne Rich writes, at the root, but split creatively, not schizophrenically?

Next, the self is only part of larger secular structures. *Familially*, what new forms are emerging? What are our forms of intimacy, care-taking, and child rearing? How can we create family forms free from the family crimes of domestic violence, incest, and the exploitation of women's work? *Educationally*, what practices work best for all women? How much is education a force for equality? *Economically*, what should women's work be like? What should its rewards be? How should the discriminatory injustices of the market be judged and erased? What should the economic position be of those who are not in the public labor force? Women and children on welfare? The home-maker? Most of these questions, of course, lunge out of that mon-strous phenomenon: the feminization of poverty, or, the pauperiza-tion of women. *Politically*, what must we do to obtain equality—if that is possible? What are the mechanisms that drive the vile ma-chinery of domination? How does gender inequity mesh with other patterns of domination and submission? Can we trust that sacred monster, the modern state, to control that machinery, or is the mod-ern state the most dangerous machine of all? Does modernization free? Enslave? Or both?

Finally, my fourth circle. Many avert their eyes from this figure. However, secular structures may only be part of vaster cosmogra-phies. In the past, women's studies has been a greatly secular enter-prise. However, some scholars and some cultural feminists have asked two questions: 1) Historically, what have been the relationships of theology, the church, and women? Have churches maimed, or saved, or both? For black women in the United States, for example, the church could be a source of political and religious salvation. 2) How might we reconcile gender equality with a sense of the sacred that gives meaning to birth, life, and death? With a sense of something-beyond-ourselves that sanctifies us? If we seek such a reconciliation, shall we abandon traditional, institutional religions and go beyond their boundaries? Shall we, for example, believe in polytheistic goddesses? Or shall we assume that institutional religion can redeem itself? Shall we be "radical monotheists"?[35]

Organized religions are bringing great pressures to bear on various societies and on the women in them. Popes, priests, preachers, and *mullahs* are demanding conformity with their interpretations of sa-cred texts. For an array of reasons, some women will find conformity comforting. At the same time, the quest, by men and women, for a source of significance beyond history, beyond culture, is intensifying.

Many people wish to transcend the profane. These two efforts—the pressure of organized religions, the quest for significance beyond history—may reinforce each other. They may also collide, as they do for many contemporary Catholic women. Women's studies, not simply feminist theologians, must understand, and no longer ignore, these contradictory patterns of reinforcement and collision.

### Opposition to Women's Studies

Despite the spaciousness of such questions; despite the scrupulousness of our answers, women's studies still meets opposition. In the 1970s, the most common responses, other than a vulgar ignorance, were those tiresome, and tiring, charges that women's studies was trivial; that women's studies was a fad; that women's studies was polemical; that only dolts did women's studies. Intriguingly, some of those dolts have gone on to garner prizes, as Suzanne Lebsock, the historian, did in 1985 when she won the Bancroft Prize in American History for her study of women in a Virginia town. The institutional events at which such responses were perhaps most destructive were faculty tenure decisions.

In the 1980s, as women's studies grew, some of these charges faltered and retired. However, other forms of opposition hopped into their place. Ironically, in some places, women's studies, once a fad, suddenly became passé. Once a flighty trollop, it became, overnight, an old crone. Both guises render women's studies an inappropriate consort for an academic patriarch.

Far more seriously, a disdain for women's studies has become a feature of a larger attack on putatively "liberal culture." The warriors in this attack wear different intellectual clothing, speak in different voices. Among the most clamorous and obvious are social conservatives, who find women's studies a horrifying cesspool of permissiveness and lesbian decadence.[36] Although social conservatives have harassed various women's studies program and activities, they have less academic respectability than a group that has since 1980 achieved not only prominence but political power. I call members of this group the neoconservative thinkers about women (the NCs).

Unlike the social conservatives, NCs accept the fact that women, even wives, can work. Women can even do intellectual work. They can publish in *Public Interest, Commentary,* and *The New Criterion.* However, NCs have at least three major, interlocking disagreements with women's studies. *First,* NCs trust the market far more than women's studies usually does. They distrust any shaking of the market's invisible hand, a shaking that they believe advocates of comparable worth dangerously desire. As a result, NCs attribute women's economic position to an alliance between market forces and women's choices, not to discriminatory practices. *Second,* NCs are suspicious of any analysis that speaks of the "patriarchy," "male hegemony" or "male dominance," or "gender inequity." Blandly indifferent to men's power over women, the NCs find women's studies grim and paranoid about the social relations of the sexes. *Third,* NCs believe that the word "family" applies only to those clusters of intimacy that blood or law creates. Far less cordial to different forms of the family and of intimacy than is women's studies, NCs inevitably valorize bourgeois family forms and its construction of a maternal role. They find women's studies, at best, insensitive to the "historical necessity" of "the family" and overly sensitive to "deviancy."

NCs are not content with disagreement. Their intellectual opponents are less antagonists than sinners. Again and again, NCs declare that women's studies provides yet more proof that the contemporary university corruptly prefers ideology to objectivity, polemics to pure thought. Peter Berger, the sociologist, whose work women's studies' practitioners have often used, grumps accusingly:

> There is a . . . division in sociology now . . . there are the ideologues, who see sociology as an opportunity for advocacy. Some are leftists, some are feminists, but whatever they are, they believe they have the answers before they have the questions. . . . It seems to me that the quality of students entering sociology today is lower than it used to be. That's due mainly to the poor job market, but I think it's also due in part to the effects of the propagandists.[37]

Although he smirks and denies political views, Allan Bloom, that elegant hysteric, also reads women's studies as moral and intellectual decay. Women's studies is a frumpy temptress to the slack. *The Closing of the American Mind,* I fear, is an example of a well-tongued hysterotely. My *Webster's New Collegiate* says that a hysterotely is a: "relatively retarded differentiation of a structure so as to exhibit a form usually associated with an earlier stage of development." Bloom is the best-seller as throwback.

Such socially conservative and NC opposition is itself hardly innocent of ideological self-interest. It has expressed itself materially in the nasty fall in federal support for research about women. From 1980 to 1983, the National Institute of Education reduced grant support for research and training projects about women and minorities from $3.4 million to $168,000. From 1981 to 1983, the National Endowment for the Humanities reduced its support for projects about women from $1.89 million to $876,000. In the same years, the National Science Foundation reduced its grants about women from $2.3 million to $1.4 million.[38] These losses are comparatively tiny in comparison to other federal budgetary commitments—be they to missiles, marching bands, or social security. However, because women's studies has never had much money, even a little loss of largess looms largely.

During the next decade, women's studies must compensate for these lapses. We can, for example, turn to individual states for funds. However, we cannot simply accept federal slaps by turning the other cheek and organizing bake sales. One of our political tasks is to insist upon a federal and national responsibility for the well-being of women and children, and for knowing about them.

Complicating that task is the appearance of still another set of speculators about women. I call members of this group the neoliberal thinkers about women (the NLs). Audaciously, but carefully, they position themselves in what they hope will be a new political center. Like the NCs, the NLs oppose the dominant politics of the post–World War II period. To them, feminism is part and parcel of those politics. However, unlike the NCs, the NLs do not simply oppose feminism and women's studies. Their responses are ambivalent. On the one hand, the NLs call themselves feminists. Associating themselves with the movement, they announce their feminist credentials. However, on the other hand, the NLs disapprove of much of the movement in which they have served their time.

The NLs now have at least two strategies for distancing themselves. First, they proclaim their sorrow that feminism and women's studies have gone astray. If women of color had to correct an obvious racism, the NLs ostentatiously name a far less obvious indifference to ordinary women, especially to heterosexual mothers. Unsurprisingly, mothering, women's most "womanly" role, attracts the otherwise conflicting forces of women's studies since the mid-1970s, the NCs and the NLs. If women of color want feminism to be more progressive, the NLs want it to be more "realistic" about the "average woman's" daily life. This means realizing that the average woman (that sturdy fiction) wants to belong to a "conventional" family— even if she is a part of the public labor force. Second, the NLs ignore much of what feminism and women's studies have actually done. Seeking both originality and the publicity that feeds on novelty, the NLs erase the complexities and accomplishments of the movements they half-embrace. They act as if they were among the very first to discover the values of pay equity, or decent child care policies, or that old war horse, flexi-time.[39] Calling for realism, the NLs deal in half-truths.

## Conclusion

Women's studies, then, confronts several sloppy, but vociferous, forces that wish to efface some of its energetic deeds, that wish to crib, cabin, and confine its energizing future. However, women's studies, like women in higher education, has proved its talent for wild patience, a capacity necessary for survival and for intellectual and moral rejuvenation. Our contests need not be our griefs. What do I do when I do women's studies in 1990? Nothing easy, but nothing less than the retyping of the thought and politics of the late twentieth century.

## Endnotes

NOTE: This paper builds upon three other essays I have recently published about women's studies and the new scholarship about women and gender: "Our 'Wild Patience': Our Energetic Deeds, Our Energizing Future," keynote speech at the Tenth Anniversary Celebration of the Wellesley Center for Research on Women, May 1985, published as Wellesley Working Paper No. 158 (1985), *Women's Studies in the United States: A Report to the Ford Foundation*, with Nina Kressner Cobb (New York: Ford Foundation, 1986); and "The Idea of Women's Studies, The Ideas of Women's Studies: An Assessment," in Tamar March and Judith Pinch, eds., *Interpreting the Humanities* (Princeton, N.J.: Woodrow Wilson National Fellowship Foundation, 1986), 2:89–105.

Women's studies and the new scholarship about women significantly overlap with feminist theory. Both take women as a central subject; both accept as basic the feminist insight that gender inequities are alive, but not well; both burnish that insight from a variety of sources (scholars, writers and artists, oral testimony). However, women's studies tends to provide ideas for institutions, be they educational, political, or cultural. Feminist theory tends to provide abstractions and intellectual direction for a movement, which is at once educational, political, and cultural. Many people seek to combine these diverging forces.

1. For a description of programs, see "Insert, Directory of Women's Studies Programs, 1985 Edition," *Perspectives: Newsletter of the National Women's Studies Association* (spring 1986). vol. 4, no. 2. The figures about sociology are from Tim Corrigan, Bob Connell, and John Lee, "Toward a New Sociology of Masculinity," *Theory and Society* (September 1985), 5:557.

2. For detail, see Joan Kelly, "Early Feminist Theory and the *Querelle des Femmes*," *Women, History, and Theory* (Chicago, Ill.: University of Chicago Press, 1984), pp. 65–109.

3. Influential examples of such work in the early 1970s include Elaine H. Pagels, "What Became of God the Mother? Conflicting Images of God in Early Christianity," published in 1976, reprinted in Elizabeth Abel and Emily K. Abel, eds., *The Signs Reader: Women, Gender, and Scholarship* (Chicago, Ill.: University of Chicago Press, 1983), pp. 97–107; and the essays in Rosemary Radford Ruether, ed., *Religion and Sexism: Images of Women in the Jewish and Christian Traditions* (New York: Simon and Schuster, 1974).

4. Florence Howe, *Myths of Coeducation* (Bloomington: Indiana University Press, 1984) is a collection of essays that traces the development of women's studies from the perspective of one of its pioneers. See, too, my essay, "Women as Knowers," *Feminist Visions: Toward a Transformation of the Liberal Arts Curriculum*, Diana L. Fowlkes and Charlotte S. McClure, eds. (University, Ala.: University of Alabama Press, 1984), pp. 15–24.

5. JoAnn M. Fritsche, *Excellence and Equity: The Scholarship on Women as a Catalyst for Change in the University* (Orono, Maine: University of Maine at Orono, 1985) is an excellent handbook about bringing about institutional change.

6. See "Facts in Brief," *Higher Education and National Affairs*, November 2, 1987, 3; Council of Graduate Schools/Graduate Record Examinations Board, *CGS/GRE Annual Survey of Graduate Enrollment, 1986 Report* (Princeton, N.J.: Educational Testing Service, December 1987). The associate professor is Susan Wiltshire; the university is Vanderbilt. Wiltshire told about her dream, with good humor, at a symposium about women's studies at Vanderbilt on April 20, 1985.

7. "The Annual Report on the Economic Status of the Profession 1986–87," *Academe*, special issue (March–April 1987), 73(2):6. George R. LaNoue and Barbara A. Lee, *Academics in Court: The Consequences of Faculty Discrimination Litigation* (Ann Arbor: University of Michigan Press, 1987) usefully surveys some notable feminist court cases. For an account of the Shaw and Paul cases, see Liz McMillen, "Legal Experts Eye Two Sex-Bias Lawsuits Brought By Women's-Studies Scholars," *Chronicle of Higher Education*, April 29, 1986, pp. 23–25. "Sex Discrimination in Academe," *Journal of Social Issues* (Ethel D. Kahn and Lillian Robbins, eds.) (1985), vol. 41, no. 4 is a solid recent survey. Liz McMillen, "Woman Who Was Denied Tenure Gets $278,000 Jury Award," *Chronicle of Higher Education*, July 23, 1986, pp. 19–20 tells of a successful tenure suit by Kathryn Gutzwiller, a classicist. See, too, "Facts in Brief," *Higher Education and National Affairs*, September 22, 1986, p. 3; Larry Rohter, "Women Gain Degrees, But Not Tenure," *New York Times*, January 4, 1987, p. E-9; an autobiographical account of a feminist scholar who ultimately left the academy, Laura Stempel Mumford, "The Painful Process of Letting Go," *Chronicle of Higher Education*, November 19, 1986, p. 104. "Learning About Women: Gender, Politics, and Power," *Daedalus* (fall 1987), vol. 116, no. 4 (Jill K. Conway, Susan C. Bourque, and Joan W. Scott, eds.) has a number of excellent articles about the contradictory experiences of women in education, intellectual life, and the professions.

8. The literature about mainstreaming is growing. It includes Marilyn Schuster and Susan Van Dyne, *Women's Place in the Academy* (Totowa, N.J.: Rowman and Allenheld, 1985); Ellen Carol DuBois, Gail Paradise Kelly, Elizabeth Lapovsky Kennedy, Carolyn W. Korsmeyer, and Lillian S. Robinson, *Feminist Scholarship* (Urbana and Chicago: University of Illinois Press, 1985);

"Reconstructing the Academy," special issue of *Signs: Journal of Women in Culture and Society* (winter 1987), vol. 12, no. 2; Janet E. Wright and Margaret A. Talburtt, *Including Women in the Curriculum: A Report to the Ford Foundation On the Current State of Knowledge About the Impact of Curriculum Integration Projects* (Formative Evaluation Research Associates, 218 North Fourth Avenue, Ann Arbor, Mich., 48104, August, 1987); Lauren D. Burnbauer, ed., *References from the Speakers' Lectures. The New Jersey Project Integrating Gender, Race, Ethnicity, and Class*, The Summer Institute, June 7–19, 1987 (New Brunswick, N.J.: Rutgers University, Institute for Research on Women, 1987).

9. A description of the intellectual errors that result from omitting women of color from women's studies is Maxine Baca Zinn, Lynn Weber Cannon, Elizabeth Higginbotham, and Bonnie Thornton Dill, "The Costs of Exclusionary Practices in Women's Studies," *Signs* (winter 1986), 11(2):290–303. Among the first of such analyses was Diane K. Lewis, "A Response to Inequality: Black Women, Racism, and Sexism," reprinted in *The Signs Reader*, pp. 169–91. Simultaneously, women of color have been showing the terrible error feminism makes when it ignores and excludes them. See, for example, Bell Hooks, *Ain't I a Woman: Black Women and Feminisn* (Boston, Mass.: South End Press, 1981), esp. pp. 119–96; Gloria I. Joseph and Jill Lewis, *Common Differences: Conflicts in Black and White Feminist Perspectives* (Garden City, N.Y.: Doubleday Anchor Book, 1981); and Paula Giddings, *When and Where I Enter: The Impact of Black Women on Race and Sex in America* (New York: Bantam, 1985; originally published in 1984), esp. pp. 299–357. The Australian journal, *Australian Feminist Studies*, published at the Research Centre for Women's Studies, University of Adelaide, G.P.O. Box 498, Adelaide, South Australia, 5001, balances in an exemplary way concepts common to women's studies in several countries and the analysis of a particular country.

10. Dorothy Smith, "A Sociology for Women," in Julia A. Sherman and Evelyn Torton Beck, eds., *The Prism of Sex* (Madison: University of Wisconsin Press, 1977), p. 169.

11. Carroll Smith-Rosenberg, "The Feminist Reconstruction of History," *Academe* (September–October 1983), 69(5):28.

12. Jane Flax, "Postmodernism and Gender Relations in Feminist Theory," *Signs: Journals of Women in Culture and Society* (summer 1987), 12(4):621–43, summarizes feminist postmodernism.

13. See "Women's Time, Women's Space: Writing the History of Feminist Criticism," *Feminist Issues in Literary Scholarship*, Shari Benstock, ed. (Bloomington: Indiana University Press, 1987), pp. 30–44; Elaine Showalter, who invented the term "gynocritics," helps to map that development. Codifying the gynocritical tradition is Sandra M. Gilbert and Susan Gubar, *The Norton Anthology of Literature by Women* (New York: Norton, 1985). The founding statement about "gynesis" is Alice A. Jardine, *Gynesis* (Ithaca, N.Y.: Cornell University Press, 1985).

14. Heidi Hartmann, "Capitalism, Patriarchy, and Job Segregation by Sex," in Abel and Abel, *The Signs Reader*, p. 193.

15. Michelle Zimbalist Rosaldo, "The Use and Abuse of Anthropology: Reflections on Feminism and Cross-Cultural Understanding," *Signs: Journal of Women in Culture and Society* (spring 1980), 5(3):400.

16. Sandra Harding, *The Science Question in Feminism* (Ithaca, N.Y.: Cornell University Press, 1986), p. 9. Harding meets at least two kinds of criti-

cism: she misunderstands the relationship of science to nature, and she misunderstands the role of women in science today. See, for example, Mary Beth Ruskai, "Letter on Feminism and Women in Science," *Newsletter, Association for Women in Mathematics* (May–June 1986), 16(3):4–6.

17. Virginia Woolf, *A Room of One's Own* (New York: Harcourt, Brace and World, 1929; Harbinger edition), p. 101.

18. Harding, *The Science Question in Feminism*, p. 243.

19. *Signs* (summer 1987), 12(4):619.

20. See, for example, *Theories of Women's Studies*, Gloria Bowles and Renate Duelli Klein, eds. (London: Routledge and Kegan Paul, 1983).

21. Myra Jehlen, "Archimedes and the Paradox of Feminist Criticism," in *The Signs Reader*, p. 71.

22. Examples of the first school are Harry Brod, ed., *The Making of Masculinities: The New Men's Studies* (Boston, Mass., Allen and Unwin, 1987) and Alice Jardine and Paul Smith, eds., *Men in Feminism* (New York and London: Methuen, 1987); an example of the second school is Frank Lentricchia, "Patriarchy Against Itself: The Young Manhood of Wallace Stevens," *Critical Inquiry* (summer 1987), 13(4):742–786. For responses, including an ebullient defense of themselves against Lentricchia's savage attack by Sandra M. Gilbert and Susan Gubar, see *Critical Inquiry* (winter 1988), 14(2):379–413. *Journal of the National Association of Women Deans, Administrators, and Counselors* (summer 1986), vol. 49, no. 4 reviews men's studies.

23. Cynthia Fuchs Epstein, "Ideal Images and Real Roles: The Perpetuation of Gender Inequality," *Dissent* (fall 1984), 31(4):441. See also Judith Lorber, "Dismantling Noah's Ark," *Sex Roles* (1986), 14(11–12):567–80.

24. My thanks to Professor Alison Jagger for help with the relationships between theories of sexual differences and theories of political equality.

25. See Carol Gilligan, *In a Different Voice: Psychological Theory and Women's Development* (Cambridge, Mass.: Harvard University Press, 1982). Among the several commentaries on Gilligan's work is Linda K. Kerber, Catherine G. Greeno, Eleanor E. Maccoby, Zella Luria, Carol B. Stack, and Carol Gilligan, "On *In A Different Voice*: An Interdisciplinary Forum," *Signs* (winter 1986), 11(2):304–33. Mary Field Belenky, Blythe McVicker Clinchy, Nancy Rule Goldberger, and Jill Mattuck Tarule, *Women's Ways of Knowing: The Development of Self, Voice, and Mind* (New York: Basic Books, 1986) sensitively extends Gilligan's theories.

26. Alice Walker, *In Search of Our Mothers' Gardens* (New York: Harvest Books, 1983), pp. xi–xii.

27. I am gratefully adapting Professor Jane DeHart-Matthews' plenary speech on "Women, Tradition, and Politics," Third Annual New Jersey Research Conference on Women, Douglass College/Rutgers University, May 21, 1985. Barbara Ehrenreich, *The Hearts of Men: American Dreams and the Flight from Commitment* (Garden City, N.Y.: Anchor Press/Doubleday, 1983) deconstructs such attitudes.

28. Alice Rossi, "A Biosocial Perspective on Parenting," *Daedalus* (spring 1977), pp. 1–33. For comment see *Signs* (summer 1979), 4(4):695–717. Rossi elaborates her theories in "Gender and Parenthood," a revision of her 1983 American Sociological Association Presidential Address, *American Sociological Review* (February 1984), 49:1–19.

29. Jane Gallop, *The Daughter's Seduction: Feminism and Psychoanalysis*

(Ithaca, N.Y.: Cornell University Press, 1982) succinctly and wittily examines the psychoanalytic foundation of much contemporary French gender theory. Adrienne Rich, "Compulsory Heterosexuality and Lesbian Existence," *Signs* (summer 1980), 5(4):631–56 (often reprinted, e.g., in *The Signs Reader*, pp. 139–68) remains one of the most cogent and eloquent statements of lesbian feminist theory. In 1976 the English translation of Hélène Cixous, "The Laugh of the Medusa," *The Signs Reader*, pp. 279–97 introduced United States audiences to "écriture féminine."

30. Mary Hartman, "Capitalism and the Sexes," *Raritan Review* (summer 1984), 4(1):133 summarizes her position.

31. Richard J. Herrnstein and James Q. Wilson, "Are Criminals Made or Born?" *New York Times* magazine, August 4, 1985, p. 32. A stinging review essay of the book *Crime and Human Nature*, which this article previewed, is Steven Rose, "Stalking the Criminal Chromosome," *The Nation*, May 24, 1986, pp. 732–36.

32. Accounts of the case include Jon Wiener, "Women's History on Trial," *The Nation*, September 7, 1985, cover page and pp. 176, 178–80; "Statistics Have Become Suspect in Sex Discrimination Cases," *New York Times*, February 9, 1986, p. 8E; Karen J. Winkler, "Two Scholars' Conflict in Sears Sex-Bias Sex Sets Off War in Women's History," *The Chronicle of Higher Education*, February 5, 1986, pp. 1, 8; Samuel G. Freedman, "Of History and Politics: Bitter Feminist Debate," *New York Times* June 6, 1986, pp. B-1, B-4; Carol Sternhell, "Life in the Mainstream," *Ms.* (July 1986), pp. 48–51, 86–91; "Women's History Goes to Trial: EEOC v. Sears, Roebuck and Company," *Signs* (summer 1986), 11(4):751–79; and Ruth Milkman, "Women's History and the Sears Case," *Feminist Studies* (summer 1986), 12(2):375–400 (a good statement of the debate between theories of sexual sameness—or equality—and sexual difference). See, too Alice Kessler-Harris, "*Equal Opportunity Employment Commission* v. *Sears, Roebuck and Company*: A Personal Account," *Radical History Review* (April 1986), 35:57–79; and Joan Hoff-Wilson, "The Unfinished Revolution: Changing Legal Status of U.S. Women," *Signs* (fall 1987), 13(1):30–33.

33. Catharine A. MacKinnon, "Feminism, Marxism, Method and the State: An Agenda for Theory," in Abel and Abel, *The Signs Reader*, p. 241.

34. The Barnard Conference, "Towards a Politics of Sexuality," (1982), whipped open the complex argument about female sexuality. Its papers are in Carole S. Vance, ed., *Pleasure and Danger: Exploring Female Sexuality* (Boston, Mass. and London: Routledge and Kegan Paul, 1984). Other important texts are Ann Snitow, Christine Stansell, and Sharon Thompson, eds., *Powers of Desire: The Politics of Sexuality* (New York: Monthly Review Press, 1983); Barbara Ehrenreich, Elizabeth Hess, and Gloria Jacobs, *Re-making Love: The Feminization of Sex* (Garden City, N.Y.: Anchor Press/Doubleday, 1986). Susan Rubin Suleiman, "Writing and Motherhood," in Shirley Nelson Garner, Claire Kahane, and Madelon Sprengnether, eds., *The (M)other Tongue: Essays in Feminist Psychoanalytic Interpretation* (Ithaca, N.Y.: Cornell University Press, 1985), pp. 352–77 lucidly surveys the nexus of psychoanalytical theory, mothering, and language.

35. I am indebted to Professor Cheryl Townsend Gilkes for this phrase, as well as for her remarks about black women and the church in her plenary speech on "Women, Tradition, and Religion," Third Annual New Jersey Re-

search Conference on Women, Douglass College/Rutgers University, May 21, 1985. Elisabeth Schussler Fiorenza, *Bread Not Stone: The Challenge of Feminist Biblical Interpretation* (Boston, Mass.: Beacon Press, 1984) intelligently seeks a feminist interpretation of the Bible.

36. A perfect example is an academic who earned degrees from the University of Chicago and Yale before migrating to Australia in 1971, Hiram P. Caton; see his wild little polemic, *Feminism and the Family* (Queensland, Australia: The Council for a Free Australia, 1985).

37. Peter Berger, "Sociologists Examine an Issue That's Very Close to Home," *New York Times*, April 28, 1985, p. 7. See, too, the ever-alarmed Michael Levin, "Women's Studies, Ersatz Scholarship," *New Perspectives* (summer 1985), 17(3):7–10. The U.S. Commission on Civil Rights publishes this journal. G. R. Elton, "History According to Saint Joan," *American Scholar* (fall 1985), pp. 549–55 is full of spleen. For an intriguing example of a supporter of women's studies and of the women's movement who still slippingly reveals patriarchal attitudes toward them, see Lawrence Stone's review of two books on women's history in the *New York Review of Books* (April 21, 1985), 32(6):21–27; two corrective letters from Mary Prior and Joan Scott, in the May 30, 1985 issue of the *Review*, pp. 52–53, and Stone's apology and explanation, especially to Scott (p. 53). My essay, "Nancy Reagan Wears a Hat," *Critical Inquiry* (winter 1987), 14(2):223–43, reprinted in a selection of my essays, *Where the Meanings Are* (New York and London: Methuen, 1988), has a more detailed account of the NCs.

38. See the *Report* of the Commission on New Funding Priorities, May 1985, from the National Council for Research on Women, located at Hunter College, New York. The cut in support for women's studies is, of course, but part of larger budget patterns. The proposed U.S. budget for FY 1987, which totalled $994 billion, had these outlays: defense, 27.5 percent; health, income security, and veterans' benefits, 45 percent; net interest, 14.5 percent; international affairs, general government, administration of justice, and revenue sharing, 3 percent; science, energy, natural resources, agriculture, 4 percent; commerce, transportation, and commercial development, 3 percent; education, social services, 3 percent. The last 3 percent includes cultural programs, which come to .05 percent of the total budget. Women's studies is attracting more money from the private sector—e.g., the Doris Stevens Foundation recently gave Princeton University $1,250,000 to establish a professorship in women's studies (*Princeton Weekly Bulletin*, May 26, 1986, p. 1). However, such philanthropy is still the blissful exception rather than the blessed rule.

39. Sylvia Hewlett, *A Lesser Life: The Myth of Women's Liberation in America* (New York: Morrow, 1986) exemplifies ambitious neoliberal thought. I owe the phrase "neo-liberal thinkers about women" to Sara Lennox, who used it during a seminar I conducted at the University of Massachusetts/Amherst, November 1985.

# 4

## Literature and Politics: Black Feminist Scholars Reshaping Literary Education in the White University, 1970–1986

### Nellie Y. McKay

*Focusing on black feminist scholars in white institutions of higher education over the past twenty years, Nellie McKay examines the position of these scholars and evaluates their influence on literary studies. McKay begins with the civil rights movement, its effect on the academy, and its consequences in making a space for black studies and increasing the presence of black scholars and students. Identifying the struggles of black feminist scholars within this larger trend, McKay explains how, paradoxically, these women often found themselves marginalized by the civil rights and women's liberation movements, each of which ignored the issues of the other. Black feminist scholars, despite these odds, fought their way into white colleges and universities, where they had and continue to have a major positive influence.*

Although black women were for a long time, extremely restricted within American education, they have always been significantly involved in it, even before the Emancipation of 1863. Through much of the nation's history they have been teachers, but until recently they had almost no opportunities to become scholars in their fields, or to determine authority over the nature of those fields. From the nineteenth century and until the 1960s, first for literate free black women in the North, and later for all qualified black women in the North and South, teaching black children, and often black adults as well, was one of the few areas that afforded them respectable gainful employment.[1] In the twentieth century it also gave them the chance to fulfill the mandate that the "talented tenth" understood as one of its prime responsibilities to the race: the elimination of ignorance through education.[2]

At the same time, beyond the middle of this century, the training of black teachers, and their careers, took place almost exclusively in black schools and colleges in the South, and black women educators were found mostly in elementary and secondary education.[3] This situation began to change with the civil rights movement of the 1960s, largely in the wake of the establishment of Afro-American studies as an intellectual discipline in northern white colleges and universities. For a large number of black people, these programs increased access to jobs in higher education and enabled contemporary black women to redefine their relationship to the national life. For the first time they perceived opportunities to have a voice in and make an impact on all areas of American education. Even today, the majority of black women educators are still involved in black education in segregated institutions, a topic richly deserving of major intellectual attention. However, my purpose here is to focus reflectively on the role that black feminist scholars have played in reshaping literary studies in white institutions of higher education over the last two decades.[4] While many of my claims can be substantiated by verifiable data. I also draw a number of conclusions from my personal experiences in the academy as graduate student and instructor from 1969 to the present. This essay begins with a retrospective view of some of the impacts that the civil rights movement had on the academy.

From its beginning in the 1950s, the movement focused a good deal of attention on the existence and importance of the ongoing black intellectual tradition which originated in the early nineteenth century.[5] The racism that permitted white people to disregard this tradition for more than one hundred and fifty years was a major ingredient in the pressure that black political activists exerted for recognition of that tradition by white America in the 1950s and 1960s. But the black agenda embodied more than nationalistic concerns for the Afro-American experience. Aside from the relatively small body of scholarly work across disciplines that was done by blacks until the 1950s, most previous explorations into black life by white scholars had little relationship to the authenticity of the black experience, and instead stressed deviance and pathology in the black community. These researchers presented blacks as objects rather than subjects: as victims who could not rise above the helplessness of inherited inferiority.[6] Pride in the achievements of the black heritage and the necessity to set the record straight were strong elements in the struggle for the creation of Afro-American studies programs. Subsequent white acceptance (however reluctant at first) of the Afro-American experience as an academic field will always be one of the signal achievements of an era when black people learned that they had group power—that collective action on their part could change the nature of the American experience for everyone. In education, as in everything else connected to their struggle, the aim was to reverse three hundred years of black dehumanization, which was as institutionalized within the white intellectual tradition as in the rest of American life.

The birth of black studies as an area of intellectual inquiry in white colleges and universities took place in a climate of national trauma, on the heels of violent confrontations between black college students and white school administrators. Encouraged by black political activism outside of the academy, in the mid-1960s these students, who had only recently been admitted to white colleges and universities in numbers that made their actions possible, "demanded" that black studies, with intellectual integrity and respect for the black experience, be included in curricula in secondary schools and white institutions of higher education.[7] These students also "demanded" that white institutions expeditiously open their doors to additional black men and women, students and faculty, and that black scholars have a prominent voice in defining the nature of black studies.[8]

As a result of the radical confrontation between black students and white policies and structures governing American higher education, as well as external political pressures from the black community, toward the end of the 1960s many white colleges and universities across the country admitted a number of black women and men, graduate and undergraduate students, and appointed a small number of black instructors to previously all-white faculties. Many of these groups were interested in black studies, for political and/or intellectual reasons, and they "invented" the first courses in the area. Although various difficulties arose and the mistakes made on all sides in the beginning led to the failure of some programs, by the mid-1970s Afro-American studies had taken firm hold inside of American education across a wide area of disciplines, and in different kinds of institutions. Today, while shrinking resources for support of the humanities, a reverse trend in national political priorities, and the decline of black student enrollment since the late 1970s threaten the stability of others, a number of strong programs exist as an integral part of the research and instructional agenda of reputable colleges and universities.[9] The more recent rise of studies in the experiences of other American ethnic groups, and of women's studies, owes much to the young black people who "manned" the barricades for black studies in the 1960s.

Many civil rights activists of the 1960s believe strongly that the movement was truncated, perhaps even displaced by the rise of the contemporary women's liberation movement that gained momentum in the 1970s. Undeniably, as the latter claimed attention, the former lost its place in the public spotlight. It is reasonable to suggest that the one was upstaged by the other because the long tradition of racism made it more palatable to white American men (as holders of power) to confront and negotiate the "demands" of angry white American women who were in search of gender equality than to face the three-hundred-year-old hostilities of black people, many of whom were determined to be denied their humanity no longer. At the same time black women, as a distinct group, were intricately linked to the political dynamics of the civil rights and women's liberation movements. In other words, they were insiders and outsiders in their relationships to both groups. As the two movements collided in competition for attention and national resources, black women found themselves at the intersection where the politics of race and gender sought to silence their voices and render them impotent. In the changing world of the second half of the twentieth century, inside and outside of the academy, politically aware black women faced the challenge of finding autonomy and ensuring black female dignity and self-worth.[10]

On issues of race, black women have a long history of cultural and political activism that goes back to the early nineteenth century.[11] As individuals, and as a group with their men, they engaged first in the struggle against the dehumanization of slavery and later in that against the inequities of segregation and racial discrimination. A few, like Sojourner Truth and Harriet Tubman in the nineteenth century, and Mary McLeod Bethune in the twentieth century, were so spectacular in their performances that the sounds of their voices could not be silenced; but the majority fared less well in the records than did black men. While black men needed and accepted their contributions to the struggles, black women seldom enjoyed the public acclaim they deserved. Names like Frederick Douglass, David Walker, Booker T. Washington, and W. E. B. DuBois were historically representative of black intellectual and political activism long before the civil rights movement of the 1960s, while those of women like Maria W. Stewart,

Frances Harper, Anna Julia Cooper, and Ida Wells Barnett have only recently come to general recognition, and then through efforts spearheaded by black and white women.[12]

Thus, while black women fought for racial justice alongside their men, they suffered sexual and gender oppression at the hands of black and white men. Consequently, for close to two centuries, they have also been in a separate struggle for black women's rights, and they have waged this struggle with the same fervor they gave to the racial struggle. Their position within the context of black and women's rights has always been unique. Gender makes their experiences significantly different from those of black men, and they have had a separate history from white women, one in which they were often oppressed by white American women. As a result, in the contemporary liberation movements, they could not divorce themselves from the male-dominated black civil rights or the white-led women's groups. In their search for equality and access, they did not have the luxury to declare themselves fully independent of black men or white women, and struggled with and against these groups.

In this respect, while sexism in the black community often strained the racial loyalties that black women shared with black men, relations between black and white women floundered on issues of race and class.[13] Too often in the white women's movement privileged feminists, who claimed to speak for all women, seemed unable to see beyond their own concerns, which were often narrowly circumscribed by class and race. In the 1960s and 1970s many black women were appalled at and openly denounced the insensitivity and/or deep-seated conscious and unconscious racism of white feminists. Consequently, at that time radical black women exercised great discretion in joining with white women and black men, leaving themselves space to raise their own voices and to plead their own cause, separate from both groups. Years later, in 1982, Gloria T. Hull, Patricia Bell Scott, and Barbara Smith published the first interdisciplinary anthology for black women's studies called *All the Women Are White, All the Blacks Are Men, But Some of Us Are Brave*, a title that paid tribute to the struggles and achievements of feminist black women in education in the 1970s even as it captured the enigmatic qualities of their situation. Today black feminist critics, as a group, recognize that both the civil rights and women's movements gave them the leverage that enabled them to achieve voice and presence within the academy, but they also enjoy the satisfaction of knowing that whatever successes have come to them individually and collectively, as well as to the area of black women's literature, were hard earned, often in the face of open resistance even from those whom they expected to champion their cause.

By the early 1970s black feminists in literature, concerned about the future of the black female experience within the intellectual tradition, were forced to come to terms with a harsh reality.[14] The gender biases of black men and the race and class biases of white women excluded the unique contributions of the black female experience from more than token representation within the new fields. At the crossroads of black and women's studies, it was clear to black women that neither black men nor white women, in decision-making positions to implement the new areas, gave serious consideration to making these fields inclusive of the black female experience.

This realization created consternation for many black women, but did not weaken their resolve to legitimate the writings of black women and to use this work toward full membership in the community of scholars. By then the number of black women graduate students and young instructors inside of white research universities and white colleges constituted a critical mass in a visible forum. Caught up in the fervor and rhetoric of liberation, they asked new questions about the meaning of black studies and women's studies as disciplines. They took advantage of the fact that the intellectual recognition of the black (male) experience as an entity in the American experience gave them access to institutions from which they were previously excluded, and that the rise of the women's movement provided a new platform within these institutions from which to make themselves heard. Black women with interests in Afro-American literature were helped considerably by the central place that literary studies occupied in the development of Afro-American studies, and did not hesitate to take their discoveries of black women writers into the battle with women's studies. As they perceived it, on one hand, in Afro-American literature, only the voices of male writers had previously served as evidence that black people had spoken out against white oppressive elements in the black experience; on the other, in women's literature, it appeared that only the voices of white women had articulated the female American experience in opposition to patriarchal oppression.[15] Black women's attacks against the new fields were leveled at the gender and race biases evident in the new research and teaching that was underway. In some cases the absence of black women's texts from reading lists was accounted for by their unavailability. Reluctant to admit their biases, the naysayers noted that as far as it was generally known, few black women had written literature, and the books of those who had were out of print. An even more openly hostile remark was that available texts did not meet prevailing standards for literary acceptance.

In fact, there were very few literary texts by black women available for classroom use in 1970. That nineteenth-century black women had written at all was yet to be discovered by almost everyone except a handful of white and black women with interests in black women's history, and even contemporary works of black women writers were almost all out of print.[16] Pressure on publishers to reprint black women's texts did not begin to make an impact until the decade was drawing to a close. Black women activist teacher-critics, in search of their experience in literature, faced the challenges of doing research, teaching, and validating the work of writers whose writings were difficult to locate, and in whom few other scholars were then interested. But these hardships also produced creative anger in the new teacher-scholars. Still, few who faced the dilemma consciously understood the dimensions of their undertaking. In contrast to the early 1970s, today black women's literature is a fully recognized field of study in white colleges and universities, and many black women writers enjoy wide national and international acclaim.[17]

The first substantial group of black women (and men) in literature to complete their training in traditional literature departments in major white universities across the country were the instructors in Afro-American literature in the early years of the 1970s. Even before the contemporary civil rights movement, American education had undergone major changes after World War II, when veterans flocked to take advantage of opportunities they received under provisions of the GI Bill, and again in the early 1960s when the "baby boom" generation came of age.[18] However, the implementation of black studies programs, and the presence of black people in so many institutions where they had not previously been, made even more far-reaching changes in the material content of teaching and in the profession. Bringing differences in perspectives to white colleges and universities, the black feminists in literature, as a new generation of teacher-critics, made a distinctive impact on students, faculty, and the educational system as a whole.

This was also a group prepared for what it wanted and needed to do. Having come of age during the most vital years of the civil rights movement, these women possessed an acute racial awareness, and for all of its shortcomings the white women's movement had awakened their feminist consciousness. They understood their position between two partly established disciplines, and the importance of hard work and confidence in their beliefs. As a beginning, they turned to each other for support, and joined with women's studies and with the men in black studies when it suited their interests. They pressured both groups to include them in their agendas, and in this way launched their own offensives against the discrimination of the systems they had entered. They searched out the out-of-print texts of the writers who truly spoke to their experiences: neglected black women writers like Lucy Terry, Phillis Wheatley, Harriet Jacobs, Frances Harper, and Zora Neale Hurston.[19] And they brought the words and voices of those whom they found into their classrooms and into the discourse of criticism. This was new territory for them and everyone else in these institutions, and in Toni Morrison's words, like countless black women before them (most under much less pleasant circumstances), they made a way where there was none. They read and talked with each other about what they read, and they used the critical tools that they had discovered in studying white male literature to begin to examine the new materials.[20]

In the 1970s these black women teacher-critics, new to faculty politics in white colleges and universities, learned their trade. They knew that the directions of their career lives depended on making themselves and the writers whom they were seeking out visible: on having the names of both groups appear as often as possible in scholarly journals and anthologies; on having their voices speak the words of the writers at academic meetings and conventions; on having their teaching reflect a dimension until then missing from the classrooms in the places where they were employed. None of this was easy, and there were casualties along the way. Some did not survive. In the meantime, each lone black woman in American or English literature in a white college or university (almost always representing all blacks in literature, and often representing black women and men in many disciplines) did these things in conjunction with her other responsibilities: teaching courses in her major discipline (unless she was an instructor in a new Afro-American studies department; serving on committees; counseling students; and learning a new area, the one she insisted existed.[21] And they won a large battle, for today black women writers are well known and many of their texts are readily available. In the early years, however, efforts to bring this material into the classroom meant "finding" those texts and relying on photocopy reproductions of out-of-print works. This latter activity defined what became a crusade to discover a past, to reclaim a history, and to establish the existence of a tradition of black women writing in America.[22] Some black women were sufficiently fortunate to find themselves in institutions where their efforts were supported by a few black men, sensitive white colleagues, and even sympathetic administrations.[23] Other women had negative experiences in this respect. As issues of race and gender have become more prominent in the classroom and in other academic settings, interest in the writings of black women, especially in fiction, has spread to a larger group of faculty, especially to white feminists, and to students.

The critical endeavor also enjoys immeasurable success from the emergence of a new generation of black women writers. Beginning in the early 1970s, this group also benefited from improved access to education and wider occupational options that the civil rights movement made possible for many black Americans and the women's movement made possible for women. In previous decades black women writers had appeared almost singly on the horizon, only to get lost to the world before they had an opportunity to become known. In contrast, the new group boasted numbers that bespoke a new era of black women's self-confidence and literary abilities.[24] Some, like Toni Morrison, June Jordan, and Toni Cade Bambara began their careers as teachers who wrote to preserve their imaginative vitality; others like Alice Walker and Gayl Jones, who also taught, struggled to make writing the focus of their lives; and still others, like Maya Angelou, found their way to writing through other art and media. All claimed a heritage in the writings of the neglected black women who preceded them, and in the words, lives, and dreams of their own mothers and grandmothers. They had in common a vision of the American cultural landscape that was different from that of black men, and from that of white women and men (which is not, of course, to say that all of these black women writers shared an identical or even similar perspective), and they created fresh and exciting autobiographical, fictional, and poetic worlds from black and black female experiences. The rise in their recognition by the American reading public was meteoric, as they captured the imagination of millions of readers. By the late 1970s publishers were eager to print their books, and readers inside and outside of the academy were anxious to read them. They received literary awards and prizes, and rapidly became artists of national and international prestige. The visions they offer, the cadences in their language, the styles they project, the morality they suggest are different from those of black men, or white women or men, and are uniquely emblematic of black female perspectives on black and white Western culture. This is their contribution to the world of literature. These writers were as much of a boon to black feminist critics as the new critics were to the writers. Previously restrictive boundaries on black women's lives in literature gave way to a past that begged restoration and a future bounded only by the receding horizon of the imagination.

In restrospect, for black feminist critics in the academy, in spite of racism and sexism, their struggles of the 1970s paid off well, and in the 1980s, although the challenges remain keen, they enjoy tangible results and rewards. For instance, the names of black women critics now appear prominently in major publications like *Contemporary Literature, New Fiction Studies, New Literary History,* and *Signs, Journal of Women in Culture and Society,* and in a wide variety of anthologies of different kinds of studies in literature compiled by men and women, whites and blacks. Their own full-length studies on the writings of black and white women and men, thematic and theoretical, are appearing with great rapidity.[25] From brave beginners in the early 1970s, they have become competent practitioners in the multiplicity of critical and theoretical approaches in today's sophisticated world of literary studies. Black women critics also appear on panels at national and international conferences, and regularly lecture in colleges and universities across the country and abroad.

Black women also shape literary education in their roles as citizens of the academic community where they bear the burdens of the double minority: as women and minority group people. University and college colleagues and administrators, inside and outside of their home institutions, constantly call on them to serve. Because there are still so few of them, they are overburdened with committee and professional work at home and abroad. Away from home they assist in the evaluation of academic programs in English and American literature and in Afro-American and women's studies, and serve on advisory and editorial boards of journals in their areas of competence. In these various capacities their suggestions make immense contributions to new directions in literary studies.[26] Attempting to fulfill the many demands that are made on them is not a minor task. Most are overworked and overextended, and depend on will, determination, and dedication to carry out their responsibilities. Their strengths, as academicians and scholars, are directly reflected in how steadily they are making their way up the professional ladder in some of the nation's prestigious institutions of higher education.[27]

Within the profession as a whole, and especially among those who work in American or modern literature in other cultures, the interest in black women's writings, especially their fiction, is now extensive. This is a phenomenon worth noting. For one thing, the power in black women's writings had never been associated with long fiction, the genre in which some of the most important and well-known American and European writers have made their fame. Such claims to literary expertise as black women writers were previously recognized for was acknowledged mainly in poetry, with Gwendolyn Brooks, the first Afro-American to receive a Pulitzer Prize in 1950, in the lead. The unanimous positive critical acclaim that fiction writers like Toni Morrison, Alice Walker, Gloria Naylor, Paule Marshall, and others have received places them among the most important American writers of this century, a situation that could hardly have been imagined a decade ago. Morrison's rhetorical question to the *Newsweek* reporter, when she learned that her photograph would be on the cover of that magazine, aptly captures the essence of the changes that have occurred: "Are you really going to put a middle-aged, gray-haired, *colored lady* on the cover of this magazine?"[28]

In the 1960s and the first half of the 1970s black male writers enjoyed an acclaim similar to that which black women have been enjoying since the middle of the 1970s. Today, black men are increasingly concerned that black male writers have been eclipsed by what they call a popular "trend" in favor of their female counterparts. The tension between black male and black female writers and literary scholars has roots in the history that excluded black women's voices from Afro-American studies and traditional departments of literature previous to and during the 1960s, when select black men's voices were included. But there are aesthetic reasons for this development as well. A colleague of mine suggests that in spite of the current conservative political climate, which seems otherwise devoted to the destruction of liberal ideologies and social programs, black women's fiction gains its new currency out of certain conditions of contemporary life. Changes in our social organization have caused more people in the dominant culture to recognize their own powerlessness and marginality (the unstated premises in the literature of that culture), and readers are drawn to works that articulate these premises. Black writers, and even more specifically black women writers, have always had to face experiences that demanded confrontation with these issues, and their literature expresses the nature of their experiences.[29] But while black men projected visions of a world in which race provided almost the only area of conflict between black and white men in the struggle for manhood and power, black women writers have always rejected such binary oppositions and created fictional worlds in which the self is in constant interaction with a variety of issues, including race. Another young critic observes that in their astuteness, black women writers have focused on and engaged the issues of political subordination in a broad spectrum. They are more concerned with the interrelations between racism, sexism, class, and other forms of oppression than many other writers. Unlike black male writers, black women seek mediation rather than challenge.[30] As a result, black women who wrote before, and those now writing, have produced an intricate and compelling literature. The conscious and unconscious recognition of this on the part of many readers and critics has given unprecedented opportunities to contemporary black women writers.

While black feminist critics rejoice with and celebrate their contemporary sister writers, perhaps their most triumphant song is in the tune of their successes in the work of recovery, of excavating the lives and writings of women, some of recent times, others from the past. The earliest recoveries were mostly of living authors whose works were little known and/or forgotten, and out of print—women like Ann Petry and Dorothy West,[31] followed by the writers of the Harlem Renaissance: poets like Alice Dunbar-Nelson and Georgia Johnson, and novelists like Zora Neale Hurston, Nella Larsen, and Jessie Fauset.[32] Following the trail back to the nineteenth century has been particularly exciting as critics recover the lives and works of women like Maria W. Stewart, the first known American woman of any color to speak on a public platform to a "promiscuous" (i.e., male and female) audience on matters of race and gender, in 1831; and Anna Julia Cooper, an early black woman graduate of Oberlin College, a feminist and civil rights activist who later earned her Ph.D. from the Sorbonne and distinguished herself as an educator.[33] These "finds" promise to be the beginning of the wave that brings new materials into use for classroom and research purposes. The discovery of a vibrant black women's tradition in literature has helped to foster the enthusiastic study of contemporary black women writers.

While this essay concentrates on the efforts and accomplishments of black feminist literary critics, I have no wish to understate the value of the encouragement and support black women received from many of their peers and colleagues. Furthermore, the early work of Dorothy Porter, Gerda Lerner, Bert Loewenberg, Ruth Bogin, and Dorothy Sterling was invaluable in tracking down "lost" women. The research and writing of other literary critics who recognized the worth of the materials before they became widely known or popular also lent support to black women. Notably, Robert Hemenway's meticulous *Zora Neale Hurston: A Literary Biography* provides the most complete source of information that we have on that writer, but more than that, it treats its subject with the intellectual seriousness few black women writers had hitherto received from anyone. More recently, William L. Andrews' anthology, *Sisters of the Spirit: Three Black Women's Autobiographies of the Nineteenth Century*, and his study of black autobiography, *To Tell a Free Story: The First One Hundred Years of Afro-American Autobiography, 1760–1865*, have enriched the scholarship of black women's literature immeasurably. The contributions these scholars made to the field come out of their intellectual engagement and appreciation for the integrity of black women's lives, as well as their respect for what black women, as teachers and critics in this field, represent.

Despite the successes this essay describes, working within an educational system that is allied to larger systems and forces in the body politic holds dangers for everyone marginal to this system, including black women writers and critics. Most importantly, these forces hold the power to effectively silence marginal voices through incorporation and appropriation. For example, I am only cautiously pleased that Harvard University now includes a course on black women writers in its core curriculum, and that the *New York Times* not only regularly publishes reviews of the works of black women writers, but acknowledges (bestows authority on) the unique tradition of black women writing. This recognition by Harvard and the *New York Times* was long overdue, but black women must not permit it to alter the fundamental nature of their social and political commitment. Black women writers and critics, taking their identity from themselves, must continue to speak out of their experiences, to use the language and idiom appropriate to the experiences that have empowered the black female self independent of external legitimization.

Also disturbing is the phenomenon of instant popularization of a work by a black woman writer, such as occurred with Alice Walker's *The Color Purple* in 1981 and 1982. Completely divorced from the merits of this book, its widespread instant appeal, at that time, made it the *one* book by a black writer to be included on hundreds of reading lists for college courses, undoubtedly to the exclusion of other important texts by both black women and men. The dangers of the kind of mainstreaming that the Harvard core course, *New York Times* recognition, and *The Color Purple* situation represent cannot be taken lightly. Among other things, the financial rewards and the professional prestige they carry with them are temptation to underestimate the degree to which black women's lives, as a group, remain marginal within the dominant culture. There is great need for the education that insists that no single black voice can represent the black or black female experience in literature.

While I noted earlier that lower black student enrollment in colleges and universities at this time will not seriously impair the health of black studies as a field, I am concerned about the small number of black men and women seeking professions in the academy. The issue is one of training young scholars to carry this work forward in the twenty-first century. Fewer young black people are continuing in higher education than in the late 1960s and early 1970s. Fewer of those who enter college are pursuing careers in the humanities or social sciences, because these areas are no longer economically attractive to black and other minority group people. In the 1980s college and university administrators are demonstrably less concerned with affirmative action policy as a way of attracting black students and faculty than they were in the 1960s and 1970s. These conditions spell trouble ahead. Much has been gained over the past two decades, but the gains are in jeopardy if the black presence is substantially lost in these institutions within the next few years.

With respect to all women's writings, Afro-American literature, and the literature of other ethnic groups, the teaching of literature in English departments and in ethnic studies programs in white colleges and universities is in the midst of a revolution. Perhaps the most concrete evidence of this is the *Norton Anthology of Women's Literature* and the forthcoming *Norton Anthology of Afro-American Literature*. At the same time, the racial/ethnic gender makeup of literature faculties is changing in positive directions, even as non–minority group faculty members engage in new aspects of intellectual development. Students can now obtain degrees in areas that were not in existence a decade ago. In many colleges and universities, the study of literature is no longer confined to a select group of writings from a select social group. A radical example of this shift has occurred in the English department at the University of Wisconsin, Madison, where there are deliberate efforts to define a graduate and undergraduate curriculum that includes all literature written in English. These changes have occurred as a result of the hard work of people inside and outside of the academy (and some of the latter are now gradually becoming insiders). Among the outsiders who invaded the halls of academic privilege in the 1960s and 1970s, black women writers, teachers, and critics have done their fair share to reshape literary education over the past fifteen years. They have made significant contributions to the reconstruction of the "canon" of American literature, through writings that emphasize the pluralism of our society and the richness that many separate voices bring to the intellectual tradition. They need to understand the dynamics of co-optation if they are to continue to have a voice and message that are effective instruments for change.

## Endnotes

NOTE, I am very grateful to my friend, Nell Irvin Painter, for her insightful reading of the first draft of this essay, and for her suggestions which helped to shape it. The essay celebrates black women literary critics across the country, especially the friends of my graduate school years: Thadious Davis, Marilyn Richardson, Barbara Smith, Hortense Spillers, and Andrea Rushing. Their work and affection continue to nourish me.

1. Teaching, lecturing, and the ministry were the occupations that offered a small percentage of black women alternatives to field labor and domestic drudgery for most of American history.

2. The "talented tenth" was a late nineteenth- and early twentieth-century term used to describe the one-tenth percentage (as it was believed to be) of black Americans who, through their education and intellectual and social aspirations (not economics) qualified as the middle class. Its usage signified an obligation of this group to spearhead the "uplift" of the black masses.

3. Most black college students continue to attend black colleges in the South. In these student-segregated institutions (white instructors have always taught in southern black colleges) educators traditionally have large classes, heavy teaching loads, small salaries, many duties, and little or no time for research and writing. They must be given the highest credit for their achievements in the face of tremendous difficulties.

4. Black feminist literary scholars (or critics), as the term is used in this essay, refers to a small handful of women across the country—perhaps less than a dozen in the beginning—who since the early 1970s have been engaged in a collective mission: the critical validation of the black female voice in literary studies. While their wide separation by geographic locations causes frustrations for them, it has perhaps minimized and neutralized many of their personal, philosophical, and even political differences. They are extremely supportive of each other, even when differences surface among them, and they are inextricably linked by their commitment to black women's literature.

5. The black intellectual tradition began in the early nineteenth century, with such documents as David Walker's *Appeal, in Four Articles; Together With a Preamble, to the Colored Citizens of the World, But in Particular, and Very Expressly, to Those of the United States of America* (1829), in *Freedom's Journal*, published in Boston.

6. Black people have been the object of study by white researchers since the late eighteenth century. For example, see George M. Fredrickson's *The Black Image in the White Mind* (New York: Harper and Row, 1971), which documents the negatively biased "Debate of Afro-American Character and Destiny, 1817–1914." In most of this research, blacks emerged as negative stereotypes. For exceptions to this pattern in early white scholarship, see Gunnar Myrdall, *An American Dilemma* (New York: Harper, 1944) and Melville Herskovitch, *The Myth of the Negro Past* (New York: Harper, 1958).

7. In the late 1950s and early 1960s, in the wake of the 1954 Supreme Court decision in *Brown v. Board* (Topeka, Kansas) overturning segregated public education, for the first time in American history a large number of black students entered white colleges and universities across the country.

8. Few white colleges and universities, including Yale and Harvard, es-

caped intense confrontations with black students in these years. Two of the most violent occurred at Cornell University and San Francisco State College.

9. In the 1960s and 1970s, several black studies programs failed (were phased out), largely as a result of institutional racism. But in other ways the field has flourished. Today, showcase programs exist in such schools as Yale University; the University of Wisconsin, Madison; Cornell University; Ohio State University; and Berkeley, where M.A. degrees in specific areas of the field have attracted black and white students from across the country and from Africa, the West Indies, and Europe. Temple University launched the first Ph.D. in the country in black studies in January 1988. In addition, some black and white scholars do rigorous "black studies" teaching and research in traditional disciplinary departments, and have a profound impact on their institutions. In spite of the continuing political importance of black studies, at the present time low black student enrollments in colleges and universities affect the black presence in the academy as a whole more than the advancement of the field. Continuing serious work by black and white scholars makes it impossible to dismiss the area. For instance, the *Norton Anthology of Afro-American Literature*, forthcoming in 1990, will insure us against future marginalization of this canon. Also see Nathan Huggins, *Afro-American Studies; A Report to The Ford Foundation* (New York: Ford Foundation, 1985) for an abbreviated history of the rise and current state of black studies in America.

10. Black women in the academy had strong counterparts outside of its walls whose efforts complemented their own. Women like Shirley Chisholm and Barbara Jordan challenged the legal and political systems, while others worked in education and in community grass-roots operations and made their voices heard in the cause of black women's lives in America.

11. Until recently, women were seldom mentioned in the nineteenth-century black intellectual tradition. Two new books, Marilyn Richardson, ed., *Maria W. Stewart, America's First Black Political Writer; Essays and Speeches* (Bloomington: Indiana University Press, 1987) and Frances Foster's forthcoming collection (New York: Feminist Press, 1988) on Frances W. Harper, are correctives to earlier historical omissions.

12. See note 11. Also see Gerda Lerner, ed., *Black Women in White America* (New York: Vintage, 1972); Bert Lowenberg and Ruth Bogin, eds., *Black Women in Nineteenth-Century American Life* (University Park: Pennsylvania State University Press, 1976); and Dorothy Sterling, ed., *We Are Your Sisters: Black Women in the Nineteenth Century* (New York: Norton, 1984) for the lives of nineteenth-century black women educational, social, and political activists.

13. Class privilege has been the primary cause of anger and hostility between black and white women in America. Black women have felt equally or more oppressed by white women than by white men in such areas as employment, since a large number of black women have traditionally been employed in domestic labor and have more contacts with white women. Since the nineteenth century, even progressive white women, in search of women's rights in a male-dominated society, unless pressed, have often neglected to take the situation of women of color into consideration. A number of scholars have addressed this problem. For instance, see Paula Giddings, *When and Where I Enter . . . The Impact of Black Women on Race and Sex in America* (New York: Morrow, 1984), p. 68.

14. In the Boston area in the early 1970s a group of black women graduate students/instructors in literature (of whom I was one), noting the exclusion of black women's writings in literature, took teaching and writing initiatives to attack that problem. We were also aware of black women in other parts of the country who did the same. Professional meetings gave us opportunities to create networks that enabled us to share information and support each other.

15. Most class syllabi from that period show that neither black men nor white women initially made efforts to include black women in their struggles for literary recognition. Obviously, there are exceptions to this generalization, such as the sensitive efforts of a number of white women at the University of Wisconson, Madison.

16. For instance, Toni Morrison was almost unknown to the larger reading public until the publication of *Song of Solomon*, her third novel, in 1978. At that time, her earlier works: *The Bluest Eye* (1970) and *Sula* (1974) were out of print.

17. International acclaim is evident in the fact that the writings of many black women, including Toni Morrison, Alice Walker, Maya Angelou, Gloria Naylor, and Paule Marshall have been translated into European and non-European languages. Their works are widely read and critiqued in these languages.

18. I am indebted to Nell Irvin Painter for pointing this out to me. Also see Huggins, *Afro-American Studies*, pp. 6–10.

19. "Bars Flight," a short comic poem about an Indian raid on Deerfield, Massachusetts in August 1746, by Lucy Terry (1730–1821), is the earliest extant writing by an Afro-American. Phillis Wheatley (ca. 1753–1784) was the first person of African origin in America to publish a book. Her *Poems on Various Subjects, Religious and Moral* was first published in London in 1773, and in America in 1786. Harriet Jacobs (1813–1897), a former slave, published *Incidents in the Life of a Slave Girl* in 1861. Frances Watkins Harper (1825–1911), born free in the North, was a feminist abolitionist poet, fiction writer, educator, and public lecturer. *Iola Leroy*, her Reconstruction novel, was published in 1892. Zora Neale Hurston (1898?–1960) was virtually unknown in the early 1970s. Her novel, *Their Eyes Were Watching God* (1937), has been applauded as the precursor to contemporary black feminist fiction. Hurston was one of the most significant figures to emerge from the Harlem Renaissance of the 1920s and early 1930s, when Afro-American literature and arts flourished as they had not done before, and would not do again until the 1960s.

20. In the early 1970s a number of black women literary critics in the Boston area met regularly to discuss books by black women writers they had "discovered" and were reading and/or teaching. These meetings provided the only forum for this activity, and the spirited discussions often went on through the night on these occasions. I suspect that the same phenomenon happened elsewhere among black women interested in black women's literature.

21. This does not suggest that a monolithic group of black superwomen literary critics existed in the 1970s. In the first place, the number of black women in literature, as in other academic fields, has always been small. In the beginning it was absolutely necessary for close friendships to develop among these women for the sake of their emotional survival in graduate schools and

in the workplace. Through the 1970s, as instructors, the graduate school friends were dispersed across the country. Each was almost invariably the only person like her in her institution. This meant isolation in places that were often hostile to their interests. Frequent communications between them created the network that enabled many, in those first years of teaching, to keep abreast of others' work and to offer the emotional support that was vital to their well-being. My own observation is that the security of success now permits more diversity of opinions (on academic as well as personal, political, and philosophical issues) among them.

22. In the 1970s black women in literature photocopied and circulated multiple copies of out-of-print texts within the group for classroom use and research. Entire courses were taught with materials duplicated in this way.

23. I am grateful to friends and colleagues, black and white, women and men, at the University of Wisconsin, Madison, for their support in my early years in this institution. University administration support of the Afro-American Studies Department and black junior faculty also deserves commendation.

24. To take black women novelists as an example, Jessie Fauset published *There Was Confusion* in 1924 and *Plum Bun* in 1927, while Nella Larsen published *Quicksand* in 1928 and *Passing* in 1929. Fauset published *The Chinaberry Tree* in 1931. Also in the 1930s, Zora Neale Hurston published *Jonah's Gourd Vine* in 1934, *Their Eyes Were Watching God* in 1937, and *Moses Man of the Mountain* in 1939. In the 1940s, Ann Petry published *The Street* (1946) and *Country Place* (1947), and in 1947, Hurston published *Seraph on the Suwanee* and Dorothy West *The Living Is Easy*. Ann Petry's *The Narrows* appeared in 1953, as did Gwendolyn Brooks's *Maud Martha*. Paule Marshall published *Brown Girl, Brown Stones* in 1959, and her second novel, *The Chosen Place, the Timeless People* in 1969. Margaret Walker's *Jubilee* appeared in 1966; eight writers spread out over four decades. In contrast, Alice Walker, Toni Morrison, Maya Angelou, Toni Cade Bambara, Gayl Jones, Louise Meriwether, Gloria Naylor, and Sherley Anne Williams are among the group that emerged in the 1970s whose names are now well known. In addition, as senior editor at Random House for a number of years, Morrison was responsible for that company's producing works of a number of black men and women, including Gayl Jones and Toni Cade Bambara.

25. For example, see Hazel Carby's *Reconstructing Womanhood* (1987); Barbara Christian's *Black Women Novelists; The Development of a Tradition* (1980) and her *Black Feminist Criticism* (1985); Thadious Davis' *Faulkner's Negro'* (1983); Mari Evans' *Black Women Writers* (1984); Trudier Harris' *From Mammies to Militants* (1982) and her *Black Women in the Fiction of James Baldwin* (1985); Bell Hooks' *Ain't I a Woman; Black Women and Feminism* (1981) and her *Feminist Theory, From Margin to Center* (1984); Gloria Hull's *Color, Sex, and Poetry; Three Women Writers of the Harlem Renaissance* (1987); Nellie McKay's *Jean Toomer, Artist* (1984); Valerie Smith's *Self-Discovery and Authority in Afro-American Narrative* (1987); and Claudia Tate's *Black Women Writers at Work* (1983). Black feminist critics have gained the intellectual respect of their colleagues by their hard work in all areas of academic life.

26. For example, at present I serve on the advisory and editorial boards of six publications, and simultaneously hold an equal number of committee positions in professional organizations. In any single year I review dozens of

manuscripts for journals and book publishers, review the work of no less than five or six scholars for tenure and/or promotion, and serve on a team evaluating English, Afro-American, and women's studies programs. This ongoing work is in addition to responsibilities and commitments to my home institution. As the only black woman in literature at this university, I hold appointments in the Afro-American studies and English departments, as well as in women's studies. I advise the general undergraduate students in M.A. and Ph.D. programs. Since the number of black women in the academy remains small, this work load is not unusual among black women in colleges and universities across the country.

27. Tenured black feminists in literature, associate and full professors, are now located in many colleges and universities across the country, including some of the most prestigious ones.

28. Toni Morrison, *Newsweek* (March 30, 1981), 97:59 (italics mine).

29. Conversation with Professor Craig Werner, Department of Afro-American Studies, University of Wisconsin, Madison, September 1987.

30. Conservation with Judylyn Ryan, black female graduate student in comparative literature, the University of Wisconsin, Madison, September 1987.

31. See note 24. Ann Petry's *The Street* and *The Narrows* were reprinted in 1986 and 1988; Dorothy West's *The Living Is Easy* was reprinted in 1982. Both women are still alive, and Petry continues to write.

32. See note 24.

33. For Maria W. Stewart, see note 11. Anna Julia Cooper's *A Voice From the South by a Black Woman from the South* was first published in 1892.

# 5

# What is the Matter with Mary Jane?
# Feminist Criticism in a Time of
# Diminished Expectations

**Kate Ellis**

*Twenty years ago, according to Kate Ellis, the goal of feminist criticism was different than it is today. Circa 1970, feminist criticism was interested in "interconnection," but today Ellis sees feminist politics and criticism moving toward difference. To be aware of the question of sex or race is to be aware of a difference and an inherent inequality. According to Ellis, feminists can face this problem in one of two ways: either they can rise above the issue of difference and inequality or they can turn away from it and reject the "dominant culture" that fosters this inequality. Looking at some of the writings of Zora Neale Hurston, Toni Morrison, Virginia Woolf, and others, Ellis examines these two "strategies" while using Frantz Fanon's definition of national culture as well as the writings of Kristeva, Irigaray, Todd, Gubar, and others. While recognizing that feminist criticism today must acknowledge the critical observations of the French and others, Ellis also questions this methodology, which emphasizes an individual rather than a collective consciousness.*

One has only to skim those old forgotten novels and listen to the tone of voice in which they are written to divine that the writer was meeting criticism; she was saying this by way of aggression, or that by way of conciliation. She was admitting that she was "only a woman," or protesting that she was "as good as a man." She met that criticism as her temperament dictated, with anger or emphasis. It does not matter which it was; she was thinking of something other than the thing itself.

—Virginia Woolf, *A Room of One's Own*

> At certain times I have no race, I am *me*. When I set my hat at a certain angle and saunter down Seventh Avenue, Harlem City, feeling as snooty as the lions in front of the Forty-Second Street Library, for instance. . . . The cosmic Zora emerges. I belong to no race nor time. I am the eternal feminine with its string of beads.
>
> —Zora Neale Hurston, "How It Feels To Be Colored Me"

**W**hen the first *Politics of Literature* came out in 1970, the aims of feminist criticism were much clearer than they are now. The academy was to be challenged, its priorities were to be reordered, and the culture into which all women woke up every morning would be variously but unmistakably altered by that endeavor. The antiwar movement had exposed the illusion of the university as an "ivory tower" and the women's movement had begun to uncover the web of sexism, drawing together aspects of daily life that had hitherto seemed unrelated. The rallying cry was not "difference" but "interconnection." The point of criticism was to make a difference in women's lives. What has happened in the intervening twenty years has been both exciting and discouraging, as might be expected. Yet as we move through the 1980s and into the 1990s, both feminist politics and feminist criticism have turned toward a celebration of difference. This may up to a point be a necessary compensation for previous denials of difference, but there are undertones of conservatism that need to be examined.

The shift in emphasis represents a new angle from which to look at the same problem: inequality. Consciousness of sex, or consciousness of race, cannot be a neutral matter so long as it involves a consciousness of inequality. One may respond to the inequality by answering back in the ways that Woolf attributes to her nineteenth-century predecessors; or one may soar above it, as Hurston claimed to do, and as Woolf hoped that women writers of genius might all do one day. But as long as inequality is present in the world where books are written, published, and read, it forms a context with which writers outside the dominant white male culture must come to terms. One way to demonstrate that one is "as good as a man" is to do what he does as well as he does, a strategy that carries within it the assumption that the differences between men and women are not significant with respect to the task at hand. An emphasis on difference, on the other hand, in a context of inequality, carries within it the assumption that women are superior, if not absolutely, then at least with respect to the issue around which difference is being raised.

I would like to look at these two strategies for confronting inequality, one seeking to rise above the social dilemmas caused by one's unequal status, the other turning away altogether from the dominant culture. I have drawn on a model that I have found useful for both black and women writers. It is articulated by Frantz Fanon in *The Wretched of the Earth*, in a chapter called "On National Culture." Fanon defines a national culture as "the whole body of efforts made by a people in the sphere of thought to describe, justify, and praise the action through which that people has created itself and keeps itself in existence."[1] He is speaking of colonized Africans, and in particular those "native intellectuals" who recognize their position vis-à-vis the ruling white culture. But parallels can be drawn with the situation of women writers, who were fully aware of the obstacles they faced *as women* in a culture that disapproved of their efforts no less vehemently than white colonists disapproved of literary aspirations among their natives.

A national culture develops, in Fanon's scheme, in three phases. In the first, "the native intellectual gives proof that he has assimilated the culture of the occupying power. His writings correspond point by point with those of his opposite numbers in the mother country." The second phase, arising out of frustration with the first, is impelled by "a secret hope of discovering, beyond the misery of today, beyond self-contempt, resignation, and abjuration, some very beautiful and splendid era whose existence rehabilitates us both in regard to ourselves and in regard to others." Yet this is ultimately unsatisfactory also, since only the externals of the lost world can be recreated. Finally, "in the third phase, which is called the fighting phase, the native, after having tried to lose himself in the people and with the people, will on the contrary shake the people. Instead of according the people's lethargy an honored place in his esteem, he turns himself into an awakener of the people, hence comes a fighting literature, a revolutionary literature, and a national literature."[2]

By placing these phases in a linear relationship, Fanon implies sequential development from one to the next. Such optimism may have been misplaced even for the colonial situations Fanon was describing, since the first stage, in which "the native intellectual gives proof that he has assimilated the culture of the occupying power," seems to have persisted in much of African society after the departure of white rule. Here I would prefer to draw on Kristeva's description of a third phase as "a *signifying space* . . . which does not exclude—quite to the contrary—the parallel existence of all three in the same historical time, or even that they be interwoven with one another."[3] The usefulness of talking about "phases" in this way is that the notion of linearity is removed. A "signifying space" is an interpretive context, a container into which utterances with designated common features can coexist and interact. By this designation, no culture would ever *be* in phase three totally. The other two would be present as boundaries against which phase-three writing would be constantly and continually defining itself.

My reading of the feminist critical enterprise in the 1980s and 1990s is that it is deeply engaged in issues of language and representation that, about fifteen years ago, seemed much simpler and more directly connected to women's lives than they do now. The feminist antipornography campaign is a case in point: a critique that was initially radical and directed toward a key site for the production of patriarchal ideology, but which, by refusing to acknowledge its own contradictions, now finds itself in alliance with the Right. I would like to focus my attention primarily upon phase two in my tripartite scheme because I see "pure" feminist criticism, split off from the concerns of Marxism—the material conditions of women's lives—suffering from some of the limitations that characterize the antipornography movement. What is needed is to ask what might characterize phase three, where, I will suggest, a number of women writers are in fact working.

It is easy enough, looking back, to see the weaknesses of *A Room of One's Own*. "Virginia Woolf was extremely sensitive to the ways in which female experience made women weak," remarks Elaine Showalter, "but she was much less sensitive to the ways in which it made them strong."[4] From one angle, Woolf's prescriptions for bringing "Shakespeare's sister" into being can be read as urging for women writers a situation that corresponds "point by point" with that of white male writers. Members of an elite have, presumably, no need of "saying this by way of aggression, or that by way of conciliation." We know how Woolf lived out the contradictions of her desire to write "as a woman, but as a woman who has forgotten that she is a woman, so that her pages were full of that curious sexual quality which comes only when sex is unconscious of itself."[5] We know also that she shifted her thinking about women to a phase-two strategy recommending, in *Three Guineas*, that women opt out of middle-class male institutions and form their own "outsiders' society."

This could be a progressive or a regressive proposal depending on the context into which it was spoken. A writer who covers both possibilities is Zora Neale Hurston, who is useful for our purposes not only because she is black and female, but also because she came into prominence as a writer at a time when black writers were achieving unprecedented visibility, and saw themselves as a cultural and political vanguard. How does one present one's people, to themselves and to their oppressors, in a way that furthers the goals of the group as a whole? For the question of audience is inevitably present as a context in which writers of any cultural minority choose and shape their material, gain or do not gain recognition. The writers of the Harlem Renaissance succeeded in creating a white audience for their work. Writing in 1925, Alain Locke, one of the mentors and spokespersons for the movement, asserted that the "New Negro" has "carried the folk gift to the altitudes of art."

> Gradually too, under some spiritualizing reaction, the brands and wounds of social persecution are becoming proud stigmata of spiritual immunity and moral victory. Already enough progress has been made in this direction so that it is no longer true that the Negro mind is too engulfed in its own social dilemmas for control of the necessary perspective of art, or too depressed to attain the full horizons of self and social criticism. Indeed, by the evidence and promise of the cultured few, we are at last spiritually free, and offer through art an emancipating vision to America.[6]

By "America" Locke means, of course, white America, a still segregated country. Art for him, as for Virginia Woolf, could not be produced by a group "engulfed in its own social dilemmas." Superceding the minstrel tradition, a white creation featuring the "happy darkie," was an essential precondition for the success of this project, and Hurston was sometimes criticized by her contemporaries for presenting black characters who exhibited the qualities attributed to them in that tradition.

Yet Hurston wanted as much as Woolf did to avoid constantly "meeting criticism" from the white world, and to be "spiritually free" of the damaging effects of racism. But she proceeded in a different direction from Locke and W. E. B. DuBois, who counted on a "talented tenth" of their race to speak *for* black people *to* the much more numerous educated white world. Writing in 1928, the year in which Woolf delivered the lectures that became *A Room of One's Own*, Hurston declared:

> But I am not tragically colored. There is no great sorrow dammed up in my soul, not lurking behind my eyes. I do not mind at all. I do not belong to the sobbing school of Negrohood who hold that nature somehow has given them a lowdown dirty deal and whose feelings are all hurt about it. Even in the helter-skelter

skirmish that is my life, I have seen that the world is to the strong regardless of a little pigmentation more or less. No, I do not weep at the world—I am too busy sharpening my oyster knife.[7]

Hurston had grown up in Eatonville, Florida, an all-black town owned by blacks and run by black elected officials. She therefore did not have to draw back into an imagined, or barely remembered, world antecedent to the coming of white supremacy. She saw from her earliest years the strengths and weaknesses of black people not as they were thrown up against the hostile white world, but as they showed up in the course of daily life. In *Mules and Men*, her collection of Eatonville folk tales, black characters often use a "trickster" strategy in which they outwit whites by playing up the stupidity and laziness that is expected of them, but turning this performance to their own ends.

In aiming to give black people a culture that was theirs, Hurston turned away from the black middle class as subject matter for her work, and was deeply critical of writers (Fanon would put them in phase one) who used that subject matter to advance the cause of black equality through books addressed primarily to whites. In 1926 she, along with Langston Hughes and Wallace Thurmon, published a magazine called *Fire!!* as an expression of protest against the artistic creed of Locke's *New Negro*, expressing their frustration with the impulse toward respectability (defined by whites) that they saw in an older generation of black intellectuals. Yet as Robert Hemenway comments, "while self-consciously mining the proletariat, *Fire!!* required a bourgeois black readership for its aesthetic and moral revelations to make any sense."[8] In attempting to create that audience, and to awaken it to the dangers of phase one of its own culture, *Fire!!* partook of the aims of phase three: liberating black readers from their captivity within a set of white cultural values. But to carry them out, phase two, the discovery of a set of antecedent black cultural values, must be undertaken.

Hurston's writings, and particularly her collections of folk tales, are not written to show that black people are as capable of creating high art as white people. They are written to give her own people a sense of their own traditions and their own culture. Her writings show black people operating in an autonomous black culture that is different from, and by implication superior to, an absent white world to which it is completely indifferent. Because she was not speaking for the "talented tenth," or showing white audiences the effects of the "color line" on her people, she was seen as "out of phase" with her fellow native intellectuals of the Harlem Renaissance. In her lifetime her books sold poorly and at the time of her death none were in print. It took not only the Black Power movement of the 1960s, but also the women's movement that arose at the same time, to bring them back into print and to create the audience to which she now speaks so powerfully.

But phase two had a conservative side, and we can see it in Hurston's later career, when the lost culture of the past is held up as superior to anything that can occur in the potentially compromised future. Hurston's support, toward the end of her life, for Republican politicians, and her opposition to the *Brown* v. *Board of Education* Supreme Court decision is an extension of her belief that black culture was really superior to the defensive posturing of the white world. Integration in Hurston's eyes implied that black students could learn only if they sat next to whites.[9] Assimilation would mean that the culture, and even the characters, from which she drew her inspiration would cease to exist. This is the irreducible paradox that Fanon saw at the heart of creating a "national culture," that "whole body of efforts . . . to describe, justify, and praise the action through which that people has created itself and keeps itself in existence."[10] Too much emphasis on its commonality with the host culture undermines the basis for its existence. On the other hand, too much emphasis on difference, with its hidden claim of superiority, pulls in a conservative direction, in both the positive and negative senses of that word.

Thus there are dangers in making phase two more than a phase. Its danger, Fanon warns, comes from the same source as its appeal: its avoidance of the present, whose deeply rooted contradictions, once discovered, can seem insurmountable. In feminist criticism, the turn to a "very beautiful and splendid era" involved, in the early 1970s, a spirited discussion of the possibility of primitive matriarchies.[11] Then, when that debate dead-ended, a strand of feminist theoretical thinking, emanating particularly from France, shifted the site of female power untouched by the invading law-of-the-father from the domain of our collective prehistory to that of the individual. If the imposition of the law-of-the-father is analogous to the arrival of the Western colonial power, the space of the other is the female body with which the pre-Oedipal child experiences oneness, the body of the mother as it lives in the memory of the pre-Oedipal psyche.

Given that a child's awareness of sexual difference is constituted by the Oedipal break between mother and child, this "splendid era" is free of the division between the sexes and the inequality built into the Oedipal triangle. Looking to represent the possibility of a world freed from the tyranny of binary oppositions, with their built-in relationships of dominance and subordination, some women writers have set out to describe that era to us. Most of this writing takes the form of fantasy and science fiction, but given the asysmmetry of power relations, it is not surprising that, when women have taken up these genres, they "have struggled—sometimes exuberantly, sometimes anxiously—to define a gender-free reality behind or beneath myth, an ontological essence so pure, so free that 'it' can 'inhabit' any self, any costume."[12]

But can this gender-free reality exist anywhere except in the head, or in utopias such as Woolf's *Orlando*, Marge Piercy's *Woman on the Edge of Time*, or Ursula Le Guin's *The Left Hand of Darkness?* If gender is constructed, it can be constructed differently to *mean* something different. But for gender to become meaningless, we must imagine either a flight from the body or else a flight into the body, so that the body becomes either nothing or everything. The latter choice seems to be very much in evidence in much contemporary French feminist thinking, which has taken up and celebrated the category of "the other" created by male philosophers and psychoanalysts. "This *other than themselves*," as Alice Jardine has remarked, "is almost always a space of some kind (over which the narrative has lost control), and this space has been coded as *feminine*, as *woman*."[13] Until fairly recently, these lacunae were valued negatively, so the feminist strategy can be seen as taking that which has been rejected or marginalized and making it central: "other is beautiful," indeed superior.

American readers are by now familiar with descriptions of the female body such as Irigaray's:

> But woman has sex organs just about everywhere. She experiences pleasure almost everywhere. Even without speaking of the hystericization of her entire body, one can say that the geography of her pleasure is much more diversified, more multiple in its differences, more complex, more subtle, than is imagined—in an imaginary centered a bit too much on one and the same.[14]

The *jouissance* women's sexuality offers becomes a metaphor for that which disrupts a male economy of pleasure based on identity and difference. Julia Kristeva has called its language the semiotic, the pre-Oedipal organization of drives that "connect and orient the body to the mother."[15] The body out of which women are urged to write is at times the mother's body, at times the daughter's, since the separation between the two has not yet been accomplished. What women

want in this space where men are not is the nurturing that patriarchal culture has denied them. As Hélène Cixous puts it in "The Laugh
of the Medusa": "In women there is always more or less of the mother
who makes everything all right, who nourishes, and who stands up
against separation; a force that will not be cut off but will knock the
wind out of the codes."[16]

Since the suppression of woman's eroticism and her exclusion from
the symbolic order that is language occur in the same invading moment, the recovery of both, known as *jouissance,* disrupts both the
linguistic and sexual codes that keep patriarchy in place. For Kristeva,
this disruption is most obvious in poetic language "since, for there
to be a transgression of the symbolic, ther must be an irruption of
the drives in[to] the universal signifying order, that of 'natural language' which binds together the social unit."[17] So poetry should be
at the cutting edge of feminist practice not because of any particular
content, but rather because it has established a nonlinear linguistic
practice. But is this true? Or has the disruption of syntax that is the
hallmark of both modernism and postmodernism served men as they
have sought to maintain control of linguistic production even as the
ground on which they have been standing becomes less and less firm?

Alice Jardine argues that this is precisely the direction in which
critical theory has moved. Speaking of the "crisis of legitimation" in
Western philosophy, she shows how male philosophers and other theorists have sought to dismantle the equation of "the place of the other"
with "feminity," and to claim that space "of that which is not" for
themselves.[18] The master narratives of the West have been built on
three beliefs: belief in a unified self, belief in a "truth" that can be
arrived at through a systematic process like the dialectic, and belief
in the possibility of accurately representing something not present.
As these beliefs are picked away by various sciences, the space of the
other, which eludes both "truth" and representation, and which exists prior to the unified self, begins to look like the best game in town.
Or, to return to Fanon, once the occupying power discovers the rich
culture that the native intellectual has uncovered, he appropriates it
for his own purposes.

But what does it mean, to stand up against separation? We have
learned from Nancy Chodorow that asymmetry with respect to separation is fueled by a division of labor in which women are the primary caretakers of children, and are thus the ones from whom both
sexes must separate. We know that failure to separate carries a different meaning for male and female children: it is overemphasized
for the male because his gender identity depends on becoming the

*opposite* sex from his primary caretaker, while it is problematized for the girl child because she and her mother are the *same* sex. Carol Gilligan makes a similar point when she notes that the paradigm of growing up in novels privileges separation and renunciation over attachment, with its attendant feelings of ambivalence and pressures for compromise.[19] But if separation has been overdetermined by a male fear of women, beginning with the mother, do we want to circumvent it completely? Irigaray speaks of a mother-daughter bond that is negated, frozen, but which she dreams back into existence, a connection that need never be sundered. Accustomed as we are to mitosis as a model for growth and autonomy, this is a disturbing prospect. Do we want one not to stir without the other?

In her groundbreaking *Of Women Born*, Adrienne Rich argues that "the mother-child relationship is the essential human relationship," and that "in the creation of the patriarchal family, violence is done to this fundamental human unit."[20] Recuperating the mother-daughter bond would therefore seem to be a vital step in the development of women as individuals and in the creation of a "national culture" that would break up the interconnected systems of patriarchal power. But the "beautiful and splendid era" that lies outside of these systems is an imagined creation. It is grounded in a present that, for the reader, is probably not always beautiful nor splendid, a present in which the relationship between oppressed and oppressor probably involves some mutual complicity. In fact, the compromise-ridden present is just what needs to be avoided in stage two, because that situation has been offered up to the "native population" as the "natural" state of affairs.

We can see the value, but also the limitation, of the phase-two project in Susan Gubar's provocative essay, "The Blank Page," in which Gubar takes a story with this title by Isak Dinesen to develop a theory of female creativity. The nuns in the story make linen that is used for the bridal sheets of the neighboring royal houses. These sheets are then mounted, framed, and displayed for all to see: the blood on them is at once a sign of the princess' virginity and a pigment that transforms their blankness into art. As such, the sheets represent women's art as it conforms to the demands of patriarchal culture, in which male control over female sexuality ensures the existence of a legitimate line of offspring who can inherit the male name and property. Gubar's point is that women under patriarchy, denied access to the male preserve of artistic creation, write with their bodies, their bodily fluids, their blood. Or rather, they are written upon, just as the sheets created by the nuns are written upon by the blood that issues forth after the prince has penetrated his virgin bride. Women's bodies *are* the blank page awaiting the script of the male pen/penis.

But what, then, is the meaning of the blank page, the sheet with no blood on it? Noting that silence often denotes suppression (as it does in Tillie Olsen's *Silences*), Gubar suggests that "blankness here is an act of defiance, a dangerous and risky refusal to certify purity. The resistance of the princess allows for self-expression, for she makes her statement by not writing what she is expected to write. Not to be written on is, in other words, the condition of new sorts of writing for women."[21] The question is: can a woman's body ever truly be a blank page? Not to be written on would be to exist outside of culture, to posit something called nature that preceded culture, as Susan Griffin and Caroline Merchant do in their explorations of scientific discourse, and as Griffin again does in her book on pornography.[22] If it is more accurate, as I believe it is, to say that nature is a distinct entity only when it is paired with its opposite, culture, then the premise of an unmarked female space is itself brought into question. In that case, women will have to go into battle against male culture, as Maxine Hong Kingston's woman warrior does, with the scars of a patriarchal script decorating her body.[23]

Gubar suggests that these markings, like the blood on the sheets, restrict or render painful female creativity.

> In Dinesen's story, the creation of female art feels like the destruction of the female body. Because of the forms of self-expression available to women, artistic creation often feels like a violation, a belated reaction to male penetration rather than a possessing and controlling. Not an ejaculation of pleasure but a reaction to rending, the blood on the royal marriage sheets seems to imply that women's paint and ink are produced through a painful wounding, a literal influence of male authority. If artistic creativity is likened to biological creativity, the terror of inspiration for women is experienced quite literally as the terror of being entered, deflowered, possessed, taken, had, broken, ravished—all words which illustrate the pain of the passive self whose boundaries are being violated.[24]

What is not questioned in this metaphor of creativity is the assumption of female passivity in sex—and the assumption that, given this passivity, women experience being entered by a man as a violation of their boundaries. Earlier in the essay Gubar comments that for Dinesen's princesses, their bridal night is a "blood wedding" which "transforms the marriage bed into a kind of coffin in which the virgin is sacrificed," implying "that many women in a patriarchy experience a dread of heterosexuality."[25]

Unfortunately, the assumption that under patriarchy women can never be sexual subjects has become a dominant strand in feminist thinking, producing a serious split in the movement around the issue of pornography. In my view the feminist campaign against pornography is regressive because it tries to build a female eros upon a dread of penetration. Whether or not this dread is common among women, a female erotic that assumes an absence of pleasure and agency in sex invokes a deeply antifeminist view of women: the pure maiden, childlike and closer to nature than the brute male whom she encounters with fear and trembling. Thus what begins with "a hope of discovering some very beautiful and splendid era whose existence rehabilitates us" ends by offering models of pre-Oedipal bonding and silence as a precondition of authentic female speech. Elaine Showalter warns against this valorization of silence when she says that "the holes in discourse, the blanks and gaps and silences, are not the spaces where female consciousness reveals itself but the blinds of a 'prison-house of language.' "[26]

Modernism, which challenges the assumption that language "represents" a prior, nonlinguistic reality, sees as its project the creation of doors and windows in this prison house. If we cannot escape from the given structure of language that we inherit, we can at least break it open, and thus deprive it of its final, coercive authority. That women have a greater need than men to take apart the walls of their prison has been a point of departure for the feminist endeavor that Showalter calls "gynocritics."[27] But the hint that we can write from somewhere other than inside this prison appears in rhapsodic moments of feminist criticism both in France and in this country. Helene Cixous, in an essay entitled "Sorties," counterposes civilization to the female body and finds her heroine in Shakespeare's Cleopatra.[28] Gubar's essay offers the possibility that women can refuse to speak the language they have learned. She suggests that from their silence emerges the possibility of an alternative speech more closely tied to women's bodies and the experience of "the female community."

The assumptions about women's writing that Gubar shares with her collaborator, Sandra Gilbert, have been brilliantly addressed in Toril Moi's *Sexual/Textual Politics*. Moi points to an axiom of *The Madwoman in the Attic* that it shares with much American feminist criticism: it is that, underneath what women writers have said, a hidden meaning can be discovered by a feminist eye—hidden because the patriarchal culture in which they are writing will not allow women to tell it straight.[29] The nineteenth-century writers who are the subject of *Madwoman* hide their real meaning, telling it "slant," to use the adjective that Gilbert and Gubar take from Emily Dickinson. Silence, in Gubar's essay, is a way of going beyond this strategy. The task of the feminist critic is then one of interpreting the silences, the gaps in the symbolic order, translating them into the words that are *really* there, unperceived by our nonfeminist habits of reading/seeing. She will uncover, that is to say, some very beautiful and splendid interpretation "whose existence rehabilitates us both in regard to ourselves and in regard to others."

The cost of this discovery of the "real meaning" of a text is that it closes the hermeneutic process down, and thus recreates the problem that feminist criticism was trying to address in the first place. The text is not opened to an unfolding of new insights played off against a dynamic present that is being shaped by political struggle. Rather it is fixed, and thus taken outside that struggle, stamped with a seal of political correctness. Moreover, if feminist hermeneutics discovers a text that has not been "written on" by male interpreters, the interpretive process is arrested in the signifying space we are calling phase two: a context that existed prior to the arrival of the colonial power interposing its law-of-the-father between the original dyad of mother and child. To valorize this space is a recuperative move in the face of patriarchal disregard for women's bodies and women's subjectivity. But having done this, we need to move on.

Instead, both Cixous and Gubar celebrate female activity as a kind of virgin birth. Gubar specifically mentions Mary, who "in her readiness for rapture . . . represents the female community, and its blank page is therefore hers." Similarly, the nuns in Dinesen's convent "spend much time in silence, seeking to duplicate Mary's receptivity to bearing and giving birth to the Incarnate Word. Thus the blank space, the female inner space, represents readiness for inspiration and creation, the self conceived and dedicated to its own divinity." This is pregnancy without being entered, deflowered, possessed, taken, had, broken, or ravished. We want images of a self-generated female creativity and female eroticism, but is virginity and prepubescent sexuality the only place where these images can be found? Is the symbolic order, and the interrelated social structures it supports and reinforces, utterly all of a piece? Or is it always a patchwork, striving to achieve a simulacrum of unity in much the same way that Lacan's infant, having seen its reflection in the mirror, strives to achieve the unified self it sees "out there?"

Kristeva has in fact moved to deconstruct that unified, imaginary identity, and has elaborated conflicts within the "very beautiful and splendid era" preceding the separation of the infant from its mother. Before there is language, Kristeva maintains in *The Powers of Horror*, there is undifferentiated pleasure and pain, the *unnameable* against which the forming, fragile ego, not yet separate and therefore not yet constituted in relation to an object, defends itself against its fear (of devouring, of being devoured) through abjection, revulsion, loathing. Since a "clean and proper self" is an ideal of this ego in its presymbolic ("mirror") phase, it ab-jects not only the mother's body but, I would add, the functions of its own body over which it has no control, not even the power of naming. I believe that this theory of the abject has enormous implications for women, for whom separation from the mother is so deeply problematic. It also enables us to begin to see what is revolutionary about that category of artists that Kristeva has thus far refused to discuss: women.

In looking to move beyond phase two, I propose that we look first at the ways in which language chooses its readers, not only through its content but also through its overloading of words so that they include some readers in their audience and exclude others. Language does this by generating what Barthes calls a second-order semiological system, a metalanguage in which signs themselves divide into signifiers and signifieds which come together at the level of myth. In one of his examples from *Mythologies*, wine is both a drink and something that French people appreciate in a way that defines them as a "we."[31] An American might be the polo horse that is found on certain articles of clothing. Participation in the myth of the horse creates power, both for its creator, who brings the group into being, and for the wearers of the clothing. This power flows in a highly fluid, Foucaultian manner, through deployment of the sign, not only between Ralph Lauren and his customers but between that group and others more powerful and less powerful than it, and between all of these and outsiders.

It is at this second level of meaning production that it is appropriate to speak of intention. Language used to indicate that an audience is not representing phenomena out in the world but *organizing* its audience into a group, including some and excluding others. That indeed is its *intention*, whether the language is a horse on a polo shirt or a piece of poetry. This intention is separable from what any individual (including the author) thinks the horse or the string of words *means.* Organizing a group is simply what writing does, and some writers have consciously foregrounded their awareness of function. Take, for instance, Toni Morrison's use of the pronoun "we" in the following passage from *The Bluest Eye:*

> We tried to see her without looking at her, and never, never went near her. Not because she was absurd, or repulsive, or because we were frightened but because we had failed her. Our flowers never grew. . . . All of us—all who knew her—felt so wholesome after we cleaned ourselves on her. . . . We honed ourselves on her, padded our characters with her frailty, and yawned in the fantasy of our strength.

The "we" shifts from the two girls, Claudia and Frieda, to the community in the novel: "all of us who knew her." But in the next paragraph the "we" widens out:

> And fantasy it was, for we were not strong, only aggressive; we were not free, merely licensed, we were not compassionate, we were polite; not good, but well behaved. We courted death in order to call ourselves brave, and hid like thieves from life. We substituted good grammar for intellect; we switched habits to simulate maturity.[32]

The burden of Morrison's addresses to the members of her wider community is that it was not just black children who wanted blue eyes. "We" in the black community in 1939–1941, the time period covered by the novel, wanted them too, and, by implication, we are still not free of our desire for them.

I remember a reading Toni Morrison gave in which she said that as she was writing *The Bluest Eye* she wanted her own community to nod their heads in recognition of what she was saying. Most black writers until that time, she observed, had been addressing white audiences. Of course Morrison did not create a large, educated black audience for black writers to address. It was created not only by the civil rights movement (a struggle from which Hurston distanced herself, having developed the very techniques that a generation of black women writers are now building on) but also by the Black Power and women's movements. Morrison gave it an articulation as a "we" that was so materially grounded in a common present that it could include a large number of readers who would not nod their heads with the same kind of recognition for which Morrison hoped from her black audience. Through her use of the "we" she brings this audience into her book even as she includes her narrator, Claudia, in the community being criticized. The criticism thus originates from within, from a member of the family, so to speak.

Moreover, this strategy of inclusion is being enacted in the context of the larger white audience that must be assumed to exist for a novel published in America by a mainstream publisher. That audience is being neither exhorted nor attacked. The white world is present only implicitly, through its artifacts (the dolls, the movie stars, Dick and Jane from the first-grade reader), which Pecola is expected by her community to admire. None of the black characters are strong enough to win in the battle against circumstances. Indeed, in their attempts to hang onto something worth living for they hurt one another. And Morrison's white readers are shown a world they do not normally get to see, from a vantage point that is not theirs. For if black readers have "cleaned" themselves on the abjected body of Pecola Breedlove, the white reader who is also constituted by Morrison's "we" has abjected Pecola not only unconsciously but deliberately. In a world where racism is so powerfully present, this gesture of a black writer on behalf of her community is a revolutionary one.

Any writer imagines an audience of those who are moved and enlightened by her work, and this intended audience may be signaled in the text. If it is not, if the "we" is assumed to be universal, this too is present in the writing. Barthes envisions, as his "phase three," a "writing degree zero" which "takes its place in the midst of all those ejaculations and judgements, without becoming involved in them; it consists precisely in their absence."[33] This zero degree, "equally far from living language and from literary language proper," was initiated by Camus in *L'Etranger*, whose narrator reports on his actions and state of mind without becoming involved in "ejaculations and judgements" about them. This style has become very fashionable, a celebration of our diminished possibilities, our inability to empathize with others in a surreal and flattened world.

The style of *L'Etranger* was undoubtedly politically potent in the context of occupied France in 1942, the year of its publication. But in 1987 the situation of fiction seems closer to Fredric Jameson's comment on the fate of structuralism in the French academy, where "the older option of an absolute solitude is lost, and the essentially political tension of the concept of zero degree tends to cool into old-fashioned scientific objectivity: what was once a differentiated lack, felt as such, now little by little becomes simply a non-registered, non-functioning absence."[34] Denying a speaking subject whose point of view "distorts" the object under observation is tantamount to claiming for the observed phenomena the status of *truth*. But this, to return to Fanon, is the assertion the colonizing culture always makes. A revolutionary mode of writing that made the same claim would thus only be giving proof that it had assimilated the culture of the occupying power, the hallmark of phase one.

I want to suggest that the signals that Barthes would go beyond, those that position the writer in relation to his or her readers, might be considered to be one defining feature of phase-three writing. Morrison's use of "we" in *The Bluest Eye* implied two groups of readers: those whose shared experiences had not been previously held up so that they could nod their heads, and those who have not participated in those shared experiences. Both are invited to encounter the language of the novel without judging its content, and this might conceivably alter the relationship between the two groups. Those included in the "we" can see strength and sensitivity in events that a racist society uses to support its image of black inferiority. The excluded white audience is invited to expand its experience of black people beyond its own learned judgments and the limited experiences of black people that are a corollary to those judgments.

White women writers in the 1970s were impelled by a similar imperative: *No More Masks* was the title of an anthology of women's poetry published in 1973. Many of the poems published in this and other collections from that time are angry: angry at men, and angry at the roles women are expected to play, at their trivialization in a patriarchal culture. The point being made is not that, under the "images of women" that men (and male writers) have imposed upon them, there is a preexisting truth represented by this anger. Rather, it is that, where power is unequally distributed, it is dangerous for the less powerful group to express certain feelings, or to own certain experiences.

Revolutionary writing takes on this danger. It does so by making public what has been secret knowledge. The writer situates herself on the borderline that divides the group possessing this knowledge from the more powerful outsiders who do not have it. For people who lack power, secret knowledge is a compensation, but one that keeps the unequal situation in place. Therefore both groups gain when such knowledge is shared. The revolutionary phase of a "national culture" would seem to me to involve constantly bringing into view the shared myths and secrets around which a "we" has been generated because, by exposing them, as Morrison does, the "we" ceases to be an absolute, exclusive category existing in nature, and becomes a construction, partly created by the "we" and partly imposed upon it. Making

its boundaries explicit is a political act inasmuch as a political consciousness is a consciousness of their operation, a denaturalization of
the political nature of group formation. Rather, a reader who is not
a member of the privileged "we" can situate herself upon the borderline between her community and the one being described. By
opening up the possibility of linkage based on a common "border,"
the phase-three writer fulfills her revolutionary mission.

This constant dissolution of an exclusive "we" has no final desti-
nation or synthesis. I suspect that the field of language will always
be a contested terrain, never the "zero degree" of pure "white writing" that Barthes postulates and that Derrida implies, a text from
which author and audience have been removed. If neither author nor
audience is the source of a text's meaning, if the "we" is created by
the writing rather than represented in it, there is no need on the part
of the writer to defend it or to tear it down. Then the text becomes
the space where a "we" is created that takes in both. White readers
of Morrison's text can enter it because she is not hiding anything from
them. In an unequal encounter, the weaker adopts strategies of con-
cealment. But the writer who sees clearly and conceals nothing undermines the inequality at the root.

What is seen is, of course, always a matter of interpretation. Alice
Walker and Ntozake Shange have been criticized for giving a distorted and thus politically harmful picture of black men, and men in
general.[35] But these are political discussions, discussions that attempt
to forge literary theory not in a domain inhabited by male French
philosophers and psychoanalysts, but in a context of women's lives
in the present. And while this is going on, writers have little choice
but to speak to readers in ways that clarify and expand their possibilities in the present. One tendency that Naylor and Erdrich share
with a number of other writers is the shift away from an individual
heroine who either does or does not get what she wants, toward a
more collective definition of freedom and empowerment. Rather than
probing even more deeply into the disjointed processes of individual
consciousness, as modernist writers have done, they use the tools of
narrative to reveal the shared histories of a group.

My final point is that none of these novels are written in the avant-
garde style that attempts to destroy narrative. Feminists have reason
to suspect literary methodologies that claim to be natural or to represent a "reality" that exists prior to its interpretation in language.
But we should also be suspicious of calling any style of writing "revolutionary" outside of considerations of content, on the one hand, and
audience on the other. To hold up the disruption of syntactical co-

herence as itself a revolutionary practice irrespective of content, as Kristeva seems to suggests, is to avoid what is really difficult about writing, which is to bring forth into the fleeting present what would not otherwise exist, to imagine possibilities that, without writing, would remain concealed and uncommunicable. The novelists I have mentioned are writing at the intersections of multiple formerly "colonized cultures" and creating new possibilities for political alignment through the act of writing itself.

Let us reimagine, therefore, the metonymically linked string of signifiers that Morrison's text invites, where body, subject, and community are envisioned neither as bounded autonomous entities, each owning particular properties that cannot legally be taken away, nor as unbounded beings reunited with the body of a mother who is strong enough to protect us against the suturing knife of patriarchy. Rather, it is circulated in language in a way that includes and adds to these two rather than canceling them out in a synthesis. For the resistance to slavery, for instance, is thoroughly grounded in the ideology of inviolable individualism, and this struggle is the foundation upon which subsequent liberation movements have been built. Morrison's body/subject/community is gendered *and* powerful: it takes the Other in and transforms both. It is our capacity to reimagine ourselves in this way upon which, so much—as the poet says—depends.

### Endnotes

I would like to thank the following people for their support and comments on this paper at various stages of its evolution: Carolyn Burke, Terry Burke, Harriet Davidson, Elin Diamond, Alicia Ostriker, Elaine Showalter, Cheryl Wall, Judy Walkowitz, Susan Wolfson, the rest of the members of the Rutgers University Gender Group, and the editors of *The Radical Teacher*. I owe a special debt of gratitude to Barbara Masakela, now working with the African National Congress, for demonstrating to me the usefulness of Fanon's paradigm for feminist criticism.

1. Frantz Fanon, *The Wretched of the Earth*, Constance Farrington, trans. (New York: Grove Press, 1968), p. 233. I have chosen to use Fanon's rather than other tripartitions of feminist politics and feminist writing—Elaine Showalter's "feminine," "feminist," and "female," in *A Literature of Their Own* (Princeton, N.J.: Princeton University Press, 1977) or Julia Kristeva's three "generations" in "Women's Time," *Signs* (fall 1981), 7(1):13–35—because I think that Fanon's distinctions encompass these and take them to another political level.

2. Fanon, *The Wretched of the Earth*, pp. 222–23.

3. Kristeva, "Women's Time," p. 33.

4. Showalter, *A Literature of Their Own*, p. 285.

5. Showalter, *A Literature of Their Own*, p. 96.

6. Alain Locke, "Negro Youth Speaks," *The New Negro* (1925; New York Athenaeum, 1974), p. 53.

7. Zora Neale Hurston, "How It Feels To Be Colored Me," in Alice Walker, ed., *I Love Myself When I'm Laughing* (Old Westbury, Conn.: Feminist Press, 1979), p. 153.

8. Robert Hemenway, *Zora Neale Hurston* (Urbana: University of Illinois Press, 1978), p. 49.

9. *Ibid.*, p. 333.

10. Fanon, *The Wretched of the Earth*, p. 233.

11. See Helen Diner, *Mothers and Amazons*, J. P. Lundin, trans. (New York: Julian Press, 1965); Elizabeth Gould Davis, *The First Sex* (New York: Putnam, 1971); Eleanor Leacock, "Introduction" to Frederick Engels, *The Origin of the Family, Private Property and the State* (New York: International, 1972), pp. 7–66. See also Kristeva, "Women's Time," pp. 32–33.

12. Sandra Gilbert, "Costumes of the Mind: Transvestism as a Metaphor in Modern Literature," in Elizabeth Abel, ed., *Writing and Sexual Difference* (Chicago, Ill.: University of Chicago Press, 1982), p. 196.

13. Alice Jardine, *Gynesis* (Ithaca, N.Y.: Cornell University Press, 1985), p. 25.

14. Luce Irigaray, "Ce sexe qui n'est pas un," Claudia Reeder, trans., in Elaine Marks and Isabelle de Courtivron, eds., *New French Feminisms* (New York: Schocken, 1981), p. 103.

15. Julia Kristeva, *Revolution in Poetic Language* (New York: Columbia University Press, 1984), p. 27.

16. Hélène Cixous, "The Laugh of the Medusa," *Signs* (1976), 1:882.

17. Kristeva, *Revolution*, p. 62.

18. Jardine, *Gynesis*, pp. 159ff.

19. Carol Gilligan, *In a Different Voice* (Cambridge, Mass.: Harvard University Press, 1982), p. 156ff.

20. Adrienne Rich, *Of Woman Born* (New York: Norton, 1976), p. 127.

21. Susan Gubar, "The Blank Page in Feminist Criticism," in Elaine Showalter, ed., *The New Feminist Criticism* (New York: Pantheon, 1985), p. 306.

22. Susan Griffin, *Woman and Nature: The Roaring Inside Her* (New York: Harper and Row, 1978); Caroline Merchant, *The Death of Nature* (San Francisco: Harper and Row, 1980); Susan Griffin, *Pornography and Silence* (New York: Harper and Row, 1981).

23. Maxine Hong Kingston, *Memoirs of a Girlhood Among Ghosts* (New York: Vintage, 1977), pp. 41–42, 62–63; Gubar, "The Blank Page," p. 299.

24. Gubar, "The Blank Page," p. 302.

25. *Ibid.*, p. 301.

26. Elaine Showalter, "Feminist Criticism in the Wilderness," in Elaine Showalter, ed., *The New Feminist Criticism* (New York: Pantheon, 1985), p. 256.

27. Elaine Showalter, "Toward a Feminist Poetics," in Elaine Showalter, ed., *The New Feminist Criticism* (New York: Pantheon, 1985), pp. 131ff.

28. Hélène Cixous, "Sorties." In Hélène Cixous and Catherine Clement, *The Newly Born Woman*, trans. Betsy Wing, (Minneapolis: University of Minnesota Press, 1986), pp. 122–30.

29. Toril Moi, *Sexual/Textual Politics* (New York: Methuen, 1985), pp. 57–69.

30. Susan Gubar, "The Blank Page in Feminist Criticism." In Elaine Showalter, ed., *The New Feminist Criticism*, (New York: Pantheon, 1985) p. 327.

31. Roland Barthes, "Wine and Milk," in Roland Barthes, *Mythologies*, Annette Lavers, trans. (New York: Hill and Wang, 1972), pp. 58–61.

32. Toni Morrison, *The Bluest Eye* (New York: Pocket, 1972), p. 159.

33. *Ibid.*, p. 77.

34. Fredric Jameson, *The Prison House of Language* (Princeton, N.J.: Princeton University Press, 1972), p. 161.

35. See, for instance, George Stade, "Womanist Fiction and Male Characters," *Partisan Review* (1985), 52(4):264–70.

# THREE

## REFLECTIONS ON THE CANON: THEORY AND PRAXIS

*The study of the canon has been one of the most important issues to come out of recent examinations of the institution of literary studies. The political implications of the very existence of a literary canon and what that canon means in terms of gender, race, class, nationality, and ideology are enormous. It is no coincidence that the current public debates over the quality of education and the success or failure of Western civilization hinge on the issues stirred up by revising the canon.*

*These public debates tend to focus either on the dangers of decentering the "central" texts of "our" civilization or on the demand, on the other side, for various previously marginalized groups to be admitted to a newer, more progressive canon. While the concrete contribution of the New Left was to open up the canon to blacks, Hispanics, Native Americans, Japanese, Chinese, women, gays, and lesbians, the politics of current discussions on the Left have more to do with how to conceptualize the process of canon formation and how to counter the hierarchical nature of such formations.*

*In this section Paul Lauter and Lillian Robinson treat the theoretical aspect of opening the canon, while Constance Coiner and Barbara Harlow offer literary readings of the work of previously marginalized authors.*

# 6

# Canon Theory and Emergent Practice

## Paul Lauter

*Paul Lauter's discussion of the canon is not derived particularly from theory but from the concrete praxis of black studies programs, open admissions policies, and women's studies programs. This concrete element is important to note because, as Lauter says, intellectuals tend to formulate theories without regard to pedagogy. So, for Lauter, the answer to discussions about the canon will come from nothing short of a movement to reread and decenter canonical texts from the perspective of the noncanonical.*

I want to begin with what some might cite as a characteristic move of the socialist intellectual in capitalist society: namely, biting the hand that feeds you. In the course of explaining to me the rejection by the board of the National Endowment of the Humanities of a highly rated proposal for a seminar for college teachers, the NEH program officer wrote that "some reviewers were concerned that the focus on the canon, while doubtless an important issue for teachers of American literature, lacked the kind of scholarly significance generally expected of Summer Seminars. . . ." Pursuing this theme, he later wrote that my "application was rather more thesis-driven than most of our seminar proposals."

I discover everywhere signs of this division. On the one side, we find the supposedly pedagogical or professional problems raised by the question of the canon, and on the other side what is valorized as "of scholarly significance," or, more simply, criticism or theory. In a recent "Newsletter for Graduate Alumnae and Alumni" issued by the Yale English Department, for example, Cyrus Hamlin writes that "precisely how this procedure of hermeneutical recuperation" he is proposing "should affect the canon and the curriculum of our institution is difficult to say," and he proceeds to ignore the question. In the same document Margaret Homans suggests why he does so. "At Yale," she writes, "while poststructuralism has proven to be intellectually more unsettling than liberal humanism, the feminist versions of post-structuralism are institutionally more easily accommodated than some of the projects of liberal feminism, such as challenging the content of the canon we teach, with its vast preponderance of white, male authors." Interestingly, Homans here appropriates the project of canon revision solely to the domain of "liberal feminism," a common enough way of trying to limit the scope of this intellectual movement to a supposed clique of uppity middle-class women. Like the characterization of canon revision as dominantly a "pedagogical" issue, and thus a matter only slightly removed from teacher college trivialities, defining it as a project of "liberal feminism" must be seen simply as one more move in the academic political struggle which I shall try to characterize here.

This division between the concerns of what I have come to call "canonical criticism" and those of what is called "theory" is, I think, one fact of current literary practice in the United States. Elsewhere I have attempted to trace the very different histories of canonical and academic criticism since the late 1960s;[1] I do not wish to pursue that story here, except to underline the fact that canon criticism was initially an effort to carry the politics of the 1960s social movements into the classroom. Thus it initially influenced curricula and scholarship most heavily, and more slowly touched publishing and textbooks. Somewhat later, it has come to affect the selection of texts about which graduate students and critics write, and more slowly still to affect the texts sufficiently revered to find their way into footnotes, indices, or other measures of academic weight. Such has been the history of books like Frederick Douglass' *Narrative*, Charlotte Perkins Gilman's "The Yellow Wallpaper," or, more recently, Harriet Jacobs' *Incidents in the Life of a Slave Girl*. In the most recent stages of this process, as I shall point out below, some of the concerns of canonical criticism have converged with those arising from academic "theory." Even so, this division is only one of those that need to be explored. If one were at a convention of educators, one might be struck by the conflict between those advocating and those denouncing the canonical proposals of former education secretary William Bennett. If one were at the National Women's Studies Association conference, one would probably notice the differences *among* those committed to changing the existing canon. Here, I want to chart the multiple conflicts that have arisen as the question of the canon has come to play a larger role on the intellectual stage.

A recent (Fall 1986) issue of *Salmagundi* concentrating on "Cultural Literacy: Canon, Class, Curriculum" provides a useful, if unlikely, starting point. A section of the issue contains an essay by Robert Scholes called "Aiming a Canon at the Curriculum" and a set of responses to Scholes' articles. For Scholes, the problem is to resist efforts by William Bennett (and, presumably, E. D. Hirsch) to impose upon educational institutions a particular canon of great books. Scholes' essay can be taken as representative of the general reaction of the academic community to the cultural prescriptions of Reaganism.[2] "What I am opposing," he writes, "is the learning of a set of pious cliches about a set of sacred texts."[3] Most readers are sufficiently familiar (not to say bored) with Bennett's ideas on this subject, so I need not rehearse Scholes' well-drawn critique, except to say that he emphatically surfaces the right-wing politics that fuel Bennett's analysis as well as his solution. Scholes approvingly quotes T. S. Eliot's formulation of the matter: "to know what we want in education we must know what we want in general, we must derive our theory of education from our philosophy of life. The problem turns out to be a religious problem."[4] Seen in this light, the question of the canon becomes a conflict of values, and therefore, translated into public policy, of politics.

Of course, the issue is seldom joined in these terms; neither side in this debate puts forward explicitly political criteria for choosing texts they think worth studying. Bennett claims that the "great books" simply emerge over time through some kind of consensus among the properly educated. The opposition is formulated in terms of resisting the imposition of an essentially narrow vision of "Western Culture as a single coherent object, constructed of masterpieces built by geniuses," which is how Scholes characterizes the Bennett doctrine.[5] Bennett would not explicitly claim that Twain, Faulkner, and Martin Luther King, Jr., whose work he includes on his list, among them sufficiently "cover" the issue of racism in America; but in practice, adoption of that list as a basis of curricula effectively marginalizes, if it does not altogether silence, the oppositional voices of writers like

Harriet Jacobs, William Lloyd Garrison, Frances Harper, W. E. B. DuBois, or Malcolm X. Against this effort effectively to narrow the limits of significant debate, all of the commentators on Scholes' piece stand united on what amounts to a platform of liberal pluralism. Even E. D. Hirsch, who has embodied his idea of "cultural literacy" in a sixty-four-page list of words and phrases that "every American should know," essentially joins Scholes on this score. Indeed, a broad consensus exists among literary practitioners against efforts like those of Bennett's successor in the National Endowment for the Humanities, Lynne Cheney, to "politicize" criteria for selecting panels and projects.

But this consensus soon unravels. In her criticism of Scholes' position, Marjorie Perloff correctly points out that he assumes, against this federal effort to impose curricula, an existing "geniune freedom of choice as to what texts shall be read." On the contrary, Perloff argues, there is "a canon operative in our current humanities programs, however reluctant professors and educators are to admit it."[7] Perloff examines the subjects of articles in recent issues of *PMLA* to illustrate the content of that canon; she also demonstrates how pervasive in these articles are certain intellectual touchstones, notably Derrida, Freud, Barthes, Plato, and Foucault, among others one could quickly name. Thus she concludes—no surprise—that today's "professors themselves carry on the traditions they themselves learned not so long ago in graduate school" with respect both to the imaginative texts worth studying and the language and procedures by which they ought to be studied. Perloff's comment invokes a second, equally familiar front of the canon controversy: the effort within the academic community to *extend* the range of texts—not to speak of the modes for encountering them—about which we think, write, and teach.

On this front, those who were united in opposition to the Bennett prescriptions may well part company. For it is precisely at this point that those dominantly concerned with what is called "theory" turn with a shrug back to "hermeneutical recuperation." While it might not seem to matter precisely which texts one subjects to psychoanalytic, semiotic, or deconstructive analysis, and that thus even the most hardened poststructuralist might in theory join the effort to broaden the canon, it turns out that in practice few have participated in reconstructing the canon, at least when one looks beyond the work of some feminist and black critics. Barbara Herrnstein Smith has effectively argued in her essay "Contingencies of Value" that the positivistic stance and universalizing tendencies of academic criticism make it largely irrelevant to, and its practitioners finally uninterested in, the issues of valuation that are central to the question of the canon.[8] Further, it is sometimes argued by enthusiasts of "theory" that deconstruction, in particular the work of Foucault, introduced the issue of power into literary discourse and thus raised the problem of canon formation. But the idea that cultural structures, like a reading list or a set of criteria for admission to higher education, embody and sustain power relationships was quite clear long before poststructuralist theory emerged on the French, much less the American, scene. It was no accident that Mao Tse-tung's final effort to overcome the institutions of class in China was called the "cultural revolution"; the core of his ideas on that subject are contained in his 1942 "Talks at the Yenan Forum on Art and Literature." Further, demands for "open admissions" and "black studies" shook American universities long before Foucault's name had become a household word. The notion that debate over the canon derives from poststructuralist theory expresses something of the insulation of the academy. The general irrelevance until quite recently of the work of most American practitioners of "theory" to the debates about the canon also suggests something of the profound conservatism of the academy, in which the citation of precedent and authority ("as Derrida proposes in *Épirons* . . .") weigh far more heavily in the scales of tenure than the presentation of an intellectual tyro like Frances Ellen Watkins Harper. Such qualities exemplify the problem Mao tried to address, badly or well—that is, how to bring into the open and thus into question the power relationships embedded in the consciousness of academics as well as in the cultural institutions we inhabit. And they suggest that part of the importance of the effort to widen the canon is precisely the need to counterweight the tendency of academics to absorb social conflict into debates—over language and form, for example—that they can more easily control.[9]

A useful illustration of the problem is offered by an anonymous comment on this essay provided to Columbia University Press. The reviewer complains that "Lauter offers up the thoroughly critiqued (and dismissed) view that the institution of literature and literary studies change simply by adding more texts by third world and minority writers. . . . Thus Lauter completely ignores the more important question of how one reads, what contexts one reads in, who the reader is and other problems that have been brought to critical attention through the debate over the canon." Anyone who has been engaged in adding minority and white women's texts to syllabi, reading lists, and anthologies and in the closely related problem of adding women and minority men to faculties and enrollments will know that there is nothing "simple" in these processes. In fact, they have entailed meaningful changes in literary, and other, forms of study, as the numerous books tracing significant alterations in academic paradigms and priorities indicate.[10] But such changes are generally "dismissed" by literary academics for whom problems of epistemology ("how one reads") are self-evidently "more important" than what one reads. They miss the dialectical relationship between, on the one hand, the subjects and authors of texts, and, on the other, those who teach and read them in the educational systems of American capitalism— or, indeed, those who make it into, or in, those systems.

If the second front of the debate is about *extending* rather than constricting the canon, the third front involves the substantial conflicts among those of us who work to change the existing canon; once again, I think, different political agendas translate into differing cultural priorities. One position is that taken up by cultural pluralists: we are many in these United States and any canon, any curriculum, ought to be "representative." I do not wish to disparage this answer, for in many respects I agree with it; indeed, I think that the currently fashionable attacks on cultural pluralism, exemplified by Werner Sollors' "A Critique of Pure Pluralism," are badly misplaced.[11] I shall return to the Sollors essay and to the book in which it is found shortly, but first I want to clarify differences among those committed to changing the canon.

Formulating the case for pluralism simply by asserting the value of representation obscures what is in question. For how can any canon be fully representative? Even if one ignores the problem of room at the inn—and I would be the last to deny that in anthologies, curricula, and literary histories this *is* a problem, although not always an insuperable one—do not the very processes of canonization necessarily reflect the structures of social and political power and thus embed in their product an unrepresentative, if widened, set of texts organized even at best along hierarchical lines? Does it not follow, then, that the goal must be to abolish canons altogether and to substitute, rather, the authority of various individual or ethnic group experiences freed from the constraints of any official discipline? It is to this issue that the most interesting essay in *Salmagundi*, that by Elizabeth Fox-Genovese, is addressed.

Fox-Genovese is altogether uninterested in my first front; she refers to Bennett only in her concluding paragraph. As for the second front, she has little patience with the moves of elite white academic theorists, of whom she writes (and I cannot resist quoting):

> They share an explicit distate for "bourgeois humanism" and for the personal subject or author. They are offering us society as text and text as society and both as process or system. They are contributing to the disillusionment with values that had been tailored to the measure of man. Yet they have done little or nothing to reestablish the accountability of the Humanities to a pluralistic society. . . . From the perspective of those previously excluded from the cultural elite, the death of the subject or the death of the author seems somewhat premature. Surely it is no coincidence that the Western white male elite proclaimed the death of the subject at precisely the moment at which it might have had to share that status with the women and peoples of other races and classes who were beginning to challenge its supremacy.[12]

But her primary argument is with those who wish to abolish all canons. While our students, she contends, may feel "colonized in relation to that elite western culture that has constituted the backbone of our humanistic education," throwing out the canon "does not solve their problem any more than expurgating all traces of western technology solves the problem of colonial peoples." Transforming "the canon and the surveys in response to changing constituencies has less to do with rewriting the story than with reinterpreting it," she concludes (pp. 135–36).

How to accomplish this goal? Fox-Genovese's proposal is to reread canonical texts as much for what they do *not* say as for what they make explicit. The work of Hobbes and Locke, for example, can be read from a gendered perspective: "we can teach elite culture from the perspective of gender, race, and class if we are prepared to accept attention to issues of gender, race, and class as proxies for the subjective testimony of those excluded from the most exalted cultural roles" (p. 140).[13] While this strategy is important, a problem with it inheres in the word "we," and in Fox-Genovese's implicit methodology. Again: "we can transform the entire focus of conventional courses by the themes we select" (p. 141); or, shifting pronoun, but retaining the teacher-dominant tactic, "one can *present* the individual as the problem rather than the solution" (p. 141; my italics). In effect, Fox-Genovese is shifting the ground of the debate from *what* is taught to *how* it is presented. Her assumption here seems to be that certain teachers can approach texts with a degree of consciousness about gender, race, class, sexuality, nationality—marginality generally— sufficient to enable them to "present" the texts from these angles of vision. That seems to me rather more complicated than her essay allows, which may emerge more clearly by looking at the results of curriculum "integration" projects, as they are called.

In these projects, faculty members, usually white and male, whose specialities are *not* women's studies or minority or ethnic studies develop new courses or units which "integrate" the findings of scholars in those areas with more traditional disciplinary materials. Such projects, which have largely been initiated by women's studies programs, have produced a good deal of interesting curricular work, particularly within the California State University system and at the University of Arizona, Wheaton College, and Towson State University, but they have also regularly encountered two difficulties. First, because they are in general marginally familiar with the shifts in disciplinary paradigms insisted upon by women's and minority studies, the faculty members engaged in such projects seldom alter their course frameworks, and thus their presentations of traditional materials. They might, for example, begin to include works like Jean Toomer's *Cane* and H. D.'s *Trilogy*, Meridel Le Sueur's *The Girl*, or Zora Neale Hurston's *Their Eyes Were Watching God* in a course on the 1920s and 1930s, but that seldom affects their approach to Eliot, Pound, and Hemingway. At the same time, incorporating noncanonical works has not necessarily guaranteed that they, much less traditional texts, are presented from a gender- and/or race-conscious perspective. The question of the canon can thus end by being narrowed to the problem of what one has time to add to an otherwise unaltered course. Further, as a range of critiques have indicated, consciousness about gender does not guarantee consciousness about race, and vice versa. The problem, then, is how "we" can develop that consciousness necessary to carry out Fox-Genovese's approach.

To be sure, the process of engaging in curricular change does help to alter consciousness. One learns something about marginality and about what is really at stake in academic structures through efforts to change them; if you would "know the taste of a pear, you must change it by eating it," a smart theorist said. And classroom discussions can act like consciousness-raising groups, particularly when they are dealing with texts with which instructors are relatively unfamiliar and about which, therefore, student responses may be more vigorous. But Western schooling assumes that we learn primarily by reading. In his 1845 *Narrative*, for example, Frederick Douglass writes:

In the same book, I met with one of Sheridan's mighty speeches on and in behalf of Catholic emancipation. These were choice documents to me. I read them over and over again with unabated interest. They gave tongue to interesting thoughts of my own soul, which had frequently flashed through my mind, and died away for want of utterance. . . . The reading of these documents enabled me to utter my thoughts, and to meet the arguments brought forward to sustain slavery. . . .[14]

I suspect that the central reason why it is necessary to read noncanonical texts is that they *teach us* how to view experience through the prisms of gender, race, nationality, and other forms of marginalization. For example, Rolando Hinojosa's Klail City Death Trip series, while being strikingly postmodernist texts, uncover the racist myths that virtually hide the realities of Texas border conflicts from Anglo and in some degree even from Mexicano consciousness. Reading, I want to reiterate, is not the only way we learn about how power is structured, and how those at the margins define their own relationships to such structures; there is no substitute finally for eating the pear of social change. Still, reading is a vital way in a literate society—which is why marginalized groups have always had to struggle against usage or law to obtain access to the power of literacy, or, having obtained it, to get a hearing for their literary productions. Which returns us to the question of the canon.

While I think that Fox-Genovese is right about the importance of rereading the traditional canon, it also seems to me that the best lens for that rereading is provided by noncanonical works themselves. For their outlook is likely to be less constrained by the deep conservatism of academia than that of professors, however progressive. In a sense, what seems to me to be involved is a reversal of the usual process by which noncanonical texts are appraised from the perspective, and in the terms, of those long established; rather, we are learning to reread—and thus to decenter—canonical texts, like *The Great Gatsby* and *A Farewell to Arms*, from the perspectives provided by noncanonical works, like *The Girl* and *Their Eyes Were Watching God*. We have used as the slogan of the Reconstructing American Literature project the statement "so that the work of Frederick Douglass, Mary Wilkins Freeman, Agnes Smedley, Zora Neale Hurston and others is read with the work of Nathaniel Hawthorne, Henry James, William Faulkner, Ernest Hemingway and others." I offer that not as an article of pluralist faith, but as, in the first instance, an epistemological proposition. And, in the second place, a challenge to theory and to history: what are the theoretical conceptions, the critical practices, the historical designs, the ideas about function and audience, that must be reconstructed *so that* these works can, indeed, be read?

Materials with which to answer those questions are being provided in a number of ways. First, I think, through the republication of lost or abandoned works, like those so notably recovered to us in Judith Fetterley's *Provisions* (Bloomington: Indiana University Press, 1985) and in Mary Helen Washington's *Invented Lives* Garden City, N.Y.: Anchor, 1987), in the Rutgers University Press American Women Writers series, in the volumes Cathy Davidson has edited (and written) for Oxford University Press (like Susanna Rowson's *Charlotte Temple*), and in the two black women writers series being issued by Beacon and Oxford University presses. These volumes force on us very different conceptions of American literary and cultural history, simply in order to account for the existence, much less the characteristics, of such texts. They also insist on a revised understanding of certain formal features, as well as of the functions of and audiences for such works. Further, many new voices from outside the academic literary circuit are being given opportunities to be heard by specialized presses, like Arte Publico of Houston, Thunder's Mouth of New York, or The Crossing Press of Trumansburg.

The republication of a range of noncanonical writings and the wider distribution of a variety of new voices make possible, indeed insist upon, a different range of historical and theoretical studies focused on the question of the canon, books like Jane Tompkins' *Sensational Designs* (New York: Oxford, 1985), Hortense Spillers and Marjorie Pryse's *Conjuring* (Bloomington: Indiana University Press, 1985), Hazel Carby's *Reconstructing Womanhood* (New York: Oxford, 1987), and essays like Carolyn Karcher's splendid introduction to Lydia Maria Child's *Hobomok and Other Writings on Indians* (New Brunswick, N.J.: Rutgers University Press, 1986) and Elizabeth Ammons' comparison of Edith Wharton and Jessie Redmon Fauset (*College Literature* [1987], 14:207–18), to name only a few. Such works are notable for a number of reasons: they demystify the processes by which reputations and canons are constructed; they offer fundamentally altered accounts of literary history and cultural relations; they define the origins and changing characteristics of the literary practices engaged in by noncanonical writers; they bring into focus contrasting readings of American history and culture provided for us by canonical and noncanonical works; and they reveal the material supports—or their lack—that prove critical not only to literary production but to the survival of works of art, a point to which I shall return below.

By contrast, I want to look briefly at the collection *Reconstructing American Literary History* edited by Sacvan Bercovitch (Cambridge: Harvard University Press, 1986). While the volume contains a number of interesting essays, when read in terms of the question of the canon it produces more problems than it resolves. There is, to begin with, the title. "Reconstructing American literature" is a phrase that has been defined by a movement for change within the profession as meaning an effort to revise the canon—as in the Northeast Modern Language Association section, called Reconstructing American Literature. The use of this title for Bercovitch's volume illustrates how what is effectively a defense of the traditional canon can screen that fact by appropriating a sign invested with a certain power by a movement for change. A sign, but *not* what it has come to signify. For almost all of the essays in this collection, brilliant as some of them are, focus upon the canonical stalwarts, Emerson, Melville, Whitman, James, Eliot, and the like.

In the main the essays consist of *explications de textes*, elaborated by detailed analysis of the contemporary implications of key words and images and of the historical interrelationships between canonical figures like Emerson and the Jameses. Almost all of the analysis of noncanonical work, apart from that assigned to the category "popular," is found in Robert Stepto's important essay on African-American ambivalence about literacy. To justify the title of the book, or even, in fact, to realize the potential of the essays, most of their authors needed to step outside of the canon. A truly reconstructed view of the "ideologies of poetic modernism," to use, for example, Frank Lentricchia's title, might more clearly emerge by using the work of Charlotte Perkins Gilman, W. E. B. DuBois, and Jose Martí as lenses to understand aspects of Emerson, the male Jameses, Royce, and Santayana.

The thrust of Santayana's attack on the genteel tradition might then be seen as critical to the construction not of modernism but of male modernist sensibility. For in a 1911 talk, Santayana converted what was initially an architectural metaphor into a gendered definition of the intellectual currents he discerned:

America is . . . a country with two mentalities. . . . This division may be found symbolized in American architecture: a neat reproduction of the colonial mansion—with some modern comforts introduced surreptitiously—stands beside the sky-scraper. The American Will inhabits the sky-scraper; the American Intellect inhabits the colonial mansion. The one is the sphere of

the American man; the other, at least predominantly, of the
American woman. The one is all aggressive enterprise; the other
is all genteel tradition.[15]

Lentricchia claims that the works of Santayana, James, and Royce
"are themselves collaborative modernist texts, the original meta-
poetic idiom of the youth of Eliot, Frost, and Stevens," that they are,
in fact, "more expansive, detailed, and precise expressions of theory
than anything written in prose by any of the important modern
American poets."[16] If so, then surely it is essential to explicate the
gendered character of their writing, especially in light of the most
recent reconstructions of American poetic modernism by critics like
Marianne DeKoven and Alicia Ostriker.[17] They make problematic what
Lentricchia seems to take for granted, that is, the identities—"Eliot,
Frost and Stevens"—of the "important modern American poets," as
well as the character of their work. Further, the racial exclusivity of
"mainstream" modernism, not to speak of the deeply disturbing connections between modernist and colonialist sensibilities, can and
should be illuminated by noncanonical writers like DuBois and Martí.

Canonical issues emerge by virtue of what Lentricchia does *not*
say; Werner Sollors' essay, however, engages more directly the institutional implications of a changing canon. The bulk of Sollors' piece
is, unfortunately, an assault on a straw man, Horace Kallen, an early
advocate of cultural pluralism. To be sure, Kallen shared most of the
racialist attitudes of his early twentieth-century contemporaries, but
his resemblance to any living intellectual really eludes me. Further,
by foregrounding Kallen's racist ideas, Sollors largely misses the progressive impact of early pluralists, especially given the reactionary
boosterism of post–World War I America.

Apart from the dubious issue of the paternity of cultural pluralism
or the significance of such paternity, Sollors does touch upon some
central issues. First, he correctly argues against the notion that you
have to be Jewish to bake or evaluate Levy's rye bread, and also against
the theory that ethnic (and one can read, as well, minority or female)
writing can be defined entirely *within* a specific ethnic culture—as
if one's marginalized status were an insulation against the power of
so-called mainstream culture to shape consciousness and art. Indeed,
marginalized writing responds both to "internal" and "external" cultural influences, and the impact of those influences changes over time.
That should be obvious.

What is murky, however, are the implications of these realities for
curricula, academic programs, literary histories, or anthologies. Sol-

lors complains that "literary pluralists" display a "dislike of mix-ings" and "would like to construct a mosaic of ethnic stories that relies on the supposed permanence, individuality, and homogeneity of each ancestral tradition."[18] He also doubts that "the very same categories on which previous exclusivism was based" should "really be used as organizing concepts."[19] I take it from these and other of his comments in this article that Sollors would be skeptical of the value of separate black studies or women's studies departments, of volumes devoted exclusively to the work of Chicanas, of surveys of or entries in literary histories on the writings of American women, of American literature anthologies that, for instance, present as a sep-arate unit the work of the Harlem Renaissance writers. These seem to me to be not very helpful, indeed dangerous, conclusions implicit in Sollors' position.

The fact is that neither separation nor integration provide wholly satisfactory methods for presenting or studying marginalized cul-tures. On the one hand, simply to integrate the writing of Jean Toomer and Nella Larsen—to speak of the most problematic—with Pound, Hemingway, and Eliot misrepresents the milieu from which and in which they created; on the other hand, to place them solely within the context of the Harlem Renaissance underplays their qualities and influence as "modernist" writers. A separate women's studies, African-American, or Chicano studies department runs the risk of falsifying the actual experience of all women and men of color in America; and also may contribute to the ghettoization of female and minority stud-ies as well as to the indifference of academics in other departments to such concerns. On the other hand, without such centers of intel-lectual work and hubs for political struggle, the culture and experi-ences of the marginalized will even more systematically be margin-alized, or so the experiences of curriculum "integration" projects, not to speak of American history, strongly suggest. Few in this country are very comfortable with the notion of assigning jobs or housing on the basis of race or ethnicity, but without specific numerical goals and timetables, the effects of racism persist even unto a generation cured—as this is not—of racism. So is it, as I have argued elsewhere, with respect to culture: the distinctive qualities of the arts of the mar-ginalized need to be determined and celebrated by viewing them to-gether even as we acknowledge how much male and female, as well as black, brown, and white cultural traditions in the United States, overlap.[20] That requires processes *both* of separation and integration. Sollors' critique of pluralism in this volume seems to me an obstacle to this dual process.

His position, as expressed in his own book, is somewhat more complex. But the choice of this essay to represent the approach of the Bercovitch volume to ethnicity and literature illustrates how the book appropriates from the universe of discourse on ethnicity an element that casts a narrowing political shadow—or, perhaps, rationalizes an approach to writing literary history that differs sharply from that of the new Columbia volume edited by Emory Elliott. Eliott's book has been mocked (in the *New York Times Book Review*, for example) for taking multiple approaches, especially to noncanonical authors. But that seems to me one of its strengths. For while some of Sollors' strictures against the oversimplifications of cultural pluralism are well taken, the thrust of his argument is finally disabling to the effort to change existing power relationships in the literary community.

I have tried to suggest that the effort to reconstruct the canon involves a set of complex struggles: against the reactionary effort to impose a narrowed view of Western traditions on all; against the practice of academic formalism, which habitually views such issues as "pedagogical" and avoids them; with the parochialism of those who would simply substitute a local or individual set of texts for any canon; with the process—illustrated by the very names in the "reconstructing American literature" slogan quoted above—by which reconstructions harden into new canons; and even, sometimes, with allies, when their work seems to reenforce existing definitions of significance and thus of power. Those, I believe, have been the issues, and it is important to emphasize that they continue to be sharply contested. The competitive demands of academic life, like those of other markets under consumer capitalism, forever impel practitioners (like the Columbia University Press reader) to foreclose "old" debates in order to offer new products: corn toasters, orange corn toasters, cranberry-orange corn toasters; studies of minority texts, studies of the conditions of study of minority texts, studies of the studier studying the conditions of study of minority texts. . . . Further, looking at a document like the annual program issue of *PMLA* might lead one to conclude, given the enormous diversity of sessions at the Modern Language Association convention, that the effort to expand the canon has triumphed and the issues I have charted can safely be laid to rest as we frantically try to make criticism new. That would be a mistake, for in the ongoing contests for cultural authority it would be as foolish to assume that these questions are permanently decided as it would have been to suppose that Reconstruction or perhaps the civil rights movement had settled the issues of race relations in the United States.

Still, it is useful to note some of the newer directions that the continuing arguments about the canon have begun to take. One asks: does it really matter whether students read Harriet Jacobs or Nathaniel Hawthorne, Fitzgerald or Le Sueur in class, since it is not at all clear what they do and do not learn by studying any of them? Or, more generally, does the reading of canonical stalwarts necessarily imply the transmission of elitist values, or the study of working-class texts dependably yield working-class consciousness? These are interesting empirical questions, perhaps mainly for educational sociologists. They evoke the studies of the late 1950s which suggested that collegiate learning affects the values, at least of the students examined, marginally, if at all. Such skepticism extends the critique post-structuralist critics have mounted against the too easily presumed value of revolutions, or even of revolutionary movements, organizations, and goals. One problem with the questions is that they invite broad generalizations about *all* students in *any* circumstances. In fact, a good deal of evidence, mainly anecdotal, suggests that students of diverse class and racial backgrounds respond quite differently to books like *The Girl* and *Daughter of Earth*, although the character of such responses has changed somewhat over the last decade and a half. It can be extremely important for students from marginalized backgrounds to know that the domain of literature belongs as much to them as to others. But the main problem with skeptical social critiques, reasonable as they may seem, is that they too easily lead to political paralysis, and they play into reactionary ideologies which, for example, deny any value to radical change, whether retrospectively in Cuba or prospectively in South Africa. In the context of canon debate such skepticism over the value of altering canons can hardly help but provide fuel for those indifferent or hostile to such change. The argument then becomes: let us await persuasive evidence that it makes a difference before we disrupt the rooted norms of academic study. It is important to call into question exaggerated claims for the effects of canon change. Still, the assumption that such change matters with regard to what readers experience, envision, and believe seems to me a useful intellectual and pedagogical hypothesis on the basis of which to act. Only through such action do we find in social practice whether or to what extent and under what conditions our hypothesis is valid.

A more promising, and more challenging, direction seems to me to be that offered by cultural critics who question the privileging of "literary" texts that is implicit in debates over a canon. If presumed aesthetic value no longer determines our choice between reading Henry

James and Elizabeth Stuart Phelps, why read novels at all rather than, say, nineteenth-century medical or legal texts? They are, after all, often as interesting, and surely as reflective and probably more determinative of cultural assumptions about gender as fictions. Still, it would be shortsighted to slight the emotional power of narratives and of poetic language, or the prestige with which such forms have been invested in our culture. It is, I think, precisely to the socially constructed differences between, say, the authority of legal texts and the prestige of fiction, the power of *Roe v. Wade* to affect lives and the capacity of *The Color Purple* to invoke conflicted feelings, that cultural study can most usefully lead us.

For my own part, the most interesting frontiers of canon study have to do, in theoretical terms, with the implications of the material conditions of authorship and, in pedagogical terms, with the comparative study of canonical and marginalized texts. In her well-known article "Why Are There No Great Women Artists?" Linda Nochlin offered an institutional analysis of the processes by which art is created and valued. "The question 'Why are there no great women artists?'" leads, she wrote,

> to the conclusion that art is not a free, autonomous activity of a superendowed individual, "influenced" by previous artists, and, more vaguely and superficially, by "social forces," but rather, that art making, both in terms of the development of the art maker and the nature and quality of the work of art itself, occurs in a social situation, is an integral element of the social structure, and is mediated and determined by specific and definable social institutions, be they art academies, systems of patronage, mythologies of the divine creator and artist as he-man or social outcast. . . . By stressing the *institutional*—that is, the public—rather than the *individual* or private preconditions for achievement in the arts, we have provided a model for the investigation of other areas in the field.[21]

Literary practitioners have, on the whole, been slow to take up the analytic challenge. Nina Baym has examined the "Melodramas of Beset Manhood" that provide a kind of exclusionary mythology. Jane Tompkins and Cathy Davidson have explored the impact of particular publishing houses and practices, as well as the effect of peer networks, on the estalishment and maintenance of reputations and thus of canons in the nineteenth century. Hazel Carby has explored the relationship of specific audiences and educational objectives to the texts of black women writers. More recently, Richard Brodhead has begun looking at how specific opportunities to enter the profession of authorship carried with them certain restrictions as to audience, subject, and convention—and thus, implicitly, access to forms of composition, including those generally defined as significant or major. I have examined the effect of the post–World War I decline of women's literary clubs, and the enormous network they informed, on the radical reshaping of an American literary canon.[22] Increasingly, we can come to see canon formation and change in terms of concrete institutional developments at particular historical junctures. That kind of history can, in turn, inform how we engage in efforts to *reconstruct* canons.

The distinctive historical experiences of marginalized groups, the recent theoretical interest in *difference*, and essays like the Karcher and Ammons pieces to which I referred above, have suggested the pedagogical importance of a comparative approach, especially to the teaching of American texts. Reading together works from the 1920s and 1930s, like those of Fitzgerald and Le Sueur, or novels like Twain's *Pudd'nhead Wilson* and Charles Chesnutt's *The Marrow of Tradition*, or collections of stories like *The Country of the Pointed Firs* and *Winesburg, Ohio* or *In Our Time* offer what may be the most useful strategy for addressing the problems of marginality, difference, and affinity in canonical and noncanonical texts. I do not want to elaborate here on the value of this approach, but only to point out that an increasing number of syllabi that come to my attention show that teachers are building a range of courses around such comparative studies.

Finally, however, canon study ought to be able to lead us out of a narrowly construed set of professional concerns and back into the broader social and political world. The efforts to keep noncanonical work in print and to provide for its wider distribution, the controversies over literary prizes, like that recently involving Toni Morrison, the debates over whether, or to what, the "American mind" is closed make it clear that canonical issues are not simply matters of academic dispute. Like any meaningful cultural concern the question of the canon directly affects lives. There is a vital dialectic between the recognition of a writer like Morrison and the need to understand her predecessors, like Frances Ellen Watkins Harper, Nella Larsen, Ann Petry, and Gwendolyn Brooks; but more, between the creative aspirations of such writers and the lived experience of black women in American society. What is at stake, after all—to return to the initial problem with the cultural maven of Reaganism, William Bennett— is what a society sees as important from its past to the construction of its future, who decides that, and on what basis.

Still, at this juncture, the ways to reunite canon study and political action in practice may seem obscure. At one point, the demand to take up and take seriously Frederick Douglass, W. E. B. DuBois, Charlotte Perkins Gilman, and Agnes Smedley could, and often did, precipitate sharp conflicts, not only in curriculum committees but in the wider communities concerned with education. Today, canon study is perhaps as popular a subject for academic disquisitions as post-structuralist "theory," and the issues are publication and promotion, not black power and sexual politics. It should be no surprise that an institution like the academy could thus largely absorb a serious challenge to its assumptions and structures. After all, the *New York Review of Books* found the diagram of a Molotov cocktail useful to selling magazines. But if the ideas that canons are socially constructed *by* people and *in* history, that they have always changed and can be changed, that they are deeply shaped by institutions and the material conditions under which writing is produced and consumed—if these and related ideas have essentially triumphed within the academy, they remain deeply conflicted outside scholastic walls. It is all but impossible, I am told, to convince a congressperson of the importance of studying Zora together with, God forbid in place of, Ernest. That is no defeat; it says to me, in fact, that while the advocates of a broad, multicultural canon have consolidated our position within most educational institutions, the Bennetts and Blooms have been hard at work in the public arenas. To me the next challenge is to shift the locus of struggle precisely to such public forums, even now as the academic right wing bemoans the triumph of heterogeneity in the university. For all the academic fascination with hermeneutics and epistemology, it is in the realms of ethics and politics that the question of the canon must now be contested.

When we look back at the defeat of the Left in the United States after the 1930s, we recognize organized anticommunism as being primarily responsible. But we must also acknowledge the complicity of the Left in its own demise. That complicity has been named *Stalinism.* In rather an imprecise way the word invokes the Left's down side: authoritarian, secretive, tailist, sectarian. Today, we need to ask what tendencies in the intellectual Left cooperate in our marginalization by Reaganism. Many of these—obscurantism, careerism, sectarianism, defeatism—gather glumly under the banner of "theory." In the 1960s we consciously marched from campus bases into the great conflicts of the day; and what we learned on picket lines and in freedom schools transformed what we did back on campus—transformed most notably, for teachers of literature, the canon. If activism is not the mode of public discourse today, that doesn't mean that there are no debates into which the Left can forcefully enter. On the contrary, some of the most intense conflicts in our society are being argued out in the arena of culture. If we are not players in these debates, the fault, dear Martin, lies not with Bill Bennett, but with ourselves. It is time we carried the lessons we have learned in changing the academic canon into the public debate over cultural policy.

## Endnotes

1. Paul Lauter, "The Two Criticisms," in Betty Jean Craige, ed., *Literature, Language and Politics* (Athens: University of Georgia Press, 1988), pp. 1–19.

2. See Paul Lauter, "Looking a Gift Horse in the Mouth," *San Jose Studies* (winter 1986), 12:6–19.

3. Robert Scholes, "Aiming a Canon at the Curriculum," *Salmagundi* (fall 1986), no. 72, p. 116.

4. *Ibid.*, p. 107. The Eliot quote is from "Modern Education and the Classics."

5. Scholes, "Aiming a Canon," *Salmagundi* (fall 1986), no. 72, p. 114.

6. Marjorie Perloff, "An Intellectual Impasse," *Salmagundi* (fall 1986), no. 72, p. 126.

7. *Ibid.*

8. Barbara Herrnstein Smith, "Contingencies of Value," in Robert von Hallberg, ed., *Canons* (Chicago, Ill.: University of Chicago Press, 1984), pp. 5–39.

9. Not to belabor the point, but many of these issues of the social functions of criticism and the political character of what was not then called the "canon" were being discussed in the late 1960s among those who contributed to the original volume called *The Politics of Literature*.

Further, the use of the term "theory" to designate the various structuralist and poststructuralist forms of criticism currently being ground out by literary intellectuals amounts to an effort to appropriate to such writing alone what has become an academic honorific. It suggests that those of us who wrote in the 1960s or before had no "theory"; that we were, as critics both of the Right and the Left have suggested, mindless activists, chirruping onto our innocent pages our "native woodnotes wild." One is tempted, considering the Columbia connection of this volume, to resurrect Mark Rudd's favorite words to describe this kind of "intellectual history," but I will refrain.

10. For example, Susan Hardy Aiken et al., *Changing Our Minds: Feminist Transformations of Knowledge* (Albany: State University of New York Press, 1988); Patricia Hill Collins and Margaret L. Andersen, *An Inclusive Curriculum: Race, Class, and Gender in Sociological Instruction* (Washington, D.C.: American Sociological Association, 1987); Adelaida R. Del Castillo, *Women's History in Transition: Theory, Methods and Content in Mexican/Chicana History* (Los Angeles: University of California Chicano Studies Research Center, 1985); Ellen DuBois et al., *Feminist Scholarship: Kindling in the Groves of Academe* (Urbana: University of Illinois Press, 1985); Diane Fowlkes and Charlotte McClure, eds., *Feminist Visions: Towards a Transformation of the Liberal*

*Arts Curriculum* (Tuscaloosa: University of Alabama Press, 1984); Elizabeth Minnich, Jean O'Barr, and Rachel Rosenfeld, eds., *Reconstructing the Academy* (Chicago, Ill.: University of Chicago Press, 1988); Bonnie Spanier, Alexander Bloom, and Darlene Boroviak, eds., *Towards a Balanced Curriculum* (Cambridge, Mass.: Schenkman, 1984); Dale Spender, ed., *Men's Studies Modified: The Impact of Feminism on the Academic Disciplines* (New York: Pergamon Press, 1981).

11. Werner Sollors, "A Critique of Pure Pluralism," in Sacvan Bercovitch, ed., *Reconstructing American Literary History* (Cambridge: Harvard University Press, 1986.

12. Elizabeth Fox-Genovese, "The Claims of a Common Culture: Gender, Race, Class and the Canon," *Salmagundi* (fall 1986), no. 72, p. 134.

13. An excellent illustration of this approach is provided in a reading of Aristotle's *Politics* provided by Elizabeth Victoria Spelman in *Inessential Woman: Problems of Exclusion in Feminist Thought* (Boston, Mass.: Beacon Press, 1988).

14. *Narrative of the Life of Frederick Douglass, an American Slave, Written by Himself* (New York: Signet, 1968), pp. 54–55.

15. George Santayana, *The Genteel Tradition: Nine Essays* Douglas Wilson, ed. (Cambridge, Mass.: Harvard University Press, 1967).

16. Frank Lentricchia," Ideologies of Poetic Modernism," in Bercovitch, ed., *Reconstructing American Literary History,* p. 223.

17. Marianne DeKoven, *A Different Language: Gertrude Stein's Experimental Writing* (Madison: University of Wisconsin, 1983); Alicia Ostriker, *Stealing the Language: The Emergence of Women's Poetry in America* (Boston, Mass.: Beacon Press, 1986).

18. Sollors, "A Critique of Pure Pluralism," p. 274.

19. *Ibid.,* p. 255.

20. Paul Lauter, "The Literatures of America: A Comparative Discipline," paper prepared for the Soviet-American Symposium on the Literature of American Ethnic Groups, Philadelphia, 1985, forthcoming in *New American Literary History* (Modern Language Association).

21. Linda Nochlin, "Why Are There No Great Women Artists?" pp. 493, 509.

22. Nina Baym, "Melodramas of Beset Manhood: How Theories of American Fiction Exclude Women Authors," in Elaine Showalter, ed., *The New Feminist Criticism: Essays on Women, Literature and Theory* (New York: Pantheon, 1985), pp. 63–80; Jane Tompkins, *Sensational Designs* (New York: Oxford, 1985); Cathy Davidson, *Revolution and the Word: The Rise of the Novel in America* (New York: Oxford, 1986); Hazel Carby, *Reconstructing Womanhood* (New York: Oxford, 1987); Richard Brodhead, in a paper delivered at the 1988 convention of the Modern Language Association, New Orleans, Louisiana; Paul Lauter, in an unpublished paper, "Clubs and Canons: Nineteenth-Century Women's Study Groups and 'American Literature'" (1989).

# 7

# Canon Fathers and Myth Universe

## Lillian S. Robinson

*Lillian Robinson also takes up the issue of the canon, but from a feminist point of view. Robinson's essay examines how women outside universal white, male myths have been silenced, rendered without identity or voice. Robinson's essay demonstrates how the very nature of feminist criticism opens up the canon. For Robinson, feminist criticism, with its gender concerns, forces us to rethink our literary tradition, forces us to consider not only the works of women but also the works of all of those other excluded groups who do not fit into the established norms of what great literature ought to be.*

In the subtext of this essay are two questions that, together, constitute the pretext for what follows. The first of these questions is that of the reader who asks, *What the hell does that title mean, anyway: Canon Fathers and Myth Universe?* Well, it refers to the generally patriarchal literary canon, the literally patriarchal biblical one that is the source of the canon metaphor, the Fathers of the Church, whose patristic writings include the bases of canon law, the Anglican cathedral clergy, whose title is "canon" and who may be addressed as "Father," and, of course, the military imagination, with its fecund visions of can(n)on fodder. And then there are the notions of a uni-

This article first appeared in *New Literary History* (fall 1987), vol. 19 and is reprinted with the permission of the Johns Hopkins University Press.

versal myth, the *dominant* myth of a human universal that turns out to be male, and the sexist international competition for Miss Universe. My title is at once the portmanteau that contains all that conceptual baggage and the background upon which the essay itself is projected.

The other question in my sub- and pretext is one that I have been asking myself with increasing insistence whenever I accept an invitation to give a guest lecture under the aegis of a department of English or comparative literature. Crudely expressed (which is exactly how it *is* expressed in the depths of my consciousness), my question goes: *Shall I choose a subject in feminist criticism or in "regular" criticism?*

First, however, the elephant seals. An elephant seal, which I once heard a lecturer describe as looking, in motion, like a cross between a walrus and a waterbed, belongs to a species of belatedly protected wildlife that lives in the Pacific Ocean. Every January, they all come up to Año Nuevo Beach near Santa Cruz, California, and to an island just off its shore, to mate. Every year, thousands of human visitors descend on Año Nuevo in a spirit of learned voyeurism to find out about the elephant seals and their environment. The actual mating takes place on the island, so it is something of an exaggeration to say, as people tend to, "We're going to see (or *watch*) the elephant seals mate." What you do see are seals, asleep, tending their young, or galumphing about, and sometimes interacting with one another. To interpret this set of observations and particularly the interactions, there is an army of volunteer docents, as well as a mass of posters, bulletin boards, and fliers. What emerges from the surfeit of natural history is a picture of male elephant seals fighting it out for dominance over one another in order to be able to control territory and hence to control females. The largest, most aggressive, and dominant males, we are told, win big harems for the mating season, those who are less so get less space and fewer females in the harem, and the adolescents—old enough to mate but not large enough to compete—join the pups and the wimps in hanging out on the beach. Elephant seal behavior that may appear random, playful, or at least neutral to the lay observer is invariably characterized in terms of this rigid lexicon of dominance, hierarchy, territory, and harems.[3]

This is a genuine question. On the one hand, my reputation and intellectual identity have both been informed by my work as a feminist critic. But the invitation is frequently at the instance of a search committee, as part of the hiring process. As a professional who is not gainfully employed, ought I not to show that I can do regular criticism too? So the question is heartfelt and authentic. Yet it horrifies me. For criticism should not be served, like coffee, in "regular" and "variant" versions, In fact, though, depending on the region of this country in which you order it, "regular" coffee is interpreted as meaning that the cream has been added or, conversely, that it has not. (Regular, that is, is the opposite of both black and white—depending on where you stand.) Surely, I have been telling myself, I can construct an argument to show why, at this time, the proper project of "regular" criticism is the one with the feminism *in* it.

In the context in which it originated, my project was clearly something of a peace initiative, an attempt to demonstrate that feminist criticism is not fundamentally different from (and hence in no way a threat to) dominant critical modalities. In its evolution, however, that irenic effort asserted its true identity, coming to resemble a declaration of permanent difference, if not precisely of war, more than the patching-over I intended. For I find that, despite having the most pacific intentions, I am still asking to what extent a feminist perspective necessarily challenges all of the previous assumptions and conclusions of the critical tradition.

It is on this basis that I inaugurated the Visiting Humanities Chair I occupied at Albright College a few years ago by delivering a lecture entitled "Why Studying Women Means Studying Everything." The anecdotes with which I began that lecture, although they are drawn from other fields, have a special pertinence to the study of literature. Despite that global title, these anecdotes deal modestly enough with my nephew Ian and the elephant seals. They are two distinct stories, but both have their ramifications, and those ramifications turn out to touch each other at a number of points.

When Ian was a teenager, I was invited from Paris to New York for a series of interviews and took advantage of that time for several marathon work sessions with my collaborators on the book *Feminist Scholarship: Kindling in the Groves of Academe.*[1] I was accompanied on my travels by my infant son, who acquired three new teeth in the two weeks we spent in America. As you can imagine, I was much in need of and very grateful for the heroic hours of babysitting provided by Ian and his younger brother. In order to help me in this way, Ian had to refuse requests for his services from his regular clients. He expatiated to me on the relative thickness of blood and water. Then, referring to the neighbor he'd just turned down for the second or third time that week, he added, "Besides, your work is more important than hers. She's just writing some book about women in the French Revolution." Reluctant as I would have been to lose or even share my sitter, I had to know: "Why was he so prepared to dismiss this work? "Well," he explained, "it can't be very important. I mean, *I* never heard of any women in the French Revolution!"[2] In the fine tradition of child psychology represented by Ring Lardner's line " 'Shut up,' I explained," *I* explained at the top of my lungs that it was precisely to prevent fourteen-year-old smart asses from being so sure that women were absent from the great events of history that such intellectual work *was* important. This story turns out to have a range of applications to literary study, and I shall be discussing some of them further on in this essay.

First, however, the elephant seals. An elephant seal, which I once heard a lecturer describe as looking, in motion, like a cross between a walrus and a waterbed, belongs to a species of belatedly protected wildlife that lives in the Pacific Ocean. Every January, they all come up to Año Nuevo Beach near Santa Cruz, California, and to an island just off its shore, to mate. Every year, thousands of human visitors descend on Año Nuevo in a spirit of learned voyeurism to find out about the elephant seals and their environment. The actual mating takes place on the island, so it is something of an exaggeration to say, as people tend to, "We're going to see (or *watch*) the elephant seals mate." What you do see are seals, asleep, tending their young, or galumphing about, and sometimes interacting with one another. To interpret this set of observations and particularly the interactions, there is an army of volunteer docents, as well as a mass of posters, bulletin boards, and fliers. What emerges from the surfeit of natural history is a picture of male elephant seals fighting it out for dominance over one another in order to be able to control territory and hence to control females. The largest, most aggressive, and dominant males, we are told, win big harems for the mating season, those who are less so get less space and fewer females in the harem, and the adolescents—old enough to mate but not large enough to compete—join the pups and the wimps in hanging out on the beach. Elephant seal behavior that may appear random, playful, or at least neutral to the lay observer is invariably characterized in terms of this rigid lexicon of dominance, hierarchy, territory, and harems.[3]

I have been to see the elephant seals a number of times, and my irritation was at first inflamed by the racist description of the Indians who used to inhabit that section of the coast, a racism presented in the same blandly factual tone as the ecology lecture. (They "disappeared," we were told, but their mysterious evanescence was no great loss, for they were not particularly "interesting" Indians. Lacking a sense of history, it seems, they "had no culture" worth speaking of!)

It was this rhetoric that made me compare what was said and written, which is to say *interpreted*, about the elephant seals—as text, if you will—with what could actually be observed. I concluded that all that really can be stated, more humbly but far more honestly, about the elephant seals is that they do come back to Año Nuevo to mate and that not much is really understood about their behavior, their motives, or their community. Perhaps one could add that male elephant seals seem to feel a need for a lot of space around them at mating time and that females prefer to be closer together at that time, as well as at the subsequent birthing of the pups. That is absolutely all we know, and the rest is projecting an oppressive anthropomorphic scenario on those poor creatures who are just trying to go about the business of reproducing their species.

Within the general framework of canon formation, re-formation, and reformation consequent upon the emergence of feminist criticism, I take the exemplary tale about my nephew and the revolutionary Frenchwomen to embody certain truths about the recovery of women's role in *literary* history. The elephant seals I take as emblematic of the problems—but also the opportunities—encountered when we bring women's reclaimed role into relation with the literary tradition as it has hitherto been perceived.

If you've never heard of any women in the French Revolution, this is a commentary on historical scholarship and even on historians, not on women in the French Revolution. That, of course, is the gist of what I yelled at my nephew. And so, too, in literary studies, where an impressive labor of intellectual reappropriation has begun to document the existence of a continuous tradition of women's writing in English, as well as in a number of other European literatures, a tradition extending well back into the centuries before the Industrial Revolution. Feminist scholarship has also challenged canonical definitions of literature itself by exploring women's private writings— letters, journals, personal memoirs—as literary texts. And it has sought access to mass female experience by considering popular genres produced by women for the female audience as a possible component of the newly acknowledged entity "women's literature." This inclusiveness, where there was once only a brief but oft-rehearsed litany of great names, has also meant a slow opening of the emerging female tradition to the voices of women of color, lesbians who write from and of that experience, and women writing out of the (literal) history of colonization and its aftermath.

But what about "the" canon, the regular canon, so to speak? How, to use my analogy from the study of history, do we *fit* the recently

uncovered activities of women into the old story of the French Revolution? There are two quite different approaches to this question.
The first is simply to add the new information about what women
did to the body of information already in our possession. The second
is to raise a more thoroughgoing question: How does what we have
learned about the role of women *change* what we know or believe we
know about the French Revolution in general? To situate it in the
literary context: How does the newly uncovered material by seventeenth-century women affect our previous generalizations about the
literature of the seventeenth century? And the answer to that question turns out to depend on essentially aesthetic considerations. As I
point out elsewhere, it is really a question about

> the extent to which challenges to the male-dominated canon also
> entail challenges to the dominant stylistic, thematic, and aes-
> thetic norms. As the archaeological aspect of feminist scholar-
> ship is pursued to good purpose, the academic world in general
> is increasingly likely to admit to us that, yes, after all, there
> were some women writing in the seventeenth century. But how
> many of them, we will be asked, we will ask ourselves, were any
> good? How many of them are good enough to deserve a place
> in an honest "coed" canon? How many are good enough to de-
> serve to (deep breath) displace some gentleman on "the" syl-
> labus for seventeenth-century literature? These are by no means
> rhetorical questions; their answers are not obvious. It all de-
> pends on what we mean by "good," on how far scholarship alone,
> simply uncovering the lost or never-heard voices of women of
> past centuries, suggests or even dictates a new set of aesthetic
> principles. How do we know that it is as good? Do we leave the
> definitions untouched and demonstrate, as is clearly possible in
> some cases, that a given woman meets all the existing criteria
> for goodness? Or do we implicitly or explicitly modify the aes-
> thetic compact?[4]

These questions, significant as they are for how we think about,
say, seventeenth-century poetry, become even more crucial as we
consider the various nontraditional *kinds* of texts—the diaries, the
sensational or domestic novels—that are part of the women's canon.
Does the act of reclamation itself imply a new aesthetic? If so, what
is that new aesthetic? What are its new limits?

Similarly, once women's literature includes the writing of women
of color, generalizations about "the female" imagination have to be
modified accordingly. When this happens, what about "the" canon

as it is confronted with the sensibility of the formerly colonized, domestic or foreign? (Here, of course, we are approaching elephant seal
territory.) Certainly, one's sense of the present world-historic moment
in literature—in English, but also in other national traditions—is
quite different depending on the degree to which one is open to this
global perspective.

As it happens, moreover, students of women's role in the actual
French Revolution have brought to light a most extraordinary series
of texts, the *cahiers des plaintes et doléances* (documented complaints)
written on behalf of women as women. Remarkably modern documents, insofar as they raise the issues that we today would label "sexual harassment" or "the right to a career," they are also a remarkable
piece of eighteenth-century history, speaking as they do *of* the condition and *in* something very like the voice of the fishwife, the flower
seller, the laundress of that period.[5] Unlike the *cahiers* prepared by
males familiar with legal forms and conventions, these documents
manage to deal with issues as various as the nature of citizenship,
the rights of illegitimate children, and the adulteration of laundry
soap, maintaining all the while a clear focus on the connections between and among them in creating the lives of women.[6]

My own impulse would be to admit these documents as women's
literature, thus making my French Revolution anecdote part of *my*
critical text, rather than a metaphor stretched in a number of different directions. But when women's literature starts including the previously inarticulate, the semiliterate, the consumer of popular literature, the literature she consumes, and the writing she does on the
basis of that "bad" stylistic model, it offers a challenge to "the" canon.
It is a challenge to open its own frontiers not only to excluded social
groups, but to the widest range of expression of those groups' experience. The result would be to see our whole past, the seventeenth
and eighteenth centuries, for starters, as experienced authentically by
two sexes and all classes, or our present moment as experienced by
all sorts of people with very different relations to the dominant culture and the fact of dominance. And it would be to understand this
seeing as a legitimate part of our activity in the world of literary
interpretation, not belonging to some other mode of apprehension
outside the proper boundaries of criticism.

And here we are right down on the beach with the elephant seals,
trying to determine how many of the truths about our culture that
we have absorbed can survive such an intellectual upheaval. The confusion starts, of course, with that word *our*, for, as Jane Flax has succinctly put it, "only recently have scholars begun to consider the pos-

sibility that there may be at least three histories in every culture—
'his,' 'hers,' and 'ours.' 'His' and 'ours' are generally assumed to be
equivalents."[7] What I have been doing in questioning that equiva-
lency is to imply the existence of something very like the Outsiders'
Society that Virginia Woolf unforgettably creates in *Three Guineas*.
My assumption is that the logic of feminist scholarship and criticism,
because they invariably bring one social category, that of gender, into
relation with traditional critical categories, necessarily entails re-
thinking the entire literary tradition in order to place centrally into
it not only an entire excluded sex—which is an enormous enough
task—but also excluded classes, races, national groups, sexual minorities, and ideological positions. (I have also felt free, for the purposes of this ideal system, to ignore both the congruences *and the
conflicts* between and among the various groups defined by their enforced cultural marginality.) What this means is a more truly comparative literature, one that could, in fact, comfortably be called *our*
literature, rather than allowing the universe of cultural expression to
remain, in the words of the Nigerian social critic Chinweizu, "the
West and the rest of us."[8]

But, as I have indicated, feminist criticism can approach the traditional standards for canonicity, which are supposed to constitute
"our" common aesthetic, either by demonstrating how the female
tradition conforms to that aesthetic or by challenging the aesthetic
itself. Similarly, in speaking of those previously excluded from elite
definitions of culture, we ought to recognize where those groups both
do and do not partake of "the" tradition. It is this question, both sides
of it, that has impelled me to consider the myths that recur in the
Western (which is to say, the white Euro-American male, high cultural) literary tradition. I am principally concerned with them *as* part
of literature, that is, not so much as archetypes as *stories* that get told
over and over and whose retellings according to the imperatives of
different generations depend on the long history of previous tellings.

From this point of view, as you switch perspectives from "insiders"
to "outsiders," you note different priorities and preoccupations. Women
writers, for instance, do not compulsively retell the history of the Tro-
jan War and its aftermath, not even adapting the myth to fit female
conditions. Indeed, in a brilliant paper at the 1984 MLA convention,
Carolyn Heilbrun contrasted the literary projects of Joyce and Woolf,
citing *Ulysses* as the closing off, in our century's terms, of one myth,
while Woolf's work opened new mythopoeic areas for women. In a
simpler vein, I find it impossible to imagine *The Odyssey au féminin*
because, in the travels of any female, the sexual question looms larger

and creates new difficulties of its own. Whom Does She Sleep With? becomes so central as to block out all of the other questions such a myth is supposed to answer. It may be that Erica Jong has something like *The Odyssey* in mind as she serializes the adventures of Isadora Wing, particularly in her latest version, *Parachutes and Kisses*, which involves the artist's wanderings and her search for identity through reclamation of the life of the dead artist-patriarch, her grandfather. But Jong's obsessive answering and answering the Whom-Does-She-Sleep-With question obscures the rest for us, and makes all of her work at least as picaresque as her intentional eighteenth-century pastiche, *Fanny*. Meanwhile, for most women writers, the Ulysses myth has proved even less useful, remaining essentially external to any central female project.

However, certain words, forms, and stories from the insiders' tradition *have* been usefully appropriated by the outsiders, and transformed in the process. When the Nigerian novelist Chinua Achebe told us in the very title of his first novel that *Things Fall Apart*, he meant things quite different from what Yeats meant in *his* colony. The use of that title signaled a simultaneous joining of the dominant tradition and an appropriation of it to different needs. The final irony in this deeply ironic novel is that it ends with the colonial district commissioner contemplating *his* eventual text. Speaking of the central character, the last *African* voice in the novel has "ferociously" told him: "That man was one of the greatest men in Umuofia. You drove him to kill himself; and now he will be buried like a dog. . . ." Then the speaker's "voice trembled and choked his words." The administrator, by contrast, thinks that the hero's story "would make interesting reading. One could almost write a whole chapter on him. Perhaps not a whole chapter but a reasonable paragraph, at any rate. There was so much else to include, and one must be firm in cutting out details. He had already chosen the title of his book, after much thought: *The Pacification of the Primitive Tribes of the Lower Niger.*"[9] Achebe ends his novel just here, but, in taking his title where and as he does and adapting the novel both to the external conditions and the inner life of a member of one of those "primitive tribes," he shows us who may *really* have "the last word."

To take a more elaborate case, John Gay's *The Beggar's Opera* includes some sharp social commentary. After all, toward the end, the Beggar comments that, "Had the Play remain'd, as I at first intended, it would have carried a most excellent Moral. 'Twould have shown that the lower Sort of People have their Vices in a degree as well as the Rich. And that they are punish'd for them."[10] But Gay's work, for all its intentional reversals, finally remains so securely inside the formal and ideological guidelines of the canon as to be able to play with them. The "lower sort of people" remain the playwright's objects, not his subjects or his audience. Brecht's *Threepenny Opera* extends these limits considerably in adapting Gay's story to social relations after the Industrial Revolution, and by considering those conditions from a perspective that is at once proletarian and experimental. These changes are part of the generational reformulation of a familiar story. To the extent that this story about class, sexuality, power, and reversed expectations claims that status, Brecht's representation represents a familiar *myth*. But Brecht is by now securely part of the European canon, too.

The noncanonical stage of the process occurs when Wole Soyinka transports Macheath and Polly to Nigeria in his *Opera Wonyosi*, combining them with traditional African and contemporary political elements to make a searing commentary on neocolonial dictatorships. With "Mack the Knife" playing in the background, Dee-Jay, the narrator, opens the play with a rap on its title:

> One time we called it the Way-Out Opera—for short, Opera Wayo. Call it the Beggar's Opera if you insist—that's what the whole nation is doing—begging for a slice of the action.
> . . . You know what, why don't you just make up your own title as we go along because, I tell you brother, I'm yet to decide whether such a way-out opera should be named after the Beggars, the Army, the Bandits, the Police, the Cash-madams, the Students, the Trade-unionists, the Alhajis and Alhajas, the Aladura, the Academicas, the Holy Radicals, Holy Patria[r]chs and Unholy Heresiarchs—I mean man, in this way-out country everyone acts way out. Including the traffic. Maybe we should call it, the Trafficking Opera. Which just complicates things with trafficking in foreign exchange.[11]

As Dee-Jay segues into an Africanized and overtly political version of Kurt Weill's lyrics, we are left to realize that the "opera" in fact has none of those proposed titles, but rather is named for "the famous Wonyosi," an absurd and absurdly expensive lace version of an African *agbada*, which is to serve as the Emperor's (literal) new clothing.

As his play develops, it becomes apparent that Soyinka is simultaneously using and permanently altering the tradition, including the radical tradition, for he openly critiques Brecht's rigid class analysis in order to strengthen a position that is at once fiercely nationalist

and what we in the Euro-American world would call liberal humanist. There is a sense in which Brecht, for all his formal iconoclasm
and social radicalism, was a good son of his literary father, whereas
Soyinka is a rebellious one, asserting a new and radically different
reality.

Another example of what I mean might be the quest myth. Women
of the metropolis and exotic peoples of both sexes often figure in quests,
but as objects, not subjects. It is hard, in our cultural context, to
imagine the female, rather than the male, serving as representative
of the human spiritual norm, Everyone instead of Everyman, for the
female, to us, remains Everywoman, and Everywoman is inevitably
sexualized. Thus, in *Surfacing*, Margaret Atwood uses themes as old
as the *Gilgamesh* epic, joining them with rituals from native Cana-
dian Indian traditions, in an attempt to ally herself with *that* Outsider community, as well. Her quest as descent into the watery world
becomes a metaphor for the fundamental female experience of childbirth (motherhood betrayed and finally accepted), creating a version
of the thing that is new in an entirely different *dimension* of newness.

Dante recognized his debt to a long insiders' tradition when he
created the special quest that is his *Commedia*. The role of Vergil both
embodies and reflects the poet's sense of participation in a tradition.
But Dante expands the tradition exemplified by Vergil's own use of
the prophetic visit to the underworld by connecting human history
and politics simultaneously to the largest spiritual forces in the universe and to the inner life of actual individuals. Those who have used
Dante's themes have always built on this enlarged sense of the meaning of a journey to the world of the dead. In the twentieth century,
the *Inferno* has spoken more directly to our inner life than either the
*Purgatorio* or the *Paradiso*. When "outsider" writers make use of Dante's
myth, therefore, it is not to take the tour of *any* part of the afterlife,
but to show us Hell transplanted to the here and now, the social here
and now, and its consequent distortion of individual psyches.

I think, for instance, of the way the American left-wing novelist
Sol Yurick gives us a Brooklyn hospital as Inferno in his *Fertig*, in
which the indifference, incompetence, and cruelty that kill the protagonist's child are played out and recalled in a setting that is consciously modeled on Dante's imagery, from the symbolic beasts
on down to the frozen center. More recently, Gloria Naylor's novel
*Linden Hills* has been criticized for adapting the "white male Christian myth" of the *Inferno* to her allegory of black bourgeois life. Why
not use African or Afro-American symbolic systems, one reviewer asked,
instead of that same old high European culture? If there is a flaw in

*Linden Hills*, I would not locate it in Naylor's extraordinarily powerful rendering of Dante's hellish vision. These characters are living in Hell, some of them at its very depths, and it is only fitting that the objective image representing their Hell be drawn from the demonic white culture in which they are all so heavily implicated and that constitutes their damnation as surely as Dante's characters experience their sin and their suffering as a single, organically organized concept.

Clearly, there are many ways of appropriating the insiders' charter myths, the ones that were always *supposed* to be universal, as long as one accepts a particular definition of the universal human. For women, as I have indicated, even white, economically privileged Western women, certain of those myths are more readily adapted than others. But it is more problematic to consider whether women writing in the Western tradition may be said to have a characteristic myth of their own. If they have, I believe that it is not rooted in the bodily difference between the sexes, but rather in the *social* experience of that bodily difference. More specifically, the myth resides in the cultural experience of being forcibly silenced and hence being left without access to language as a source of identity, a means of expression, or a modality of change.

Feminist writers and critics have adapted and retold the myth of Procne and Philomel as a representation of our condition. Jane Marcus' essay "Still Practice" is perhaps the most salient example of feminist critical theory built on this myth of women using the means available to them, speech denied, to tell of the brutal violation visited upon one of their number and on the sex as a whole.[12] Ovid tells us that Philomel, her tongue torn out by her rapist, makes a tapestry and sends it to her sister to show her what has happened. In *Titus Andronicus*, Shakespeare has Lavinia, who has had her hands chopped off as well as her tongue cut out, point with her stumps to the passage in the *Metamorphoses* that describes the rape of Philomel, using the text to explain her plight, and then, with her uncle's staff in her mouth, write the names of her own violators in the sand. To plunge from these sublime heights, another male author, John Irving, in *The World According to Garp*, gives us the actual experience of eleven-year-old Ellen James and the stupid, fanatical self-multilation of the Ellen Jamesian feminists as complementary propositions in this same dialectic.

From Virginia Woolf's creation of Shakespeare's sister, equally gifted but born in a female body, to Tillie Olsen's discussion of motherhood and female creative incapacity in *Silences*, the emphasis on *not* writing, on being *prevented* from writing, underlies critical discussion of what is and has been written. The next step in the theoretical process is for the female nontext to *become* the text, as in feminist treatments of Freud's *Dora*. As reflected in the lengthy bibliography to Bernheimer and Kahane's *In Dora's Case: Freud, Hysteria, Feminism*,[13] the obsession with this turn-of-the-century text, with its central *agon* between Freud and the hysterical adolescent girl who was his early patient, is not unlike the tradition's recurrent reference to classical myths. *Dora* may be our *Odyssey* and our *Metamorphoses* in one. The reason for this recurrence is that the principal symptom of the sexually molested girl Freud called Dora was aphonia. Freud tried hard to put words in her mouth—a proceeding that could be construed as benevolent only by someone entirely unfamiliar with our English idioms. From Hélène Cixous on out, however, feminist creative artists, critics, analysts, and historians have wanted to give the young girl back her own voice—and, in so doing, give one to all of us.

One of the things Alice Walker achieves in *The Color Purple* is to supply a voice to the inarticulate in a more concrete but also more sophisticated way. At the start of the novel, Celie is fourteen years old, barely literate, and with neither the vocabulary nor, seemingly, the capacity to describe her experience of rape by the man she believes to be her father. The rapist's words, which serve as epigraph to the first letter and hence to Celie's beginning to speak—"You better not tell nobody but God. It'd kill your mammy"—constitute the profoundly ironic permission to take the rape and (as in the Philomel myth, *Titus Andronicus*, and the feminist recreations of *Dora*) create a text out of one's own pain and oppression, written in one's own blood, if necessary.[14] The epistolary form, one of the earliest narrative strategies for the novel, is here appropriated as a source of empowerment for a woman who has no access even to the words that properly name violated parts of her own body. Some of us have always had our suspicions of Pamela, or rather of Samuel Richardson, even though he does get the sex and class dynamics right. For Pamela's complex relationship to the act of narration and the parental audience to whom the narrative is addressed is by no means a story of empowerment by means of the text. Celie shows us why our suspicions were justified, as, taking hold of that pen to write first to God, later to her sister in Africa, and finally to "Everything," she becomes the black woman entering a world where telling is an *event* and writing can make something happen.

For, as the woman whose tongue is ripped out may find an unmutilated sister to tell her story, the woman writer at her best feels her hand guided, like Alice Walker's by the woman who cannot write her own story because she cannot write at all. As long as, according to UNESCO, 80 percent of the world's illiterates are women, this is not a piece of pretentious rhetoric but a true responsibility. When the woman writer writes within the boundaries of what we already have been taught to recognize as literature, using, even participating in traditional canonical forms and myths, while asserting the specifically female myth, she surely extends our *common* literary heritage.

It is hard to disagree with Audre Lorde's much-cited dictum that the Master's tools will never dismantle the Master's house.[15] But people have to live in a house, not in a metaphor. Of *course* you use the Master's tools if those are the only ones you can lay your hands on. Perhaps what you can do with them is to take apart that old mansion, using some of its pieces to put up a far better one where there is room for all of us. One where no one asks me and I need not ask myself, as I talk about its fine proportions and human significance, whether I'm engaging in feminist criticism or the real thing.

### Endnotes

1. Ellen Carol DuBois, Gail Paradise Kelly, Elizabeth Lapovsky Kennedy, Carolyn W. Korsmeyer, and Lillian S. Robinson, *Feminist Scholarship: Kindling in the Groves of Academe* (Urbana: University of Illinois Press, 1985). The collective nature of the completed study has attracted a good deal of comment. For the five authors, the intellectual difficulties of collaboration were enhanced and complicated by the fact that at no time after we decided to write a book "together" did all of us live in the same place.

2. A version of this anecdote appears, with different applications, in Lillian S. Robinson, "Feminist Criticism: How Do We Know When We've Won?" *Tulsa Studies in Women's Literature* (1984), 3:143–51, reprinted in Shari Benstock, ed., *Feminist Issues in Literary Scholarship* (Bloomington: Indiana University Press, 1987), pp. 141–49.

3. The analogous and more destructive generalizations about and *from* the behavior of apes have begun to be roundly challenged by such feminist primatologists as Sarah Blaffer Hrdy. I do not know whether revisionist arguments are also being advanced in the case of the elephant seals. See Sarah Blaffer Hrdy, *The Woman Who Never Evolved* (Cambridge, Mass.: Harvard University Press, 1981).

4. Robinson, "Feminist Criticism," p. 147.

5. Paule-Marie Duhet points out in the preface to *Cahiers des doléances des femmes en 1789 et autres textes* (Paris: Des Femmes, 1981) that there are also a number of (readily distinguishable) "false" *cahiers*, petitions, and so on purporting to have female authors, and she comments on the various motives— often satirical, conservative, antifeminist, or anticlerical—behind this widespread assumption of the female persona. One distinction Duhet makes be-

tween real women and their impersonators is that: "Les femmes ont trop à dire . . . elles ne peuvent pas prendre la distance que suppose le maniment sarcastique de l'écriture. Leurs textes sont toujours marqués par une impatience, une indignation retenues, un souci de dominer les maux présents en y portant remède." (Women have too much that needs saying . . . they can't establish the distance presupposed by sarcastic handling of the written word. Their texts are marked by an impatience, a restrained indignation, a concern to surmount present evils by finding a remedy for them"; p. 16, my translation.)

6. See, e.g., in *Cahiers:* Anonymous, "Du sort actuel des femmes," pp. 115–23; Madame Grandval, "Pour les droits des enfants naturels," pp. 151–57; and "Doléances des blanchisseuses et lavandières de Marseille," pp. 43–46.

7. Jane Flax, "Postmodernism and Gender Relations in Feminist Theory," *Signs: Journal of Women in Culture and Society* (summer 1987), 12(4):629.

8. Chinweizu, *The West and the Rest of Us: White Predators, Black Slavers and the African Elite* (New York: Random House, 1975).

9. Chinua Achebe, *Things Fall Apart* (New York: McDowell and Obolensky, 1959), pp. 214, 215. The title, epigraph, and themes of Achebe's next novel, *No Longer at Ease* (New York: Astor-Honor, 1960) reinforce these observations.

10. John Gay, *The Beggar's Opera*, in John Fuller, ed., *Dramatic Works* (Oxford: Oxford University Press, 1983), 3:13.

11. Wole Soyinka, *Opera Wonyosi* (Bloomington: Indiana Univesity Press, 1981), p. 1 (scene 1).

12. Jane Marcus, "Still Practice, A/Wrested Alphabet: Toward a Feminist Aesthetic," *Tulsa Studies in Women's Literature* (1984), 3:79–98, reprinted in Shari Benstock, ed., *Feminist Issues in Literary Scholarship* (Bloomington: Indian University Press, 1987).

13. Charles Bernheimer and Claire Kahane, eds., *In Dora's Case: Freud, Hysteria, Feminism* (New York: Columbia University Press, 1985).

14. Alice Walker, *The Color Purple* (New York: Harcourt Brace Jovanovich, 1982).

15. Audre Lorde, "The Master's Tools Will Never Dismantle the Master's House," in Cherríe Moraga and Gloria Anzaldúa, eds., *This Bridge Called My Back: Writing by Radical Women of Color* (Watertown, Mass.: Persephone, 1981), pp. 98–101. The essay is also contained in Audre Lorde, *Sister Outsider: Essays and Speeches* (Trumansburg, N.Y.: Crossing Press), 1984, pp. 110–13.

# 8

## Literature of Resistance: The Intersection of Feminism and the Communist Left in Meridel Le Sueur and Tillie Olsen

### Constance Coiner

*Constance Coiner's article concentrates on the working-class literature of Meridel Le Sueur and Tillie Olsen. Although members of the Communist party in the 1930s, these two writers, according to Coiner, wrote in spite of male party ideology when they portrayed such feminist concerns as work, relationships, and most particularly reproduction and family. Coiner's essay takes a careful look at some of Le Sueur's and Olsen's works and locates feminist experiences within the Marxist tradition while showing how these writers attempted to identify not one but many facets of struggle.*

> He confuses me about writing, for one thing.
>
> —Josephine Herbst, about her reluctance to
> get emotionally involved with Michael Gold[1]

This essay places two American working-class writers, Meridel Le Sueur (1900–) and Tillie Olsen (1912– or 1913–) in a contemporary critical context, addressing the complex intersection of feminism and the political Left as refracted in these writers' literary texts. Le Sueur's and Olsen's lives and literary texts span two generations of radical women, those affiliated with the Old Left and those who came of age with the New Left and the most recent women's movement. One of the salient features of the 1930s was the failure of any leftist organization to develop women's militance into a self-conscious feminism. Yet in more or less covert ways, Le Sueur's and Olsen's literature from the late 1920s and 1930s anticipates the concerns of feminists a generation later. We see in their texts a prescient if latent consciousness. During the 1930s Le Sueur's and Olsen's literature was considered "proletarian," the term generally reserved for working-class literature produced during the Depression decade. This essay adopts Paul Lauter's definition of the broader term, "working-class literature," as texts by *and* about the working class that coincide with other literary categories such as literature by women and people of color.[2]

Women's working-class literature provides a valuable historical record that is not as self-evident as many of its detractors—and its sympathizers—would have us believe. Cultural products refract rather than reflect history, suggesting the limits, in a given social formation, within which meanings are constructed and negotiated. But when 1930s leftist critics mined novels for their "revolutionary social content," their critical apparatus did not allow for the complicated mediation of social reality operating within the texts. Thus there is a need for a renewed historical and critical exploration of women's working-class literature.

Few scholars have examined American working-class literature since its flourishing in the 1930s. Since then, working-class literature has been generally considered crudely tendentious and aesthetically inferior to bourgeois literature. Impatient with this assumption, Lauter points out that the American literary canon has been defined by a privileged elite, primarily males of Anglo-Saxon or northern European origin. This essay implicitly supports the efforts of Lauter and others (people of color, women, radicals) to expand the canon and to examine the aesthetic and political bases on which it is constructed.

My approach, however, is also based on the premise that moments of textual conflict, often viewed as examples of "inferiority" or "weakness" in canonical, popular, or working-class literature, may be historically resonant, sometimes suggesting more about a given historical period than those moments that formalist critics might consider evidence of aesthetic excellence. Far from constituting a coherent reflection or central meaning, a piece of working-class literature, like any form of discourse, displays conflicting and contradictory meanings.

This is not to say that flaws exist in Le Sueur's and Olsen's literature that they should have recognized and corrected. Any writer is enmeshed in history and partially blind to the full range of events shaping that history. History precedes form, and tears in the textual fabric indicate the pressure that historical content brings to bear on form. That any text is "flawed" or incomplete, however, does not mean that the critic should fill in the missing pieces; the critic's task is not to repair or complete the text but to identify the *principle* of its silences, "flaws," conflicted meanings.[3]

In Le Sueur's and Olsen's 1930s literature, this principle lies partly in these writers' response to the sexism of the American Communist party, an organization to which they were deeply committed. On the Communist Left, "proletarian" and "manly" were nearly synonymous; the worker-protagonist in proletarian literature "almost by definition was male; proletrian prose and criticism tended to flex their muscles with a particularly masculinst pride."[4] The androcentrism of Communist literary policy reflected that of the Communist party as a whole. Party organizing during the early 1930s, for example, focused on the workplace, when only about 20 percent of women worked outside the home, and throughout the decade Party union activity centered on the mining, steel, maritime, and auto industries, in which few women were employed. The Party at least tacitly endorsed the traditional sexual division of labor, and domestic issues, when they counted at all, were not priorities.

However, the Party's work among women in the 1930s should be carefully evaluated as part of the struggle for women's liberation in the United States. Many women developed an awareness of their own potential, a sense of collectivity, and an understanding of America's social system through Party-related activities. Peggy Dennis, for fifty years an active Party member, and the widow of Party leader Eugene Dennis, reflects the views of Olsen and Le Sueur when she summarizes the contradictory experience of Party women: "Male Communists often responded to discussions of the 'woman question' with derision or condescension, but there were few other organizations in the country at the time in which women would even consider it their right to challenge such attitudes."[5] That Party leadership was overwhelmingly male and that its bureaucracy functioned undemocratically "from the top down" is a matter of record, but the history of the rank and file, including its women, has yet to be thoroughly explored. Le Sueur's and Olsen's literary texts comprise an important part of that history.

Le Sueur and Olsen were at once loyal Party members and emerging feminists; their literature, straining toward and away from Party prescriptions, reveals conflicting impulses which I term "official" and "unofficial." Their texts addressed the physiological and sexual experiences that shape women's lives—sexual initiation, pregnancy, childbirth, miscarriage, sterilization, battery, rape—at a time when these topics seldom appeared in literature, including working-class literature. Olsen's emphasis on domestic labor in *Yonnondio*, a novel begun in 1932, implicitly questions orthodox Marxism's primacy-of-production theory and its concomitant privileging of the workplace and the industrial worker as the loci of struggle. During the 1930s the Party generally characterized psychological and emotional categories as unmaterialist, as unrelated to "real" politics, labeling introspective novels febrile, self-indulgent, and bourgeois. Despite this, Le Sueur and Olsen made familial relations, emotional deformation, and the developing consciousness of children the central subjects of their literature, overcoming the restraints of the very revolutionary organization that fostered them. Le Sueur's and Olsen's conscious and unconscious movement between official and unofficial categories was not limited, however, to the subjects and themes of their texts. Each writer also experimented with varying literary forms.

Because Le Sueur and Olsen subvert not only bourgeois but also orthodox Marxist categories, "literature of resistance" in the context of this essay means something directed not only against the dominant culture but also against restrictive elements within a leftist subculture. Le Sueur's and Olsen's texts foreshadowed, if only in a muted, provisional sense, questions about Marxism and Leninism that theorists, including feminists, have much more recently and more explicitly raised. They implied that "the personal is political" long before that phrase became a household slogan among younger feminists. By now old news, this slogan is nevertheless still timely.

One of my richest sources about the 1930s have been the writers themselves, whom I extensively interviewed. But writing about living subjects, especially those with whom one feels political and personal solidarity, is a touchy, even painful, business. Attempting to be at once sensitive and critical, I resemble a character in Joanna Russ' *The Female Man* who thinks of herself as standing in a puddle of water, holding two alternating electrical currents.[6] The women's movement has made archetypes of Le Sueur and Olsen, who have become emblematic figures as much as historical ones, and yet I have more patience now than I once did with interviews that tend to be honorific rather than penetrating. I beg my subjects' forebearance while claiming that their rightful place is in history, not myth.

Conflicts between Le Sueur's "official" and "unofficial" views emerge in the tension between her theory and practice of literature.

Le Sueur first publicly expressed her position on how radicals create a literature of resistance in "The Fetish of Being Outside" (1935). Written in the twilight of the Communist party's proletarian period (or Third Period, 1928–1935), this essay adopts the Party line that it is not only possible but requisite for enlightened middle-class writers wholly to leave their own class and to become *ex officio* members of the revolutionary working class. "The Fetish," which was a reply to Horace Gregory's defense of some middle-class writers' reluctance to join the Party, does not allow for oscillation between complicity and critique with regard to class sympathies. Le Sueur's language suggests rebirth, a baptismal cleansing of original sin, a Kierkegaardian leap of faith: "You cannot leave it by pieces or parts; it is a birth and you have to be born whole out of it." The "creative artist" must be "willing to go all the way, with full belief, into that darkness." With "a new and mature integrity" the writer does "not react equivocally."[7] The view expressed in "The Fetish" was popular among Party members and sympathizers. Sherwood Anderson, for example, thought it possible for intellectuals to join in a form of group suicide. In 1932 he declared: "If it be necessary, in order to bring about the end of a money civilization and set up something new, healthy and strong, we of the so-called artist class have to be submerged, let us be submerged."[8] And Joseph Freeman's autobiography, *An American Testament* (published in 1936 but "in progress" for nearly ten years), attempted to show that an intellectual committed to proletarian revolution could break irrevocably with the middle class.

Some of Le Sueur's "unofficial" literary texts, however, contradict the position articulated in "The Fetish of Being Outside." As a feminist within a male-dominated movement, she herself experienced, and expressed in her literature, the conflicting impulses for which "The Fetish of Being Outside" does not allow. In three short stories—"Our Fathers," "Annunciation," and "Corn Village"—Le Sueur frankly examines her own experience with the dual vision and divided loyalty that "The Fetish" proscribes. After providing some biographical information about Le Sueur, I will address these three texts.

Le Sueur was born on February 22, 1900 in Murray, Iowa, into a white, middle-class, and educated family. One of the most prominent women writers of the 1930s, she endured red-baiting, blacklisting, and twenty-five years of obscurity to become, in the 1970s, a regional folk heroine and nearly an archetypal figure within the women's movement.

Le Sueur has written extensively about her maternal grandmother, Antoinette Lucy, "one of the first settlers, gun in hand, of the Oklahoma territory," who had divorced her husband for "drinking up the farms her father left her."[9] Le Sueur's vivid memories of her grandmother, so full of the woman's courage and self-reliance, are nevertheless shadowed by a recognition of her emotional and sexual repression. Le Sueur has described Antoinette Lucy's "graceless intensity"; she was "earnest, rigid . . . spare as the puritan world."[10] Lucy always dressed in black, considering bright colors sinful, and bathed in a loose-fitting shift. Her only emotional outlet was singing Protestant hymns, which she did with a telling fervor—through this hymn singing, Le Sueur has said, her grandmother made love to Jesus. But the hymn singing revealed other repressed feelings, as well, Le Sueur believes: "Only through these songs did I know . . . her terrible loneliness, her wish to die, her deep silence. Sometimes I heard her cry in the night, but I could not humiliate her by going to comfort her. In the day there would be no sign."[11]

Le Sueur has said of her mother and grandmother that "their experience of this world centered around the male as beast, his drunkenness and chicanery, his oppressive violence."[12] Meridel was ten when her mother, Marian Wharton, left her first husband, William Wharton, a Church of Christ minister. Le Sueur describes him as "a charming womanizer, the village sex symbol . . . a raconteur, a vivant," as well as heavy-drinking, violent, and physically abusive.[13]

As a single woman Marian Wharton earned a living by lecturing on women's issues. While a lecturer, she was arrested for disseminating birth control information and for participating in the suffrage fight. Marian later headed the English department at the People's College in Fort Scott, Kansas, where she met and married socialist Arthur Le Sueur, president of the college (Eugene Debs was the chancellor). The school strove to attract working-class students and to teach from a working-class perspective. Marian and Arthur edited the college magazine, which bore the slogan "to remain ignorant is to remain a slave." Through her mother and her stepfather, both active socialists, Meridel was exposed as a girl to Populists, Wobblies, anarchists, union organizers, and members of the Socialist party, the Non-Partisan League, and the Farmer-Labor party; through her parents she met luminaries such as Debs, Emma Goldman, Alexander Berkman, John Reed, Mabel Dodge, Margaret Sanger, Theodore Dreiser, and Carl Sandburg. She joined the Communist party in 1924.

On the basis of her long, admirable life as a radical, writer, and feminist, Le Sueur has become an emblematic figure, a "socialist tribal mother," as one admirer put it.[14] Le Sueur both enjoys this status and finds it disturbing. "I haven't really revealed the brutality of . . .

my own life," she has admitted. "And I think the women's movement has helped me to cover it up. . . . *Ms* [*Magazine*] wanted to present me as [a] role model, [as a woman] who made it, who succeeded. . . . They don't tell the horrible violence of women's lives" (interview). When Le Sueur speaks candidly about her life, she reveals details that add rough edges to her public persona. But with a few exceptions, the popular feminist and leftist press has treated her as an ideal without contradictions, shortchanging not only Le Sueur but also students of women's history and the American Left.[15]

Le Sueur is known for her reportage, especially "Women on the Breadlines" and "I Was Marching," which I categorize as "official" proletarian literature. However, "Our Fathers" is one text in which an "unofficial" Le Sueur emerges.[16] She has described "Our Fathers," which is somewhat autobiographical, as "one of the few [of my] stories that's not covered up. . . . It [is] really a naked cry" (interview). Through the fictional characters, she confronts her grandmother's, her mother's, and her own emotional deformation. Adolescent Penelope, the story's protagonist, rebels as Le Sueur did against ascetic Protestanism. Penelope insists on knowing and feeling what her mother and grandmother have repressed, forgotten, denied.[17]

"Our Fathers" takes place immediately before the funeral for Penelope's father, Tim, who had been active in the Unemployment Council and shot in a demonstration. Despite his irresponsibility toward his family, Tim had fostered his daughter's developing political consciousness. But Penelope is as disturbed by her grandmother's "triumphant" bitterness as she is by her father's death. The old woman sneers at a photograph of a man she left after twenty years of marriage: " 'Samuel that no account. If I'd known what I do now about men it would a been different. Men . . . men. . . .' She was only glad to remember in order to deride him." Penelope wants desperately to know the stories of the forebears in the old photographs, to feel some connection to them, but the grandmother, revealing little, begins to quaver, "Jesus lover of my soul." She was "like a spouse of the Lord being betrayed by earth's little men."[18]

Tim's death has intensified Penelope's adolescent search for her identity. Studying the family photographs, she tries to comprehend her past and imagine her future by placing herself in a genealogy of immigrants, settlers, bitter women, rakes, and rebels. As a result "Our Fathers" has a searching, dreamy quality strikingly different from Le Sueur's "official" proletarian literature. The didacticism of "Women on the Breadlines" and "I Was Marching" is muted in "Our Fathers," except for Penelope's memory of Tim's identifying the class struggle

and the proper side to support. Rather than providing slogans, solutions, and clear demarcations, "Our Fathers" permits questions,
doubts, and fears to emerge and suggests that some aspects of life
may remain mysterious to Penelope, despite her craving to know.

The threat is not simply the "wheat, lumber, and coal kings" about
which Tim had sermonized: Penelope senses that she will not escape
the "bitter drouth" so affecting her mother, grandmother, and the
stern women in the photographs, and she fears that eventually she,
too, will taste the "brew" and "never be cured of it."[19] "Our Fathers"
acknowledges some of the complexity of the emotional/sexual legacy
Le Sueur and other women of her generation inherited.

One can wish that Le Sueur had further explored the marks left
on her by the towering presence of an absent father and by a grandmother who could not cry unless "her bad eye" ran water, "as if
weeping alone, unknown to her."[20] Le Sueur explains that she became
a writer to speak for the "oppressed, mute, forgotten, or lost," specifically identifying her grandmother: "My grandmother was mute.
She had no words for her terrible life" (inteview). While we get a
valuable glimpse of unemployed women during the Depression in Le
Sueur's reportage, we do not come to know these women as we come
to know Penelope and her forbidding grandmother. Le Sueur's reportage is perhaps limited by her class. She does not penetrate the
consciousness of the characters in "Women on the Breadlines" or "I
Was Marching," but does so acutely in "Our Fathers," whose characters were based on people she knew only too well.

"Annunciation" departs even more than "Our Fathers" from typical proletarian literature. The title alludes to the angel Gabriel's announcement to Mary that she will give birth to the Son of God (Luke
1:26–38), and Le Sueur originally wrote the story in 1928 to her first,
unborn child. Set in the Depression, this narrative prose poem represents a pregnant woman's dreamlike state of mind, imposing a theme
of fertility and regeneration upon a secondary theme of contrasting
deprivation.

Because pregnancy, labor, the moment of birth, and the nurturing
of a newborn are among life's most profound experiences, it is strik-
ing that they appear so rarely in literature. One explanation for this
silence is supplied by Hortense Calisher, who, in referring specifically
to labor and delivery, also describes the experiences surrounding them:
"Childbed is not a place or an event; it is merely what women do."[21]
"Annunciation" suggests the powerful, inexplicable bond between
mother and unborn child, a bond at once common and singular in
women's experience and yet almost entirely excluded from proletar-

ian as well as canonical literature. And the story's lush, sensual, evocative language is hardly the stuff of "official" proletarian literature: "I look at myself in the mirror. . . . My hips are full and tight. . . . I am a pomegranate hanging from an invisible tree with the juice and movement of seed within my hard skin. I dress slowly. I hate the smell of clothes. I want to leave them off and just hang in the sun ripening . . . ripening."[22] Images move in circles—the magnolia tree, pear tree, and landlady appearing, disappearing, and reappearing—as opposed to the linear progression Le Sueur associates with masculine form. Here we see one of Le Sueur's deliberate subversions: she intends this style as the "antithesis of what she sees as the male style of linear movement toward a 'target,' or a conclusion to be 'appropriated.' "[23]

"I've never heard anything about how a woman feels who is going to have a child," observes "Annunciation" 's narrator.[24] When Le Sueur wrote the story, pregnancy was considered unacceptable as a literary subject, as much by *New Masses* as by the magazines that gave that reason for rejecting her manuscript (*Scribner's Magazine* and the *Atlantic Monthly*). Although the story has been frequently reprinted, it was originally published only in a small private edition (Los Angeles, Calif.: Platen Press, 1935). A favorite Le Sueurian anecdote recalls her retort to the editor at Scribner's who, as he rejected the story, suggested that she write more like Hemingway: But "fishin', fightin', and fuckin'," she quipped, "are not the sum of my experience" (interview). "Annunciation" similarly defies protocol.

Like "Annunciation," "Corn Village" (*Scribner's Magazine*, 1931) has little in common with orthodox proletarian realism or reportage. In writing about Midwest farmers, Le Sueur was not writing about workers considered by the Party during the Third Period to be the key to revolution; the Party gave priority in this period to organizing efforts among workers in basic industry because of its assumed importance to the economy. In "Corn Village" Le Sueur has consciously or unconsciously almost wholly discarded the Party discourse. "Official optimism" and its corollary, what I term "official certainty" ("we know that not pessimism, but revolutionary elan will sweep this mess out of the world forever") are noticeably absent from the text.[25] Like Penelope's grandmother, corn villagers have no love song other than "Jesus, Lover of My Soul." Their bodies are awkward, "held taut for some unknown fray with the devil or the world or the flesh" (15). Sexual and emotional repression are the human equivalent of the barren, frozen landscape, which is colorless and lifeless—all whites, grays, "emptiness and ghostliness." In Corn Village, it is "as if some malignant power were in the air."[26] Mystery, uncertainty, and fear prevail.

"Corn Village" also departs formally from Le Sueur's consciously proletarian literature. In her reportage and her novel *The Girl*, for example, Le Sueur resisted lyricizing experience, partly as a response to the problem of poeticizing oppression. She also felt her writing should take a revolutionary form presumably divorced from bourgeois forms. Some 1930s Marxists considered unembellished prose an act of good faith, a break from bourgeois writing, and regarded stylistic experimentation suspiciously. "Corn Village," however, subverts the Party aesthetic. Like "Annunciation," it is less a short story than an evocative prose poem, a vortex of incident, image, and symbol. Moreover, the didacticism evident in her "official" literature is noticeably absent from the text, while it acknowledges the complexity of "the people," who were often romanticized in Party—and in Le Sueur's own—discourse.

"Corn Village" is not constrained by the limited understanding of ideology that characterizes much of proletarian realism and reportage. For example, in Le Sueur's "I Was Marching," ideology is seen as merely a superstructure produced by an economic base, a false consciousness obscuring society's "real" structures. In contrast, ideology pervades "Corn Village," prefiguring the more current understanding of ideology as the way in which we actively but unconsciously perform our roles within the social totality. The story supports Gramsci's notion of dominance and subordination as a "whole lived social process" saturating even the most private areas of our lives and consciousness. If we accept Wendell Berry's definition of regionalism as "local life aware of itself,"[27] "Corn Village" qualifies as an extraordinary piece of regionalist writing precisely *because* Le Sueur adopts the double consciousness and the oscillation between complicity and critique that "The Fetish of Being Outside" condemns as neither possible nor desirable for the radical writer. Le Sueur resides at once within the corn village culture and outside it, negotiating difference and sameness with divided loyalty and consciousness.

This text seems as authentic as it does, I suspect, largely because it examines Le Sueur's own experience. She chronicled the lives of other oppressed people, sometimes at the expense of exploring her own oppression as a middle-class woman and a member of the male-dominated Communist party. "I don't know how to write about women. I feel like I have to learn to write the final book about myself as a woman," Le Sueur has said, even though she has been writing about women for over seventy-five years, ever since she first recorded bits of conversation while hiding under the quilting frame as a ten-year-old (interview). Yet we sense that in "Corn Village" Le Sueur's untold story begins to emerge.

Le Sueur's motives for adopting the working class as her literary milieu were overdetermined: surely a strong sense of justice and collective responsibility sparked her concern; she also disliked the strains of ennui, nihilism, and self-absorption in twentieth-century American literature; and she was influenced by the Party's focus during the Third Period on the proletariat as the key to overturning capitalism and by its contradictory attitudes toward women. As a whole, Le Sueur's treatment of the working class contributes to American literature and social history a valuable record of people whose lives have rarely been chronicled. Yet in pieces such as "Our Fathers," "Annunciation," and "Corn Village," an unofficial Meridel Le Sueur appears, moving toward the oracular voice she sought but did not achieve in her "official" proletarian literature.

We can understand why demarcations seemed clear in the midst of the sharpening class struggle that accompanied the economic crisis in the 1930s. However, we have moved beyond 1930s Marxist assumptions about working-class literature that place a resistance culture in binary opposition to bourgeois culture. Working-class literature is, at best, a subspecies of bourgeois literature, just as any culture of resistance remains, for the historical moment, a subspecies of bourgeois culture. Leftist criticism must try to account for the conscious and unconscious movement of working-class literature between marginality and inclusion and view working-class literature relationally, gauging which of its forms oppose, which strategically adopt, and which unconsciously borrow the forms of "high" and mass culture. As we have seen, some of Le Sueur's own texts subvert the reductive opposition she established in "The Fetish of Being Outside" and support a more contemporary view of how we might usefully approach elements of a resistance culture. In "Our Fathers," "Annunciation," and "Corn Village" we see that discourse lives, as Bakhtin suggests, on the boundary between its own and an alien context, and that one culture "can define itself only by becoming imbricated in another."[28]

This complex intersection of feminism and the Old Left is also refracted in illuminating ways in Tillie Olsen's literary texts. Olsen's career includes two periods: All of her 1930s publications appeared in 1934, when she was only twenty-one; her "second period" dates from 1953, when the youngest of her four children entered school.[29]

Olsen's writing from the 1930s, like Le Sueur's, is marked by a tension between official and unofficial views of proletarian literature.

Olsen's writing from her two "periods" also represents two distinct types of oppositional form. Whereas the content of her 1930s literature is culturally and politically agitational, the discursive model has been borrowed, unmodified, from dominant modes of representation, taking the processes of signification for granted. These texts foreground the "message" rather than the production of meaning. Openly tendentious, Olsen's published 1930s writing is marked by an uncontested authorial voice and a completion and closure of meaning. In what Bakhtin terms monological discourse, these texts directly address the reader, anticipating responses and deflecting objections; meanings are seen as delivered, unchanged, from source to recipient. In the tradition of muckraking, social journalism, and reportage, Olsen's writing during this period, like Le Sueur's "Women on the Breadlines" and "I Was Marching," was intended to spark political resistance. At the same time, however, its didacticism, like that of Le Sueur's more tendentious writing, actually limits involvement by undercutting the reader's role as an active producer of meaning. As we will see, Olsen's *Silences* (1978), on the other hand, challenges the ideological character of the signification process itself. The production of meaning, as much as the message, becomes a site for dissent.

Olsen's birth was not recorded, although she has determined that she was born either near Mead or in Omaha, Nebraska in either 1912 or 1913. Her parents, Samuel and Ida Lerner, were Jewish working-class immigrants who had participated in the abortive 1905 Russian revolution. Although the family was poor, the Lerners' active socialism added a rich dimension to Tillie's childhood. She became politically active in her mid-teens as a writer of skits and musicals for the Young People's Socialist League. In 1931, at eighteen, she joined the Young Communist League, the youth organization of the Communist party.

Olsen did not share the problem of the enlightened middle-class writer who, like Meridel Le Sueur, contemplated in the 1930s how best to identify with the working class. Hers was a different dilemma: whereas our social system defines Olsen's intellectual and professional aspirations as middle class, her personal and emotional identification remained, profoundly, with the class of her birth. Olsen appreciated the power of class origin, which Le Sueur unintentionally trivialized in "The Fetish of Being Outside." Both intellectual pursuits and the struggles of working people to improve their lives were crucially important to Olsen, and how to live in both worlds remained her insoluble riddle.

Like Meridel Le Sueur, Olsen recognizes the debt she owes the Communist Left for nurturing her writing. The Party provided publishing outlets for beginning writers and established the John Reed Clubs specifically to encourage unknown young writers and artists. Although Olsen was occasionally obliged during her years as an activist to write short pieces "on demand" for political events, her 1934 publications were not consciously written to accommodate the Party literary credo. Olsen was well aware that proletarian realism was "the standard that was set . . . by the leading columnists and polemicists" of New Masses, which she read "faithfully—sometimes lovingly, sometimes angrily," but she insists that the Party literary line "did not touch" her.[30] Nevertheless, Olsen's published writing in 1934 is consistent with the tenets of proletarian realism, which the Communist party promoted from 1930 to 1935. Her literature shows "the *real conflicts* of men and women who work for a living"; includes details of the workplace; and portrays the "horror and drabness in the Worker's life" while emphasizing that "not pessimism, but revolutionary elan will sweep this mess out of the world forever."[31]

That hopes were high among leftists in 1934 is evident from the notes about contributors when Olsen's short story, "The Iron Throat," appeared in Partisan Review: "Tillie Lerner is at work on a novel of mining life. She is a 21-year-old Nebraska girl at present living in Stockton, Calif. Last year she took a leave of absence from the Young Communist League to produce a future citizen of Soviet America."[32] As Olsen began her writing career, workers started pouring into the available unions. Section 7A of the New Deal's National Industrial Recovery Act (1933) guaranteed workers the right to organize and bargain collectively, and many workers felt that "the tide of history had finally turned" (even though the NRA was skirted far more often than it was enforced by the establishment of "company" unions, and was declared unconstitutional in 1935).[33] Three major strikes of 1934, the year in which all of Olsen's publications from the 1930s appeared, demonstrated the great potential for working-class militancy. In February nine-hundred National Guardsmen failed to break a massive picket of ten-thousand workers from the community surrounding the Toledo Auto-Lite plant. The San Francisco maritime strike, which involved Olsen directly, began in May. And in July the Minneapolis teamsters strike, chronicled in Le Sueur's "I Was Marching," closed down the trucking industry and tied up the entire city.

As one might expect, then, Olsen's 1930s publications are more polemical, more akin to orthodox proletarian literature than her later writing. The two poems she published during the 1930s—"I Want You Women Up North To Know" (*The Partisan*, March 1934) and "There Is a Lesson" (*The Partisan*, April 1934)—are representative.[34] In these poems Olsen consciously resists lyricizing experience. She works in the muckraking and reportage tradition, wanting her readers "to see and feel the facts"—to "*experience*"—oppression's iron heel.[35] The source of the discomfort that these poems cause for readers is, however, ambiguous. While the texts succeed in forcing us to confront oppressive working conditions in the United States and the rise of fascism in Europe, they are also unsettling because their exhortatory language preempts our emotional and moral responses. Marked by closure, the poems resist a reader's collaboration in constructing meaning. This earlier writing is marked by a didacticism, an "us/them" opposition, and an "official certainty" absent from the later period. Olsen's 1934 publications respond soberly to grave historical conditions and buoyantly to a working class that was on the move. These texts deal less with the complexity of consciousness and more with the economic causes of oppression than do her more recent works.

As Deborah Rosenfelt points out, however, this tension between discursive models is already apparent in *Yonnondio*, which Olsen began in 1932 at nineteen.[36] The novel, which provides a bridge formally and politically between Olsen's 1934 literature and her more recent writing, comprised her most important literary effort during the 1930s. Olsen completed the first four chapters, or almost half, of the novel before regretfully abandoning it after the birth of her second child in 1937. In 1972–1973, Olsen completed *Yonnondio* "in arduous partnership" with "that long ago young writer." The first four chapters, in final or near-final form, presented only minor problems. The succeeding pages, which became four more chapters, were increasingly difficult to reconstruct. "But it is all the old manuscripts— no rewriting, no new writing," Olsen explains in a note appended to the novel. She felt that she "didn't have any right" to revise what "that long ago young writer" had intended for print (interview). *Yonnondio*, then, is more a cultural product of the 1930s, when it was written, than of the 1970s, when it was published. Varying tendencies coexist uneasily within the text (some elements adhere to the tenets of proletarian realism while other elements subvert them), indicating Olsen's increasing ambivalence about the Party aesthetic, as Rosenfelt suggests. But this tension also hints at fundamental problems within the 1930s Communist party and Marxism itself.

*Yonnondio* confronts one of the differences within the working class that the 1930 Communist party minimized—the divisive effects of sexism. At a time when Avram Landry, representing Party leadership, denied "any conceivable antagonism" between working-class women and men, the novel implicitly emphasizes the way in which the sexual division of labor militates against working-class unity.[37] While Jim Holbrook descends into "the iron throat" of a Wyoming coal mine, Anna Holbrook, lacking the barest essentials, struggles to care for their growing family. A psychic division of labor accompanies the material one. Anna frets that her children will go uneducated and does not dismiss a friend's wish that their daughters enter convents rather than live in poverty and bear more children "to get their heads blowed off in the mine." Jim, on the other hand, wonders "what other earthly use can a woman have" except childbearing. As a man he must never reveal his fear of the mine, and when Anna pushes him to consider its dangers he tells her, "Quit your woman's blabbin."[38] The novel depicts Jim and Anna taunting one another and his abandoning the family for days at a time. Jim "struck Anna too often to remember," and, at one point, raped her while their young daughter, Mazie, listened in terror (p. 15).

Since tensions between Anna and Jim ease considerably during their one brief period of relative prosperity, *Yonnondio* implies that gender-based antagonisms are related in a simple cause-and-effect way to economic oppression. According to the prevailing view of 1930s Party members, a socialist revolution would sweep away sexual oppression in its wake (one *Daily Worker* headline proclaimed about the Soviet Union: "All [Sex] Inequality Abolished by the October Revolution"), and Party women tended to defer their hopes for a feminist future.[40] Nevertheless, whatever Olsen's intention at the time, *Yonnondio* provides evidence that the social construction of gender is an entrenched, unconsciously reproduced phenomenon that will not overturn itself simply by "tailing" a transformation in economic relations.

The novel includes four didactic intrusions by an omniscient narrator, separated typographically from the text, that contain several conventions of proletarian literature. One such passage appears after an explosion occurs at the mine. While miners' families wait anxiously for survivors to emerge and for bodies to be dug out, the editorial voice, like a Greek chorus, interjects:

And could you not make a cameo of this and pin it onto your aesthetic hearts? So sharp it is, so clear, so classic. The shattered dusk, the mountain of culm, the tipple; clean lines, bare beauty—and carved against them, dwarfed by the vastness of night and the towering tipple, these black figures with bowed heads, waiting, waiting.

Surely it is classical enough for you—the Greek marble of the women, the simple, flowing lines of sorrow, carved so rigid and eternal. (p. 30)

This interjection attacks formalism, which elevates aesthetic concerns over sociopolitical ones. The standard call to revolution, in the form of an imaginary letter threatening the mining company, occurs later in this passage: "Dear Company . . . Please issue a statement; quick, or they start to battle through with the fists of strike, with the pickax of revolution" (p. 31). Three of the novel's four interpolations echo this battle cry, and a reference to Marx, common in proletarian novels, functions as a refrain in the fourth insertion ("nothing to sell but his labor power" [pp. 77, 78]). Olsen views her art as pedagogical; "I was writing the reason why we have to have a revolution," she has said about *Yonnondio*. She did not trust the novel, if stripped of these didactic passages, fully to affect her readers, to make them "feel the impact," and to indicate the causes and remedies for the Holbrooks' misery, which they themselves perceive and articulate only in a limited way (interview). Olsen may also have been unconsiously adhering to one of the principles of proletarian realism, which, as defined by Edwin Seaver in *New Masses*, demanded that the writer "take a conscious part in leading the reader through the maze of history toward Socialism and the classless society."[41]

These four passages interrupt *Yonnondio*'s narrative much a Brecht's *Verfremdung* disrupt his plays (although, since Brecht's literary work had not yet been translated into English and circulated in the United States, it is unlikely that Olsen knew that she was employing a Brechtian device). Such intrusions counter traditional realism, in which the present social order appears as natural, static, and immutable rather than contradictory, discontinuous, and, potentially, the object of revolutionary change. The interpolations also announce the gulf between art and reality, which realism effaces but Brecht's epic threater foregrounds. Conventional realism assumes the reader to be a passive recipient of a representation, whereas Brecht and Olsen attempted to jolt the audience/reader into an active spectatorship that may lead to their questioning the status quo.

However, Olsen's Brechtian intrusions support as well as undermine the classical ideologies of representation. Although the interpolations are politically and culturally oppositional, they draw upon a culturally dominant form—the dualistic rhetorical model of a message conveyed, unchanged, from an authoritative source to a compliant recipient. They announce themselves as the official "reading" of the novel, attempting to impose a closure of meaning on the reader. These editorial passages, then, like Olsen's 1934 publications, at once attempt to activate and to constrain the reader.

The editorial voice of the intended passages is joined by those of three other narratives—Mazie, Anna, and Jim. Together these four comprise a collective protagonist, which Rachel Blau DuPlessis defines as a way of structuring a text so that neither an individual nor a heterosexual couple dominates the novel.[42] One of the progressive effects of the collective protagonist is a merging of the public and private spheres that a patriarchal and capitalist system would have us keep separate. The use of a collective protagonist also implies that problems that bourgeois culture would have us view "as individually based are, in fact, social in cause and in cure."[43] Since form is profoundly dependent on historical change, the best working-class literature can do is prefigure postindividual forms in some diminished, provisional sense, and *Yonnondio*'s four narrators represent an attempt to move beyond an individual point of view toward more collective forms—in narrative structures suggesting possibilities for social change.

The presence of a feminist voice in the novel also pluralizes the text. Writing over thirty years before the existence of the women's movement that would welcome *Yonnondio*'s publication in 1974, Olsen countered Communist party literary prescriptions by focusing on domestic labor and the point of *re*production. Her unsentimental presentation of institutionalized motherhood has forced on the American literary canon a subject hitherto forbidden except in idealized form.

What Jim derisively calls "woman's blabbin'," in a variety of forms, is central to the novel. Mazie, with her special sensitivity to language, lists the words she knows, tells her brother stories, recites poetry. Moreover, she vocally opposes the sexual division of labor, even though neither of her parents does: "Why is it always me that has to help? How come Will gets to play?" (p. 142). In the penultimate, packing-house scene, it is a woman "who [has] a need to put things into words," who chants the workers' plight in kitchen imagery (p. 144). And when Mis' Kryckski takes care of the children after Anna's miscarriage, she sings them "not lullabies, but songs of her own country in which her fierce anger flashed" (p. 90). The novel concludes with baby Bess announcing and celebrating her emerging identity by banging a fruit jar lid.

As any other text of working-class literature, *Yonnondio* remains subsumed by bourgeois form and content. However, it subverts elements not only of bourgeois culture but also of the 1930s Communist party and orthodox Marxism. While *Yonnondio*'s critique of capitalism is foregrounded and full-blown, its prescient questioning of some tendencies of party politics and orthodox Marxism—such as productivism and its concomitant privileging of the industrial worker; the separation of public and private spheres; the subordination of gender-related issues to those of class; and the teleological notion that revolutionary struggles will achieve an ideal, static "state"—is only half-realized. In *Yonnondio* Olsen strains away from her early 1930s "official" proletarian literature, her evolving lyrical style lending itself readily to the novel's two major themes—working-class familial relations and the complexity, susceptibility, and potential of human consciousness. Despite the Party's minimizing of consciousness as a site for ideological struggle, *Yonnondio* suggests that "one of the major powers of the muted is to think against the current."[44] "Reader, it was not to have ended here," Olsen laments in the note appended to the unfinished novel. On the contrary, in *Yonnondio* Olsen has written "beyond the ending."[45]

While Olsen's "message" continues to be oppositional in her more recent writing, the rhetorical model is more dialogic than that of her 1930s publications, challenging the signification process itself. Culturally mainstream modes of representation lend themselves to forms of domination that can be countered by alternative modes of representation such as those prefigured in *Silences* (1978), a nonfiction book that catalogues impediments to a writer's productivity. By now a classic of American feminism, *Silences* employs the strategy of a pluralized text, suggesting one form that a literature of resistance might take.

When the authorial voice is granted exceptional status, writers appear to need no complement, as Bakhtin has noted; the natural state of being appears to be solitary, independent of others. *Silences*, however, subverts unicentered discourse and the concept of textual ownership, affirming the reader not as an object but as another subject, a reciprocal "thou." Whereas dominant discursive practices take for granted that the act of reading will be a *subjection to* a fixed meaning, *Silences* offers an alternative way of conceiving the writer's and reader's roles: it foregrounds the process by which it constructs meaning, disrupting and activating its reader-subjects while subverting authorial control. *Silences* implicitly acknowledges that in the act of reading, reader-subjects engage in an active, complex, and creative process not unlike that of writing. An anticonjurer, Olsen refuses to lull her readers with the illusion of mimetic representation. The reader is no longer simply a consumer, a passive receiver of a representation. In the tradition of Brecht's theater and Jean-Luc Godard's cinematic montage, *Silences* turns readers into collaborators.

The first half of the book comprises three essays by Olsen; the second half is a montage including excerpts from writers' diaries and letters spliced together with Olsen's headings and commentary. Crossing gender, race, and class boundaries, Olsen quotes male and female, white and black, known and unknown writers. By extensive use of citation, *Silences* undercuts the conventional rhetorical model of speaker/message/listener by adding not only a third voice but dozens of voices. Both writer and reader must address themselves not simply to each other, but to the extra, complicating party or parties. This third (or fourth, fifth, etc.) speaker in the language act changes the discourse from a dualistic exchange to a complex social one.[46]

The fact of work and production, one of the keys to historical thinking, is a carefully concealed secret of commodity cultures, which by definition efface the signs of work on production. *Silences* demystifies book-as-final-product by recalling its own often precarious progression from silence to speech (two of the three essays derived from unwritten talks) to writing. More important, *Silences* unmasks the hidden labor that often supports literary production, exposing the class and patriarchal character of the structures in which literature is produced. Olsen foregrounds domestic labor and especially child care, which may be the most "naturalized," invisible labor of all, the secret *most* carefully concealed.

In Olsen's *oeuvre* we see a shift from one form of cultural resistance to another. This was not a deliberate, conscious shift. "I never *thought* in terms of form," Olsen insists, her voice resonating. "I thought in terms of *content*. When people ask me about form, I'm still that way. . . . I don't *think* in terms of form" (interview). Form is not, however, the initial mold from which a writer starts but the final articulation of content.[47] *Silences*' democratic content realizes itself in its multivocal form, resisting the present social order at the level of narrative. Olsen may not be conscious of a relationship between her own antiauthoritarian impulses and the way she constructs a text; and when she has "completed" a work, she may not be aware of all of its implications, especially its formal ones. A writer's intention, after all, does not circumscribe the range of meanings evoked by a text. That Olsen may not be fully aware of her own achievement does not lessen it, however. Olsen's later texts proclaim, with works like Virginia Woolf's "The Leaning Tower": "Literature is no one's private ground; literature is common ground. . . . Let us trespass freely and fearlessly and find our own way for ourselves."[48]

Le Sueur and Olsen asserted their difference within the forced unity and closure of not only the dominant culture but also an androcentric Communist party, providing a wedge into problems that have historically plagued the Left. In so doing, they prefigured a younger generation of feminists. Politically and culturally, Le Sueur and Olsen's texts represent what Raymond Williams describes as a *"pre-emergence*, active and pressing but not yet fully articulated, rather than the evident emergence which could be more confidently named."[49]

Their texts resist, for example, orthodox Marxism's reduction of the social terrain's heterogeneity to centers and margins, such as males in the industrial workplace and women in the domestic sphere. At a time when the "proper" subjects and settings of working-class literature were workers waging strikes in the factory, *Yonnondio*, for example, focused largely on working-class familial relations and ended with an image of a baby realizing her power by gleefully banging a fruit jar lid.

Against the transcendent Party, Le Sueur and Olsen asserted the importance of their own concrete experience. They implicitly questioned Marxism's primacy-of-production theory, which defines production as *the* distinctively human activity. This theory encodes activities carried out in the home, to which women have historically been disproportionately consigned, as less valuble than men's activities outside it. When Michael Gold challenged proletarian writers to "write with the courage of [their] own experience," addressing himself to machinists, sailors, ditch-diggers, and hobos, he thought he was speaking broadly, inclusively.[50] Ironically, it is as if both Le Sueur and Olsen took Gold at his word: their texts subvert the Party's productivism and sexism, legitimating the point of *re*production, work that Olsen terms "the maintenance of life."[51]

One critical element of this "maintenance of life" may be the crucible of the women's movement: responsibility for children. This issue has not been a priority for the movement because during the 1960s and 1970s many feminists forewent or delayed childrearing. With the 1980s baby boom, however, even the women whom the movement has most helped to advance, its educated professionals, have with a sense of *deja vu* felt that old shock of sudden recognition, that familiar "click": equal professional opportunity collapses around the issue of who will take care of the kids. Olsen's and Le Sueur's literature illuminates the cracks in an idealized, good-housekeeping Comrade/ Wife, a creature not unrelated to today's mythic Superwoman, who, politically mainstream or Left, can presumably "do it all." That more women than men have valued Le Sueur's and Olsen's iconoclasm reminds us that textual meaning, rather than being absolute, is a consequence of a reader-subject's being in a particular situation in the world.

The American Communist party was not a monolith; democratic centralism notwithstanding, the views and daily experience of rank-and-file women often varied from those of male Party bureaucrats, as Tillie Olsen and Meridel Le Sueur insist. And yet, despite valuable documentaries made during the 1970s and 1980s, such as *Union Maids*, *With Babies and Banners*, *The Life and Times of Rosie the Riveter*, and *Seeing Red*, the history of rank-and-file Party women remains largely unrecorded. Le Sueur's and Olsen's literature, and that of other radical and working-class women writers, comprises an important part of that record. This literature suggests that a counterhegemony created by connecting many different forms of struggle—including those not primarily "public" and "economic" as well as those within "the fibres of the self and in the hard practical substance of effective and continuing relationships"—would lead to a more profound and compelling sense of revolutionary activity.[52]

### Endnotes

1. This appears in a letter from Herbst, who was widely regarded during the 1930s as one of the decade's most important leftist women writers, to writer Robert Wolf. Cited in Elinor Langer, *Josephine Herbst: The Story She Could Never Tell* (Boston: Little, Brown 1984), p. 68. Exemplar of a new proletarian tradition in American literature, Gold, was from 1926 to 1932 one of the editors of *New Masses*, a Communist party journal. During the early 1930s Gold was "perhaps the best known Communist writer and critic," and at the 1935 American Writers' Congress, he was hailed as "the best loved Americian revolutionary writer"; the first quote is from James Burkhart Gilbert, *Writers and Partisans: A History of Literary Radicalism in America* (New York: Wiley, 1968), p. 119, the second from Walter B. Rideout, *The Radical Novel in the United States, 1900–1954* (New York: Hill and Wang, 1956), p. 168. Gold's classic proletarian novel, *Jews Without Money*, which has been translated into sixteen languages, went through eleven printings in the first year of its publication (1930) and six more by 1938.

2. Paul Lauter, "Working-Class Women's Literature: An Introduction to

Study," *Radical Teacher* (December 1979), 15:16, designates as members of the working class those who sell their labor for wages, have relatively little control over the nature or products of their work, and are not professionals or managers. He includes not only factory workers but also slaves, farm laborers, and some of those who work in the home.

3. Terry Eagleton, *Marxism and Literary Criticism* (Berkeley: University of California Press, 1976), p. 35.

4. Deborah Rosenfelt, "From the Thirties: Tillie Olsen and the Radical Tradition," *Feminist Studies* (fall 1981), 7:395. Reprinted in Judith Newton and Deborah Rosenfelt, eds., *Feminist Criticism and Social Change* (New York: Methuen, 1985).

5. Maurice Isserman, *Which Side Were You On? The American Communist Party During the Second World War* (Middletown, Conn.: Wesleyan University Press, 1982), p. 141.

6. Joanna Russ, *The Female Man* (New York: Bantam Books, 1973), p. 138.

7. Meridel Le Sueur, "The Fetish of Being Outside," *New Masses* (February 26, 1935), 26:23.

8. Sherwood Anderson, "A Writer's Note," *New Masses* (August 1932), 8:10.

9. The first quote is from Elaine Hedges, ed., *Ripening: Selected Work, 1927–1980* (Old Westbury, NY.: Feminist Press, 1982), p. 2; the second is from Le Sueur, "The Ancient People and the Newly Come," in Chester G. Anderson, ed., *Growing Up in Minnesota: Ten Writers Remember Their Childhoods* (Minneapolis: University of Minnesota Press, 1976), p. 22. In *Ripening* Elaine Hedges provides extensive biographical information about the writer.

10. Le Sueur, "Ancient People," pp. 31, 33.

11. *Ibid.*, p. 34.

12. *Ibid.*, p. 23.

13. Personal interview conducted by Constance Coiner, March 26, 1985. Subsequent quotations from this interview will be identified parenthetically in the text.

14. This term appeared in "Meridel Le Sueur," a poem by Will Inman included in an unpaginated anthology commemorating Le Sueur's eightieth birthday; see Mary McAnally, ed., *We Sing Our Struggle: A Tribute to Us All for Meridel Le Sueur* (Tulsa, Okla.: Cardinal Press, 1982).

15. Among the exceptions: Elaine Hedges, cited above; Jan Clausen's several reviews of Le Sueur's texts, appearing in *Motheroot Journal* (spring 1980) and in *Conditions* (1978), vol. 3; and Blanche Gelfant's "Meridel Le Sueur's 'Indian' Poetry and the Quest/ion of Feminine Form," included in a book by the same author, *Women Writing in America: Voices in Collage* (Hanover, N.H.: University Press of New England, 1984).

16. The pieces of reportage originally appeared in *New Masses* (January 1932) and September 18, 1934, respectively. Le Sueur began "Our Fathers" in the 1920s and continued working on it in the 1930s; it was published on February 1, 1937 by the *Intermountain Review of English and Speech*. These texts have been reprinted in Elaine Hedges, ed., *Ripening: Selected Work, 1927–1980* (Old Westbury, N.Y.: Feminist Press, 1982). "Our Fathers" comprises part of the first chapter of *I Hear Men Talking*, a novel that Le Sueur completed in the mid-forties but revised and published in 1984 (Cambridge, Mass.: West End Press).

17. Le Sueur's grandmother reproached her for writing the truth about women's lives. "I've spent all my life trying to conceal it," she complained, viewing her granddaughter as a saboteur (interview).

18. Meridel Le Sueur, "Our Fathers," in Hedges, *Ripening*, pp. 120, 122.

19. *Ibid.*, pp. 114, 117.

20. *Ibid.*, p. 115.

21. Quoted by Tillie Olsen in *Silences* (New York: Dell, 1978), p. 230.

22. Meridel Le Sueur, "Annunciation," in Meridel Le Sueur, *Salute to Spring* (1940; New York: International, 1977), p. 86. "Annunciation" was originally published by the Platen Press, Los Angeles (1935).

23. Hedges, *Ripening*, p. 251.

24. Le Sueur, "Annunciation," p. 86.

25. Michael Gold, "Notes of the Month," *New Masses* (September 1930), 6:5.

26. Meridel Le Sueur, "Corn Village," in Meridel Le Sueur, *Salute to Spring*, pp. 15, 10, 11.

27. Wendell Berry, "The Regional Motive," *Southern Review* (October 1970), p. 975.

28. Jon Klancher, *The Making of English Reading Audiences, 1790–1832* (Madison: University of Wisconsin Press, 1986), p. 103.

29. The 1934 publications include two poems discussed here, "I Want You Women Up North to Know" and "There Is a Lesson"; "The Strike," a piece of reportage (*Partisan Review*, September–October); "The Iron Throat" (*Partisan Review*, April–May), a short story that became 60 percent of the first chapter of *Yonnondio;* and "Thousand Dollar Vagrant" (*The New Republic*, August 29), an essay chronicling Olsen's arrest for her role in the 1934 maritime strike. Olsen's "second period" publications include *Tell Me a Riddle* (1961); "Requa I," which appears in Martha Foley and David Burnett, eds., *The Best American Short Stories 1971*, and *Silences* (1978). Olsen wrote *Yonnondio: From the Thirties* in the 1930s but recovered and published it in the 1970s, as I subsequently explain.

30. Personal interview conducted by Constance Coiner, July 11–12, 1986 and by Deborah Rosenfelt, December 20, 1980. Subsequent quotations from these two interviews will be identified parenthetically in the text, without distinguishing between them. I wish to thank Deborah Rosenfelt for generously allowing me to use her taped interview of Tillie Olsen to supplement my own. Rosenfelt's essay (see note 4), the touchstone for Olsen criticism, provides a wealth of biographical information about the writer. I am indebted to Meridel Le Sueur and Tillie Olsen for their permission to quote from the taped interviews—and for their legacy of courageous resistance.

31. These are some of the elements of proletarian (or socialist) realism outlined by Michael Gold in "Notes of the Month," *New Masses* (September 1930), 6:5.

32. Tillie Lerner, "The Iron Throat," *Partisan Review* (April–May 1934), 1(2):2.

33. James R. Green, *The World of the Worker: Labor in Twentieth-Century America* (New York: Hill and Wang, 1980), p. 143.

34. These poems have been reprinted in Selma Burkom and Margaret Williams, "De-Riddling Tillie Olsen's Writings," *San Jose Studies* (1976), 2:65–83. "I Want You Women Up North To Know" and Olsen's "The Strike" have

been recently reprinted in Charlotte Nekola and Paula Rabinowitz, eds., *Writing Red: An Anthology of American Women Writers, 1930–1940*, New York: Feminist Press at The City University of New York, 1987). Le Sueur's "The Fetish of Being Outside" has also been reprinted in this valuable collection.

35. Granville Hicks et al., eds., *Proletarian Literature in the United States* (New York: International, 1935), p. 211.

36. Rosenfelt, "From the Thirties," pp. 389–399.

37. Robert Shaffer, "Women and the Communist Party, USA, 1930–1940," *Socialist Review* (May–June 1979), vol. 86.

38. Tillie Olsen, *Yonnondio: From the Thirties* (New York: Dell, 1974), p. 10. Further page references to this novel will be given in the text.

39. Friedrich Engels, *The Origin of the Family, Private Property, and the State*, excerpts from which appear in Robert C. Tucker, ed., *The Marx-Engels Reader* (New York: Norton, 1978), p. 744.

40. This proclamation appears as a secondary headline in an article credited only to "Irene" and titled "Legend of the 'Weaker Sex' Effectively Smashed by the Position of Women in the Soviet Union" (*Daily Worker*, September 2, 1935, p. 5).

41. Edwin Seaver, "Socialist Realism," *New Masses* (October 22, 1935), 17:23–24.

42. Duplessis, *Writing Beyond the Ending*, p. 163.

43. *Ibid.*, pp. 179–80.

44. *Ibid.*, p. 196.

45. This phrase and concept are borrowed from Duplessis's *Writing Beyond the Ending*, which defines "writing beyond the ending" as "the invention of strategies that sever the narrative from formerly conventional structures of fiction and consciousness about women" (x). However, I believe "strain away from" is often more accurate than "sever."

46. Jon Klancher, "Dialogue from Rhetoric to Literature: Bakhtin's Social Text," paper presented at College Composition and Communication Convention, New Orleans, Louisiana, 1986, p. 4.

47. Fredric Jameson, *Marxism and Form* (Princeton, N.J.: Princeton University Press, 1971), pp. 328–329.

48. Virginia Woolf, "The Leaning Tower," in Virginia Woolf, *The Moment and Other Essays* (London: Hogarth, 1952), p. 125.

49. Raymond Williams, *Marxism and Literature* (Oxford, England: Oxford University Press, 1977), p. 126.

50. Gold, "Notes of the Month," p. 5.

51. Olsen, *Silences*, p. 217.

52. Williams, *Marxism and Literature*, p. 212.

# 9

# Memory and Historical Record: the Literature and Literary Criticism of Beirut, 1982

**Barbara Harlow**

*Barbara's Harlow's essay takes a crucial moment in the history of the Middle East as a basis for her study. Focusing on August 1982, when the leadership and troops of the Palestine Liberation Organization decided to leave Beirut following the earlier Israeli invasion of Lebanon, Harlow examines some of the literature and literary criticism that came out of Lebanon during this momentous time. The essay, which illuminates the interaction between politics and literature, looks at some of the writings of such authors as Elias Khouri, Mahmud Darwish, and others, while revealing their literary responses to the upheaval in their country.*

Having made a strong impression regionally and internationally during the years 1970 to 1982, the Palestinian narrative . . . is now barely in evidence. This is not an aesthetic judgement.

> —Edward Said, "Permission to Narrate" (1984)

Who knows? . . . Maybe one day people will study the bitter, isolated experience of the Arab intellectuals in a heroic battle and young people and future generations will learn from our position. . . . In any case, it is an experience which will not pass quickly.

> —Saadi Yusuf, "Writing in a Time of Killing" (1983)

Studies of occupation and resistance present today what is perhaps an enormous political and intellectual heritage. What is certain is that the only way to confront occupation is to resist it. Resistance is always possible, whatever

the conditions, however much the occupation might try to play with civil
war or ignite sectarian madness.

—Elias Khouri, *The Time of Occupation* (1985)

Yahya Yakhluf, a Palestinian writer, was in Lebanon's Bekaa Valley
with the Palestinian commandos positioned there in August 1982 when
the news of the decision of the Palestine Liberation Organization (PLO)
leadership to leave Beirut together with its fighting forces was officially announced. This decision had been taken following nearly three
months of Palestinian and Lebanese resistance to the Israeli invasion
of Lebanon, which had begun on June 6, 1982. Yahya Yakhluf's short
story, "The Gentle Sparrows," was written on August 24, 1982 in the
mountains around the valley and describes the final acts of fighting
in that area. Midway through the story the fateful announcement
reaches the small group of *fedayeen*, the Palestinian fighters, as they
sit exhausted, reminiscing about childhood days in the village and its
popular wisdom and speculating on the death of their comrade Majdi,
whose body had just been found.

Then one morning news of the departure hit.

We're leaving Beirut. The announcement from central operations reached us. The Murabbitun radio station went on broad-
casting patriotic music.

They're leaving Beirut. And what are we supposed to do here
in the Bekaa? Where are we supposed to depart to? When does
the journey end? From Amman to Damascus. From Damascus
to Beirut. From Beirut to the slaughterhouse. And the islands
and the straits. The narrows. Suffocation and strata-
gems . . . !! Oh you gentle sparrows . . . Oh you gentle sparrows."[1]

A year and a half later Yahya Yakhluf was himself in Damascus with
Abu Musa, who had led the revolt against the leadership of Yasser
Arafat, a revolt that began in the Bekaa in May 1983. In the meantime
those fighters who had left Beirut in the preceding fall and who remained loyal to Abu Ammar (as Arafat is known within the Palestinian movement) were scattered and confined in isolated camps
throughout the Arab world, from Yemen and the Sudan to Tunisia.

The distances, as Yahya Yakhluf describes them, were indeed long.
In 1948 the exodus from Palestine began in the midst of the violent

confrontations which surrounded the establishment of the Israeli state when Britain terminated its mandate in the area. In 1970 during Black September, when King Hussein's army launched its brutal drive to remove the PLO from Jordan, the liberation movement proceeded to transfer its operations to Lebanon. And in the course of the 1970s more than one PLO leader spent time in a Syrian prison. In Lebanon, meanwhile, the Palestinians too had been brought into the factional fighting during the 1975–1976 civil war. For over a decade then, when Israel invaded in 1982, the PLO had been headquartered in Lebanon, where it had established not only a military command, but hospitals, schools, research centers, factories, welfare agencies, and other social services that administered to Palestinians living in Lebanon as well as to the Lebanese population seeking the PLO's aid. Many Lebanese, however, like the Jordanians before them, came to fear what some considered to be the threatening emergence of a Palestinian "state within a state." These Lebanese, who included Muslim Shi'ites and the Christian Phalange, welcomed the Israeli invasion of Lebanon when it came on June 6, 1982.

Within days of the initial incursion, the massive Israeli military machine had reached the outskirts of Beirut. Having ravaged the cities and towns of southern Lebanon and devastated the Palestinian refugee camps there, the Israel Defense Forces (IDF) began a two-month siege of Lebanon's capital city, a siege that consisted not only of indiscriminate shelling and bombing raids, but of the cutting off for long periods of time of water, electricity, food, fuel, and medical supplies to the western half of the city. On August 21, three days before Yahya Yakhluf wrote "The Gentle Sparrows," the PLO began its departure from Beirut. Posters and banners could be seen among the throngs of people assembled to see them off, reading "Palestine or Bust," "Beirut Was and Always Will Be Faithful," and "This Is Not Good-Bye." For all the reluctant leavetaking, however, the evacuation was completed two days ahead of schedule, on September 1. On September 10 the multinational forces of France, Italy, and the United States, which had been called in, as part of the agreement between Philip Habib and Yasser Arafat, to oversee the departure and the welfare of those left behind also withdrew, ten days before the expiration of their mandate. On September 14, Bashir Gemayel, the newly elected president of Lebanon, was assassinated, and within hours the Israeli army had entered West Beirut. From September 15 to 18 they oversaw the massacres that took place in the Palestinian refugee camps of Sabra and Shatila. From Beirut to the slaughterhouse: Yahya Yakhluf was ominously prophetic in his narrative. The continued assault on the Palestinian refugee camps in Beirut, the *harb al-mu-khayyamāt* or "war of the camps," is further testimony to the suppressed history of struggle and resistance being waged in Lebanon.

"The Palestinian narrative," as Edward Said maintained in 1984, two years after Yahya Yakhluf's short story was written, "is now barely in evidence."[2] As Said goes on to assert, however, this absence of a Palestinian entry in the historical record is not simply an "aesthetic" question. Rather it is a function of an unequal distribution of political power in the global arena which has succeeded in maintaining its dominant narrative of events, one that seeks to suppress contesting histories in the interests of what Noam Chomsky has referred to as an "ideologically serviceable history."[3]

Distorted or neglected as the Palestinian narrative may be in the Western media's sanitized versions of current events or the official histories that legitimize and sanction continued "unequal development" on behalf of United States foreign policy or Israeli designs in the region, that narrative, while not the only scenario, has been critical to the contemporary Middle East. Modern Arabic literary history is articulated, not primarily in terms of "world wars" and a United States–European chronology, but according to decisive junctures in what has been called the "Arab-Israeli conflict." The year 1948 and the creation of the state of Israel, designated in Arabic historiography as the *nakba* (disaster), and the June 1967 war, termed the *naksa* or "setback," mark crucial moments in the sociopolitical evolution of Arab history. These dates concatenate just as significantly in the cultural arena: post-1948 writing, the post-1967 generation of intellectuals. The Camp David agreement and Egypt's separate peace with Israel in 1979 signal perhaps a similar rupture. The consequences of Beirut 1982 have yet to be played out.

Muhammad Beniss, a Moroccan critic, suggested in an article published in 1984 and entitled "Toward the 'Question of Modernity'" that it often seemed in contemporary Arabic writing "as if reality were more modern than poetry."[4] It was almost two decades earlier, in 1966, that the Palestinian novelist and critic Ghassan Kanafani had first defined Palestinian literature as "resistance literature" (*adab al-muqāwama*). In his study, *Literature of Resistance in Occupied Palestine 1948–1966*, followed two years later by *Palestinian Resistance Literature Under Occupation 1948–1968*, Kanafani examined the relationship between literary production and the historical and material conditions of the Israeli occupation of Palestine that informed this literature. For Kanafani, literature was not an academic enterprise, the task solely of literary critics, but an active arena of struggle.

In the intervening years between Kanafani's critical studies and Beniss' interrogation of Arab literary "modernity" following the siege of Beirut and the dispersal of the Palestine Liberation Organization, Arab writers and theorists have continued to problematize the intersection of culture and political struggle. That discussion has taken place within the immediate context of the historical and political events that still riddle the contemporary Middle East.

While it is a much addressed, although little redressed, phenomenon that the popular representation of the Arab in the U.S. media and public imagination is that of one-dimensional stereotypes coincident with a dominant ideology and U.S. policies, still less attention has been paid in the academic arena to the cultural production issuing from within the Arab world that would challenge the ascendant historical narratives and curricular disciplines. The few anthologies of poems and short stories and the several novels by largely mainstream Arab writers that have been translated and have made their way onto the lists of some few publishing houses in the United States hardly represent the full spectrum of literary and theoretical issues that focus Arab intellectual debate and ideological controversy. Such concern as there is with modern Arabic literature and culture attempts, as if according to some intellectual or academic version of the international division of labor, to understand these issues largely according to the terms and paradigms provided by theoretical developments in the hegemonic Western world. The Arab world, like the "Third World" more generally, is seen to provide the raw materials for the "First World"'s critical apparatus that will transform that material into consumable commodities for its properly schooled readership. It is thus important now for us to complicate that record, for the "First World" to understand and come to terms with the internal debates and contradictions, the histories, that sustain non-Western strategies of theory and their decisive challenge to Western forms and paradigms of domination.

Elias Khouri, a Lebanese writer and critic, articulated the problem in his paper "Writing the Present":

> Writing is self-dialogue and dialogue with others. But when the "other"—the Third World—is part of "oneself," the dialogue becomes a one-sided dialogue. In other words, an Arab text dialogues with the West, but the West does not dialogue with it. [Is this] an attempt to jump from history to legend, to make the present of the Third World into the past of the West or its covert folklore? This would be to establish a non-historical affiliation

with the center, to fabricate novels of fashion or turn the novel into a news item. Rather than the history of the Marquezian world, history would become shattered pieces in the mirror of western consciousness which consumes everything.[5]

The story of the Palestinian resistance in Beirut during the summer months of 1982, and the cultural strategies of that struggle, provide an exemplary, although not unique, situation for the examination of the challenge presented by "Third World culture" to the pedagogical and disciplinary practices of the United States academies. The teaching of works that emerge out of a world deeply and decisively riven by political issues, as was Beirut in 1982, raises fundamentally different problems from those posed by the teaching—even a politically conscious teaching—of already canonized texts. The insertion of works such as those written out of Beirut in 1982, works so thoroughly penetrated by the political, into a curriculum distinguished by its allegiance to aristocratic social structures calls into question the very distinction between literary and nonliterary which still provides the theoretical foundation for "literary studies" in the United States academic system. How does such a project, one that inquires into the questions raised by the historically-specific relationships between "literature and Beirut 1982," enter into the literature curriculum? Can a place be made for it without radically altering the premises and received definitions of literature, genre, and literary history? This essay is intended to suggest examples of some of the issues that a literary curriculum would have to contend with in attempting to assimilate "Beirut 1982" into the idea of the "literary" or even into "literary interpretation." The military resistance in Beirut to the Israeli siege of the city was also a cultural resistance to the assimilationist tendencies, what Armand Mattelart has called "ethnocentric cosmopolitanism,"[6] of a particular practice of Western cultural politics, that of domination and control.

Beirut 1982 marks a decisive chronological moment, much as did 1948 or 1967, in modern Arab history: the Israeli invasion of Lebanon and the departure of the PLO from Beirut and its dispersal throughout the Arab world. The subsequent literary and critical responses to these events are as significant as the political ones. Indeed, the literary and the political cannot here be separated. Rather than a study that would recover the political from an already acknowledged corpus of literary texts, that would reveal that Fredric Jameson has called the "political unconscious" of the canon, the cultural strategies elaborated in Beirut demand of the Western reader and critic a new way of engaging with its corpus, an engagement that is both partisan and participatory, and that responds to the historical exigencies and urgency of "Third World" literary production. At stake here is not just the presentation of the world in literature, but the political task assumed by literature in the global context,—literature, that is, not as an artifact, but as a transitive activity.

Mahmud Darwish is a Palestinian poet. His homeland is now become the State of Israel, but in 1982 he had been living in exile in Beirut for the previous ten years. He too spent the summer of Israel's invasion and siege in Beirut, quitting the city only after the last of the *fedayeen* had departed. He was a poet, he said, not a fighter, and he would exit separately. In an interview in the magazine *Kul al-Arab* following his own leavetaking of Beirut, Darwish answered questions about what the war had meant for his poetry and writing. "Throughout the war I wrote nothing of importance," he said, and then went on: "But I am certain that this experience will radically alter what writing is, my own writing at least. And I am confident that it is going to change. What I wrote before Beirut was derivative. The experience demands a new kind of writing, because what happened in Beirut is more than just the ordinary experience of a people's history. It is more even than just an earthquake."[7] The Israeli siege of Beirut through the summer months of 1982 occasioned critical questions for Arab writers, whether, like Yahya Yakhluf, they struggled alongside the commandos, or, like Mahmud Darwish, they sought to redefine the task of the poet in terms of the immediate struggle and the exigencies it imposed.[8]

The debate on the relationship between the pen and the gun took on a new urgency during the siege. Beirut, long an intellectual capital and publishing center for the Arab world, in 1982 provided the setting for an historical reexamination of the role of the writer in the resistance movement. According to Ahmad Abu Matar, a Palestinian critic who lived the siege in Beirut, it was precisely the abstention of the intellectuals from the activities of the liberation struggle that had to be considered in order to understand the setbacks suffered thus far by the movement. "It seems to me," he wrote, "that among the reasons for the setbacks of the Arab national movement and its failures over the last fifty years even on the level of struggle is the aloofness of intellectuals and writers from an active participation. Either they have withdrawn or they remain the dependent appendages of an official leadership or of a revolutionary national leadership."[9]

Beirut 1982 witnessed, however, a transformation in the role of the intellectual in the resistance movement; new possibilities emerged and were elaborated in experience. In the case of Ali Fodeh, a young Palestinian poet and editor of the journal *Rasīf* (Sidewalk), the experience was fatal. Ali Fodeh was killed in August 1982 by Israeli bombs while distributing his journal on the sidewalks of West Beirut. In other cases, however, the experience generated new collective forms of cultural production, such as the *Al-Ma'raka* (The Battle), or *Rasīf*. The story of these publications is an important one, recounting as it does their changing locations following bombing raids, their distribution among the people and the fighters, their role in the analysis and dissemination of political and military information, and the publication of poems, interviews; and drawings from the besieged inhabitants of West Beirut. That story which has been told by various of its participants, such as Ahmad Abu Matar or the Egyptian writer Hilmi Salim in *Culture Under Siege* (1984),[10] points out the direct role played by culture in the arena of struggle. Beirut subsequently, however, has become a scene of strife and contention on another level: the ideological battle over the representation of Beirut.

Like Mahmud Darwish, Ahmad Abu Mattar, or Ali Fodeh, Thomas Friedman too spent the summer of 1982 in West Beirut. As a reporter Friedman covered the Israeli invasion for the *New York Times*, eventually receiving a Pulitzer Prize for his reporting of the war from Lebanon. Since that time, however, Friedman has been transferred by his editors to Jersualem, and he now writes from Israel. In December 1985 the journalist reviewed *Under Siege* for the *New York Times Book Review. Under Siege;* by Rashid Khalidi, a Palestinian historian who, as a professor at the American University of Beirut, was in Beirut at the time of the invasion, is a documentary study and narrative of the political and diplomatic processes whereby the PLO leadership eventually came to its historic decision to leave Beirut. According to Khalidi in his introduction to the book,

> Little written so far about the 1982 war has used documents or interviews to illuminate the actions of the parties involved. The reasons are easy to find. In Israel, the war has been a matter for bitter, partisan dispute since it began, coloring the large amount of material which has been published so far. Lebanon is still torn by war, while the Palestinian movement has been riven by dissension. As a result, few Lebanese or Palestinians have had the chance to record their view of events in 1982.[11]

Friedman, for other reasons, recommended the book to his *New York Times* readership, claiming that for students of the Middle East, [Khalidi's] generally objective, lucid and incisive account of PLO decisionmaking fills a critical void in the literature about the Israeli invasion—the Beirut side of which has been dominated by angry, and not particularly useful accounts by journalists and memoirs in Arabic by PLO officials. If Mr. Khalidi's book is read alongside Ze'ev Schiff and Ehud Ya'ari's excellent account of Israeli decisionmaking, *Israel's War in Lebanon,* a reasonably complete picture of events can be drawn.[12]

Thomas Friedman's critical appreciation of *Under Siege* presupposes not only a set of generic distinctions sanctioned by Western literary traditions, which would seem to dismiss diaries, memoirs, and journalistic narratives—the "angry, and not particularly useful, accounts by journalists and memoirs in Arabic by PLO officials"—as legitimate sources for establishing the historical record, but a national bias as well: Israeli accounts like that of Schiff and Ya'ari, themselves journalists, are considered by Friedman to be more reliable, even "reasonable," than those presented by Arab participants in the war.

The siege of Beirut, however, was a crisis for Israeli historiography and its own narrative as well. As is pointed out by Tony Clifton, a reporter for *Newsweek* in Beirut during the summer of 1982, the author with Catherine Leroy of *God Cried,* one of the journalistic accounts dismissed by Friedman, it is perhaps remarkable that one doesn't "see the generals and cabinet ministers of Israel writing the sort of triumphant books about 'Operation Peace for Galilee' that followed the Six Day War or the Yom Kippur War. . . . Will General Rafael Eitan come up with his memoirs called *Beirut Victory,* or Ariel Sharon with something along the lines of *The Man Who Smashed the PLO?"* Rather than annals of victory, critiques proliferated within Israel, such as Jacobo Timmerman's *The Longest War;* Amnon Kapeliouk's *Sabra and Shatila: Inquiry Into a Massacre; My War Diary* by the Israeli colonel Dov Yermiya; or even the controversial Kahan Commission's *Final Report* on the events in Sabra and Shatila. The dominant narratives were, for the moment at least, being challenged. That challenge persists still in the writing of Palestinian and Lebanese critics and intellectuals for whom 1982 articulated a decisive juncture in the historical record of the resistance movement and its attendant cultural struggle. The "reasonably complete picture of events" that Thomas Friedman would like to have drawn remains historically unfinished, with its various dimensions not yet adumbrated, its consequences yet to be elaborated.

In his review article, "Permission To Narrate," Edward Said recollects how he asked family and friends living in West Beirut during the 1982 siege to record their experiences of the invasion.

> I recall during the siege of Beirut obsessively telling friends and family there, over the phone, that they ought to record, write down their experiences; it seemed crucial as a starting point to furnish the world some narrative evidence, over and above atomised and reified TV clips, of what it was like to be at the receiving end of Israeli "anti-terrorism," also known as "Peace for Galilee." Naturally, they were all far too busy surviving to take seriously the unclear theoretical imperatives being waged on them intermittently by a distant son, brother or friend. As a result, most of the easily available written material produced since the fall of Beirut has in fact not been Palestinian and, just as significant, it has been of a fairly narrow range of types: a small archive to be discussed in terms of absences and gaps— in terms either pre-narrative or, in a sense, anti-narrative. The archive speaks of the depressed condition of the Palestinian narrative at present.[14]

The journals and newspapers produced in West Beirut throughout the siege did succeed in some measure in providing an important collection, for the inhabitants at any rate, of accounts of the daily lives of the people, fighters, and writers during that period. Since then the reflections and analyses of the cultural and political significance of Beirut 1982 have continued to accumulate, according to changing circumstances, both from within the Palestinian movement and in the larger Arab world. These debates remain important, according to the Saudi novelist Abdel Rahman Mounif, because "it is necessary that we not repeat the situation which occurred after 1967. What happened after that defeat was that, for the most part, all discussion of the reasons which led to the defeat stopped. Criticism and self-criticism were nonexistent."[15] Abdel Rahman Mounif's article, "Some Lessons from the War of Beirut," appeared in the April 1983 issue of *Al-Tarīq*, a journal affiliated with the Lebanese Communist party. For Faysal Darraj, however, writing from Damascus in 1985 in a special issue of *Al-Hadaf*, the publication of the Popular Front for the Liberation of Palestine (PFLP), the issues presented themselves somewhat differently. Darraj, in Syria, saw the consequences of Arafat's policy of diplomacy and negotiation as being critical in determining the direction of the Palestinian struggle. In his article, "Palestinian Culture Between the Tragedy of Impotence and the Comedy of Decay," which dealt with the Arab cultural situation in the aftermath of Beirut, Darraj accepts the premise of continued and renewed armed struggle, but maintains that the "task of social culture" is "not to spring from the barrel of a gun, but to determine the direction taken by the bullet."[16]

The narrative of the departure of the PLO from Beirut at the end of August 1982, the dispersal of its forces, and the subsequent splits that have divided the organization against itself is much contested. These events, together with the Israeli occupation of Lebanon following the PLO evacuation and the successful popular resistance to that occupation, especially in the south, are recorded differently according to the narrative that reconstructs them. As Raymond Williams has claimed, the "struggle for and against selective traditions" is itself a "major part of all contemporary cultural activity."[17] The "Palestinian narrative" is not only struggling against the dominant histories of the West, but it participates as well in the attempts to reconstitute the history of a Middle East conflicted by sectarian strife, competing nationalisms and the interests of world capitalism in the region. The story of Beirut 1982 and its aftermath is critical to that narrative. It is part of what Edward Said referred to as its "theoretical imperative."[18]

The Israeli siege of Beirut placed critical demands on the Arab writers and intellectuals for whom the Lebanese capital had provided an important center of publication, distribution, and exchange. The nature of those demands changed with the termination of the siege and the implementation of an Israeli occupation of the country. The imperative was no longer resistance alone but reconstruction as well. The question of the form such reconstruction would take was further complicated by the different assessments that were made of the situation and the disposition of the critics with respect to the central events. Mahmud Darwish, for example, had left Beirut only in late September. Elias Khouri, however, had been abroad throughout the siege. Khouri, a Lebanese Christian who was active in the Arab Nationalist movement and the Palestinian resistance, is a major novelist, critic, and journalist in the Arab world. He served, as well, as co-editor from 1977 to 1979 of *Shu'un Filastiniyya* (Palestine Affairs), the journal published by the PLO Research Center. In addition to his 1979 novel *The Lost Memory*, he has published four novels, two volumes of literary criticism, and a volume of short stories set in Beirut in the aftermath of the 1982 Israeli invasion.

When Khouri returned to Beirut in the fall of 1982, many of those

Palestinian and Lebanese men and women to whom Rashid Khalidi, in *Under Siege*, had given a "little more substance by describing their actions during the summer of 1982 through the imperfect medium of diplomatic telex messages and recollections recorded over a year after the event"[19] had left the city, either with the fighters or, like Mahmud Darwish, in the aftermath of the human destruction in the Palestinian refugee camps. Shortly after his return to the Lebanese capital, a volume that collected Khouri's critical studies and essays over the previous ten years was published by the Institute for Arab Research under the title *Al-dhākira al-mafqūda* (The Lost Memory). These articles, which appeared originally in various Arabic literary and political journals, ranged from analyses of Palestinian resistance poetry to presentations of individual authors or more general cultural critiques. Basic to Khouri's critical project over the preceding period was the assumption of "literature as critical history."[20] For Elias Khouri, the Arab historical memory had been either lost through negligence, or confiscated by force over the short decades of the recent past, decades that had produced war, internecine sectarian strife, and bureaucratic systematized repression in much of the Arab world. The Arab peoples were consigned by their politicians and official ideologues to the limited choice between a return to the classical heritage or *turāth* on the one hand, or the material acquisition of modern Western technology on the other. The dichotomous opposition between "traditionalism" (*asāla*) and "modernism" (*hudātha*) as articulating the options for an "underdeveloped" world is an ideological construct that has been much critiqued by progressive Arab intellectuals. The very opposition, when deployed in the contemporary global context, only reinforces relations of dependency and unequal development by its legislation of a universal model of linear stages of development. This model serves in turn to provide a legitimating ideology for neocolonialism. "When modern Arabic writing," according to Elias Khouri in his paper "Writing the Present," "tried, in the course of its renaissance, to put together the past—which is dominated by the miraculous nature of the Koran and poetry—and the future which is devoured by something like a miracle created by the West through which it exerts supreme authority over our countries, wars broke out. . . ."[27]

"The history of Arab criticism," according to Khouri in the introductory title essay to *The Lost Memory*, must be linked to a "critique of history."[22] Criticism, he maintained furthermore, can only study the "problems of literary creation" when it is allowed to study the "problems of society" and its forms of oppression.[23] "Can we," Elias

Khouri asks, "develop a criticism of the literary text, if the government power stands above criticism and study?"[24] And in an interview with the journal *Al-Nada'* in November 1982, in the wake of the siege of Beirut and in the face of the continued Israeli occupation of Lebanon, Khouri reiterated the urgent need for renewed self-criticism on the part of the Arab intellectual: "the memory which I have lost is the ideological organization which controls Arab writing and which is connected to the illusions of the nationalist period. These have become manifest as illusions with the continuous massive defeats ever since 1967."

For nearly two years following his return to Lebanon—from January 1983 until November 1984—Elias Khouri went on to contribute a series of articles to *Al-Safīr*, a Lebanese leftist newspaper and the only regular Lebanese daily to have published without interrruption throughout the Israeli army's siege of Beirut. The articles from this regularly featured column, entitled *Zaman al-ihtilāl* (The Time of Occupation), were collected and published as a book with the same title in 1985.

The first essay written "in the time of occupation," dated January 18, 1983 and titled "A Moment of Clarity," opens with the departure of the Palestinian resistance from Beirut—the departure announced to Yahya Yakhluf in the Bekaa Valley—and the beginning of the Israeli occupation of Lebanon. The intellectual and political scene in Lebanon, like the human lives being lived there, is one of destitution, disarray, and vacuity. According to Khouri,

> the hidden debate which revolves around the cultural issue in Lebanon after the Israeli occupation of Lebanon remains a timid, confused and uncertain debate. The confusion over the rapid developments—the destruction, the siege of Beirut, the departure of the resistance, the election of Bashir Gemayel and his assassination, the massacres, the negotiations, the sectarian war in the mountains, the fear in Beirut—places the debate in the context of seemingly total deperdition. It consists in the total absence of any basic points.[25]

The same essay, however, ends with a call to renewed resistance, an appeal for a reconstruction of the organized opposition struggle that would respond, not to the inherited paradigms of the past, but to the new exigencies of the present.

Similar ideas were being expressed in other forms and shaping a different critique by those who had been compelled to leave Beirut at summer's end in 1982. In renewed Palestinian exile, Mahmud

Darwish, who had then relocated in Greek Cyprus together with many other Palestinian intellectuals and the cultural institutions they represent, composed his long "Poem in Praise of the Tall Shadow," which he recited in 1983 in Tunis, where the PLO had reestablished its headquarters and which had received many of the Palestinian *fedayeen* as well. Darwish's poem describes the Palestinian effort

> To present the east with
> The notion of collectivity,

but goes on to present the different disposition of the Palestinian now exiled from Lebanon:

> Two names we are for unity
> We wanted to exist by our own will
> So that people in this world
> Are not turned into chattel.
> People of Lebanon, farewell!

Yet for Elias Khouri, who returned to remain in Beirut as writer and editor to the literary supplement for *Al-Safir*, it was necessary to defend the city. What must be defended, he wrote in "Normalization and Culture" (January, 1983), is the "cultural role of Beirut . . . Cultural normalization [of the kind that Israel wanted to impose on Egypt following the Camp David Accords] is the attempt to put an end once and for all to Beirut's cultural role, to transform it from the capital of resistance and intellectual activity into a small irrelevant city, a suburb of Israel."[26]

Mahmud Darwish, the Palestinian poet, suffered the loss of Beirut. Elias Khouri, the Lebanese writer, suffered the occupation of Beirut. In both cases, however, the destruction of the city betokened catastrophic consequences for intellectual and cultural production throughout the Arab world, consequences that are still being recorded today.

In their study of one of West Beirut's neighborhoods, *Hamra of Beirut: A Case of Rapid Urbanization*, Samir Khalaf and Per Kongstad pointed to the Lebanese capital's obvious significance as a commercial and financial center. Their study, published in 1973, two years before the outbreak of the Lebanese civil war, however, reads today with a certain prophetic irony. Although they focus on the Hamra district, a more developed, more commercialized area of West Beirut, the two urban sociologists describe Beirut as a whole as a "mosaic" of distinct urban communities. They further insist on its role as a cultural center, citing as evidence the fact that no less than eight institutions of higher learning are located there and emphasizing the "diverse origin of its universities and the varied cultural traditions they represent."[27] Khalaf and Kongstad were able then, in 1972–1973, to maintain in the introduction to their study that

> throughout its history Beirut has been an effective organ for the fusion of different ethnic, confessional and socio-economic groups. With increasing urbanization it has absorbed and assimilated successive waves of migrants and political refugees without any apparent degree of mass violence or urban strife. Dispossessed socio-economic groups and aliens currently out of favor with the political regimes in adjacent Arab states continue to seek refuge in the relatively permissive political atmosphere of Beirut. Ras Beirut's side-walk cafes and snack bars have in fact become notorious for sheltering the so-called coffee-house intellectuals with varying political shades and ideological leanings. Beirut, as a result, is perhaps the only Arab capital which has been able to absorb politically divergent and ethnic groups without much tension or dissent.[28]

Thus, while Beirut maintained, even throughout the civil war, its reputation for modernity, night clubs, and the latest in European fashion, it remained also the the case that Beirut represented perhaps the only secular, cultural capital in the Middle East to which writers throughout the region could look—whatever their political persuasion or religious or ethnic affiliation—for a place where they would be able to publish and distribute their work. A recent novel, for example, by the Egyptian writer and member of the Nasserite opposition party in Egypt, Sonallah Ibrahim, combines both of these once dynamic features of the Lebanese city: its Western-style decadence and its political secularism. *Beirut Beirut*, published in 1984,[29] is set in the period of the Lebanese civil war and tells the story of an Egyptian writer who travels to Beirut in order to see to the publication of his latest novel there. Sonallah Ibrahim's own previous novels, many of them originally proscribed in Egypt, would often, like the writings of many progressive Arab intellectuals, appear first in Beirut. *Beirut Beirut*, by contrast, was published in Cairo, bitter evidence of the changed historical circumstances of Arab intellectual activity.

During the months of the siege, a new collective resistance and common steadfastness (*sumūd*) had enjoined the writers and intellectuals present in Beirut to reorganize their cultural activity. In his book-length study, *Culture Under Siege*, Hilmi Salim analyzes the transformation of Beirut literary production occasioned by the Israeli assault on the city and their attempt to isolate its inhabitants. Prior to the siege, Salim points out, Beirut suffered from a seemingly chronic "information indigestion" (*al-tukhama al-'alamiya*). West Beirut, with a population of approximately half a million persons, produced nearly one hundred regular publications,—daily, weekly, monthly, etc.,— representing the different ideological positions and political parties in the city. "The printing presses ran day and night." And there were books as well. "Are there readers," Salim asks, "for all these publications?"[30]

Under siege, this diversity, often conflicting and contentious, became a common cultural front, part of the combined resistance to the invasion. It was not, according to Hilmi Salim, "a time of poetry, but rather a time of collective confrontational work."[31] Those writers already in Beirut, like Mahmud Darwish, Ahmad Abu Mattar, Fawaz Trabulsi, or the Iraqi poet Saadi Yusuf, were joined in the course of the summer by others, such as the Palestinian Muin Basisu or the Egyptian Abu Bakr Yusuf, who arrived from Moscow. They came, one and all, to participate in the resistance. Abu Bakr Yusuf, for example, translated Russian poetry from the siege of Leningrad to be published in the journals and newspapers now printed and distributed on a daily basis.[32] Saadi Yusuf recalled in his memoir "Writing in a Time of Killing:" "I was amazed at this clear, shared language which gathered the Palestinians together in a time more conducive to dissension, discord and disunity."[33] Writing in Egypt following the siege, Mahjub Amr commented in his book, *The People and the Siege*, that "day after day Beirut was changed from the name of an Arab capital into a theater of war. Onlookers anticipated the results. The unity of the peoples of Beirut intensified."[34] The siege of Beirut in the summer of 1982 was a critical, if short-lived, moment in the development of Beirut's role as a cultural capital and ideological topos in the Arab world. A larger narrative frames it. In her article "Lebanon as a Mirror of Arab Transformations," Mona Anis opens with a quotation from Elias Khouri: "Lebanon was a mirror reflecting the Arab transformations evolving outside it. The Lebanese interior was the Arab outside par excellence."[35] The siege ended, the PLO departed, and the Israeli occupation began.

Following the departure of the Palestinian resistance, Israeli occupation, working in cooperation with the Christian Phalange government under Amin Gemayel and with the moral and military support of the Reagan administration, brought about the closure or relocation of a number of cultural institutions, publishing houses, and research centers that once functioned in Beirut. A car bomb explosion, for example, seriously damaged the PLO Research Center in January 1983. Whereas the number of printings and publications in Beirut prior to the summer of 1982 had often seemed to exceed, according to Hilmi Salim, the number of reading inhabitants in the city, the subsequent imposition of direct and indirect censorship in Lebanon, during the Israeli occupation and while the Phalange managed to maintain its control over the city, dramatically altered the programs of publication in many institutions. In his essay "Democracy and Modern Despotism," (1978), Elias Khouri had already criticized the tendency of the *comprador* Arab bourgeoisie to "transform the people into folklore and tourism."[36] That critique finds a further elaboration in Khouri's later article, " 'Arabization' and Intimidation."[39] " 'Arabization' and Intimidation" first appeared *Al-Safir* in May 1983, at a moment when the Phalange government's censorship of literary and intellectual production in Lebanon was especially intense following the controversial agreement negotiated by U.S. secretary of state George Shultz between Israel and the Christian Lebanese government. Because of this highly contested treaty arrangement (which eventually collapsed), the Lebanese regime of Amin Gemayel was particularly interested in maintaining the political and, more importantly perhaps, financial support of its "sister Arab states."

Although the Christian population in Lebanon had historically insisted on its geneology as "Phoenician" rather than "Arab," "Arabization" in the cultural sphere now became part of the government program. This "Arabization" was, however, according to Khouri, construed in such a way as to satisfy the more conservative Arab oil regimes. Whereas Beirut had once served as the center for the dissemination of radical Arab thought, what was now to be exported was the traditional Arab cultural heritage, the classical *turāth*, "leatherbound books with their titles embossed in gilt."[38] In the name of "Arabization," furthermore, there began what Khouri describes as a "purification of the Lebanese University of those professors who had imported ideas. Although 'we,' " as the critic writes with a certain irony, "are capable of economic openness and readiness to import commodities even from New Zealand in order to re-export them to our sister states, we are not yet ready to receive western-imported ideas. Ideas must be 100% local manufacture."[39]

Khouri ends his article of May 27, 1983 by indicating that, in the face of such pressures from within and without, only two choices are available: the first, "isolationism," he rejects despite its apparent historical ascendancy of the moment. The second option, he insists, is the only lasting one, even given the difficulties it entails,—the option, that is, of resistance. The word for resistance used here, *mu'ārada*, translates the term *muqāwama* (conventionally used in Arabic to suggest popular, organized resistance to colonial occupation or imperialist oppression) and gives a literary-critical implication to the idea of resistance. *Mu'ārada*, while it does have the literal meaning of confrontation, opposition, or resistance, is also the designation given to a classical Arabic literary form, according to which one person will write a poem and another will retaliate by writing along the same lines, but reversing the meaning. This translation into Arabic of the Arabic word for resistance suggests a larger and collective political agenda for the Arab writer and intellectual. It describes now a critical strategy of cultural resistance practiced by other contemporary writers of the "Third World." *Season of Migration to the North*, by the Sudanese novelist Tayeb Salih, for example, is a form of riposte to *Othello*, in much the same way that Jean Rhys' *Wide Sargasso Sea* responds to *Jane Eyre*, or Chinua Achebe's *Things Fall Apart* rewrites Joseph Conrad's *Heart of Darkness*. Such a genre as *mu'ārada*, which evolves out of the indigenous cultural tradition of the Arab world, has critical implications for an enlarged, more global, definition of literature and literary practice than that devised exclusively by the educational institutions of the West.

Khouri reacted to the political and cultural collapse of Beirut in his capacity not only as political intellectual and writer but as a journalist as well. In "Writing and Silence," Khouri raised the question of the connection between writing and action and pointed to the curious phenomenon that the only place where the question of this connection seemed to be articulated was the "daily newspaper." It is, however, according to Khouri, "as if the newspaper were nothing but a means for disseminating writing and questions of creativity." In such circumstances, newspapers become just another means of diverting attention from historical reality. What, then, he goes on, is the "role of writing and the newspaper during war?"[40] This particular article was written in fall 1983, at the moment when sectarian fighting in the Shuf mountains between Druze and Christian forces was particularly intense, fighting that was further aggravated by the shelling from the USS *New Jersey* in the Mediterranean. Khouri describes the prohibition on Lebanese reporters, who were not permitted access to the events in that region. Lebanese reporters were considered "biased," and it was assumed that they probably belonged to one sect or another involved in the fighting and thus could not possibly entertain any distance or objectivity in their reportage. Accordingly, Khouri goes on,

> the foreign reporter could go to the region, observe and then write. Our only sources about the Shuf or the barracks, then, become foreign newspapers and our references for the long Lebanese war are thus largely foreign references.
>
> The issue I want to raise here is precisely the apparent lack of objectivity as regards the capacity of the Lebanese writer to write about the situation he is living in, to see and be able to reveal, to record and bear witness.[41]

The result, for Khouri, of such legislated proscriptions is the renewed "anthropologization" of Lebanese history. The Orientalists, this time in the guise of foreign correspondents, were determining the nature of the Lebanese historical narrative.

The series of articles that make up *The Time of Occupation* are part of a collective project to reconstruct the terms and priorities of that historical record. The destruction of the city of Beirut—from within as well as from without—destroyed one of the major geographical centers of cultural and intellectual resistance to foreign domination and cultural imperialism in the modern Middle East. Such a narrative of the recent history of Beirut as that proposed in *The Time of Occupation* suggests that the city's significance is not only invested in the construction of its buildings and its economic infrastructure, but in its cultural and ideological superstructure as well. The material and intellectual realities of Beirut, in the meantime, find a revealing intersection in the "writing on the walls" that remain standing, as Nadia Rachid Koleilat points out in her study *War Graffiti in Beirut (1975–1982)*,[42] to narrate the city's ravaged history. Should the fighting ever stop and reconstruction begin, not only might a fuller account emerge of the number of people killed in the refugee camps of Sabra and Shatila (as one officer from the Lebanese Forces mockingly put it, such a count will be available only if the city planners decide to build a metro in Beirut), but perhaps a new historical narrative as well. Such a narrative appeals for a new vision. In an article published in the March 17, 1986 issue of *Al-Yawm al-Sābi'*, (an Arabic weekly printed in Paris) entitled "A Pressing Longing for Beirut," Mahmud Darwish offered what he described as an "addendum to the blueprint for the reconstruction of the Shatila camp." The article began with a questioning of historical necessity:

You may return to Beirut, you may return to writing, but no one can return to what was. If one did return, then one would find neither it nor oneself as they were. Perhaps it is the truth of poetry to go back to the use of magic as a tool to make or control absence or the unknown. But no one returns to what was. What is the hold of this city on us, as if it were the beginning of our history, as if it were our childhood? We restrain the longing in us, for it is not for us to reveal it, if for no other reason than this, that it is a threatened longing.[43]

Historical necessity is part of the "theoretical imperative" enjoined by the assault on Beirut.

"Unity and diversity," Elias Khouri wrote in the spring of 1983. "Is it possible that after all this tragedy we could dream of transcending the wounds of civil war in order to confront the danger of occupation? This is our choice, our one reality, that before the wave of retreat and decay, we manifest our commitment to the vision of resistance, that we seek the pulsebeats in the rubble of the ravaged cities and villages." These lines appeared in the journal Al-Tarīq, published by the Lebanese Communist party. In a special issue in June 1983 the feature topic was "Israel in Lebanon" and the articles, testimonies, and interviews that appeared there all bore witness to the physical, human and cultural devastation that had been wrought upon the city. Elias Khouri's essay in that issue is entitled "Questions of Culture and Questions of Occupation," and in it he describes the transformation of the city from a "revolutionary laboratory" into a "laboratory of death." The society, he wrote had "discovered its own inability to narrate itself."[44]

A year and a half earlier, in the article "The Optimism of the Will" (April 2, 1983), Elias Khouri had questioned the significance of the destruction of Beirut: would it mark an endpoint or a turning point in the historical narrative of Palestinian and Arab resistance: "The deep meaning of the confrontation of the summer of 1982," he wrote, is "its transformation from an endpoint of confrontation into a new direction for confrontations with the occupying country, with ourselves and with repressive Arab regimes. . . . We will write anew," Khouri concluded then, "our stories without end."[45] In "Death of the Symbol" (June 14, 1983), though, there seemed to be "no connection between the first story and the last story, between the second story and the seventh, between the ceasefire and the child reported found in California. Nevertheless, Khalil Hawi [a Lebanese poet who killed himself a few short days after the IDF launched its invasion] had committed suicide; Sharon had reached the walls of the Presidential Palace; the Lebanese Cabinet went on to approve overwhelmingly the Shultz Agreement; and so on. . . . "[46]

Is there, the question remains, a literary-historical narrative that would make sense of these disparate, conflicting, but simultaneously occurring *faits divers,* a narrative that would reorganize the historical circumstances and transform the divisive sectarian consequences of the dominant master narrative into a collective struggle against further domination and exploitation? What this essay has tried to suggest is that the answer to that question lies not in the research institutes or academies of higher learning of the West, nor even in its literary history and critical traditions, but in the global politicization of the very idea of "literature" as it is being waged in the historically specific struggles, such as that of the Palestinian resistance, on the staging grounds of the world today. As Elias Khouri claimed, in his introduction to *The Time of Occupation,* "studies of occupation and resistance present today what is perhaps an enormous political and intellectual heritage."[47] It may be that the practice of a politics of literature for the 1990s and beyond in the United States academies will be learned from the strategic arenas of struggle and confrontation in what is currently referred to as the "Third World."

This essay was written in the fall of 1986. As the essay goes to press in the fall of 1989 the dire situation in Beirut and the concurrent relocation of the struggle to the Palestinian *intifada* in the occupied territories of the West Bank and the Gaza strip suggest once again the contemporary urgency of the intersections of historical events and cultural production.

### Endnotes

NOTE: This paper owes much to conversations with Abd Bibi, Shafeeq al-Ghabra, Taghreed al-Qudsi, and Jamal al-Hibri. All translations from Arabic are my own, unless otherwise indicated.

1. Yahya Yakhluf, "An al-'asāfīr al-hanūna" (The Gentle Sparrows), *Al-Karmal* (1983), 7:133.

2. Edward Said, "Permission To Narrate," *London Review of Books,* February 16–29, 1984, p. 14.

3. Noam Chomsky, "Middle East Terrorism and the American Ideological System," *Race and Class* (1986), 28(1):17.

4. Muhammad Beniss, "Lī 'musā'ala al-hudātha' " (Toward the "Question of Modernity"), *Al-Karmal* (1984), 12:51.

5. Elias Khouri, "Writing the Present," paper presented at the Conference on the Challenge of Third World Culture, Duke University, September 1986.

Reprinted in Arabic as "Kitāba al-hādir," *Al-Safīr*, October 11, 1986. The conference at which Khouri's paper was presented was attended by prominent writers and intellectuals of "Third World culture," and provided an important and controversial testing ground for the problematized and conflicted role of the "Third World writer" in the academies of the "First World."

6. Armand Mattelart, "Communication in Nicaragua Between War and Democracy" in *Communicating in Popular Nicaragua*, ed. Armand Mattelart (New York and Bagnolet: International General, 1986), p. 7.

7. Mahmud Darwish, interview with Shabul Daghr, *Kul al-Arab*, November 13, 1982.

8. See Barbara Harlow, "Palestine or Andalusia: The Literary Response to the Israeli Invasion of Lebanon," *Race and Class* (1984), 26(2):33–43.

9. Ahmad Abu Mattar, "Al-Muthāqqafūn al-'arab fi hisār Bayrūt" (Arab Intellectuals in the Siege of Beirut), *Fikr* (1985), 6:64.

10. Hilmi Salim, *Al-thaqāfa taht al-hisār* (Culture Under Siege) (Cairo: Dar al Shahdi, 1984).

11. Rashid Khalidi, *Under Siege: P.L.O. Decisionmaking During the 1982 War* (New York: Columbia University Press, 1985), p. 5.

12. Thomas Friedman, review of Rashid Khalidi's *Under Siege, New York Times Book Review*, December 15, 1985, p. 3.

13. Tony Clifton and Catherine Leroy, *God Cried* (London: Quartet Books, 1983), p. 14.

14. Said, "Permission To Narrate," p. 15.

15. Abdel Rahman Mounif, "Ba'd al-durūs min harb Bayrūt" (Some Lessons from the War of Beirut), *Al-Tarīq* (April 1983), 1:79.

16. Faysal Darraj, "Al-thaqāfa al-filastiniyya bayn ma'sāh al-'ajz wa kumidiyya al-inhitāt" (Palestinian Culture Between the Tragedy of Impotence and the Comedy of Decay), *Al-Hadaf*, December 23, 1985, p. 207.

17. Raymond Williams, *Marxism and Literature* (London: Oxford University Press, 1977), p. 117.

18. Said, "Permission To Narrate," p. 14.

19. Khalid, *Under Siege*, p. 6.

20. Elias Khouri, *Al-dhākira al-mafqūda* (The Lost Memory) (Beirut: Institute for Arab Research, 1982), p. 14.

21. Elias Khouri, "Writing the Present," paper presented at the Conference on the Challenge of Third World Culture, Duke University, September 1986, p. ; reprinted in Arabic as "Kitāba al-hādir," *Al-Safīr*, October 11, 1986.

22. Khouri, *Al-dhākira al-mafqūda* (The Lost Memory), p. 9.

23. *Ibid.*, p. 17.

24. *Ibid.*

25. Khouri, *Zaman al-ihtilāl* (Time of Occupation), p. 7.

26. Elias Khouri, "Normalization and Culture," *Zaman al-ihtilāl*, p. 14.

27. Samir Khalaf and Per Kongstad, *Hamra of Beirut: A Case of Rapid Urbanization* (Leiden: Brill, 1973), p. 19.

28. *Ibid.*, pp. 2–3.

29. Sonallah Ibrahim, *Bayrūt Bayrūt* (Beirut Beirut) (Cairo: Dar al-Mustaqbal al-Arabi, 1984).

30. Salim, *Al-thaqāfa taht al-hisār* (Culture Under Siege), p. 12.

31. *Ibid.*, p. 82.

32. *Ibid.*, pp. 174–75.

33. Saadi Yusuf, "Al-Kitāba fi zaman al-qatl" (Writing in a Time of Killing), *Al-Badīl* (November 1983), p. 102.

34. Mahjub Amr, *Al-nās wa al-hisār* (The People and the Siege) (Cairo: Al-Arabi, 1983), p. 88.

35. Mona Anis, "Lubnān mir'ah al-tahāwwalāt al-'arabiyya" (Lebanon as a Mirror of Arab Transformations), *Al-Muwājaha* (1985), 5:56.

36. Elias Khouri, "Democracy and Modern Despotism," in Khouri, *Al-dhākira al-mafqūda* (The Lost Memory), p. 57.

37. Elias Khouri, "'Arabization' and Intimidation," in Khouri, *Zaman al-ihtilāl* (Time of Occupation), pp. 67–71.

38. *Ibid.*, p. 69.

39. *Ibid.*, p. 68.

40. Elias Khouri, "Writing and Silence," *Zaman al-ihtilāl*, p. 112.

41. *Ibid.*, p. 116.

42. Nadia Rachid Koleilat, "War Graffiti in Beirut" (1975–1982), M.A. thesis, University of Texas at Austin, 1985.

43. Mahmud Darwish, "Hanīn makbut ila Bayrūt" (A Pressing Longing for Beirut), *Al-Yawm al-Sābi'*, March 17, 1986.

44. Elias Khouri, "As'ila al-thaqāfa wa as'ila al-ihtilāl" (Questions of Culture and Questions of Occupation), *Al-Tarīq* (June 1983), 2:101.

45. Elias Khouri, "The Optimism of the Will," *Zaman al-ihtilāl*, p. 44.

46. Elias Khouri, "Death of the Symbol," *Zaman al-ihtilāl* p. 78.

47. Khouri, *Zaman al-ihtilāl* (Time of Occupation), p. 5.

# FOUR

## TRACINGS: DEVELOPMENTS AND TRENDS IN NONCANONICAL LITERARY TRADITIONS

*One of the aims of this anthology is to acquaint and reacquaint readers with political developments in literary studies over the past years. With the opening up of the canon, we all have to master so many more traditions than simply the "great tradition." Because the very noncanonical literature that is partly the subject of this anthology—African-American, Chicano, Palestinian, feminist—would not have been the stuff of articles and general books thirty years ago, most of us have to be both specialists and generalists of a very new sort. The political goal is more exhaustive, and there is a general assumption that we must all be familiar with what were previously alien traditions.*

*In a move to present alternative "surveys" of this literature, the authors of the following pieces refer to a countercanon of their tradition. These essays do not analyze closely the works of individual writers or particular literary pieces. Rather, they have a broader focus and present a "tracing" of the trends and accomplishments of Chicano, lesbian, and African-American literary critical traditions.*

# 10

## At the Crossroads of History, on the Borders of Change: Chicano Literary Studies Past, Present, and Future

### Héctor Calderón

*Héctor Calderón's article begins by acknowledging the literary and political benefits derived from the opening of the canon. However, he laments that, despite the strides made in canon studies, the literatures of Native American, Asian-American, Puerto Rican, and Chicano men and women have not received the kind of attention they deserve.*

*Specifically, Calderón argues that Chicano literature should be seen as a branch of American literature that offers, in its literary pursuits, a valid picture of the history and politics of the American Southwest. With this in mind, Calderón goes on to give an insightful overview of and introduction to the many and varied accomplishments and contributions of Chicano literature.*

> The U.S.-Mexican border *es una herida abierta* where the Third World grates against the first and bleeds. And before a scab forms it hemorrhages again, the lifeblood of two worlds merging to form a third country—a border culture.
>
> —Gloria Anzaldúa, *Borderlands/La Frontera*[1]

**M**uch has happened to literary studies in this country since the 1960s, especially if we note the conferences, publications, books, and special issues of journals devoted to women and cultural groups whose creative and scholarly work had been ignored for too long by the academy. Yet much still needs to be done, especially in the field of Chicano literature; although many fine women and men have entered the academy, our literature and scholarship have not received full institutional support or national attention. Certainly, other fields have benefited from the widening of the literary canon, most notably women's studies and Afro-American studies. That these areas of research have received the most attention from the academy and its allied publishing sector can be verified by strolling through the book exhibits at the annual Modern Language Association National Convention or by noting the names of women and Afro-American scholars present on the editorial boards of legitimating literary journals. I encourage and support this interest in African American and feminist scholarship, for it arises out of concrete social conditions and will eventually influence classroom teaching and the emergence of an alternative canon. However, I lament the fact that such recognition has not been achieved by Chicano, as well as by Asian-American, Native American, and Puerto Rican men and women.

It is, indeed, a sad commentary on American studies in this country that Chicano literature and art enjoy greater interest from non-Chicano scholars in Europe, Mexico, and Latin America than in our universities. Indicative of this growing internationalization of Chicano studies are the biennial conferences in Germany (1984), France (1986), and Spain (1988) sponsored by the European Association pour la Diffusion et l'Etude des Cultures Latines en Amérique du Nord, the "Semana Chicana" in Mexico City (1987) and the participation of Chicana and Chicano artists, film makers, and theater groups in festivals throughout Latin America.

By way of introduction to my contribution, I would like to begin with a brief autobiographical sketch.

I was born in 1945 a short five blocks from the U.S.—Mexican border in Calexico, California of working-class parents who as children had left Mexico during the revolution. My mother came from a migrant worker family who managed to settle permanently in the 1940s; prior to me, all of the males in my father's family had earned their living working for the Southern Pacific Railroad. Although I was educated in English-speaking schools, my early home environment was Mexican-*mestizo*, with strong ties to Catholicism and a rich oral tradition. I was the first of my family to receive a college education. That was in the 1960s at hip and liberal UCLA. I developed an interest in folklore and literature while working (in the Work Study Program) for three years for Wayland D. Hand, director of the Center for Folklore and Mythology at UCLA. In 1965 I happened to come across what was for me the first book written by a Mexican-American, *"With His Pistol in His Hand"*: *A Border Ballad and Its Hero*, the now classic study of Texas border balladry by one of the founders of Mexican-American studies, Américo Paredes. What ensued during the following years was a general awakening of interest in alternative cultural expressions and political ideologies—most notably the Chicano movement and the Cuban Revolution, and a worldwide 1960s counterculture, all eventually leading me to complete an M.A. in Spanish at UC-Irvine and a Ph.D. in Latin American literature with a minor in comparative literature at Yale University in 1981.

I am relating this bit of personal history because it is exemplary of the origins and development of Chicano literature and criticism. Almost every Chicano writer and scholar is bicultural and bilingual with Mexican-*mestizo*, working-class roots. Although Chicano literature courses have been present in the undergraduate curriculum for over a decade, for the most part they are still excluded from graduate programs. Thus, like myself, many scholars have had no training in Chicano literature. All of us have formal ("legitimate") training in other fields of specialization and have taken on Chicano literature as both a personal and a political commitment. Although we entered the academy during the expansion of literary studies and our work reflects the recent 1970s boom in literary theory, our field is still very marginal.[2] And even though we may hold positions of power and relative autonomy as associate and full professors, whatever gains we may have achieved for our field as a legitimate institutional area of study in the 1970s and 1980s are now threatened by the decade of the Reagan revolution, a period of political retrenchment whose conservative point of views are echoed in literary studies through Richard Rodriguez' right-wing stance on bilingual education, William J. Bennett's Eurocentric great tradition, E. D. Hirsch's middle-class cultural literacy, Allan Bloom's conservative classicism, and the reemergence of the college core curriculum.

I am dismayed when E. L. Doctorow is often mentioned as one of the few American writers who deals with history and politics. As I will demonstrate, ours is an American literature that emerged literally almost overnight in the midst of a political movement. As in the early work of Tomás Rivera and Rolando Hinojosa, the emphasis on social struggle is carried on today by writers such as Cherríe Moraga, Gloria Anzaldúa, and Helena María Viramontes, who have not only suffered at the hands of their own patriarchal culture but have also suffered exclusion from Anglo-American feminism.[3] And because of our relationship to Anglo-American society our field of criticism is constantly threatened and questioned. The field can serve as an example of social and cultural struggle in this country, for what may seem mundane situations for others—whether it be teaching a text in the classroom, getting work published in "legitimate" journals or by mainstream presses, or receiving tenure—are for us political battlegrounds. Since a Chicano point of view was absent from the first version of this collection, let me survey the history of this field before assessing its present condition and its prospects for the future as we approach the last decade of this century.

Chicana and Chicano cultural production is an expression of a social group that has given *the* distinctive cultural feature to the American West and Southwest. If we limit this literature to political boundaries, it has existed in oral and written form first since the Texas-Mexican War (1836) with greater awareness of cultural differences from Mexico after the U.S.-Mexican War (1846–1848). Although Spanish and Mexican cultures in the Southwest date back to the mid-sixteenth century and beyond, taking into account Native American *mestizo* roots, the literature produced by these two groups should be ideologically and institutionally placed within the national literatures of Spain and Mexico. After all, a Spanish chronicler of the Southwest, like Cabeza de Vaca or Coronado, writing in the sixteenth century, regardless of whatever sympathy he may have had for Native Americans, is not a Chicano but a Spaniard. A similar situation holds true for Mexican writers. While Mexican literature flourished in the Southwest prior to and after 1848, until recently Mexican writers, expatriots, and travelers through the United States have taken a dim view of their northern brethren, judging them as inauthentic (I am referring to the Mexican term *pocho*) Mexicans.

And although the largely "unsettled" West may have been discovered for Anglo-Americans at the turn of the twentieth century by easterners such as Charles F. Lummis (*The Land of Poco Tiempo, A New Mexico David*)[4] with greater knowledge of native cultures through research on Spanish balladry in Spanish departments in Western universities (I am referring to such works as Aurelio Espinosa's "Romancero nuevomejicano"[5] and Arthur L. Campa's "Spanish Folksong in the Southwest")[6] and the development of Western folklore societies (see J. Frank Dobie's *Flavor of Texas*),[7] these efforts stressed either an uninhabited landscape or else a romantic Spanish past (see A. Paredes, "Folk Base of Chicano Literature")[8] at the expense of recently arrived Asian-Americans and Native Americans and Mexicans, many of whose ancestors had lived and worked the Western soil for centuries. This past, viewed by many Anglo-Americans (including critics) as the golden age of Hispanic culture in the Southwest, has continued to flourish to the present in the Anglo-American popular imagination in literature, mass media images, and Hollywood films and in the celebration of Spanish fiesta days throughout the Southwest.

This same romantic, even quaint, view of Mexican experience on both sides of the border was held by many Mexican-American writers, both men and women, during the first forty years of this century. Raymund D. Paredes has repeatedly written (see "Evolution of Chicano Literature," "Mexican American Authors and the American Dream," and "Promise of Chicano Literature")[9] on such writers of English expression as María Cristina Mena, Nina Otero de Warren, Jovita González, and Josephina Niggli. Although I have a great deal of respect for this historical research, it is important to point out that these writers, in large measure, held conventional Anglo-American views of their culture. This is a vital area of research which awaits further scholarship with a greater knowledge of history and a grasp of theory beyond plot summaries in order to make these texts meaningful for our historical moment. For example, Genaro Padilla has recently argued for a rereading of early folkloric autobiographies by New Mexican upper-class Hispanas within the context of cultural imperialism, within the network of cultural and discursive practices invented by Charles F. Lummis through his work in the development of the New Mexico Folklore Society.[10] Given such domination and self-deceit, Padilla has set himself the task of finding moments of lucidity and resisitance in texts written by Fabiola Cabeza de Baca and Cleofas Jaramillo. In sum, I am arguing for a Mexican-American or Chicano intellectual perspective, as found in the Arizona writer Mario Suárez, who wrote short stories and sketches about his Tucson barrio for the *Arizona Quarterly* in the 1940s.[11] We must posit that such a point of view must have emerged somewhere in the mid-nineteenth century when Mexican-Americans or mestizos began to project for themselves a positive, yet also critical, rendering of their bilingual and bicultural experience as a resistive measure against Anglo-American economic domination and ideological hegemony.[12]

For many compelling historical and sociological reasons, including overt racism, economic exploitation, and the lack of educational opportunities, it is not surprising that Mexican-American experience, thought, and writing did not receive their proper share of attention from universities prior to the Chicano movement of the 1960s. We must, however, with all due respect, pay to tribute to some outstanding scholars who later gained wide recognition after the Chicano movement but who through their individual efforts laid the groundwork for Chicano research and writing.

Ernesto Galarza rose from poverty to become the first of his cultural group to receive a doctorate in this country.[13] He became an expert in Latin American politics, an ardent social activist, and noted author, poet, and writer of children's literature. He was born in Jalcocotán in the State of Nayarit, Mexico in 1905 and as a child migrated with his family to Sacramento, California. In 1927 he graduated from Occidental College with Phi Beta Kappa honors, followed in 1929 by a master's degree from Stanford in Latin American history and in 1932 by a doctorate in political science from Columbia University. During the Spanish Civil War he was a fervent supporter of the Abraham Lincoln Brigade. He traveled throughout Latin America and combined his research and writing to argue on behalf of Latin American workers. For his efforts he was awarded the government of Bolivia's "Order of the Condor Medal," the highest honor given to a noncitizen for promoting human rights and democracy in the Americas. During the next three decades, he turned his attention to the plight of migrant farm workers in this country. He not only was one of the promoters and organizers for the National Farm Workers Union AFL-CIO, but he also produced a series of books—*Merchants of Labor, Spiders in the House and Workers in the Fields, Farm Workers and Agri-Business*—whose arguments helped to end the exploitative *bracero* program and exposed the harmful effects of agribusiness on Chicano workers. His autobiography, *Barrio Boy*, has become one of the early classics of Chicano narrative.[14]

Of equal stature is the singer, poet, journalist, and folklorist Américo Paredes who in the 1950s, as a graduate student in the English department at the University of Texas, took on the deeply entrenched, Anglo-Texan, white supremacist views expressed through state-supported institutional studies of Texas folklore and history.[15] Born in Brownsville, Texas, where his family had arrived with early Spanish settlers, Paredes directed his scholarship to the oral tales and songs that he had heard as a child. He applied Anglo-American, Spanish, and Mexican folklore scholarship to his study of the popular Mexican *corrido*, a tradition that first began to flourish not in Mexico proper but along both sides of the Rio Grande since Anglo-Texan occupation of the region in the nineteenth century. Paredes' dissertation, "With His Pistol in His Hand" (now the film "The Ballad of Gregorio Cortez") was more than just a piece of research. Like Bakhtin's research on folkloric satire directed against the Stalinist state's view of the Russian epic tradition, Paredes' work was also a bold imaginative political statement that told from the Texas-Mexican perspective the tale of Gregorio Cortez, a Mexican *vaquero* and rancher who had been wrongly accused of killing a Texas sheriff in cold blood in 1901. Through his humor, storytelling, and scholarship, Paredes struck at the heart of Anglo-Texan myth making as published in the scholarly works of J. Frank Dobie and Walter Prescott Webb.[16] Along with demystifying the Texas rangers, Paredes produced a theory of border culture as resistance and struggle expressed through the heroic *corridos*.

The work of these two scholars along with others such as longtime labor activist and scholar Bert Corona[17] speaks well for individual scholarly research combined with the interests of a bicultural, working-class community, a combination that has helped to mold Chicano studies today. The reputation for moral courage that the media and the political right wing have accorded to Richard Rodriguez (*Hunger of Memory*) for shedding his Mexican, working-class identity for that of a middle-class "American" male pales in comparison to the struggles and achievements of these early Mexican-American scholars.

The tradition of Chicano literary scholarship that I inherited as I began my teaching career in the late 1970s is owed, certainly, to the efforts of the above mentioned scholars but also to the social upheavals of the decade of the 1960s, the major political and cultural consequences of which for Chicanos, in my view, was the widespread institutionalization of their experience.

The Chicano movement of the 1960s was an intellectual watershed, an historical awareness of our place in our native land. We were no longer Mexicans as opposed to "Americans" or *pochos* as opposed to authentic Mexicanos. We were Chicanos and we shared much with the militancy and the ideologies of such diverse manifestations as the American Indian, Black Power, civil rights, and antiwar movement, the development of the New Left, an international student movement, and the liberation struggles in the Third World.[18] It is not easy to define the movement, which encompassed divergent ideologies, nor even the term Chicano. Like many Anglo-Americans, conservative Mexican-Americans denounced the strategies of activists; and the term *Chicano* was never totally accepted by all regional groups. Even its etymology is still debated.[19] However, what was certain was that repercussions of the movement, especially a new ethnic pride, were felt at every level throughout the Mexican-American community and dramatically transformed it.

The movement crystallized around the "Plan de Delano" and the farm workers' strike, which were organized by César Chávez in 1965. Other important events were to follow: the armed struggle for property rights guaranteed by the Treaty of Guadalupe Hidalgo (1848) of the New Mexican Alianza, led by Reies López Tijerina; Rodolfo Gonzales' Crusade for Justice in Colorado; and the founding of the Raza Unida Party in Crystal City, Texas. However, it was the Delano strike that seized the public's imagination and mobilized many sectors of the Mexican-American community. Many students rallied and joined forces with farm workers on the picket lines. This turned out to be a decisive moment, for it was the youth, high school, and university students who were to give these regional events the sense of a broad social movement.

Almost overnight a new consciousness emerged. Popular ballads of the Mexican Revolution were rewritten to express the farm workers' struggle. The Teatro Campesino organized by Luis Valdez, a student himself at San Jose State College, performed its first *actos* in Delano with farm workers portraying the roles. The Teatro Campesino was eventually taken to the university campus to rally support for the cause. In this early period, the majority of Chicano artistic production appeared as broadsides and chapbooks or in local journals and alternative newspapers. One of the better-known journals, *El Malcriado* (literally "uncivil"), allied with the Delano farm workers, published short stories and traditional poetic pieces. Chicano artists and writers chose public forms of expression. Much of this literature was enjoyed in an oral, communal setting. These community readings endure today. As in one of the founding poems of Chicano literature, "El Louie" by José Montoya, a new pride in the language was reflected by writers who have continually returned to the lived speech act to capture in print the oral quality of Chicano Spanish and English vernaculars. Following Mexican artistic traditions from pre-Columbian art to the muralists Orozco, Siquieros, and Rivera, artists chose for murals and posters easily recognizable icons—the *mestizo* or *campesino*, the *pachuco*, religious figures, and Mexican revolutionaries—to reflect a new ethnic militancy.

By the end of the decade three key events would give cohesion to Chicano literary studies. These were the first National Chicano Youth Conference held by the Denver Crusade for Justice, where an ideology for the movement was formulated, the gathering of intellectuals at the Santa Barbara campus of the University of California, whose goal was to formulate a master plan for Chicano studies, and the establishment in Berkeley, California of the first Chicano publishing house.

As in the case of the farm workers' strike, the leaders for these events made effective use of a rhetoric borrowed from Mexican traditions. The Plan Espiritual de Aztlán, which was drafted in March 1969, was the crucial document for defining a Chicano brand of cultural nationalism or Chicanismo.[20] The plan was a recognition of a history of exploitation, a call for collective action to redress social injustice, and an affirmation of a *mestizo* cultural identity. Referring for the first time to the Southwest as Aztlán (in Aztec myth the northern point of origin for the Aztecs in their journey to central Mexico), Chicanos stressed their Native American roots. Whatever ambiguities had been present in Mexican-American literary characterization prior to the 1960s were politically solved by the idea that Chicanos were no longer foreigners but part of a border region that had served as a centuries-old crossroads between what is now the Southwest and Mexico.

Prior to the meeting in Denver, California university students had taken the lead in the development of Chicano studies. In response to student demands, administrators at California State College, Los Angeles, had agreed to the first department of Mexican American studies in 1968. Although some centers were already in existence by the end of 1968, the Chicano Coordinating Committee on Higher Education in California consisting of student leaders, faculty, staff called for a statewide three-day conference in April 1969 at UC-Santa Barbara to develop a coordinated plan for Chicano access to higher education. The meeting was restricted to one hundred participants. Twenty-nine campuses sent two official student representatives. The other forty-two were faculty, or university staff and community activists involved in educational programs in Chicano communities. Topics in workshops included recruitment, support programs, funding and legislation, Chicano studies curricula, and the institutionalization of Chicano studies programs.

For conference participants, Chicano studies programs, as the institutional arm of the movement, would play an important role in the recruitment of Chicano faculty and administrators, the development of curricular programs pertinent to the Mexican-American experience, the coordination of student services such as the Equal Opportunity Program (EOP), and the establishment of centers with research and publication components as well as cultural and community action programs. The meeting also produced the umbrella organization, El Movimiento Estudiantil Chicano de Aztlán (MEChA), for virtually every student organization across the nation. Later that same year, in October, the Chicano Master Plan was published in a

155-page document as *"El Plan de Santa Bárbara."*[21] In general, the plan called for an alternative ideological framework as a means of recapturing our own image with less emphasis on the way that the culture had interacted with Anglo-American institutions. A rhetoric of authenticity and cultural nationalism replaced the Anglo-American ideals of the melting pot and assimilation.

Two Berkeley academicians, Octavio I. Romano-V. (behaviorial sciences) and Herminio Ríos-C. (comparative literature), independent of their institutional affiliations, founded Quinto Sol Publications in 1967 and began publishing *El Grito: A Journal of Contemporary Mexican-American Thought,* the first journal of Chicano writing, followed in 1969 by *El Espjeo/The Mirror,* the first anthology of Chicano literature. The latter event has prompted many to say, in good humor, that we had an anthology before we had a literature. On a more serious note, however, these events reveal that the development of a literature is never a natural process. Literatures, of course, have their institutional histories growing and developing through the efforts of committed individuals. Certainly, the American literary anthologies and the canon itself from which Chicana and Chicano writers are excluded are defined by aesthetic as well as political choices within the institutions of "higher learning."

The founding of Quinto Sol Publications (named after the present age, the fifth sun, in Meso-American culture) would be decisive not only of the way that Chicano literature would develop in themes and forms but also in establishing a canon. This early history of the literature may never be written, but regardless of the rationale for selection, the narrative works published in 1971, 1972, and 1973 are still widely read. In 1969 Quinto Sol announced the First Annual Premio Quinto Sol. Of the manuscripts received in 1970, the editors elected to award the first prize to ". . .y no se lo tragó la tierra" /" . . . And the Earth Did Not Part," a novel/short story collection written in Spanish by Tomás Rivera, a professor of Spanish, influenced by the Mexican writer Juan Rulfo. After the publication of this work in August 1971 in a bilingual edition, critics could no longer question the existence of Chicano literature.

For me, this slim volume (less than one hundred pages in each language) combining both short story and novel forms ranks with the most highly advertised works of the worldwide 1960s explosion in Third World literature. Written in a Chicano Spanish vernacular rich in nuances, the narrative retells in their own voices the experiences of Texas migrant farm workers in their travels throughout the Midwest. Enriching the individual characterization of the novel with a multiplicity of voices, Rivera portrays a young anonymous protagonist and the ways in which his community's problems lead him, through acts of individual rebellion, away from a centuries-old Mexican colonial mentality to a new historical awareness. Moreover, Rivera forced readers to travel along with the protagonists in a shifting narrative composed of fourteen stories and thirteen vignettes. The narrative was also emblematic of a shift from oral traditions to Chicano print culture, from the exemplary tale to the novel. Assuming the stance of an oral poet in the ending frame piece, the artist Rivera allows the individual consciousness of his protagonist to recede into the background as the collective voices of the narrative return to speak through him.

There is still some question about the editors' reordering of the "original" manuscript (an act worthy of theoretical consideration), so I will conclude that both Quinto Sol and Rivera were right on target in capturing the utopian feelings already present in the Chicano movement. Within a wider comparative context, Rivera effected a deconstruction of the subject, not toward the nihilism of recent theory but toward what should be termed a Third World postmodernist, postindividualistic narrative.

The two following works to receive the Quinto Sol prize, Rudolfo A. Anaya's *Bless Me, Ultima* and Rolando Hinojosa's *Estampas del valle y otras obras* (*The Valley* is the English version), published respectively in 1972 and 1973, showed clearly that Quinto Sol was effectively pursuing a distinct version of Chicano culture, one tied to the soil (migrant workers, farmers, or ranchers) in isolated but well-established rural communities. Readers would find in Anaya's New Mexico of the 1940s and Hinojosa's Rio Grande Valley that although change was evident in the culture, there were also some irreplaceable elements from older Mexican-*mestizo* traditions. And, indeed, the culture was radically changing as the 1970s arrived, for henceforth Chicano writers would benefit, as no Mexican-American writers had before, from a small but growing group of academic readers whose dominant language would be English. Rivera would cease writing and pursue a career as a university administrator (at his death in 1984 he held the position of chancellor at the University of California at Riverside), but Anaya and Hinojosa would continue writing into the 1980s as the most prolific writers in Chicano literature.

Despite the Quinto Sol bias for their own brand of Chicano literature, this publishing house had made it possible almost overnight for many unknown Mexican-Americans, who had dedicated their careers to writing, to find outlets for their work. The 1970s witnessed non-Chicano presses publishing two important writers of the California urban scene, Oscar Zeta Acosta and Ron Arias.

Acosta's two autobiographical books, *The Autobiography of a Brown Buffalo* (1972) and *The Revolt of the Cockroach People* (1973) published by Straight Arrow Books of *Rolling Stone* magazine are radical, self-indulgent, digressive, and hallucinogenic satires belonging as much to Chicano literature as to the general counterculture movements of the 1960s.[22] In the first book, San Francisco's neighborhoods, divided among ethnic and marginal groups, serve as backdrops for Acosta's rejection of the American solution to ethnicity, the melting pot, and the acceptance of his Chicano identity. The second chronicles his involvement with Chicano activists in east Los Angeles and his battles with the California judicial system.

Part humor, part invective, and part politics, the books mirror in rich detail Acosta's own outrageous life-style. Indeed, he was a crazy, suicidal, larger-than-life figure—a practicing lawyer, activist, and self-proclaimed terrorist who once almost set fire to a judge's house in Santa Monica, California. He also ran for sheriff of Los Angeles County as a candidate of the Raza Unida party. He scribbled his last will and testament as well as the plot for his next but never-to-be-published book, *The Rise and Fall of General Zeta*, from the University of Southern California hospital, and disappeared in Mexico sometime in 1974. Acosta's friend and partner in crime, Hunter S. Thompson, who fictionalized him as the Samoan in *Fear and Loathing in Las Vegas*, wrote a fitting eulogy ("The Banshee Screams for Buffalo Meat") in the tenth anniversary issue of *Rolling Stone*. Acosta has not received his due from Chicano and non-Chicano critics, and should be given credit along with Thompson, for creating "gonzo" journalism, a 1960s surrealism mixing politics and aesthetics, written under "fire and drugs." Despite the efforts of Acosta's son, Marco, *Autobiography of a Brown Buffalo* and *The Revolt of the Cockroach People* remained out of print until Vintage Books reissued them in 1989. These books make a valuable addition to an American studies course on 1960s culture.

The publication of Ron Arias' *The Road to Tamazunchale* in 1975 by the West Coast Poetry Review was heralded as a breakthrough in Chicano fiction. It was a whimsical and satirical view of Mexican culture's obsession with death that revealed the influence of Latin American magical realism. Arias had been a reader of Latin American writers prior to their commercialization in the United States. As a traveler and journalist in South America, he had read García Márquez' *One Hundred Years of Solitude* immediately after its publication in

1967; prior to that, in Buenos Aires, he had attended a course on British literature taught by Jorge Luis Borges. Like much Latin American fiction, Arias' book is about borders—borders between the real and imagined, between what is and could be. He brought the simultaneity of various historical planes to his story of the former Spanish settlement of Nuestra Señora la Reina de Los Angeles, Alta California. This place name, as well as the real Elysian Park and Los Feliz (the happy ones) Theatre, served as worldly planes on which could be superimposed otherworldly and outrageous but socially critical events such as the border crossing at Tijuana of an army of "wetbacks" who make their way through the promised land of Anglo-America by playing dead.

Arias' book was evidence that a cross-fertilization between Chicano and Latin American creative artists was emerging. To be sure, the Teatro Campesino's revival of an earlier form of a Mexican itinerant tent theater occasioned a similar phenomenon in Mexico's urban scene, refocusing the public's attention from middle-class bourgeois theater to street performances. And the most popular poet of this early period, Alurista, born in Mexico City, enriched his original use of code-switching between English and Spanish with Meso-American symbols and motifs. But perhaps the major literary event of the 1970s was the awarding in 1976 of the Cuban *Casa de las Américas* International prize for Novel to Rolando Hinojosa's *Klail City y sus alrededores*.[23] The jury for the prize was composed of some very well-known Latin American writers, including Juan Carlos Onetti of Uruguay. Unbeknownst to the American literary academy, Chicano literature had received the most prestigious prize in Latin American literature and had unquestionably arrived on the international scene.

The *Casa de las Américas* journal and press, as most Latin American scholars and Chicanos have known for some time and as Anglo-American Marxists are beginning to discover, has been the dominant voice for Marxism in the Americas. As an institutional arm of the Cuban Revolution, *Casa de las Américas*, under the direction of Roberto Fernández-Retamar, had been waging, through its publications, festivals, and prizes, a cultural struggle against North American imperialism since the 1960s. As the trend toward conservative literary studies in this country was spurred on by Jacques Derrida, Paul de Man, J. Hillis Miller, and the deconstructionist movement, Chicano scholars found in Fernández-Retamar's now classic 1971 article, "Calibán: Apuntes sobre la cultura en nuestra América" (Caliban: Notes Toward a Discussion of Culture in Our America),[24] a source for widening their intellectual horizons to encompass all *mestizo* cultures of our Americas. Henceforth Caliban would serve not as the inarticulate half-man, half-monster envisioned by Shakespeare but as a representative of the slaves who resist oppression using their master's language.

The influence of Fernández-Retamar was felt in one of the first important articles on Chicano culture, "On Culture," authored by Juan Gómez-Quiñones.[25] After making a survey of Mexican and border culture, this Chicano historian turned to the role of the intellectual in social struggles. Against a "lumpen destructive anti-intellectual bias" still evident in Chicano thought and writing, Gómez-Quiñones reaffirmed the importance, for a culture under domination, of the intellectual as a source of resistance against ideological hegemony. Echoing the Cuban scholar's call for a union between Caliban and Ariel, the figure of the native slave-turned-intellectual in defense of the culture, Gómez-Quiñones urged fellow Chicano intellectuals to return to the source—to Mexican and Latin American history, knowledge, writing, and art—and ally themselves with workers' struggles. To this day a spirit of cooperation exists between *Casa de las Américas* and Chicano intellectuals, many of whom have traveled or studied in Cuba. Like Hinojosa, other Chicano works would receive awards from *Casa*, including, most recently, Cheech Marín's film "Born in East L.A."

By the mid-1970s no one could question the existence of Chicano literature, but what about its criticism? To the two or three original Chicano studies courses (usually in history, sociology, or political science) taught by graduate students or instructors were added courses in literature taught by assistant professors housed in either departments of English or Spanish, depending upon administrative decisions. Because these courses were demanded by students, departmental administrators did not receive these appointments with open arms. However, I am still amazed at the growth of Chicano literary studies, for almost overnight critics emerged in campuses not only in the West and Southwest, but also in the Midwest, at the University of Indiana, where the *Revista Chicano-Riqueña* was founded by Luis Dávila and Nick Kanellos, and even at Yale, where Chicano literature was taught first by Ramón Saldívar (as a graduate student) and then by Juan Bruce-Novoa and me (at the level of assistant and associate professors).

Like individual university departments, the national academy was puzzled about what to do with Chicano literature. Articles written in Spanish appeared in the Latin American section of the MLA bibliography; those in English appeared in the American section. The MLA solved this language issue by conferring discussion group status on

Chicano literature as a subform of American literature. The many sessions that Rolando Hinojosa almost singlehandedly organized for the 1979 San Francisco meeting of the MLA National Convention were proof of the healthy status of Chicano literary criticism.

In the early 1970s, two important strains of criticism emerged—historicist and formalist. Without a readily available context for Chicano literature, the logical direction in which to look for some affirmation of a tradition was toward Mexico. Early critics, to their dismay, tried to pursue a Chicano viewpoint in the work of the Mexicans José Vasconcelos, Octavio Paz, and Carlos Fuentes. Beyond some musings on *pochos* and *pachucos*, Mexican writing did not offer much for Chicanos. For many critics, however, the founding article on Chicano literature was authored by the well-known Mexicanist scholar Luis Leal,[26] who supplied the periodization and the necessary historical documentation for an uninterrupted tradition of Chicano literature that descended from Spanish chroniclers of the Southwest. In this early Mexicanist viewpoint that Leal has repeated on other occasions, he emphasized that Chicano literature had derived its forms, both popular and erudite, and its spirit of rebellion from Mexican literature. Stressing writers in English, Raymund Paredes also wrote a brief history of the literature.[27]

While I value this scholarship and understand the need to establish legitimacy for Chicano literature, I am troubled by its idealist notions of history as well as those of literary traditions and genres. How many Chicano writers, for example, can trace their writing directly back to the Spanish chroniclers? Shouldn't we also read these accounts in their original context as military dispatches of the conquest, the Spanish *relación*, and not as modern imaginative literature that did not gain ascendancy until the late sixteenth and early seventeenth centuries? Future studies, some already underway by Genaro Padilla, Rosaura Sánchez, and Lauro Flores,[28] will concentrate on the institutional, ideological, and artistic affiliations of the literatures of the Southwest. Américo Paredes' study of the border ballad is still the best example of a reinterpretation of an earlier historical moment in order to make it meaningful for Chicanos.

Juan Bruce-Novoa of Yale established himself in 1975 as the leader in Chicano literary theory with his "The Space of Chicano Literature."[29] Borrowing from Mircea Eliade, Georges Bataille, and the Mexican writers Juan García Ponce and Octavio Paz, Bruce-Novoa displayed an independence from Anglo-American theorists, especially those at Yale. Yet his thought was in some ways a return to the mystification and myth criticism of the late 1960s. Bruce-Novoa conceived of writer and literature as existing outside of society and politics; this space of Chicano literature was sacred and inviolable. Bruce-Novoa, however, has always been a strong promoter of Chicano literature. Tired of the neglect of Chicano literary studies by Americanists in this country, he was a cofounder of the Association pour la Diffusion et l'Etude des Cultures Latines en Amérique du Nord, and should be partly credited with arousing the international interest that now exists in Chicano literature.

Throughout its brief history, Chicano studies, to the detriment of literary studies, has been confined largely to history and the social sciences. These fields have received more press coverage than has the study of Chicano literature and some scholars have been published by prestigious eastern publishers. In the annual meetings of the National Association of Chicano Studies (NACS), literature was treated as some poor relation that had to be invited. However, two recent phenomena have placed Chicano literature and criticism at the forefront of Chicano studies. One was the almost star status and attention given to younger writers, most of them women, and the other was the maturing of Chicano literary criticism to rival not only the literature but also the allied fields in Chicano studies.

Arte Público Press of Houston and Bilingual Press/Editorial Bilingüe of Tempe, Arizona should be given credit for the expansion of the literary canon. Under the direction of Nicolás Kanellos and Gary D. Keller, respectively, these presses have not only taken the lead in publishing early writers like Rolando Hinojosa, but they have also made a concerted effort to seek out and publish Chicana writers.

Indeed, a series of talented feminist writers in drama, poetry, and narrative has emerged in the 1980s, including Gloria Anzaldúa (*Borderlands/La Frontera: The New Mestiza*), Ana Castillo (*The Mixquiahuala Letters*), Lorna Dee Cervantes (*Emplumada*), Denise Chávez (*The Last of the Menu Girls*), Sandra Cisneros (*The House on Mango Street*), Pat Mora (*Chants*), Cherríe Moraga (*Loving in the War Years, Giving Up the Ghost*), Cecile Pineda (*Face*), Gina Valdés (*There Are No Madmen Here*), Evangelina Vigil (*Thirty an' Seen a Lot*), and Helena María Viramontes (*The Moths and Other Stories*); these writers have taken center stage, displacing older patriarchal problematics and realigning the field once again with Third World struggles.[30] But the accomplishments of men should not be forgotten: Gary Soto (*The Elements of San Joaquin*) was the recipient of the United States Award of the International Poetry Forum, and Alberto Alvaro Rios (*The Iguana Killer*) received the Western States Book Award for

Short Fiction.[31] In addition, Rolando Hinojosa's fragmented chronicle of the mythical Belken County, now in its seventh book, has turned out to be nothing less than the complete history of the Río Grande Valley from Spanish and Mexican ranching in the eighteenth and nineteenth centuries to the large-scale farming and migrant worker culture of this century.[32]

Two writers, Cherríe Moraga and Gloria Anzaldúa, deserve further comments for their creative and critical revitalization of Chicano literature. Like other Chicana writers, both gained their sustenance from the history of women's resistance and rebellion. However, both Moraga and Anzaldúa gained prominence outside of the traditional patriarchal politics of the Chicano movement, in feminist-lesbian circles, and should be credited with the advancement of the Chicana or a woman-of-color point of view through their editorial work in *This Bridge Called My Back: Writings by Radical Women of Color* and their autobiographies.[33] The solutions to the problems of gender and sexuality led both writers to an awareness that problems of race and class could not be overcome by working within Anglo-American feminism. Multiple oppressions separated them from their white sisters and aligned them not only with Chicanas but with all Third World women. In her foreword to the second edition of *Bridge*, Moraga confessed that another *Bridge* would deal less with the relations between women and concentrate on the relations between men and women of color. Anzaldúa's *Borderlands* has fulfilled these expectations, for it begins with the history of the Río Grande Valley where Paredes and Hinojosa had left off. She offers a new historical and metaphorical vision of border crossings with an eye to the plight of her mother, the Mexican woman worker, at the *maquiladoras* along the border, and the "illegitamate" *mestizas* and *mestizos*, whether they be Chicana, Native American, black, gay, or lesbian.

The growth of Chicano literary criticism in the 1980s, increasingly utilizing the methodology of critical and cultural studies, is due both to an internal development as well as to the boom in European and Anglo-American literary theory. In this decade, men and women who had entered graduate schools in the 1970s have expanded the field with theoretical issues of representation, ideology, and subjectivity bolstered first by the writings of Lukács and later by the work of Althusser, Bakhtin, Gramsci, Raymond Williams, Fredric Jameson, Edward Said, and Terry Eagleton. This trend away from an historicist or Mexicanist perspective to one of historical materialism, which seems to have become dominant in Chicano literary criticism, was previewed by two often-mentioned articles of the late 1970s, Joseph

Sommers' "From the Critical Premise to the Product: Critical Modes and Their Application to a Chicano Literary Text" and Ramón Saldívar's "A Dialectic of Difference: Towards a Theory of the Chicano Novel."[34] Besides displaying the critical rigor of recent literary theory, both articles were also a commentary on the field.

By 1988, Chicano literary studies had unfolded in ways unforeseen in the early years, with Chicano critics reaching out to forge institutional affiliations with friendly scholars. Recent sessions organized by Chicana and Chicano scholars at the national MLA conventions have included Paul Lauter joining panelists to discuss the literary canon; Barbara Harlow discussing Chicana literature in a comparative context; and a session devoted to the work of Fredric Jameson and Chicano literature. In 1987 French Afro-Americanist Geneviève Fabre and Harvard Americanist Werner Sollors respectively chaired and moderated a conference at the Sorbonne on the representation of history in Latino discourse. Increasingly Chicana and Chicano critics are publishing their work in Spanish and English mainstream journals.

To the list of the early critical pioneers should be added the names of Rosaura Sánchez, whose work on nineteenth-century writings by California upper-class Hispanas will shed new light on that period; José David Saldívar, author of several important pieces and editor of the most outstanding critical anthology to date, *The Rolando Hinojosa Reader*; Norma Alarcón, promoter of women's literature and founder and editor of the *Third Woman* journal and press; Angie Chabram ("Conceptualizing Chicano Critical Discourse"), whose interviews with selected critics will document the institutional history of Chicano literary criticism; and my own work on narrative genres ("To Read Chicano Narrative: Commentary and Metacommentary").[35]

Would recent publications like *The Politics of Interpretation, Marxism and the Interpretation of Culture*, and *"Race," Writing, and Difference* be altered in any significant way if Chicano literature or critics had been included?[36] What would American studies as practiced in this country be like if it actually encompassed the entire hemisphere, both North and South, as well as Chicano culture. Would "real" comparative studies of world literatures, including Chicano literature, show that theories of the dominant literature would be altered by new emergent literatures? What problems of class, race, and gender evident in Chicana literature have been ignored by Anglo-American feminists? These are some of the questions that Chicana, Chicano, and non-Chicano scholars will be asking. Some recent Chicano scholarship—work on Chicano literature and the canon, Chicano narrative

and Western genres, the institutional role of Cuba in ethnic literatures of the Americas, Chicana literature in the light of Third World
feminism—is heading in that direction. And Barbara Harlow may,
indeed, be paving the way for what a non-Chicano comparative analysis should look like with her recent study of Chicana writers, workers, and prisoners in the context of South Africa and Palestine.[37]

Despite these and other potential contributions to literary studies
in this country, Americanists have continued to ignore Chicano writers and scholars. For example, readers will find little or nothing on
the problems posed by the persistence of Chicano and Mexican cultures throughout the West, Southwest, and Midwest (Chicago and
Detroit) for the traditional model of "American" culture within the
United States in Sacvan Bercovitch's *Reconstructing American Literary
History* and *Ideology and Classic American Literature*.[38] In the case of
Bercovitch's studies (see also his *American Jeremiad*),[39] if one does not
shed a former cultural identity for the "American" ideological consensus model, then, as Ramón Saldívar has noted,[40] writers can suffer
exclusion from the American literary canon. Equally negligent have
been North American scholars of Spanish-American literature in their
attempts to portray multinational perspectives. Editors Bell Gale
Chevigny and Gari Laguardia, in their introduction to *Reinventing the
Americas: Comparative Studies of Literature of the United States and
Spanish America*, express and regret their failure to deal with the increasing number of writers of Hispanic background who write in
English or with the extraordinary re-Hispanicization of United States
culture.[41]

In the future, Chicano literary studies will face challenges arising
from its own evolution as well as from recent historical changes.
Through the two decades of its existence, Chicano literary discourse,
both creative and critical, has reflected the interests of a largely homogeneous group born in the struggle for equal economic and social
participation. Some of these early goals have been realized with the
emergence of a middle class. Regardless of the ethnic and cultural
affiliations formed (although I doubt that many will seek the road of
assimilation, as Richard Rodriguez has), this phenomenon represents
a departure from the peasant and working-class origins of the movement. A parallel change is the advancement of Chicano critics to the
level of tenured professors and office holding members of the academy. As we go about the business of our profession, are we to be distanced from those who nurtured us, both personally and politically?[42]
I hope not. For it should be the role of the intellectual as well as of
other committed individuals to continue to point out that although

some "have made it," the disparity between the privileged and underprivileged in this country—including Chicanos, Mexican-Americans (the term is resurfacing), and millions of Mexicans and other Latino groups—has never been greater.

We are also witnessing dramatic demographic changes in the West, Southwest, and northern Mexico that will play a decisive role in determining the future of Chicano studies. Since the 1950s (for a little over thirty years) the population of major Mexican border towns from Tijuana, on the Pacific Ocean, to Matamoros, on the Gulf of Mexico, has more than quadrupled. Many Mexican men and women are flocking to Mexican border cities to work for U.S. companies. Because of the U.S. cultural or economic influence in Mexico or because of northward migrations, we are now hearing from a frank Mexican historian that every Mexican national is a potential Chicano. A similar phenomenon is occurring on the northern side of the border. California, for example, we are being told, is fast becoming a Third World state; soon after the year 2000 the Anglo population will be reaching minority status. If current population trends and birth rates continue, California will experience a complete reversal from its 1945 ratio of whites to nonwhites. Thus, a centuries-old border culture with new social and economic realities extending from San Francisco in the West and Chicago in the Midwest to the northern states of Mexico reasserts itself on the U.S. national scene.

There exists, however, the real possibility that some regions of this country, especially in the case of California, like other Third World countries in Latin America and, indeed, South Africa, will be composed of a ruling minority and an underprivileged majority. One hopes that we will see a narrowing of the gap between professional duties and public involvement as Chicano intellectuals, institutions, and associations (an assertive NACS) reflect the interests of an emerging domestic Third World majority and defend any threat to its rightful political power. A revitalized Chicano movement, without the rhetoric of authenticity and cultural nationalism, should return to its original unfilfilled goals of economic and social justice and equal access to higher education—this time around, one hopes, with more political clout and know-how. And Chicano studies, now without the stigma of minority status, should assume a greater role in a university curriculum sensitive to Third World cultures. As Gómez-Quiñones once indicated, we should work toward a Chicano cultural literacy (including Mexican- and Latin American intellectual traditions), this time for all university students.

Given our present historical juncture—a shrinking hemisphere, the rapid influx of Third World immigrants, and the increasingly multicultural nature of this country—we can no longer ignore the centuries-old Mexican-*mestizo* presence in the Southwest. Any future models of American culture or reconstructions of American literary history that fail to take into account this historical fact will of necessity be incomplete.

## Glossary

BRACERO: one who "lends an arm," or a peon. The word is commonly used to refer to Mexican nationals contracted in large numbers by the U.S. government to work as farm laborers during World War II. The program lasted from 1942 to 1964. The word is now used to refer to anyone crossing the U.S.-Mexico border to work as a farm laborer.

CORRIDO: A traditional ballad originally sung in Spanish, usually by men, which had as its theme the exploits of legendary heroes. These ballads, in eight-syllable quatrains, were first sung during the latter half of the nineteenth century in the Río Grande Valley, and must have developed out of the Spanish ballad tradition brought to the Americas from Europe.

MAQUILADORA: Derived from *maquila*; both terms refer to an assembly plant established under the Border Industrial Program, whose goal was to stabilize the Mexican border economy. Established in 1968 the program called for American manufacturers to construct plants in Mexico in which American products would be assembled by Mexican nationals and then shipped back into the United States. Over 75% of workers at these plants are women, and are also referred to as *maquiladoras*.

PACHUCO: Refers to Mexican-American youths who formed their own subculture of resistance complete with manners, style, dress, and language as a response to both Mexican and Anglo-American cultures. Also known as "zoot-suiters," this group originated in the barrios of El Paso, Texas in the early 1940s and spread throughout the metropolitan centers and rural communities of the Southwest.

POCHO: A Spanish term originally meaning faded or discolored. The term, since the second decade of this century until the Chicano movement of the 1960s, was used by Mexican nationals to describe a Mexican "Americanized" in manners, dress, and language. Although being a *pocho* was a middle-class phenomenon, anyone who had "airs" of being superior because of acculturation to Anglo-American ways was called a *pocho* by Mexican-Americans and Chicanos.

RELACIÓN: A Spanish narrative genre derived from the Spanish *relato*, meaning case, account, or narrative. This is the form that the early chronicles of the Americas assumed in order to establish historical veracity through an eye witness account. The *relación* was also, in fact, a legal document, a form of deposition or notarized statement, upon which rested the colonial bureaucracy after the conquest.

VAQUERO: Literally, cowboy. The term refers to a Spanish and Mexican-*mestizo* way of life that emerged after the Spanish conquest. Although ranchers and horsemen were prevalent throughout the Southwest, they played a particularly crucial role in the pastoral economy of California, New Mexico, and Texas.

### Endnotes

1. Gloria Anzaldúa, *Borderlands/La Frontera: The New Mestiza* (San Francisco, Calif.: Spinsters/Aunt Lute, 1987) p. 8.
2. Luis Leal, "Literary Criticism and Minority Literatures: The Case of the Chicano Writer," *Confluencia* (1986), 1(2):4–9.
3. Norma Alarcón, "The Theoretical Subject(s) of *This Bridge Called My Back* and Anglo-American Feminism," in Héctor Calderón and José David Saldívar, eds., *Chicano Literary Criticism: New Studies in Culture and Ideology* (forthcoming) Duke University Press.
4. Charles F. Lummis, *The Land of Poco Tiempo* (New York: Scribner's, 1893); Charles F. Lummis, *A New Mexico David and Other Stories and Sketches of the Southwest* (New York: Scribner's, 1891).
5. Aurelio Espinoza, "Romancero Nuevomejicano," *Revue Hispanique* (1915), 33(84):446–560; (1917), 40(97):215–27; (1917), 41(100):678–80.
6. Arthur L. Campa, "The Spanish Folksong in the Southwest," *University of New Mexico Bulletin* (1933), vol. 4, no. 2.
7. J. Frank Dobie, *The Flavor of Texas* (Dallas, Tex.: Dealy and Lowe, 1936).
8. Américo Paredes, "The Folk Base of Chicano Literature," in Joseph Sommers and Tomás Ybarra-Frausto, eds., *Modern Chicano Writers: A Collection of Critical Essays* (Englewood Cliffs, N.J.: Prentice-Hall, 1979), pp. 4–17; Américo Paredes, *"With His Pistol in His Hand": A Border Ballad and Its Hero* (Austin: University of Texas Press, 1958).
9. Raymund D. Paredes, "The Evolution of Chicano Literature," *MELUS* (1978), 5:71–110, reprinted in Houston Baker, Jr., ed., *Three American Literatures: Essays in Chicano, Native American, and Asian-American Literature for Teachers of American Literature* (New York: Modern Language Association, 1982), pp. 33–79; Raymund D. Paredes, "Mexican American Authors and the American Dream," *MELUS* (1981), 8:71–80; Raymund D. Paredes, "The Promise of Chicano Literature," in Dexter Fisher, ed., *Minority Language and Literature: Retrospective and Perspective* (New York: Modern Language Association, 1977), pp. 29–41.
10. Genaro Padilla, "Imprisoned Narrative? Or Lies, Secrets, and Silence in New Mexico Women's Autobiography," in Héctor Calderón and José David

Saldívar, eds., *Chicano Literary Criticism: New Studies in Culture and Ideology* (forthcoming).

11. Mario Suárez, "El Hoyo," "Senor Garza," "Cuco Goes to a Party," "Kid Zopilote," *Arizona Quarterly* (1947), 3(2):112–15, 115–121, 121–127, 130–137, respectively; "Southside Run," "Maestria," *Arizona Quarterly* (1948), 4(4):362–368, 368–373, respectively; "Mexican Heaven" *Arizona Quarterly* (1950), 6(4):310–315. Mexican American writer John Rechy, who is one of the better-known gay novelists in the United States, had an early essayistic, sketch of El Paso, Texas, and should be included along with Suárez as anticipatory of future Chicano themes and forms. See John Rechy, "El Paso del Norte," *Evergreen Review* (1958), 2(6):127–140.

12. Juan Rodríguez, "Notes on the Evolution of Chicano Prose Fiction," in Joseph Sommers and Tomas Ybarra-Frausto, eds., *Modern Chicano Writers: A Collection of Critical Essays* (Englewood Cliffs, N.J.: Prentice-Hall, 1979), pp. 67–73.

13. Carlos Muñoz, Jr., "Galarza: Scholar on the Ramparts," foreword to the Ernesto Galarza Inaugural Commemorative Lecture, presented by Américo Paredes (Stanford, Calif.: Stanford Center for Chicano Research, 1987), np.

14. Ernesto Galarza, *Farm Workers and Agri-Business in California* (Notre Dame, Ind.: University of Notre Dame Press, 1977); Ernesto Galarza, *Merchants of Labor: The Mexican Bracero Story* (Santa Barbara, Calif.: McNally and Loftin, 1964); Ernesto Galarza, *Spiders in the House and Workers in the Field* (Notre Dame, Ind.: University of Notre Dame Press, 1970); Ernesto Galarza, *Barrio Boy* (Notre Dame, Ind.: University of Notre Dame Press, 1971).

15. For more on Paredes, see José E. Limón, "Mexican Ballads, Chicano Epic: History, Social Dramas and Poetic Persuasions," SCCR Working Paper Series No. 14 (Stanford, Calif.: Stanford Center for Chicano Research, 1986); José E. Limón, "The Return of the Mexican Ballad: Américo Paredes and His Anthropological Text as Persuasive Political Performance," SCCR Working Paper Series No. 16 (Stanford, Calif.: Stanford Center for Chicano Research, 1986); and José David Saldívar, "Texas Border Narratives as Cultural Critique," SCCR Working Paper Series No. 19 (Stanford, Calif.: Stanford Center for Chicano Research, 1987).

16. See José David Saldívar, "Texas Border Narratives as Cultural Critique."

17. See Bert Corona, "Chicano Scholars and Public Issues in the United States in the Eighties," in Mario T. Garcia et al., eds., *History, Culture, and Society: Chicano Studies in the 1980s* (Ypsilanti, Mich.: Bilingual Press/ Editorial Bilingüe, 1983), pp. 11–18.

18. See Tomás Ybarra-Frausto, "The Chicano Movement and the Emergence of a Chicano Poetic Consciousness," in Ricardo Romo and Raymund Paredes, eds., *New Directions in Chicano Scholarship* (La Jolla, Calif.: Chicano Studies Program, University of California at San Diego, 1978), pp. 81–109.

19. *Chicano* is a term that has existed in Spanish probably since the conquest of Mexico. It is said to have derived from the shortened form of Mexicano, Xicano, from the Nahuatl language of the Aztecs, who were also known as Mexicas. The present spelling reflects the *sh* fricative or *ch* affricative sounds of Nahuatl, which in sixteenth-century Spanish corresponded to the letter *x*. Prior to the Chicano movement in the United States, the term was used, usually in the diminutive (*chicanito*), by Mexican-Americans to refer to recently

arrived working-class Mexicans. During the 1960s the term was given new ideological resonance by Mexican-American students to refer to their own working-class Mexican-*mestizo* culture and to affirm their Native American roots.

20. See Alurista, "Cultural Nationalism and Xicano Literature During the Decade of 1965–1975," *MELUS* (1981), 8(2):22–34.

21. Chicano Coordinating Council on Higher Education, *El Plan de Santa Bárbara: A Chicano Plan for Higher Education* (Oakland, Calif.: La Causa Publications, 1969).

22. See Héctor Calderón, "To Read Chicano Narrative: Commentary and Metacommentary," *Mester* (1983), 13(2):3–14.

23. Rolando Hinojosa, *Klail City y sus alrededores* (La Habana: Casa de las Américas, 1976). The bilingual edition is *Generaciones y semblanzas* (Berkeley, Calif.: Editorial Justa Publications, 1977); the English edition is *Klail City: A Novel* (Houston: Arte Público Press, 1987).

24. Roberto Fernández-Retamar, "Calibán: Apuntes sobre la cultura en nuestra América," *Casa de las Américas* (1971), 68:124–51. This article was published in English as "Caliban: Notes Towards a Discussion of Culture in Our America," *Massachusetts Review* (1974), 15(1–2):7–72.

25. Juan Gómez-Quiñones, "On Culture," *Revista Chicano-Riqueña* (1977), 5(2):29–47.

26. Luis Leal, "Mexican American Literature: A Historical Perspective," *Revista Chicano-Riqueña* (1973), 1(1):32–44.

27. Paredes, "The Evolution of Chicano Literature."

28. Padilla, "Imprisoned Narrative?"; Rosaura Sánchez is currently writing a book-length study of writing by nineteenth-century California Hispanic women and Lauro Flores is conducting research on Chicano autobiography from the nineteenth to the twentieth century.

29. Juan Bruce-Novoa, "The Space of Chicano Literature," *De Colores* (1975), 1(4):22–42.

30. Anzaldúa, *Borderlands/La Frontera;* Ana Castillo, *The Mixquiahuala Letters* (Binghamton, N.Y.: Bilingual Press/Editorial Bilingüe, 1986); Lorna Dee Cervantes, *Emplumada* (Pittsburgh, Pa.: University of Pittsburgh Press, 1981); Denise Chávez, *The Last of the Menu Girls* (Houston, Tex.: Arte Público Press, 1986); Sandra Cisneros, *The House on Mango Street*, 2d rev. ed. (Houston, Texas: Arte Público Press, 1988); Pat Mora, *Chants* (Houston, Tex.: Arte Público Press, 1984); Cherríe Moraga, *Giving Up the Ghost* (Los Angeles, Calif.: West End Press, 1986); Cecile Pineda, *Face* (New York: Viking Penguin, 1985); Gina Valdés, *There Are No Madmen Here* (San Diego, Calif.: Maize Press, 1981); Evangelina Vigil, *Thirty an' Seen a Lot* (Houston, Tex.: Arte Público Press, 1985); Helena María Viramontes, *The Moths and Other Stories* (Houston, Tex.: Arte Público Press, 1985).

31. Gary Soto, *The Elements of San Joaquin* (Pittsburgh, Pa.: University of Pittsburgh Press, 1979); Alberto Alvaro Rios, *The Iguana Killer: Twelve Tales of the Heart* (New York: Blue Moon/Confluence Press, 1984).

32. Following are the book installments that comprise Hinojosa's The Klail City Death Trip Series: *Estampas del valle y otras obras* (Berkeley: Quinto Sol Publications, 1973), and in Hinojosa's English version *The Valley* (Ypsilanti, Mich.: Bilingual Press/Editoiral Bilingüe, 1983); *Klail City y sus alrededores* (La Habana: Casa de las Américas, 1976), published in a bilingual edition in

the United States as *Generaciones y semblanzas* (Berkeley: Editorial Justa, 1977), and in Hinojosa's English version *Klail City: A Novel* (Houston: Arte Público Press, 1987); *Korean Love Songs* (Berkeley: Editorial Justa, 1978); *Mi querido Rafa* (Houston: Arte Público Press, 1981), and Hinojosa's English version, *Dear Rafe* (Houston: Arte Público Press, 1984); *Rites and Witnesses: A Comedy* (Houston: Arte Público Press, 1982); *Partners in Crime: A Rafe Buenrostro Mystery* (Houston: Arte Público Press, 1985); *Claros varones de Belken/Fair Gentlemen of Belken County* (Tempe, Ariz.: Bilingual Press/Editorial Bilingüe, 1986).

33. Cherríe Moraga and Gloria Anzaldúa, eds., *This Bridge Called My Back: Writings by Radical Women of Color* (New York: Kitchen Table/Women of Color Press, 1983); Gloria Anzaldúa, *Borderlands/La Frontera: The New Mestiza* (San Francisco: Spinsters/Aunt Lute Press, 1987); and Cherríe Moraga, *Loving in the War Years: Lo que nunca pasó por sus labios* (Boston: South End Press, 1983).

34. Joseph Sommers, "From the Critical Premise to the Product: Critical Modes and Their Application to a Chicano Literary Text," *New Scholar* (1977), 6:34–50; Ramón Saldívar, "A Dialectic of Difference: Towards a Theory of the Chicano Novel," *MELUS* (1979), 6(3):73–92.

35. José David Saldívar, ed., *The Rolando Hinojosa Reader: Essays Critical and Historical* (Houston, Tex.: Arte Público Press, 1985); Héctor Calderón, "To Read Chicano Narrative: Commentary and Metacommentary," *Mester* (1983), 13(2):3–14; Angie Chabram, "Conceptualizing Chicano Critical Discourse," in Héctor Calderón and José Saldívar, eds., *Chicano Literary Criticism: New Studies in Culture and Ideology* (forthcoming) Duke University Press. Calderón, "Rudolfo A. Anaya's *Bless Me, Ultima*. A Chicano Romance of the Southwest," *Crítica* (1986), 1(3):21–47.

36. Cary Nelson and Lawrence Grossberg, eds., *Marxism and the Interpretation of Culture* (Chicago: University of Illinois Press, 1988); Henry Louis Gates, Jr., ed., *"Race," Writing, and Difference* (Chicago, University of Chicago Press, 1986); W. J. T. Mitchell, ed., *The Politics of Interpretation* (Chicago: University of Chicago, Press, 1983).

37. Barbara Harlow, "Sites of Struggle: Immigration, Deportation, Prison, and Exile," in Héctor Calderón and José David Saldívar, eds., *Chicano Literary Criticism: New Studies in Culture and Ideology* (forthcoming: Duke University Press).

38. Sacvan Bercovitch, ed., *Ideology and Classic American Literature* (New York: Cambridge University Press, 1986); Sacvan Bercovitch, ed., *Reconstructing American Literary History* (Cambridge, Mass.: Harvard University Press, 1986).

39. Sacvan Bercovitch, *The American Jeremiad* (Madison: University of Wisconsin Press, 1978).

40. Ramón Saldívar, "Narrative, Ideology, and the Reconstruction of American Literary History," in Héctor Calderón and José David Saldívar, eds., *Chicano Literary Criticism: New Studies in Culture and Ideology* (forthcoming: Duke University Press).

41. Bell Gale Chevigny and Gari Laguardia, *Reinventing the Americas: Comparative Studies of Literature of the United States and Spanish America* (New York: Cambridge University Press, 1986).

42. See Sánchez, "Ethnicity, Ideology and Academia."

# 11

# The Third Plane at the Change of the Century: The Shape of African-American Literature To Come

Pancho Savery

*Pancho Savery's article begins by questioning the very fact that in the earlier Lauter and Kampf anthology the "voices" of African-Americans were noticeably missing. He then goes on to present a history of the Harlem Renaissance and the Black Arts movement leading up to what Savery calls the "Third Plane"—a movement that encompasses the years of the late 1960s through the present and that acknowledges the indigenous African-American tradition but is also aware of the pluralistic nature of the larger culture. For Savery these Third Plane writers, such as Ishmael Reed, Toni Morrison, and Albert Murray, to mention a few, have not only produced important works of literature but herald what is to come in African-American literature.*

### Preface[1]

I bought my copy of Kampf and Lauter's *The Politics of Literature* in the fall of 1973. The book was helpful then and it is helpful now. Most significant for me, however, was my own invisibility in its pages. On no level were any of its authors really speaking for me. One of the four white-authored essays that dealt with "black culture" spent half of its text on Tennessee Williams and André Malraux, and came to the not revolutionary conclusion that "oppression [was] not amusing or ironic to those who [were] actually oppressed."[2] While I understood the racist history of African-American exclusion from most anthologies, journals, and classrooms, I expected a great deal more from radicals, and my disappointment with *The Politics of Literature* was acute. It was especially so because the introduction "explained" the absence of any African-American voices from its pages, acknowledging that "it might be asked why there are no essays in this book on black literature or by black writers." Two answers are given. The first is that the "essays we print came out of the collective experience of a group of white literary intellectuals."[3] Why did this collective experience of a group of intellectuals include only white ones? And even if it did, why was African-American literature not on any of their agendas? And even if it wasn't, why couldn't they have decided that it was an issue that needed to be dealt with and found someone to do it for the volume? None of these issues is addressed in the introduction. All we are told (and this is the second reason given) is that "the need during the past years for black radicals to work separately is well known, and has its source in the sharp differences of black and white social experience in the United States."[4] "Black radicals need to work separately; therefore, African-American literature can be ignored" is, to me, an unacceptable equation, as is, "Black and white social differences exist; therefore, African-American literature can be ignored." Rather than constituting justifiable reasons for the exclusion of African-Americans, this sounds to me like more of the same old thing. And whose formulations were these anyway? Did the editors make a serious attempt to have African-Americans included in the volume and were told these things by black radicals who were unwilling to participate? Or did they just come to these conclusions on their own? There is no way of knowing, since the introduction passes over the issue so quickly. Given the mood of the times—after the deaths of Malcom X, Martin Luther King, Mark Clark, Fred Hampton, and George Jackson, not to mention the presence of the Black Power movement and the attempt at articulating a black aesthetic—it would have been understandable if black radicals had expressed reluctance to participate in a largely white enterprise. But again, had an attempt to include them been made and proved fruitless, it is reasonable to assume that this would have been mentioned in the introduction.

I am left with two questions. Was *The Politics of Literature* seriously flawed, and because of that an updated version is long overdue; or did it largely reflect its time but fail to transcend its historical moment, and now a new edition is needed because times have changed? In either case, I am pleased that *The Politics of Literature* is being revised, and revised in such a way that it is no longer colorless. What follows is a brief history of the two great cultural explosions in African-American history, the Harlem Renaissance and the Black Arts movement, and a discussion of the writers of the Third Plane, writers who have come to prominence since the late 1960s.

Writing fifty years ago in his classic of literary criticism *To Make a Poet Black*, Saunders Redding pointed out that two problems plagued African-American literature. On the one hand was the desire of black people to "adjust . . . to the American environment." This created what Redding called a "literature of necessity," motivated by ends. On the other hand was the motivation of means. African-American writers were plagued by what DuBois called in *The Souls of Black Folk* "this double-consciousness." In Redding's words, "if they wished to succeed they have been obliged to satisfy two different (and opposed when not entirely opposite) audiences, the black and the white."[5] Until very recently, Redding's outline has remained true. African-American writers have been pushed and pulled, and the result has been that consistent quality has been rare. In *To Make a Poet Black* and in subsequent works Redding praises a very small number of writers working before the 1940s. Chief among these are Sterling Brown, James Weldon Johnson, Langston Hughes, Jean Toomer, and Zora Neale Hurston. What unites these writers is an "acknowledgment of their debt to the folk material."[6]

Although all these writers are associated with the Harlem Renaissance, the first major explosion of African-American creativity, it would be a mistake to place too much emphasis on this fact. While it was a period of great artistic production, it also needs to be pointed out that Hurston's work in folk material was not her most popular; *Cane* quickly disappeared after two small printings, Brown's second book of poetry was rejected by publishers, and Hughes was often criticized because his folk portrayals did not present the best possible image of blacks to white readers. The sonnets of Claude McKay, and what Redding calls the "effete and bloodless" poetry of Countee Cullen,[7] are just as representative of the Harlem Renaissance as a literary period. Not only was the period characterized by the need to prove the humanity of black America to white America through art; but when white America lost its interest in black America, the movement died. And both Hughes and Hurston had notable battles with white literary patrons about what was suitable to publish.

If the writers of the Harlem Renaissance went too far in the direction of trying to please whites, the writers of the Black Arts/Black

Aesthetic movement, or what is sometimes referred to as the "Second Renaissance," went too far in trying to exorcise any white or Western influence from their work. In Sigmund Ro's words, what was sought was "a new imaginative order purged of oppressive white influence" and "a dissociation of black America from the cultures of the First and Second Worlds and a reinterpretation of the racial experience."[8] If the earlier writers went too far in saying that there was no African-American literary tradition, the later writers went too far in saying there was only a black African tradition, and that writers who did not exemplify this in their work, Baldwin and Ellison in particular, were to be rejected. To quote Ro again, "the task was that of grafting the black American's soul, as seen through the vistas of nearly four hundred years, onto the tree of his African brother's *negritude* in a shared synthesis of consciousness and sensibility."[9] Not only did politics come before art—a work of literature had to directly aid the revolution or else it was useless—but any concern with form, technique, or craft was seen as a clear sign of reactionary backwardness. In "Black Cultural Nationalism" Ron Karenga declared that "all our art must contribute to revolutionary change and if it does not, it is invalid."[10] And in "The Literature of Black," Carolyn Rodgers connected punctuation and colonialism: "To start sentences with capitals, to end sentences with periods/to use commas etc etc etc reeks of . . . the colonizers' language, correctness, learnedness and a subtler more destructive order."[11]

In addition, there was a clear lack of historical sense about the African-American folk past. This can be seen in LeRoi Jones/Amiri Baraka's *Dutchman*, where Clay asserts:

> Charlie Parker? Charlie Parker. All the hip white boys scream for Bird. And Bird saying, "Up your ass, feeble-minded ofay! Up your ass." And they sit there talking about the tortured genius of Charlie Parker. Bird would've played not a note of music if he just walked up to East Sixty-Seventh Street and killed the first ten white people he saw. Not a note! . . . If Bessie Smith had killed some white people she wouldn't have needed that music. She could have talked very straight and plain about the world. No metaphors. No grunts. No wiggles in the dark of her soul . . . Crazy niggers turning their backs on sanity. When all it needs is that simple act. Murder. Just murder! Would make us all sane.[12]

African-American folk expression is a great deal more than merely a substitute for killing white people, and surely Baraka should know this. Gerald Early quotes Cecil Taylor, whose piano work spans the history of African-American music, as saying, "Baraka! . . . Oh, he never knew what he was talking about when he discussed my music."[13] Ron Karenga and Frantz Fanon, guru to many in the movement, are equally obtuse. For Fanon, the blues are "a modicum of stylized oppression."[14] And for Karenga, "the blues are invalid; for they teach resignation, in a word, acceptance of reality—and we have come to change reality."[15] Another notable lack of insight is found in much of the work of Addison Gayle, whose *The Black Aesthetic* (1971) and *The Way of the New World: The Black Novel in America* (1975) are perhaps the most prominent products of the movement. There are many misreadings in Gayle, but perhaps the most critical are his misreadings of Ralph Ellison's *Invisible Man*. In "The Function of Black Literature at the Present Time," Gayle accuses Ellison of attempting "to negate race either by integrating the racial idiom with that of whites, or by obliterating racial characteristics altogether."[16] In *The Way of the New World*, he asserts that Ellison's narrator's values "are not to be found in his own cultural history and heritage," and that he "chooses death over life, opts for non-creativity in favor of creativity, chooses the path of individualism instead of racial unity."[17] None of these charges is close to being true, as a careful reading of *Invisible Man* will reveal. Nevertheless, they have been echoed and reechoed by many.

In contrast to Gayle stands the work of the late Larry Neal, who in his brief forty-three years (1937–1981) established himself as one of Afro-America's great literary critics. Early in his career, Neal was one of the preeminent black aestheticians, writing for *The Cricket*, *Liberator*, *Black Theatre*, *Negro Digest/Black World*, *Black Review*, *Black Dialogue*, the *Journal of Black Poetry*, etc. And in 1968 he edited (with Baraka) *Black Fire: An Anthology of African-American Writing*. Like Baraka, Karenga, and Gayle, Neal started out attacking Ellison, although there was always some praise. But by 1970 Neal had totally turned around, coming to the conclusion in "Ellison's Zoot Suit" that "*Invisible Man* is artistically one of the world's greatest novels; it is also one of the world's most successful 'political' novels. It is just that Ellison's politics are ritualistic as opposed to secular."[18] Unlike others in the movement, Neal was able to understand the true importance of the folk/vernacular tradition in African-American culture in and from an historical perspective. This is evident not only from Neal's own writing, such as "Some Reflections on the Black Aesthetic,"[19] but also in critical essays on his work such as Houston Baker's "Critical Change and Blues Continuity: An Essay on the Criticism of Larry

Neal."[20] In addition, again unlike others, Neal realized the importance of craft; and finally, he realized the limitations of propaganda:

> The historical problem of black literature is that it has in a sense
> been perpetually hamstrung by its need to address itself to the
> question of racism in America. Unlike black music, it has rarely
> been allowed to exist on its own terms, but rather has been uti-
> lized as a means of public relations in the struggle for human
> rights. Literature can indeed make excellent propaganda, but
> through propaganda alone the black writer can never perform
> the highest function of his art: that of revealing to man his most
> enduring human possibilities and limitations.[21]

Neal's revision of his views on Ellison and the Black Aesthetic
movement is a significant moment in African-American literary history. It got him out of what Ishmael Reed and Stanley Crouch call
"the opiate of ideology" when "the romance [of black nationalism]
began to fade in face of the megalomania, the lies, the avarice, and
the interwoven monstrosities of totalitarian and opportunistic impulses."[22] Neal was able to see that in the black aesthetic, "the concept of race is substituted for the Marxist idea of class,"[23] and thus
was, in Houston Baker's terms a form of "romantic Marxism."[24] Or,
as Greg Tate sums them up, the black aestheticians' "most grandiose
scheme involved trying to transform a supremacist sense of black cultural *difference* into the basis for a racially bonding black American
zeitgeist—one that would serve blacks as Judiasm was believed to
have solidified Jews."[25] This revision allowed Neal not only to understand history, but also to be able to see the shape of African-
American literature to come.

Despite its limitations, good things did result from the period of
the "Second Renaissance" (1954–1970). African-Americans collectively engaged in a period of self-examination that directly resulted
in positive feelings of self-identification. "Black is beautiful" was much
more than a slogan. It was the culmination of a psychological, political, social, and artistic process that would not have taken place without the work of Baraka, Karenga, Gayle, Malcolm, et al. And this
"Second Renaissance," limited as it was and as incomplete as it was
in its own way, as the Harlem Renaissance, has helped give birth to
the "Third Plane."[26]

The Third Plane refers to that group of writers, primarily although
not exclusively fiction writers, who started publishing in the late 1960s
and early 1970s and who, although not specifically connected to the
Black Arts movement, nevertheless were influenced by it. Unlike the

writers of the Harlem Renaissance, the writers of the Third Plane do not question their own humanity or feel the need to prove it to white America; nor are they embarrassed by the variety and fullness of African-American life. And while, like the writers of the Second Renaissance, they acknowledge an indigenous African-American cultural tradition, they are also aware that America is a pluralistic society, that African-American writers must draw on all traditions available to them, Western and non-Western, black and white. Finally, also unlike the writers of the Second Renaissance, they bring to the task of writing both a sense of the importance of craft and a more complete historical knowledge of the African-American folk past. For these writers, participants in Afro-America's third major cultural explosion, it is the joint heritage of the Black Aesthetic and Ralph Ellison that has made their work possible. And again, it is Larry Neal who first saw and understood the real possibilities of this new African-American literature that had developed precisely along the lines Saunders Redding had emphasized in *To Make A Poet Black*, an "acknowledgment of their debt to the folk materials":[27]

> There is a new Afro-American literature in the process of developing. It has its antecedents in African-American folk culture, the folk tales, blues, spirituals, and the unrecorded and recorded oral history of the people. Langston Hughes, Zora Neale Hurston, and Ralph Ellison, to name a few, have attempted to explore this culture for all of its possibilities and ramifications. There is, however, a wider area of possibilities; and the more one proceeds towards them, the more profound is the contact with the essential reality of the Black man in the West. It is this kind of contact with fundamentals that makes Ellison's *Invisible Man* one of the most significant novels of the Twentieth century.[28]

The writers of the Third Plane all began publishing major works in the late 1960s or early 1970s; and so important is their work that it has already spawned a later generation, including such writers as David Bradley, Charles Johnson, Jamaica Kincaid, Gloria Naylor, Richard Perry, and Sherley Anne Williams. The work of the Third Plane is the shape of African-American literature to come and has influenced not only work in fiction, but also poetry, drama, and literary criticism.

Third Plane writers can be considered "disciples" of Ellison's. I label these writers "disciples" because they were conscious of Ellison's groundbreaking work and consciously chose to follow in his footsteps. In other words, to a large extent, without the example of Ellison, the "disciples" could not have written. These thirteen disciples of Ralph Ellison are: Toni Cade Bambara, Leon Forrest, Ernest J. Gaines, Gayl Jones, Clarence Major, James Alan McPherson, Toni Morrison, Albert Murray, Ishmael Reed, Ntozake Shange, Alice Walker, John Edgar Wideman, and Al Young. Among them, they published seventy books between 1964 and 1979.[29] All of these writers, with the single exception of McPherson, have published books in the 1980s. In addition, they are all relatively young and can be expected to produce a lot more exceptional work before they are through.

One of the most significant things about this list is the large number of women on it. While there were several significant women writers active during the Harlem Renaissance, most of them are somewhat obscure to many, because their work is and has been out of print. The single exception is Zora Neale Hurston; and until Alice Walker's work in reviving her reputation and Robert Hemenway's 1977 *Zora Neale Hurston: A Literary Biography*, most of her work was also out of print. If she was known at all, it was more likely to be as an anthropologist who walked the streets of Harlem measuring heads for Franz Boas. And as for the Second Renaissance's view of women, there was Stokely Carmichael's infamous comment, "The only position for women in SNCC [Student Nonviolent Coordinating Committee] is prone."

However, in addition to the positive byproducts of the Second Renaissance that I have already mentioned, there was also the establishment of African-American Studies programs and the hiring of black faculty members.[30] The research done by these academics, as well as the work done by black women writers themselves, to uncover a female literary tradition—foremothers in addition to the forefathers-only tradition of the Second Renaissance—contributed greatly to the explosion of black women writers in the 1970s.[31] This, in turn, has resulted in a great deal of secondary publication: many long-out-of-print books being resurrected and literary and scholarly anthologies of black women writers and full-length critical studies written.[32] With this critical mass of material in print and, it is hoped, with much more to come, women's voices, past, present, and future, will never again be silent or silenced.

Third Plane cultural criticism has also been characterized by a great deal of work not exclusively focused on women. In addition to excellent studies of individual authors (Kimberly Benston on Amiri Baraka, Michel Fabre on Richard Wright, Trudier Harris on James Baldwin, Robert Hemenway on Zora Neale Hurston, Nellie McKay on Jean Toomer, Stephen Milliken on Chester Himes, Robert O'Meally

on Ralph Ellison, and Arnold Rampersad on W. E. B. DuBois and
Langston Hughes, in particular), the three most significant voices are
those of Henry Louis Gates, Houston Baker, and Robert Farris
Thompson. Gates' seminal essay, "The Blackness of Blackness: A Critique of the Sign and the Signifying Monkey" and Baker's *Blues, Ideology and African-American Literature: A Vernacular Theory* (1984) argue for a totally new way of looking at and interpreting formal and
structural properties of African-American literature, based in the vernacular. Gates' theory, with Reed's *Mumbo Jumbo* at its center and
Ellison as "our Great Signifier," sees the African-American vernacular, improvisational, rhetorical practice of signifying as "our trope
for repetition and revision."[33] In other words, through signifying, "black
writers read and critique other black texts as an act of rhetorical self-
definition."[34] For Baker, a blues matrix is at the heart of African-
American culture. His book recounts "moments in African-American
discourse when personae, protagonists, autobiographical narrators,
or literary critics successfully negotiate an obdurate 'economics of
slavery' and achieve a resonant, improvisational, expressive dignity."[35] The blues is thus much more than a body of music; it is an
African-American way of being. It is based in the vernacular, has improvisation as perhaps its key element, and is inherently political.
This is all made clear in Baker's key section, a materialist interpretation of the Trueblood episode in *Invisible Man*.[36]

Thompson, an art historian who prefers the term "guerrilla scholar,"
has, most notably in his fourth book, *Flash of the Spirit: African and
African-American Art and Philosophy* (1983), delineated a black Atlantic visual and philosophic tradition that connects black persons of the
Western Hemisphere "to Mother Africa" through, among other things,
an "improvisatory drive and brilliance."[37] Thompson finds flashes of
African spirit in sculpture, religion, dance, music, funeral symbolism,
textiles, language, gesture, and ideogrammatic writing in the New
World. His work threatens Western civilization as we know it, with
its racist notion that all we are derives from Greece and Rome, and
"the condescending Western image of 'primitive Africa.'"[38] Inciden-
tally, his acknowledgements record "the names of the women and
men without whose fundamental contributions in the field of African
or African-American aesthetics I doubt this book would have been
conceived at all."[39] Among them are DuBois, Hurston, and Ellison.
The work of Thompson, Baker, and Gates is radical in both senses of
the word. It challenges the traditional and accepted ways of seeing
things, and thus points us toward the future; and, at the same time,

it pertains to the fundamental, the root, or the origin, and never lets us forget the past.[40]

While the most significant and sustained work has been done in the fields of fiction and criticism, there have also been notable achievements in poetry and drama. Drama has probably had the least impact, because plays are not published as often as poems and fiction, and also because of the outrageous costs of mounting a major production. Literary criticism can be particularly important to drama. A major step in this direction is Genevieve Fabre's *Drumbeats, Masks and Metaphor: Contemporary African-American Theatre* (1982), which essentially picks up the story of African-American drama where Doris Abramson left off in her *Negro Playwrights in the American Theatre: 1925–1959* (1969). Fabre continues from Loften Mitchell's *Black Drama: The Story of the American Negro in the Theatre* (1967), and complements Paul Carter Harrison's *The Drama of Nommo* (1972). Thus, there is no comprehensive critical history of African-American drama. Other than these texts, there is Errol Hill's two-volume *The Theater of Black Americans* (1980) in the "Twentieth Century Views" series published by Prentice-Hall, which includes essays on music and dance (including Robert Farris Thompson's "An Aesthetic of the Cool: West African Dance"), and the James Hatch and Ted Shine monumental anthology, *Black Theater U.S.A.: Forty-Five Plays by Black Americans, 1874–1974* (1974). Clearly, a great deal of work needs to be done. The major emerging voices, including those of Ntozake Shange, Charles Fuller, August Wilson, and Samm-Art Williams, need to have their work supported, produced, and published; and the many voices from the past need to be resurrected.

Poetry has fared better than drama, and a number of new writers, again a large number of them women, have made their mark. Among the most important are Ai, June Jordan, Jayne Cortez, Audre Lorde, Lucille Clifton, Marie Evans, Pat Parker, Thulani Davis, Rita Dove, Sonia Sanchez, Colleen McElroy, Sherley Anne Williams, A. B. Spellman, Larry Neal, Quincy Troupe, Lorenzo Thomas, Jay Wright, David Henderson, George Barlow, Michael Harper, and Etheridge Knight. But here too, the work of recovery must go on. Not only does more work need to be done on the generation before the Black Arts Movement (Bob Kaufman, Gwendolyn Brooks, Dudley Randall, Margaret Walker, Robert Hayden, etc.), but earlier writers such as Alice Dunbar-Nelson, Arna Bontemps, Georgia Douglas Johnson, Anne Spencer, Angelina Grimke, and Fenton Johnson need to be rediscovered, republished, and replaced before our eyes as creative models.

As has been pointed out by many commentators, the African-American cultural contribution has been greatest in music, from work songs and shouts to spirituals, gospel, blues, ragtime, rhythm and blues, soul, and jazz. More or less concomitant with the Second Renaissance was the most recent major movement in jazz, variously known as "the new thing," "the new wave," or simply the avant-garde. One could point to the year 1959 as pivotal: *Kind of Blue* by Miles Davis, *Giant Steps* by John Coltrane, and *Tomorrow Is the Question!*, *The Shape of Jazz to Come*, and *Change of the Century* (as well as parts of *To Whom Who Keeps a Record*, *Twins*, and *Art of the Improvisers*) by Ornette Coleman were all recorded in 1959. This is also the year when Ornette made his New York debut at the Five Spot. As Kimberly Benston points out in "Late Coltrane: A Re-Membering of Orpheus":

> The sounds of John Coltrane, Ornette Coleman, Sonny Rollins, Sun Ra, Cecil Taylor, Albert Ayler, Archie Shepp, Pharoah Sanders, and their fellow travelers unfolded before the black poet a new kingdom, a world which has little in common with the systematized reality around him, and in which he leaves behind all concrete feelings in order to discover within himself an ineffable longing. The "new wave" jazz—having extended and mastered the contribution of bebop—opened the floodgates of passion, anger, pain, and love, and aroused that fury for liberty which is the essence of the new black art. It joined itself to earlier, major epochs of black music by reaffirming the creative union between the improvising soloist and the total musical collective. But it also forged a new role for music in the hierarchy of black expressions—that of guide rather than mere analogue to other communicative modes.[41]

This spirit has influenced some forms of writing, criticism most notably, such as Baraka's *Black Music* (1967) and *John Coltrane: Where Does Art Come From?* (1978), and A. B. Spellman's *Four Lives in the Bebop Business/Black Music: Four Lives* (1966). It has also had a good deal of influence on poetry.[47] But in fiction it has been the spirit of the blues more than anything else that has had the most significant musical effect. The "jazz aesthetic"[43] (the spirit of improvisation, spontaneity, indefiniteness, and what Ted Gioia calls "the retrospective method"—in which one is guided by what has already been played, and in which planning ahead, blueprints, preliminary sketches, outlines, or rough drafts are not important—as opposed to "the blueprint method"[44] is often missing from African-American fiction. For all the progress and innovation characteristic of the writers of the Third Plane, this aspect is still missing. Cecil Taylor, Sun Ra, the Art Ensemble of Chicago, Anthony Braxton, Eric Dolphy, and, most importantly, Ornette Coleman—who still hasn't gotten his due credit, but who deserves to be ranked (unlike Coltrane) with Louis Armstrong and Charlie Parker as one of the three most important, innovative, and revolutionary forces in the history of jazz—are absent from the pages of African-American fiction.

There was such a potential in Henry Dumas. His short story ("Will the Circle Be Unbroken?"), about the saxophone player Probe, whose "afro-horn," played at the Sound Barrier Club, has the power to kill white people, demonstrated an extensive knowledge of and affinity for the new music. Unfortunately, a bullet from the gun of a white New York City police officer in May 1968 ended Dumas' life before he was able to reach his full potential. However much "Will the Circle Be Unbroken?" demonstrated a knowledge, a content, about the new music, the form of the prose is straightforward, unambiguous, realistic narrative.

A new voice, however, has recently appeared. And however risky and problematic it might be to single out one young writer as being the essence of the future, especially on the basis of only one novel, and one novel that is part of an ongoing series and therefore concludes inconclusively, I am willing to take such a chance. The novel is entitled *Bedouin Hornbook*,[45] and its author is Nathaniel Mackey. Mackey is the author of three volumes of poetry, *Four for Trane* (1978), *Septet for the End of Time* (1983), and *Eroding Witness* (1985). He is also editor of *Hambone*, which, along with *Callaloo* and Ishmael Reed and Al Young's *Quilt*, is the most exciting outlet around for new writing. *Bedouin Hornbook* is a series of letters by "N.," a jazz musician (saxello, contrabass bassoon, bass clarinet, and trumpet) and composer with the Mystic Horn Society (formerly the East Bay Dread Ensemble, and before that the Deconstructive Woodwind Chorus), whose music is clearly influenced by Ornette, Dolphy, and the Art Ensemble of Chicago. Mackey goes beyond Dumas by not only writing about music, but by having the open form of the music being mirrored in the novel's prose. As the novel's title makes clear, *Bedouin Hornbook* is the nomadic pursuit of life's meaning through and with "a likewise mobile, prancing, or capricious horn."[46] The text is the journey, is the music, rather than a narrative about the music. It is the difference, say, between Ezra Pound, whose *Cantos* wants to approach the condition of music, and Louis Zukofsky, whose *A* literally is music. *Bedouin Hornbook*, in addition to its musical and philosophical concerns and its open form, is part of a series wonderfully entitled *From a Broken Bottle Traces of Perfume Still Emanate*.

Apart from its beautiful lyric poetry, this title clearly points to the problem of the Second Renaissance. Again, as the writers of the Harlem Renaissance wasted too much energy trying to please and impress white America, the writers of the Second Renaissance wasted too much energy solely concentrating on racism and trying to vilify white America. Yes, America is racist; and yes, it always will be; and yes, there must be what Mackey calls in "Sound and Sentiment, Sound and Symbol" "a refusal to forget damage done."[47] Nevertheless, there is much more to the life and culture of the African-Americans than being the victims of racism. If America were to suddenly change overnight and racism were to disappear, it would not mean the end of African-American culture. Racism may have broken the bottle, but there will always be beauty and sweetness emanating from African-American life. *From a Broken Bottle Traces of Perfume Still Emanate* could well end up being African-America's first great prose epic, on the same level as *The Cantos, Paterson, A, The Maximus Poems, Passages*, and *Mountains and Rivers Without End*.

In referring to his hero Quickskill in *Flight to Canada*, Ishmael Reed notes that his "writing was his HooDoo . . . his typewriter was his drum he danced to."[48] It is this spirit and attitude that keeps African-American writers ever mindful of their roots in the folk/vernacular tradition. As we approach the change of the century, this will be the shape of African-American literature to come.

### Endnotes

1. This preface was originally part of " 'Get Down Into the Mud and Live': Invisibility in the Academy," paper presented at the Modern Language Association's annual convention, December 1986.

2. Louis Kampf and Paul Lauter, eds., *The Politics of Literature: Dissenting Essays on the Teaching of English* (New York: Pantheon/Random House, 1972); quotes are from pp. 8 and 184, respectively.

3. *Ibid.*, p. 8.

4. *Ibid.*

5. J. Saunders Redding, *To Make a Poet Black* (1939; Washington, D.C.: McGrath, 1968), p. 3.

6. *Ibid.*, p. 122.

7. *Ibid.*, p. 108.

8. Sigmund Ro, " 'Desecrators' and 'Necromancers': Black American Writ-

ers and Critics in the Nineteen-Sixties and the Third World Perspective," *Callaloo* (1985), 8:563–76; quotes are from pp. 563 and 564, respectively.

9. *Ibid.*, p. 564.

10. Ron Karenga, "Black Cultural Nationalism," in Addison Gayle, Jr., ed., *The Black Aesthetic* (Garden City, N.Y.: Anchor Books/Doubleday, 1971), p. 36.

11. Carolyn Rodgers, "The Literature of Black," *Black World* (June 1970), p. 10.

12. LeRoi Jones, *Dutchman* and *The Slave* (New York: Morrow, 1964), p. 35.

13. Gerald Early, "The Case of LeRoi Jones and Amiri Baraka," *Salmagundi* (1986), nos. 70–71, p. 343.

14. Frantz Fanon, *Toward the African Revolution* (New York: Grove, 1969), p. 37.

15. Maulana Ron Karenga, "Black Art: Mute Matter Given Force and Function," in Abraham Chapman, ed., *New Black Voices: An Anthology of Contemporary African-American Literature* (New York: Mentor/New American Library, 1972), p. 482.

16. Addison Gayle, Jr., "The Function of Black Literature at the Present Time," in Addison Gayle, Jr., ed., *The Black Aesthetic* (Garden City, N.Y.: Anchor Books/Doubleday, 1971), p. 390.

17. Addison Gayle, Jr., *The Way of the New World: The Black Novel in America* (Garden City, N.Y.: Anchor Books/Doubleday, 1975), pp. 211, 212.

18. Larry Neal, "Ellison's Zoot Suit," in John Hersey, ed., *Ralph Ellison: A Collection of Critical Essays* (Englewood Cliffs, N.J.: Prentice-Hall, 1974), p. 79; the essay is reprinted from *Black World* (December 1970), pp. 31–50.

19. Larry Neal, "Some Reflections on the Black Aesthetic," in Addison Gayle, Jr., ed., *The Black Aesthetic* (Garden City, N.Y.: Anchor Books/Doubleday, 1971), pp. 12–15.

20. Houston Baker, "Critical Change and Blues Continuity: An Essay on the Criticism of Larry Neal," in Kimberly W. Benston, ed., *Larry Neal*, special issue of *Callaloo* (1985), 8:70–84.

21. Larry Neal, "The Black Contribution to American Letters, Part II: The Writer as Activist (1966 and After)," in Mabel Smythe, ed., *The Black American Reference Book* (Englewood Cliffs, N.J.: Prentice-Hall, 1976), p. 784.

22. Ishmael Reed, "Larry Neal: A Remembrance," in Kimberly W. Benston, ed., *Larry Neal*, special issue of *Callaloo* (1985), 8:264; Stanley Crouch, "The 'Scene' of Larry Neal," in Benston, *Larry Neal*, p. 260.

23. Neal, "The Black Contribution," p. 783.

24. Houston A. Baker, Jr., *Blues, Ideology and African-American Literature: A Vernacular Theory* (Chicago, Ill.: University of Chicago Press, 1984), p. 81.

25. Greg Tate, "Cult-Nats Meet Freaky-Deke: The Return of the Black Aesthetic," *Village Voice Literary Supplement* (December 1986), p. 5.

26. I have taken the term "Third Plane" from the title of a composition by jazz bassist Ron Carter.

27. Redding, *To Make a Poet Black*, p. 122.

28. "Eleanor Traylor, " 'And the Resurrection, Let It Be Complete': The Achievement of Larry Neal," in Kimberly W. Benston, ed., *Larry Neal*, special issue of *Callaloo* (1985), 8:55.

29. Toni Cade Bambara   *The Black Woman* (1970)
        *Tales and Short Stories for Black Folks* (1971)

|  | *Gorilla, My Love* (1972) |
|  | *The Sea Birds Are Still Alive* (1977) |
| Leon Forrest | *There Is a Tree More Ancient Than Eden* (1973) |
|  | *The Bloodworth Orphans* (1977) |
| Ernest J. Gaines | *Catherine Carmier* (1964) |
|  | *Of Love and Dust* (1967) |
|  | *Bloodline* (1968) |
|  | *The Autobiography of Miss Jane Pitman* (1971) |
|  | *In My Father's House* (1978) |
| Gayl Jones | *Corregidora* (1975) |
|  | *Eva's Man* (1976) |
|  | *White Rat* (1977) |
| Clarence Major | *All-Night Visitors* (1969) |
|  | *The New Black Poetry* (1969) |
|  | *Swallow the Lake* (1970) |
|  | *Dictionary of African-American Slang* (1970) |
|  | *Private Line* (1971) |
|  | *Symptoms and Madness* (1971) |
|  | *The Cotton Club* (1972) |
|  | *No* (1973) |
|  | *The Dark and Feeling* (1974) |
|  | *The Syncopated Cakewalk* (1974) |
|  | *Reflex and Bone Structure* (1975) |
|  | *Emergency Exit* (1979) |
| James Alan McPherson | *Hue and Cry* (1969) |
|  | *Elbow Room* (1977) |
| Toni Morrison | *The Bluest Eye* (1970) |
|  | *Sula* (1973) |
|  | *Song of Solomon* (1977) |
| Albert Murray | *The Omni-Americans* (1970) |
|  | *South to a Very Old Place* (1971) |
|  | *The Hero and the Blues* (1972) |
|  | *Train Whistle Guitar* (1974) |
|  | *Stomping the Blues* (1976) |
| Ishmael Reed | *The Free-Lance Pallbearers* (1967) |
|  | *Yellow Back Radio Broke-Down* (1969) |
|  | *19 Necromancers from Now* (1970) |
|  | *Catechism of D Neoamerican Hoodoo Church* (1971) |
|  | *Mumbo Jumbo* (1972) |
|  | *Conjure* (1972) |
|  | *Chattanooga* (1973) |
|  | *The Last Days of Louisiana Red* (1974) |
|  | *Flight to Canada* (1976) |
|  | *Shrovetide in Old New Orleans* (1978) |
|  | *A Secretary to the Spirits* (1978) |
|  | *Yardbird Lives!* (1978) |
|  | *Calafia: The California Poetry* (1979) |
| Ntozake Shange | *For Colored Girls Who Have Considered Suicide/When the Rainbow is Enuf* (1975) |

|              | *Sassafrass* (1976) |
|--------------|---------------------|
|              | *For Colored Girls Who Have Considered Suicide/When the Rainbow is Enuf: A Choreopoem* (1977) |
|              | *Nappy Edges* (1978) |
| Alice Walker | *Once* (1968) |
|              | *The Third Life of Grange Copeland* (1970) |
|              | *Revolutionary Petunias* (1973) |
|              | *In Love & Trouble* (1973) |
|              | *Langston Hughes, American Poet* (1974) |
|              | *Meridian* (1976) |
|              | *I Love Myself When I Am Laughing . . . And Then Again When I Am Looking Mean and Impressive: A Zora Neale Hurston Reader* (1979) |
|              | *Good Night, Willie Lee, I'll See You in the Morning* (1979) |
| John Edgar Wideman | *A Glance Away* (1967) |
|              | *Hurry Home* (1970) |
|              | *The Lynchers* (1973) |
| Al Young     | *Dancing* (1969) |
|              | *Snakes* (1970) |
|              | *The Song Turning Back Into Itself* (1971) |
|              | *Who Is Angelina?* (1975) |
|              | *Geography of the Near Past* (1976) |
|              | *Sitting Pretty* (1976) |
|              | *Yardbird Lives!* (1978) |

30. For a full treatment of this topic see Nellie McKay's essay in this volume.

31. On this topic see Sherley Anne Williams, "Some Implications of Womanist Theory," *Callaloo* (1986), 9:303–308; and Thulani Davis, "Family Plots: Black Women Writers Reclaim Their Past," *Village Voice Literary Supplement* (March 1987), pp. 14–17.

32. Some of the women whose work has recently been reprinted are: Zora Neale Hurston, Paule Marshall, Louise Meriwether, and Dorothy West, by the Feminist Press; Nella Larsen by Rutgers; Ann Petry and Frances Ellen Watkins Harper by Beacon; and Jessie Fauset by Pandora. Recent literary and scholarly anthologies of black women writers include: Amiri and Amina Baraka, *Confirmation: An Anthology of African American Women* (1983); Roseann P. Bell, Bettye J. Parker, and Beverly Guy-Sheftall, *Sturdy Black Bridges: Visions of Black Women in Literature* (1979); Marie Evans, *Black Women Writers (1950– 1980): A Critical Evaluation* (1984); Marjorie Pryse and Hortense J. Spillers, *Conjuring: Black Women, Fiction, and Literary Tradition* (1985); Barbara Smith, *Conditions: Five, the Black Women's Issue* (1979), *All the Women Are White, All the Blacks Are Men, But Some of Us Are Brave: Black Women's Studies* (1982), and *Home Girls: A Black Feminist Anthology* (1983); Erlene Stetson, *Black Sister: Poetry by Black American Women, 1746–1980* (1981); Claudia Tate, *Black Women Writers at Work* (1983); and Mary Helen Washington, *Black-Eyed Susans: Classic Stories by and About Black Women* (1975), *Midnight Birds: Stories by Contemporary Black Women Writers* (1980), and *Invented Lives: Narratives*

*of Black Women 1860–1960* (1987). Among the significant full-length studies are: Barbara Christian, *Black Women Novelists: The Development of a Tradition, 1892–1976* (1980) and *Black Feminist Criticism: Perspectives on Black Women Writers* (1985); Gloria Wade-Gayles, *No Crystal Stair: Visions of Race and Sex in Black Women's Fiction* (1984); and Susan Willis, *Specifying: Black Women Writing the American Experience* (1987).

33. Henry Louis Gates, Jr., "The Blackness of Blackness: A Critique of the Sign and the Signifying Monkey," in Henry Louis Gates, Jr., ed., *Black Literature and Literary Theory* (New York: Methuen, 1984), pp. 285–321; quotes are from pp. 292 and 286, respectively.

34. *Ibid.*, p. 290.

35. Baker, *Blues, Ideology and African-American Literature*, p. 13.

36. On Gates and Baker see Greg Tate, "Yo! Hermeneutics!: Hiphopping Toward Poststructuralism," *Village Voice Literary Supplement* (June 1985), 1:17–19. I do want to stress here that what I say is not meant to be taken as a complete, unqualified acceptance of Gates and Baker. There are criticisms that have been and can be made: that they are writing to a limited audience exclusively composed of other literary critics, that their audience is limited even more by the fact that they employ an at times obscure poststructuralist language (a charge that at times has become an accusation that they are selling out and using the "enemy's" language), that their criticism of their critics degenerates into personal attacks, that they have been insufficiently attentive to works by and images of women, that their work threatens to depoliticize African-American literature, and that in seeming to privilege theory their work comes too close to making literature a form of science. I don't intend to enter this debate, except to say that I think that the charges of political conservatism are unfounded, and that whatever their excesses, Gates and Baker have put African-American literary criticism on a new plane that is an unquestionable "great leap forward" from most of the literary criticism of the Black Aesthetic period. Readers who want more detail on this controversy should consult the debate among Gates, Baker, and Joyce A. Joyce in the pages of *New Literary History* (1987); 18:335–84; and Theodore O. Mason, Jr., "Between the Populist and the Scientist: Ideology and Power in Recent African-American Literary Criticism or, 'The Dozens' as Scholarship," *Callaloo* (1988), 11:606–15.

37. Robert Farris Thompson, *Flash of the Spirit: African and African-American Art and Philosophy* (New York: Random House, 1983), quotes are from pp. xiv and xiii, respectively.

38. *Ibid.*, p. 3.

39. *Ibid.*, p. ix.

40. On Thompson see Greg Tate, "Guerilla Scholar on the Loose: Robert Farris Thompson Gets Down," *Village Voice*, January 10, 1984, pp. 39–40; and Frederick Iseman, "Canons of the Cool," *Rolling Stone*, November 22, 1984, pp. 23, 27–28, 81.

41. Kimberly W. Benston, "Late Coltrane: A Re-Membering of Orpheus," in Michael S. Harper and Robert B. Stepto, eds., *Chant of Saints: A Gathering of African-American Literature, Art, and Scholarship* (Urbana: University of Illinois Press, 1979), p. 415.

42. For the best treatment of this topic see Stephen Henderson, *Under-*

*standing the New Black Poetry: Black Speech and Black Music As Poetic References* (New York: Morrow, 1973), pp. 46–61.

43. This term comes from Nate Mackey's "The Changing Same: Black Music in the Poetry of Amiri Baraka," in Kimberly W. Benston, ed., *Imamu Amiri Baraka (LeRoi Jones): A Collection of Critical Essays* (Englewood Cliffs, N.J.: Prentice-Hall, 1978), p. 126.

44. Ted Gioia, "Jazz: The Aesthetics of Imperfection," *Hudson Review* (1987), 39:593.

45. Nathaniel Mackey *Bedouin Hornbook*, (Lexington: University of Kentucky Press, 1986) is volume 1 of *From a Broken Bottle Traces of Perfume Still Emanate*, an ongoing work.

46. Mackey, *Bedouin Hornbook*, p. 157.

47. Mackey, "Sound and Sentiment, Sound and Symbol." *Callaloo* (1987), 10:47.

48. Ishmael Reed, *Flight to Canada* (New York: Random House, 1976), p. 89.

# 12

# History as Explanation: Writing About Lesbian Writing, or "Are Girls Necessary?"

## Julie Abraham

*Like the other essays in this section, this one attempts to trace a trajectory in the study of previously excluded groups. Julie Abraham considers the particular difficulties raised by the history of lesbian experience and of the development of the study of lesbian writing. The aim is to expand our current understanding of the significance of and critical possibilities for lesbian criticism.*

In her 1926 essay "Composition as Explanation," Gertrude Stein argued that "composition," the form of a work, is explained by its specific historical moment. "There is singularly nothing that makes a difference a difference in beginning and in the middle and in ending except that each generation has something different at which they are all looking," Stein wrote. "Nothing changes from generation to generation except the thing seen and that makes a composition."[1] Virginia Woolf was also considering the relations between literature and history in the 1920s. In *Orlando* (1928) she observed, with an edge of satire, that "the transaction between a writer and the spirit of the age is one of infinite delicacy, and upon a nice arrangement between the two the whole fortune of his works depends."[2] It is only after her hero/ine, the ambisexual Orlando, has succumbed to the spirit of the Victorian age and married that her pen will produce anything other than the conventional pieties of the period. But the newlywed Orlando begins immediately to write what was actually Woolf's lover Vita Sackville-West's poetry:

> And then I came to a field where the springing grass
> Was dulled by the hanging cups of fritillaries,
> Sullen and foreign-looking, the snaky flower,
> Scarfed in dull purple, like Egyptian girls—

> As she wrote she felt some power . . . reading over her shoulder, and when she had written "Egyptian girls," the power told her to stop. Grass, the power seemed to say, going back with a ruler such as governesses use to the beginning, is all right; the hanging cups of fritillaries—admirable; the snaky flower—a thought strong from a lady's pen, perhaps, but Wordsworth, no doubt, sanctions it; but—girls? Are girls necessary? You have a husband at the Cape, you say? Ah, well, that'll do.
> And so the spirit passed on.[3]

Woolf recognizes that this "spirit of the age" rules on the content as well as the reputation of a writer's works, and particularly on appropriate sexual and gender behavior for authors and their subjects. She also illustrates the complex interaction between these terms: "girls" were acceptable from a woman writer if she was safely married. The marriage need only be a form. That the husband is engaged in imperial adventures "at the Cape" makes life simpler all around. So also, perhaps, does the fact that the girls are not Shropshire lasses, but are distanced by their relation to Egypt: exotic girls are both less real and more easily eroticized, from the perspective of a British spirit of the Victorian age (or the early twentieth century).

But despite a spirit of the age still—a century after Orlando's wedding—officially inimical to girls, in an often-quoted passage of *A Room of One's Own* (1929), Woolf proposed a new subject for fiction, Chloe's liking for Olivia: "Let us admit in the privacy of our own society," she wrote, "that these things sometimes happen. Sometimes women do like women."[4] Woolf actually makes use of historical reference to convey a lesbian meaning: we know that Chloe and Olivia represent more than just good friends because of the accompanying allusions to the obscenity trial of Radclyffe Hall's *The Well of Loneliness*, which was progressing as she wrote. (The Sirs Chartres Biron, Archibald Bodkin, and William Joynson Hicks, about whom she warns her readers whenever she raises the subject of women's affections, were all chief among Hall's journalistic and judicial prosecutors.)[5]

*A Room of One's Own* is often now regarded as the first work of feminist literary criticism; it is also perhaps the first work of lesbian criticism: certainly Woolf encountered the first question and fell into the first trap of lesbian criticism. The first critical question—rather like many of our personal experiences—is whether, having found one, there are any other lesbian texts or women out there. The first trap is to accept the immediate evidence of one's eyes and conclude that no, there are not. Woolf suggested that "Chloe liked Olivia perhaps for the first time in literature"[6] and framed her discussion in those terms: "For if Chloe liked Olivia and Mary Carmichael [her fictional female novelist of the 1920s] knows how to express it she will light a torch in that vast chamber where nobody has yet been."[7] But Woolf was wrong.

Her own *Mrs. Dalloway*, published four years before, Hall's earlier novel *The Unlit Lamp* (1924), and a host of less well-known fictions of the early and mid-1920s represented the growing presence of lesbian references in British fiction since the turn of the century.[8] She could also have looked back to the Victorians, to Christina Rossetti's *Goblin Market* or Henry James' *The Bostonians*, or to French literature, from the myth of George Sand and Gautier's *Mademoiselle de Maupin* to the work of Proust and Colette.[9]

As Woolf was undoubtedly aware of these predecessors and peers, her sweeping statement may have been due to the desire to mark a new self-consciousness about the literary representation of women's relationships. But her example of the first question and the first trap also bring us to the first problem of lesbian criticism: what do literary lesbians look like, what is lesbian writing—or, to quote her out of context now, "Are girls necessary?"[10] The question is still with us sixty years later; what we need to develop is a more complex approach to the issue of definition, of both subject and method, that it represents.

One of the revolutionary aspects of *A Room of One's Own* was Woolf's location of women writers and representations of women in social and political history. Whether we are referring to the old feminist criticism—its historical bases recently reemphasized by Judith Lowder Newton and Janet Todd[11]—or the perhaps not-so-new historicism, any writing about lesbian writing must also take into account the historical moment at which the work in question was produced: what that generation of women was looking at and what the spirit of that particular age was telling them. At the same time, despite the tendency of contemporary lesbian critics to assume, at least rhetorically, that history stops with us, our own discussions of lesbian writing in

the 1960s, 1970s, and 1980s have also been shaped by specific political and personal pressures, in particular a constant sense of epistemological (if not also material) present danger, an ongoing identity
crisis, which both exacerbates and parallels the critical difficulties of
defining our subject. The first step toward addressing the problem of
definition must be that any criticism of lesbian writing and representation consider its own historical moment as well as that of its
subjects, locating the critic as well as the subject in sociopolitical
space.[12]

An insistence on history, however, leads to the second problem of
lesbian criticism, the use of literary texts as historical sources. Cora
Kaplan has observed that "literature, as a cultural object, has a different place in feminist cultural and historical analysis than it does
in androcentric criticism," because it is "one of the central historical
discourses in which sexual difference is represented as both a social
and psychic reality, [and] it is also one of the few public genres in
which women themselves spoke about these questions."[13] The resulting importance of literary works is magnified in the context of specifically lesbian historical and cultural analysis, given that the representation of lesbianism remained largely confined to literary texts
until the past two decades. (It is not at all accidental that the first
cultural artifact of lesbianism many women found was a novel, usually Radclyffe Hall's *The Well of Loneliness*.) But treating literary works
as historical evidence obscures their status as the products of literary
cultures as well as of historical moments. We need to resist the easy
incorporation of lesbian literature into the narratives of lesbian history, women's history, and the history of sexuality as they have all
come to be constituted. At the same time lesbian criticism's understanding of "history" must incorporate not only social and political
but also literary contexts—the already existing possibilities for compositions and their relation to, in Stein's terms, "the thing seen," as
well as "the thing seen" itself. These contexts also include our own
literary-critical history and assumptions, in which the terms have been
set by the problem of definition and the debate it has generated.

Paralleling the development of feminist criticism as the study of
women in literature, but originating outside of the academy, lesbian
criticism in its later twentieth-century form began as a bibliograph-
ical and biographical enterprise, simultaneously discovering and creating the object of inquiry. From the beginning the bibliography and
the parameters of biographical speculation were shaped by the problem of defining the subject. Jeannette Foster took a category from the
field of psychiatry as the basis of her self-published *Sex Variant Women*

*in Literature* (1956), the first survey of the field. Arguing that "not all women recognize a sexual factor in their subjective emotional relations, particularly in the intrasexual field so heavily shadowed by social disapproval," and also recognizing that there is a distinction between acting and representing, she recorded every reference she could find to emotional as well as sexual involvements between women in literature and in the lives of women writers, from Sappho to the 1950s.[14]

Foster's work was followed by the three editions of Barbara Grier's bibliography, *The Lesbian in Literature* (in 1967, 1975, and 1981) and J. R. Roberts' *Black Lesbians* (also in 1981).[15] Grier invented an elaborate system of categorization for the hundreds of titles she listed, which involved As, Bs, and Cs for the amount of "lesbian" material in a given book plus asterisks for the quality of its treatment. (There was also T for trash, usually referring to pulp paperbacks of the 1950s and 1960s, often written by and for men.) In *Black Lesbians* Roberts used extensive annotation to situate her entries.

Literary lesbianism was treated along the lines of an earlier, certainly pre–twentieth-century model of homosexuality as a function of acts rather than lives: lesbian content was seen as something distinct within a work—books could have more or less of it, and the amount was almost always an effect of character and story. Jane Rule, herself the first of a new generation of self-conscious lesbian writers, took the bold step of organizing her 1975 study *Lesbian Images* according to author, but she was still most interested in those works by her chosen authors that contained what were by the mid-1970s called "lesbian images."[16]

Feminist criticism was engaged in its own elaboration of the study of "images of women" in fiction and the identification and recovery of "lost" women writers.[17] But its task of discovery was, at least initially, not as materially complex: before the ascendancy of deconstruction, once you found a woman writer, few would dispute that she was female. And the political pressures imposed on feminist critics by their own potential audience, although great, were arguably less than those surrounding lesbian critics. The letters Claire Morgan received after the publication of her 1952 novel *The Price of Salt*— one of the few novels about lesbians to that date without an unhappy ending—reflected an ongoing need for cultural representations predating the development of this criticism. By the late 1960s and early 1970s the continuing social and cultural invisibility of lesbians—added to the political promises of the gay and women's liberation movements—created the pressure to provide accessible "lesbian images" as quickly as possible.

At this time, paradoxically, within the framework of invisibility there already existed an a priori idea of the lesbian text that supplied a paradigm for the needed images. While Radclyffe Hall did not invent the lesbian novel with *The Well of Loneliness*, the conventional realism and willing self-condemnation of her 1928 work, and the public response it received—obscenity trials in both Britain and the United States—served to crystallize a possibility for lesbian writing.[18] As Gillian Whitlock comments, "Hall uses the scientific and medical concepts of inversion in a quite different kind of discourse, a literary and fictional one. Here these concepts achieve a different currency, of a very personal and intimate kind."[19] Hall contributed to the creation of a midcentury literary type that had the virtue of being instantly recognizable by enemies and friends alike. It could also be written by and for and be read by both enemies and friends.

In the 1960s and 1970s lesbian critics pursued an idea of the lesbian text that was still based on this older popular conception of the lesbian work, in which girls were most emphatically necessary. Within the frame of critical readings as well as for a wider audience, the only quality perhaps more important than the girls themselves was narrative. In order to be read as lesbian, on the simplest level, a work had to be about some kind of recognizable relationship between recognizable characters who were recognizably female: a girl-meets-girl or woman-meets-woman story, regardless of who gets who in the end. Literary realism was essential. So because it had been and continued to be the most accessible forum for the lesbian character and for the possible if rarely satisfying presentation of lesbian narratives, the unit of discussion about lesbian writing came to be primarily the lesbian novel.

When in the later 1970s lesbian critics began to argue about what could be considered lesbian writing (and writing to be studied from a lesbian perspective), all of the assumptions continued to be realist—the girls remained crucial. The debate centered around the definition of the lesbian—how literal a lesbian image should be, how explicitly sexual, before it could be counted. These arguments were tied to developments in the study of women's history—marked, especially, by Carroll Smith-Rosenberg's work on relationships between women in the eighteenth- and nineteenth-century "Female World of Love and Ritual" she described, and the responses her conclusions provoked.[20] But the issues, for both critics and historians, were fundamentally shaped by feminist politics. The stakes were so high partly because the battle always contained an element of response: many of the speakers also wanted to show that we were not really "those" women—the women in men's suits with slicked-back hair who hung out in bars or, in literary terms, Radclyffe Hall's Stephen Gordon, with her horses, her tailoring and her damnation. The debate went in two directions politically, toward metaphor and simultaneously toward the specific. While the Radicalesbians, in their famous position paper "The Woman-Identified Woman," were declaring that "A lesbian is the rage of all women," Del Martin and Phyllis Lyon in *Lesbian/Woman* were assuring their readers that we were the girl next door—their sisters, friends, mothers, daughters, teachers, secretaries, nurses, etc. These two courses also shaped the development of lesbian feminist criticism.[21]

As Bonnie Zimmerman observed in her 1981 survey, "What Has Never Been: An Overview of Lesbian Feminist Criticism," some critics proposed including a wide range of representations of women's relations as lesbian. This position was exemplified by Barbara Smith's well-known analysis of Toni Morrison's *Sula* in her "Toward a Black Feminist Criticism" (1977) and by Adrienne Rich both in her 1976 vision of the lesbian as the image of female creativity, "It Is the Lesbian In Us . . ." and in her 1980 proposal of a lesbian continuum in "Compulsory Heterosexuality and Lesbian Existence."[22] On the other side, Catharine Stimpson argued for a criticism based on a "severely literal" sexual definition of the lesbian "as writer, as character, as reader" in "Zero Degree Deviancy: The Lesbian Novel in English" (1981):

> She is a woman who finds other women erotically attractive and gratifying. Of course a lesbian is more than her body, more than her flesh, but lesbianism partakes of the body, partakes of the flesh. That carnality distinguishes it from gestures of political sympathy with homosexuals and from affectionate friendships in which women enjoy each other, support each other, and commingle a sense of identity and well-being. Lesbianism represents a commitment of skin, blood, breast and bone.[23]

In *Surpassing the Love of Men*, her study of lesbian history through lesbian writing, Lillian Faderman attempted to chart a central course by historicizing the question, arguing that what was romantic friendship before 1900 became lesbianism (and more likely to be sexual) in the changed political and social conditions of the twentieth century. Nevertheless, perhaps inevitably given her historical purposes, she also came down on the side of a realistic convention of lesbian representation, the presence of specific girls as a deciding factor in her choice of works to be discussed.

The battle between the lesbian as metaphor and lesbian specificity has endured. By the early 1980s, in a development that also reflected broader efforts among feminist activists and critics, specificity was ascendant: the work of women of color and Jewish women, racism and class issues, were addressed in major anthologies such as Barbara Smith's *Home Girls*, Cherríe Moraga and Gloria Anzaldua's *This Bridge Called My Back* and Evelyn Torton Beck's *Nice Jewish Girls*, as well as in individual memoirs such as Audre Lorde's *Zami* and Michelle Cliff's *Claiming an Identity They Taught Me To Despise*. Now the metaphor seems to be making a comeback, as in Marilyn Farwell's recent essay "Toward a Definition of the Lesbian Literary Imagination," in which she develops ideas derived from the 1970s work of Adrienne Rich and Monique Wittig, elaborating arguments for the lesbian as a metaphor for female creativity.[24]

The arguments about the definition of the lesbian in political, historical, and critical circles were never particularly adapted for a literary context; they conflated literature and life, disregarding the specificities of both literary constraints and possibilities. There were many questions that were dealt with implicitly rather than explicitly, and others that were not dealt with at all. For example, what is the role of the author of the literary work under consideration: does it matter if the author is lesbian, a heterosexual woman, or a straight or gay man? Are Henry James' *The Bostonians*, D. H. Lawrence's *The Fox*, Mary McCarthy's *The Group*, and Gertrude Stein's *Tender Buttons* all works of equal status?[25]

How do we define an author as a lesbian in specific biographical contexts rather than in terms of political or cultural theory? To what extent was it the case that, as Stein observed, "the reality of the twentieth century is not the reality of the nineteenth century, not at all."[26] What does marriage mean, and for how long; does it count if he was paid, does it count if there were children, and does it count if he was gay?[27] What about authors who spent their lifetimes denying their lesbianism or, like Willa Cather, their last years destroying all written traces of it?[28] What if there is simply too little information, as Deborah McDowell suggests is the case with Nella Larsen?[29]

How do we define a lesbian *writer*, once we've decided she's a dyke: what do we do about lesbians who, like Cather or the English historical novelist Bryher, did not write about "lesbian characters or action," or who, like Mary Renault, Sylvia Townsend Warner, and Patricia Highsmith, only wrote "about lesbians" once or in a scattered fashion?[30]

But then what does lesbian character or action look like in literature—given that literature is not life and has a history and conventions of its own? Are lesbians only lesbians when in love, in couples, in bed, and if more complicated than that, can lesbian writing be confined to those parameters? What about poetry as well as novels, short stories, essays, elegies, diaries, polemic, political analysis, and work that was never published: Amy Lowell's verses, the Paris letters of Janet Flanner, and the diaries of Alice Dunbar-Nelson? What about women such as Dunbar-Nelson and Angelina Weld Grimke, whose work was also shaped by the pressures of racism or class?[31] How do we create frames for lesbian subjects that take into account race and class?

What do we owe to the range of lesbian writers whose representations, politics, and choices we do not approve, including such a disparate pair as Radclyffe Hall and Djuna Barnes? There has been fierce critical battle over *The Well of Loneliness*, on the grounds of its politics and its unhappy ending. Djuna Barnes was for a long time barely mentioned because of the threatened despair in her famous *Nightwood* and perhaps also because of the explicit sexuality of the *Ladies Almanack*. Finally, what is to be done with radically experimental and thus less accessible writers, like Djuna Barnes again, Virginia Woolf, and Gertrude Stein herself, for a long time everyone's favorite unread lesbian writer? It was not until the late 1970s that work on more politically and/or stylistically difficult subjects such as Cather, Barnes, and Stein really began.

The chief casualty of the critical assumption of a more or less unproblematic connection between living and literary lesbians was the discussion of experimental fiction. Bertha Harris, a writer of experimental fiction herself, championed the work of Djuna Barnes, and in an expansive gesture proposed that the "lesbian" could be identified with the moster, so that monster novels such as Peter Benchley's *Jaws* could be considered lesbian novels.[32] At the same time, in "Toward a Female Aesthetic" Julia Penelope Stanley and Susan J. Wolfe were arguing, in an exclusionary gesture, that true lesbian writing was inevitably experimental.[33] But because of the practical hegemony of fictional "realism" neither of these arguments "took."[34] Rather, the discussion of modernist writing that did develop at the end of the 1970s was interwoven with the development of the chief convention of lesbian criticism itself, the idea of "coding."

The concept of coding allowed critics to broaden their discussions beyond the narrow range of the "lesbian novel," offering freedom from both "girls" as identifying sign and narrative as form. It was based on the ongoing assumption of the cultural repression of lesbian writing, as Zimmerman explained: "One of the most pervasive themes in lesbian criticism is that women-identified writers, silenced by a homophobic and misogynist society, have been forced to adopt coded and obscure language and internal censorship."[35] According to this interpretive paradigm, Stimpson argued, "the literary encoding does what Morse Code does: it transmits messages in a different form which initiates may translate back into the original":[36] lesbian writers encoded lesbian references in texts that to straight readers appear to be neutral—asexual, heterosexual, or exclusively concerned with the fall of the Roman Empire—but, a privileged reader or group of readers, having knowledge of the writer's sexuality or having the same sexuality, can read the "real" lesbian subject. So narrative could be bypassed completely. The "girls" should still be there, but they did not have to look like girls in a realist fashion. The concept was particularly applied to modernist writers, especially Stein: within this framework literary experimentation was often read as an attempt to obscure while expressing the lesbian subject.

Yet the idea of coding is also problematic. Associated with experimental or nonrealist fiction it creates a false demarcation—implying that there are unmediated or less mediated texts and so obscuring the extent to which Stephen Gordon's broad shoulders, narrow hips, and intellectual pretensions are as much a code as Gertrude Stein's cows and tender buttons. It does not take account of the "codes," for example references to the Greeks, that were public speech, used by both heterosexual and lesbian writers as signs of the lesbian.[37] Moreover, the dichotomy established between public and private speech obscures the possibility of a lesbian writer working unchallenged, often by simply avoiding those tropes already publicly coded as lesbian—the broad shoulders and narrow hips—or by avoiding conventional narrative, i.e., creating Clarissa Dalloway and Orlando instead of Stephen Gordon. A particular private speech was not always necessary.

The discussion of lesbian coding and modernism implies neater correspondences and simpler meanings lurking behind modernist texts than these texts can bear: it initiates searches for what are in some cases different kinds of meanings than the texts were created to convey. It deflects attention away from texts by these authors that are considered less "modernist," that are and are not less "obscure," and that certainly operate within a different system than perhaps either the discussion of coding or conventional discussions of modernism allow: Woolf's *Orlando* and *Between the Acts,* or Stein's narrative works, such as *The Autobiography of Alice B. Toklas* and *Wars I Have Seen,* hover on some other borders than those between "obscurity" and "clarity," coded and open. Finally, the critical emphasis on coding in relation to modernism itself sometimes seems to turn the modernist gesture into a negative and defensive choice—as a means of obscuring lesbian meaning—when it could as logically be read as a positive search for expanded possibilities for lesbian expression.[38]

The repression hypothesis from which coding derives tends to imply that there were other, more direct ways for saying what was being said, of writing "about lesbianism," that the writer has avoided because of social pressure—that in effect within each Clarissa Dalloway there is a Stephen Gordon waiting to come out. As Stimpson observed, "The texts these women generated were often coded rather than open; sublimated rather than straightforward; hazy with metaphors and silence rather than lucid. Women are now far more exuberantly expressive."[39] In retrospect it seems that the unexamined assumptions were double—firstly, that there could be some direct unrepressed true literary representation, but also, secondly, that we know what lesbian writing would be like if not for social repression. This glosses over the more complicated and deeper effects of oppression—that the problem created by social taboo is an absence of cultural structures for conceptualizing, understanding, and representing what is forbidden, not just fear of punishment that forces silence. Through their complex modernist experiments Woolf and Stein and Barnes were saying things that could not have been imagined without the forms they created, and through creating the forms they spoke.

But through the concept of coding modernist fiction has entered the discussion of lesbian writing. The 1980s have also seen the publication of letters, diaries, and biographical studies confirming much of what was only informed speculation in the 1970s—about Virginia Woolf, Vita Sackville-West, Janet Flanner, Alice Dunbar-Nelson, Sylvia Townsend Warner, Sylvia Beach, Djuna Barnes, Willa Cather, H. D. etc, including finally a feminist study of Natalie Barney and Renee Vivien, Karla Jay's *The Amazon and the Page.*[40] Yet there still remains a gap between, figuratively, Gertrude Stein and Radclyffe Hall—between the high modernist and the pseudo-Victorian. The question of how deal with those many writers who did not write "lesbian novels," who did not—or not more than once or not in a narrative fashion—claim their girls, has not been addressed. The definitional problem, and its assumptions, also remain, including the continuing desire to turn the lesbian into a metaphor.

Bonnie Zimmerman recorded the absence of lesbian references from the major critical studies, anthologies, and journals of feminist criticism throughout the 1970s.[41] Her own essay then became the token lesbian contribution in two of the major essay collections of the mid-1980s, Elaine Showalter's *The New Feminist Criticism* and Gayle Greene and Coppelia Kahn's *Making a Difference*, which thus responded to her critiques by incorporating them.[42] In the consolidation and review of the history of feminist criticism that took place during the mid-1980s, lesbian criticism was still marginalized (often along with black feminist criticism): Toril Moi, in her widely read *Sexual/Textual Politics* (1985), explicitly excluded both from her view, because "so far, lesbian and/or black feminist criticism have presented exactly the same *methodological* and *theoretical* problems as the rest of Anglo-American feminist criticism."[43] Most recently, in a new defense of American feminist criticism, *Feminist Literary History*, Janet Todd also connects black and lesbian critics, this time as the two sources of salvation for feminist criticism as a whole.[44] But she does not discuss either black or lesbian criticism in any more detail.

Nevertheless, within Anglo-American feminist criticism in the 1980s there has also been a shift, at least with regard to fiction, from an early concentration on the nineteenth-century novel to a new interest in the subject of twentieth-century women's writing, in extended studies such as Rachel Blau DuPlessis' *Writing Beyond the Ending*, Shari Benstock's *Women of the Left Bank*, Gillian Hanscombe and Virginia Smyers' *Writing for Their Lives*, and Sandra Gilbert and Susan Gubar's *No Man's Land*.[45] This shift has forced feminist criticism into considering writers whose lesbianism cannot be overlooked, and who, like Woolf and Stein, cannot be dismissed. So lesbians are being mentioned much more often by feminist critics, with more and less useful results.

There has been continuing resistance to marking significant distinctions between lesbian and heterosexual women writers. For example, the lesbian and the lesbian writer are used without any reference to sexual difference as metaphors for women and women's writing—Sappho as the archetypal woman writer, and Virginia Woolf as the archetypal modern woman writer—in the work of Sandra Gilbert, Susan Gubar, and Jane Marcus.[46]

Another form of this resistance that is peculiar to discussions of the modernist period is the argument that is advanced by Hanscombe and Smyers in *Writing for Their Lives* and that is implicit in Gilbert and Gubar's *The War of the Words*, the first volume of their *No Man's Land* trilogy, that the women of these generations were all sexual revolutionaries together. Hanscombe and Smyers argue that "modernism, for its women, was not just a question of style; it was a way of life":[47]

> Modernist women—writers, editors, publishers, booksellers—who wanted to fulfill their own drives with as little compromise as possible, either eschewed sexual relationships with men altogether; or dallied with them; or chose the lesbian option; or did their best (as far as they dared) before seeing the writing on the wall and deciding to leave the battlefront. There were some, though—a minority, certainly—for whom the best means of defence was indeed, attack. For these women, their sense of sanity and autonomy demanded that they keep the battle joined until heterosexual relations underwent transformation.[48]

Gilbert and Gubar engage all women writers equally in the "battle of the sexes," which they propose as "one possible metastory, a story of stories about gender strife" in twentieth-century literature,[49] which in the first half of the century took the form of conflict "between turn-of-the-century misogynists and rebellious suffragists, between modernist no-men and autonomous New Women, between midcentury he-men and ambitious independent women."[50]

In order to construct such parallel lives Hanscombe and Smyers must emphasize their subjects' shared reaction against men's incapacity to be proper partners. This only echoes the conventional explanation of lesbian as well as heterosexual women's choices in terms of the women's relations to men. Gilbert and Gubar's incorporation of lesbian and heterosexual women writers into parallel relations to determining male figures is more sophisticated. But in *The War of the Words* their use of Freud's explanation of the development of female sexuality and then a Freudian "family romance" paradigm to describe the literary relations of male and female writers to each other and to previous generations also provides a system of explanation that can contain lesbians within the same pattern of analysis as their heterosexual peers. All women writers can then be described in terms of their responses to both the father figures of male literary history and Freud himself.[51] When the lesbian in question is not being seen in relation to the father/Freud, these structures allow for the discussion of lesbian writing in terms of a "masculine affiliation complex" and "male impersonation,"[52] terms that have an unfortunately familiar ring.

In *Sexchanges*, the second volume of *No Man's Land*, Gilbert and Gubar attempt a separate and more specific discussion of lesbian writing. But they derive their paradigms for this discussion from an extraordinarily literal reading of *The Well of Loneliness*: Hall's story of Stephen Gordon's tormented life, culminating in her sacrifice of her lover to heterosexual social and literary conventions, is seen as reflecting "the fragility of the homosexual community and the homosexual couple."[53] According to Gilbert and Gubar, *The Well* "delineates the isolation that modernist lesbian writing seeks to erase."[54] But Radclyffe Hall's own decades-long union with Una Troubridge contradicts such a one-dimensional (and conventional) analysis of lesbian life.[55] Gilbert and Gubar even seem unaware that lesbian critics have been debating about *The Well* for two decades.[56]

Rachel Blau DuPlessis makes a much more successful attempt to acknowledge lesbian presences in *Writing Beyond the Ending*, partly because of her general avoidance of biographical interpretation and her interest in systemic structures, literary and social. However, because she is focusing on heterosexual romance plot conventions, her analyses of individual works and writers are inevitably constrained. Lesbianism is too often construed as a response to that plot rather than any more independent alternative possibility, as in a discussion of Virginia Woolf's *Mrs. Dalloway*, where "the use of lesbian desire" is seen as "another way . . . to pose the critique of the convention of romance."[57]

In *Women of the Left Bank* Shari Benstock tries to avoid the empirical dangers of "American feminist criticism" by employing both feminist and deconstructionist analyses. Within this framework she then addresses the fact that "thirteen of the twenty-two women of this study" were lesbian, as the basis for an exploration of differences among women.[58] Unfortunately, despite the value of her research, she fails to rethink any of the literary elements of the lesbian writer's position. Instead she adopts uncritically a range of assumptions: about "lesbian writing"—"to write as a lesbian (as Radclyffe Hall did, for instance"; heterosexual imitation—"the Gertrude Stein model: to live as a lesbian in imitation of the heterosexual norm"; and coding—Stein "writing encoded lesbian works that could not be decoded by a heterosexual reading public."[59]

But Benstock's is the most ambitious attempt to consider sexual "difference" among women writers. Toril Moi dismissed lesbian criticism in the context of a valorization of French feminist criticism. In "Gender Theory and the Yale School" Barbara Johnson addresses the ease with which women can be erased within theory, in relation to her own work as well as that of de Man, Hartman, and Bloom et al.[60] Feminist theoreticians have usually not been concerned with sexual difference, instead sharing with more empirical critics the emphasis on male/female gender difference that Teresa de Lauretis argues, in *Technologies of Gender*, "tends to recontain or recuperate the radical epistemological potential of feminist thought inside the walls of the master's house."[61]

At the same time, both Nancy K. Miller and Barbara Christian have pointed to the dangers of deconstruction for women and people of color, who have never yet been granted by the dominant culture a unified and authoritative self.[62] While some feminist critics have discovered that "woman" is not a transparent category, such a state of epistemological insecurity is not particularly new to lesbians. In *Four in America* Gertrude Stein described the United States as the oldest modern nation because it entered the twentieth century before any other country; lesbians might turn out to be the first postmodern people, having "always/already" been deconstructed. The history of lesbian criticism has been a history of construction. The debate about the definition of the lesbian, reflecting as it does the larger problem of defining our subject, is predicated on the possibility of historically real authors and politically engaged readings for historically specific readers. Much lesbian criticism has implicitly relied on the claim that our revisionary readings are the "real" or the "true," as a basic justification, even as, by existing and writing, we prove that the conventional real and true are neither. Deconstruction might free lesbian critics from the burden of impossible proofs. But there have also been lesbian writers and theorists, from Bertha Harris to Monique Wittig, who have been claiming the right to invent, to "make it up," for the last twenty years, without benefit of critical authorities.

Deconstruction promises the rediscovery of repressed meanings and marginalized subjects: its claim for what Gayatri Spivak calls "scrupulous and plausible misreadings" in the interest of "alert pedagogy" contains obvious possibilities for readers usually classed as invalid.[63] At the same time, the value of such terms as "repression" and "marginal" to the discussion of lesbian writing is questionable. As "coding" may be an unnecessarily negative construction for describing the relation between the (at least hypothetical) writer's intention and the text, with regard to lesbian writings the concept of repressed meanings may be similarly inadequate or distorting. Elizabeth Abel, for example, in her essay "Narrative Structure(s) and Female Development," discusses the lesbian element in Virginia Woolf's *Mrs. Dalloway* as repressed in terms of form ("submerged in the anonymity of the background"), as well as psychoanalytically (a "recessive narrative . . . of pre-Oedipal attachment and loss)", whereas it could equally well be argued that the lesbian story is structurally and emotionally central to the novel.[64] The history of interpretation of lesbian writing generally and *Mrs. Dalloway* in particular illustrates the extent to which the question of what is in the background and what in the foreground depends on the capacity of readers and critics. Stein responded to charges of obscurity in *Everybody's Autobiography*:

> He said that I talked so clearly why did I not write clearly. I do write clearly. That is not the answer that is a fact. I think I write so clearly that I worry about it. Not really, but a fact. However I began to explain to him then and at intervals all that winter I explained it to him and then at last I wrote him letters about it explaining to him how explanations are clear but since no one to whom a thing is explained can connect the explanations with what is really clear, therefore clear explanations are not clear.[65]

Not only should we be wary of assuming that "lesbian meaning" is repressed, but we must also be careful of unreflectively accepting the designation of marginality. White upper- and middle-class women did not necessarily lose racial and class privileges because they were lesbian. Gertrude Stein and Virginia Woolf, for example, were not marginal to the work of their generations. Amy Lowell, Willa Cather, and H. D. benefited respectively from the advantages of class, popular recognition, and high-cultural connections. And in contemporary terms, Woolf has not been marginal to either feminist criticism's theoretical formulations or its reconstructions of the history of women's writing.[66]

Lesbian writing also needs to be considered in relation to the comparatively new emphasis on "gender"—as in "gender studies"—among feminist critics. The contents of two recent essay collections, Linda Kauffman's *Gender and Theory: Dialogues on Feminist Criticism* and Elaine Showalter's *Speaking of Gender* are illuminating. In *Gender and Theory*, in which "gender" is identified with feminist criticism and females and "theory" identified with males, the pairing seems primarily to allow for strictly heterosexual exchanges (reminiscent of Gilbert and Gubar's paradigm of literary history in *No Man's Land*). Within these exchanges, the subject of lesbianism is raised once, by a gay male critic.[67] Both this relative absence and mediated presence are prophetic of *Speaking of Gender*, in which there is no essay that deals with lesbianism, but three essays about gay male subjects. In her introduction Showalter draws revealing parallels even as she insists that "most feminist critics agree on . . . the need to explore masculinity as well as femininity, and homosexuality as well as heterosexuality,"[68] confirming the impression the subsequent discussions convey, that through gender studies gay men will be incorporated, and even become central, to some feminist analyses, while lesbian subjects remain at best peripheral.[69]

At the same time, the construction of a lesbian literary history begun by Foster, Grier, Rule, and Faderman has been joined by more mainstream feminist critics, especially Gilbert and Gubar, within their all-encompassing account of twentieth-century women's writing. Such work inevitably raises the question of whether or not there is a lesbian tradition. That in turn is part of older, larger questions: whether the purpose of feminist criticism is to change existing interpretations of literary traditions as embodied in various canons, to construct alternative traditions of women's writing, or to challenge the idea of canons altogether—to promote a more flexible understanding of literary history and the teaching of literature. At the same time, there is a question about the works themselves: in what ways is it useful to consider lesbian writing in terms of a tradition?

There are biographical connections between the writers of particular generations. These appear in the work in the sense that Natalie Barney appears as Valerie Seymour in Hall's *Well of Loneliness*, and both Barney and Hall serve as subjects in Djuna Barnes' *Ladies Almanack*. Louise DeSalvo's study of the relationship between Virginia Woolf and Vita Sackville-West illustrates not only that Sackville-West inspired Woolf's *Orlando* but that Woolf also influenced Sackville-West's writing: her novel *The Edwardians* (1930), for example, has an Orlando hero/ine divided back into two characters, a Shakespearean brother and sister, Sebastian and Viola.[70] In even less specific form the relationship between Bryher and H. D. resulted in an exchange whereby, put simply, H. D. "gave" Bryher her passion for "the Greeks" as a focus of lesbian meaning and reference and Bryher "gave" H. D. her knowledge of the Elizabethans.

Less personal connections are also apparent. A pattern of reference to the transvestite heroines of Elizabethan drama can be traced from the epigraph of Gertrude Stein's 1903 first novel, *Q.E.D.*—a long quotation from Shakespeare's *As You Like It*—to the lurid-covered U.S. pulp paperbacks of the 1950s. In her brilliant essay on "Lesbian Intertextuality" Elaine Marks describes the recurrence of a "Sappho model" in French literature through, for example, the repeated use of girls' school settings and teaching paradigms.[71]

The idea of a lesbian "tradition," or "canon," "aesthetic," or "literary imagination" has been a continuing and comparatively unquestioned theme within lesbian criticism.[72] This can be seen partly as a reaction to the apparent lack of history confronting those who began the project of lesbian criticism. Information, connections, and coherence were prime necessities. Working against the silence of conventional criticism and much early feminist work, it also perhaps appeared that any formulation about lesbian writing was challenging in itself, even if its terms might be conventional. A lesbian tradition was self-evidently radical both because of the assumption—shared with other studies of women's writing and, for example, Afro-American writing—that content mattered as well as form, and because of the socially proscribed nature of "lesbian" content. But by the late 1980s we must also allow that discussion of the "lesbian" is not in itself enough, that it does not in a literary context obviate, for example, the restrictive assumptions behind canonicity.

Because of class, race, historical, and national distinctions we could only finally hope to trace traditions, not *the* tradition. And recently Biddy Martin has pointed out the dangers, in contemporary accounts of lesbian lives, of unreflectively incorporating those distinctions within a still essentially undifferentiated "feminism":

> differences, for example, of race, class, or sexuality, are finally rendered noncontradictory by virtue of their (re)presentation as differences within individuals, reducible to questions of identity within the unifying context of feminism. What remains unexamined are the systemic institutional relationships between those differences, relationships that exceed the boundaries of the lesbian community, the women's movement, or particular individuals, and in which apparently bounded communities and individuals are deeply implicated.[73]

The undifferentiated feminism might be either that of contemporary autobiographers interpreting their own lives or of contemporary biographers and critics interpreting the lives of other women, including women of previous generations. Martin sees a solution in her reading of contemporary autobiographies by women of color and white women, in that in such current work

> lesbianism ceases to be an identity with predictable contents, to constitute a total political and self-identification, and yet it

figures no less centrally for that shift. It remains a position from which to speak, to organize, to act politically, but it ceases to be the exclusive and continuous ground of identity or politics. Indeed, it works to unsettle rather than to consolidate the boundaries around identity, not to dissolve them altogether but to open them to the fluidities and heterogeneities that make their renegotiation possible.[74]

There remains in even such a self-consciously specific analysis a level of metaphor, the desire to ascribe to lesbian identity some necessary social or political power. Yet Martin's formulation that though "lesbianism ceases . . . to constitute a total political and self-identification" it yet "figures no less centrally for that shift," and her insistence on "differences . . . that exceed the boundaries of the lesbian community" offers the basis for a re-vision of the "tradition," "canon," and "aesthetic" assumptions. Moving back beyond the writing of the last two decades she is considering, historically as well we must recognize the lesbian subject as both shifting and shaped by other sets of relations—class, racial, and national. Lesbianism was never "an identity with predictable contents," and that is perhaps why it might be, as she argues, always a destabilizing factor, undercutting even our own attempts to describe its cultural effects.

The assumption of the absence of lesbian representation that Woolf articulated in *A Room of One's Own* was echoed by Djuna Barnes, also in the 1920s, when she referred in the *Ladies Almanack* to stories that "could be printed nowhere and in no Country."[75] It has been maintained as the premise of lesbian writing and criticism into the 1970s and 1980s. Since the 1960s, especially, for example, in North America and Britain, it has become possible to be a lesbian writer in a way not conceivable before—in terms of the ability to create and publish lesbian representations, a sense of history, and a sense of a lesbian audience. But the spirit of the age is still not propitious: Adrienne Rich, for example, has spoken in the 1970s and 1980s about the cultural silencing of lesbians.

Yet although the fact of oppression is unavoidable—the space to speak even now, as Teresa de Lauretis has observed, "hard-won and daily threatened by social disapprobation, censure, and denial, a space of contradiction requiring constant reaffirmation and painful renegotiation"—there they are speaking, and even if privately, publishing.[76] Bonnie Zimmerman argued in 1981 that "Lesbian criticism begins with the establishment of the lesbian text: the creation of language out of silence."[77] But because of the work lesbian and feminist critics have done, we now know that lesbians have "spoken": either in the manner of Radclyffe Hall, or the manner of Gertrude Stein, or through an infinite range of styles and solutions in between. In the twentieth century, at least, some of them made it into cultural pantheons (insofar as women ever do), and some onto best-seller lists. It seems therefore that an opposition posed between silence and speech no longer provides a useful framework for understanding lesbian writing. Silencing did not prevent speech; such contradictions should be central to our analyses. While the chief contradiction might be in existing and not existing within the culture at the same time, in this literary context we need to consider such specific contradictions as simultaneous repression and production.

This paradox brings us back again to the problem of definition. Although Toril Moi in *Sexual/Textual Politics* argued that there were no methodological issues specific to lesbian criticism, there are obviously particular methodological problems derived from both the historical/political context of lesbian writing and the history of the lesbian criticism already done. The central question particular to lesbian criticism remains that of its subject. All discussions proceed across a terrain that by the late 1980s we can see is neither temporarily nor theoretically unknown but permanently and practically unstable. The epistemological insecurity, the question of definition, and the persistent tendency toward metaphor will always be with us.

While the metaphorization of the lesbian within criticism can be connected to a similar tendency within feminist political theory, this pattern can be traced in turn into the mainstream culture and back to the beginning of this century. The lesbian was treated—for good and ill—as a sign of the "modern" by such different writers as D. H. Lawrence, in *The Rainbow* (1915), F. Scott Fitzgerald, in *Tender is the Night* (1934), and Radclyffe Hall, in *The Unlit Lamp*. From the heterosexist dominant culture this can be read as a method of both distancing and containing "the lesbian" and therefore of control. From within recent political lesbian and gay cultures, the image of the lesbian as the transcendent revolutionary, for example, replaces conventional hostile images and exclusively sexual images (which were sometimes the same thing). Within lesbian criticism, the desire to make the lesbian the revolutionary in linguistic or cultural terms reflects in part a frustration with both the limitations of accepted representations (particularly perhaps the "lesbian novel") and the debate about definition.

But metaphor does not offer a way around the question of definition, that is, a way out of culture. The debate about the relative value of metaphor or specificity in the discussion of lesbian subjects often turns on history, with charges that the metaphor is ahistorical.[78] But it is not history that divides these approaches. Each term in the debate reflects a cultural reality—and a historically circumscribed reality. In *Technologies of Gender* Teresa de Lauretis describes "Woman with the capital letter, the *representation* of an essence inherent in all women (which has been seen as Nature, Mother, Mystery, Evil Incarnate, Object of [Masculine] Desire and Knowledge, Proper Womanhood, Femininity, et cetera)" as "distinct from women, the real, historical beings and social subjects."[79] Similarly, the Lesbian is the metaphor—a complex of powerful cultural images (with, by the late 1980s, both conservative and radical sources): she is modernity; gender transgression; sexual threat; sexual fantasy; or in feminist terms, revolutionary purity. Individual lesbians are "real, historical" women who love other "real, historical" women, within the social world of daughters, aunts, mothers, sisters, and girls next door, with its divisions by race and class and gender as well as its imposition of heterosexual appearances. The lives of all lesbians are lived in some relation to the Lesbian (relations always complex and often shifting and even contradictory), but none of these women is the Lesbian.

While I do not want to deny the oppression experienced by individual women, in cultural terms it is the Lesbian that is at the same time defined and repressed. Behind the screen provided especially by mainstream cultural definitions lesbian repesentation has been most often unrecognized or unacknowledged in both literature and criticism. This is one source of the continuing contradiction between repression and production, cultural absence and presence. The question of definition is the point of connection between these terms. If we are going to be able to acknowledge and then study the literature lesbians have produced, the question of definition must itself be problematized rather than resolved.

Definition will be an ongoing task without a conclusion, shared between authors, texts and critics. It requires constant consciousness of the Lesbian and her changing forms as well as constant openness to new (or previously unrecognized) representations, and relations between individual lesbians, the Lesbian and representation. Some of the answers to the questions of lesbian identity must be individual and biographical. But, with regard to the literature, given that we do not know what lesbian writing might look like, all of the work of those who can be historically identified, not only the novels about girls, should be considered.

When Woolf's imaginary governess asks of the writing of her very real lover, "Are girls necessary?" it is a complex question. It makes lesbianism the focus of this passage about the social control of writing. As asked in this apparently comic text, the question is only vaguely hostile ("Must you say this?") but definitely controlling ("Will I allow you this?"). And the answer is not yes or no but qualified: yes, given external circumstances, the biography of the author within the text (Orlando's marriage), and the historical place and time, the foreignness of the girls in question in relation to whole patterns of cultural connections between Empire, class, race, and sexuality. Answers to the question of what can and cannot be said are always qualified and contingent, Woolf indicates. And the question itself has not even been provoked by a story of love between women, but by a possible connection between a writer and her subject, suggesting the detail of both the social policing involved and the self-consciousness it produced. In this way the question also points directly back to Woolf herself, and the text within which this passage is contained. *Orlando* began, Woolf recorded in her diary, as "The Jessamy Brides," a fantastical narrative about two women in which "Sapphism [was] to be suggested."[80] In the very different work that resulted, she-Orlando responds to other women: "if the consciousness of being of the same sex had any affect at all, it was to quicken and deepen those feelings which she had as a man. . . . if there is anything in what the poet says about truth and beauty, this affection gained in beauty what it lost in falsity."[81] But "girls," in the "lesbian novel" sense, play a comparatively small part. The central relationship of *Orlando* is that between the author and her subject, Sackville-West.[82] Woolf's question, within Woolf's text, is also a challenge to our interpretive skills.

Attempting to deny that *Orlando* is a lesbian text and Woolf a lesbian writer, Ellen Bayuk Rosenman recently argued that "although many critics today identify *Orlando* as a lesbian novel, nothing in its overt content marks it as such." It appeared in the midst of the *Well of Loneliness* scandal and was quickly linked to Sackville-West, but it aroused no controversy; it was, in fact, one of Woolf's great popular successes. Its implicit lesbian content was, in the words of Sherron Knopp, 'one of the best-kept secrets in literary history.' "[83] But that Woolf's work was not controversial while *The Well* (which was hugely successful in terms of sales) was persecuted only underlines Woolf's point about the flexibility of the distinction between what can and cannot be said. *Orlando,* of all the lesbian texts that might be considered—not only dedicated to but illustrated by photographs of its female subject—makes any distinction between "implicit" and "overt" lesbian content, and the idea of "lesbian content" itself, untenable.

Rosenman claims that she is putting the question of Woolf's sexuality into historical perspective. But she argues that because Woolf did not write like Radclyffe Hall, because she would not have identified with Hall (who represented the dominant cultural idea of lesbianism at the time), because she made ambivalent comments about lesbians, and because she did not "consider her relationship with Sackville-West a disease or perversion, as both sexologists and Hall herself would have done," Woolf cannot be considered a lesbian.[84] Such historicizing involves imposing the little we are sure of—in this case *The Well of Loneliness,* its obscenity trials, and medical views of homosexuality—over a multiplicity of possibilities, here everything Woolf wrote and all the information we have about her life. If one does not fit into the other, if Woolf does not fit into the Radclyffe Hall model, then nothing that Hall represented so publicly applies to Woolf. The alternative conclusion, however, might be that the Hall model, the public image, is not appropriate to the reality being considered. Rosenman's historical context contains no understanding of individual lesbians' responses to social disapprobation nor of the distinction and complex relations between lesbians and the Lesbian. When Woolf, as Rosenman notes, dropped a reference to Chloe and Olivia sharing a bed from *A Room of One's Own,* she muted her girls. But she described the anxiety that the subject of women together aroused, and left us the political, historical references that explain that anxiety. We have to allow, given the cultural climate in which *A Room* was produced, that to invoke the persecution of lesbian writing was as much a means of lesbian representation as referring to beds.

In pursuit of lesbian representation Teresa de Lauretis considers

> how lesbian writers and artists have sought variously to escape gender, to deny it, transcend it, or perform it in excess, and to inscribe the erotic in cryptic, allegorical, realistic, camp, or other modes of representation, pursuing diverse strategies of writing and of reading the intransitive and yet obdurate relation of reference to meaning, of flesh to language.[85]

Woolf's *Orlando* is about nothing more than gender and the erotic. But although lesbian difference may be a matter of the flesh, it is also a matter of the relation of the flesh to the social world and cultural forms. In the flesh girls may be necessary, but in the text they are not. I am not proposing critical celibacy, but rather new levels of critical complexity. After all, the "intransitive and yet obdurate relation of reference to meaning, of flesh to language" is not only expressed through attitudes toward gender. The inscription of the erotic can look like anything but girls—even, sometimes, boys. We might consider the subversion of looking for lesbian writers without looking for love, or looking for love, as it were, in all the wrong places, and be surprised by where we found sex, gender, and ourselves.

The study of lesbian writing has obviously not kept pace with the increasing number of courses, essays, books, and the developing conceptual sophistication of feminist criticism. It is a field not simply hampered by the oppression and repression of its subjects in the past, but by contemporary critics' reluctance to engage in this work for fear of personal and professional penalties. Less tangibly there is still an ongoing reluctance to name a writer lesbian, not out of intellectual doubt but because it is a term that the woman might not have chosen for herself, a term she might have vehemently rejected, and because there is still a broader critical as well as cultural discomfort not just with seeing but also with saying—unless the woman herself declared herself, and even then, it is at best still "limiting," hardly nice, hardly kind. How can you elaborate a critical discourse on that basis? How can you not?

## Endnotes

1. Gertrude Stein, "Composition as Explanation," in Carl Van Vechten, ed., *Selected Writings of Gertrude Stein* (New York: Vintage, 1972), pp. 513–14.
2. Virginia Woolf, *Orlando* (Harmondsworth, England: Penguin, 1975), p. 188.
3. *Ibid.*, p. 187.
4. Virginia Woolf, *A Room of One's Own* (New York: Harcourt Brace, 1929), p. 142.
5. See Vera Brittain, *Radclyffe Hall: A Case of Obscenity?* (London: Femina, 1968).
6. Woolf, *A Room of One's Own*, p. 142.
7. *Ibid.*, p. 146.
8. See Jeanette Foster, *Sex Variant Women in Literature* (Baltimore, Md.: Diana, 1975), and Lillian Faderman, *Surpassing the Love of Men: Romantic Friendship and Love Between Women from the Renaissance to the Present* (New York: Morrow, 1981).
9. In *A Room* Woolf proposed, taking an example from Shakespeare, that the hostility between Cleopatra and Octavia in *Antony and Cleopatra* was representative of the relations of women in literature until the arrival of Chloe

and Olivia. Yet the relationship of Rosalind and Celia—"Whose loves Are dearer than the natural bond of sisters" (1:2:292–93); "We still have slept together, Rose at an instant, learn'd, play'd, eat together; And whereso'er we went, like Juno's swans, Still we went coupled and inseparable" (1:3:76–79)—not to mention the other lesbian and gay allusions and enactments of *As You Like It*, are of course implicit in her choice of "Orlando" as the name for her fictional portrait of her own lover.

10. It is a question that has been both implicitly and explicitly present: Bonnie Zimmerman points to this as the central problem of lesbian criticism in "What Has Never Been: An Overview of Lesbian Feminist Criticism," in Elaine Showalter, ed., *The New Feminist Criticism: Women, Literature and Theory* (New York: Pantheon, 1985), pp. 200–24.

11. See Judith Lowder Newton, "History as Usual? Feminism and the New Historicism," in H. Aram Veeser, ed., *The New Historicism* (New York: Routledge, 1989); and Janet Todd, *Feminist Literary History* (New York: Routledge, 1988).

12. Bonnie Zimmerman has also argued, in "What Has Never Been," that "lesbian criticism and theory in general can only gain by developing a greater specificity, historically and culturally" (p. 215).

13. Cora Kaplan, *Sea Changes: Essays on Culture and Feminism* (London: Verso, 1986), p. 59.

14. Foster, *Sex Variant Women in Literature*, p. 12. Foster continued: "Still they often exhibit indirect responses which have all the intensity of physical passion and which quite as basically affect the pattern of their lives. Hence this study includes not only women who are conscious of passion for their own sex, with or without overt expression, but also those who are merely obsessively attached to other women over a longer period or at a more mature age than is commonly expected. If 'commonly expected' is another nebulous phrase, a species of pooled judgment is available to clarify it. During the past few decades—that is, since Freudian concepts have become a part of the common background—most works on sex guidance have taken some account of homosexuality. These agree in general that passionate attachments during puberty and early adolescence may lie within the norm, but if occurring later they constitute variance. Without here debating the absolute validity of this opinion, one may borrow it as a working criterion."

15. See Barbara Grier, ed., *The Lesbian in Literature* (Tallahassee, Fla.: Naiad Press, 1981); and J. R. Roberts, ed., *Black Lesbians: An Annotated Bibliography* (Tallahassee, Fla.: Naiad Press, 1981).

16. See Jane Rule, *Lesbian Images* (New York: Doubleday, 1975).

17. See Susan Koppelman Cornillon, ed., *Images of Women in Fiction: Feminist Perspectives* (Bowling Green, Ohio: Bowling Green University Popular Press, 1972). The implicit demand for "positive images"—role models or inspirational authors and characters—was explicitly discussed by feminist critics, who came to differing conclusions. See Josephine Donovan, ed., *Feminist Literary Criticism: Explorations in Theory* (Lexington: University of Kentucky Press, 1975).

18. See Brittain, *Radclyffe Hall*; Gillian Whitlock, "'A Martyr Reluctantly Canonised': The Lesbian Literary Tradition," *Hecate* (1984), 10(2):19–39 and "'Everything Is Out of Place': Radclyffe Hall and the Lesbian Literary Tra-

dition," *Feminist Studies* (fall 1987), 13(3):555–82; and Esther Newton, "The Mythic Mannish Lesbian: Radclyffe Hall and the New Woman," *Signs* (1984), 9:557–75.

19. Whitlock, " 'Everything Is Out of Place,' " p. 558.

20. Carroll Smith-Rosenberg, "The Female World of Love and Ritual: Relations Between Women in Nineteenth-Century America," *Signs* (Fall 1975), 1(1):1–29.

21. See Radicalesbians, "The Woman-Identified Woman," in Anne Koedt, Ellen Levine, and Anita Rapone, eds., *Radical Feminism* (New York: Quadrangle, 1973); and Del Martin and Phyllis Lyon, *Lesbian/Woman* (New York: Bantam, 1972). Blanche Wiesen Cook, " 'Women Alone Stir My Imagination': Lesbianism and the Cultural Tradition," *Signs* (1979), 4(4):718–39 offers a good example of the functional interconnections between the literary, historical, and political debates.

22. Barbara Smith, "Toward a Black Feminist Criticism," in Elaine Showalter, ed., *The New Feminist Criticism: Women, Literature and Theory* (New York: Pantheon, 1985), pp. 168–85; Adrienne Rich, "It Is the Lesbian in Us . . . ," in Adrienne Rich, *On Lies, Secrets, and Silence: Selected Prose, 1966–1978* (New York: Norton, 1979) and "Compulsory Heterosexuality and Lesbian Existence," in Adrienne Rich, *Blood, Bread, and Poetry: Selected Prose, 1979–1985* (New York: Norton, 1986).

23. Catharine R. Stimpson, "Zero Degree Deviancy: The Lesbian Novel in English," in *Where the Meanings Are: Feminism and Cultural Spaces* (New York: Methuen, 1988), p. 97.

24. Marilyn R. Farwell, "Toward a Definition of the Lesbian Literary Imagination," *Signs* (Fall 1988), 14(1):100–118. See also Lee Edelman, "At Risk in the Sublime: The Politics of Gender and Theory," in Linda Kauffman, ed., *Gender and Theory: Dialogues on Feminist Criticism* (New York: Blackwell, 1989), pp. 213–24.

25. Women's literature, as it was coming to be defined, did not include works by James, for example, who wrote of women so often. But such arguments from parallels are only partially useful, given that James himself is frequently considered a British rather than a North American author.

26. Gertrude Stein, *Picasso* (New York: Dover, 1984), pp. 21–22.

27. The best-known instance of an arranged marriage is that of Bryher to Robert McAlmon in New York in 1921, which was intended to give her access to her financial inheritance and comparative freedom from her family's control, so enabling her to continue to live with H. D. and raise H. D.'s daughter, Perdita, whom she would later legally adopt. McAlmon was able to travel to Europe, and also gained access to Bryher's money, which he used to finance various Paris publishing schemes. The different parties to the transaction have of course since given a range of explanations and justifications. See Barbara Guest, *Herself Defined: The Poet H. D. and Her World* (New York: Morrow, 1984); Shari Benstock, *Women of the Left Bank: Paris, 1900–1940* (Austin: University of Texas Press, 1986), pp. 357–62; and Robert McAlmon, *Being Geniuses Together: 1920–1930*, revised with additional material by Kay Boyle (Garden City, N.Y.: Doubleday, 1968).

28. The effect of such destruction on subsequent conventional biographical work can be seen in James Woodress, *Willa Cather* (Lincoln: University of

Nebraska Press, 1987). See Sharon O'Brien, *Willa Cather: The Emerging Voice* (New York: Oxford University Press, 1987) for a more sympathetic reading of Cather's sexuality.

29. Deborah McDowell, introduction to *Quicksand* and *Passing*, by Nella Larsen (New Brunswick, N.J.: Rutgers University Press, 1986), pp. ix–xxxv.

30. A single novel "about lesbians" in a writer's career is quite common. See, for example, Sylvia Townsend Warner's *Summer Will Show* (1936), Mary Renault's *Friendly Young Ladies* (1945), Claire Morgan (Patricia Highsmith), *The Price of Salt* (1952), and Kate O'Brien's *As Music and Splendour* (1958).

31. See Gloria T. Hull, ed., *Give Us Each Day: The Diary of Alice Dunbar-Nelson* (New York: Norton, 1984) and, for discussions of Dunbar-Nelson and Weld Grimke, Hull's *Color, Sex and Poetry: Three Women Writers of the Harlem Renaissance* (Bloomington: Indiana University Press, 1987).

32. On Djuna Barnes, see Bertha Harris, "The More Profound Nationality of Their Lesbianism: Lesbian Society in Paris in the 1920s," in Phyllis Birkby et al., eds., *Amazon Expedition: A Lesbian Feminist Anthology* (Albion, Calif.: Times Change Press, 1973); with reference to sharks, see Harris' "What We Mean To Say: Notes Towards Defining the Nature of Lesbian Literature," *Heresies* (fall 1977), 3:5–9.

33. Julia Penelope Stanley and Susan J. Wolfe, "Toward a Feminist Aesthetic," *Chrysalis* (1978), 6:55–71.

34. Stimpson discusses the rejection of experimental fiction, and Bertha Harris' work in particular, in "Zero Degree Deviancy," pp. 108–10.

35. Zimmerman, "What Has Never Been," p. 207.

36. Catharine R. Stimpson, "The Mind, The Body and Gertrude Stein," *Critical Inquiry* (1977), 3:499.

37. D. H. Lawrence, for example, uses references to the Greeks in his characterization of the lesbian Winifred Inger in *The Rainbow* (1915), and Compton Mackenzie used extensive reference to Sappho in his comic *Extraordinary Women* (1928). The Greeks also, of course, appeared as part of many literary references to gay men.

38. Formally experimental texts, from Stein's *Tender Buttons* to Kate Millett's *Flying*, might be described as somehow "more lesbian" than realistic texts, because more disruptive of the conventional literary order (for example, by Stanley and Wolfe). But it could also be implied that they were "less lesbian," because they were not confrontational but indirect, allusive, coded (as was suggested by Stimpson, for example, in "The Mind, The Body and Gertrude Stein").

39. Stimpson, "The Mind, The Body and Gertrude Stein," p. 505.

40. The publication of Woolf's letters and diaries, and of the correspondence between Sackville-West and Woolf, as well as Victoria Glendinning's biography, provided ample evidence of Woolf's and Sackville-West's relationship and of Vita's lesbianism. See *The Letters of Virginia Woolf;* vol. 3, *1923–1928*, edited by Nigel Nicolson and Joanne Trautmann (London: Hogarth Press, 1977); *The Diary of Virginia Woolf*, vol. 3, *1925–1930*, edited by Anne Olivier Bell, assisted by Andrew McNellie (New York: Harcourt Brace Jovanovich, 1980); *The Letters of Vita Sackville-West to Virginia Woolf*, Louise DeSalvo and Mitchell A. Leaska, eds. (New York: Morrow, 1985); and Victoria Glendinning, *Vita: The Life of V. Sackville-West* (New York: Morrow, 1983).

Natalia Danesi Murray recorded her own relationship with Janet Flanner in *Darlinghissima: Letters to a Friend* (New York: Random House, 1985); Gloria Hull has edited Alice Dunbar-Nelson's diaries, *Give Us Each Day;* and Wendy Mulford tells the story of Sylvia Townsend Warner and Velentine Ackland in *This Narrow Place: Sylvia Townsend Warner and Valentine Ackland: Life, Letters, and Politics, 1930–1951* (London: Pandora Press, 1988), which has been supported by Ackland's memoir, *For Sylvia: An Honest Account* (New York: Norton, 1986). Sylvia Beach and Adrienne Monnier have been written about by Noel Riley Fitch in *Sylvia Beach and the Lost Generation: A History of Literary Paris in the Twenties and Thirties* (New York: Norton, 1983); Djuna Barnes by Andrew Field in *Djuna: The Life and Times of Djuna Barnes* (New York: Putnam's, 1983); and Willa Cather by Sharon O'Brien in *Willa Cather: The Emerging Voice.* Barbara Guest recorded H. D.'s relationship with Bryher in *Herself Defined.* See also Karla Jay's *The Amazon and the Page: Natalie Clifford Barney and Renée Vivien* (Bloomington: Indiana University Press, 1988).

41. Zimmerman, "What Has Never Been," pp. 200–3.

42. Gayle Greene and Coppelia Kahn, eds., *Making a Difference: Feminist Literary Criticism* (London: Methuen, 1985). For a discussion of the place of Showalter's collection within the history of feminist literary criticism see Janet Todd, *Feminist Literary History.*

43. Toril Moi, *Sexual/Textual Politics* (New York: Methuen, 1985), p. 86.

44. Todd, *Feminist Literary History,* pp. 5, 94.

45. Rachel Blau DuPlessis, *Writing Beyond the Ending: Narrative Strategies of Twentieth-Century Women Writers* (Bloomington: Indiana University Press, 1985); Gillian Hanscombe and Virginia L. Smyers, *Writing for Their Lives: The Modernist Women, 1910–1940* (Boston, Mass.: Northeastern University Press, 1987); Sandra M. Gilbert and Susan Gubar, *The War of the Words,* vol. 1 of *No Man's Land: The Place of the Woman Writer in the Twentieth Century* (New Haven, Conn.: Yale University Press, 1988).

46. Gilbert, Gubar, and Marcus actually seem to be in struggle over the term "sapphistry," which lesbian readers may be most likely to connect with Pat Califia's sex manual of that name: *Sapphistry* (Tallahassee, Fla. Naiad Press, 1981). See Susan Gubar, "Sapphistries," *Signs* (1984), 10:43–62 and Jane Marcus, *Virginia Woolf and the Languages of Patriarchy* (Bloomington: Indiana University Press, 1987), pp. 138 and 207, n. 5, and chapter 8, "Sapphistry: Narration as Lesbian Seduction in *A Room of One's Own."*

47. Hanscombe and Smyers, *Writing for Their Lives,* p. 11.

48. *Ibid.,* p. 247.

49. Gilbert and Gubar, *The War of the Words,* p. xiv.

50. *Ibid.,* p. 121. The heterosexual assumption shaping their view of literary history is also apparent in more individual terms. They discuss, for example, "a kind of scribbling sibling rivalry . . . [which] may have been established between mutually admiring pairs like James and Wharton, Yeats and Lady Gregory, Hemingway and Stein, Lawrence and Mansfield (or H. D.), Wells and West (or Richardson), Eliot and Woolf, Graves and Riding, Miller and Nin" (p. 149).

51. For example, discussing the responses of modern women writers to their female precursors, Gilbert and Gubar argue that, "the woman writer who engages with her autonomous precursor in a rivalrous struggle for pri-

macy often learns that the fruit of victory is bitter: the approbation of the father is almost always accompanied by his revulsion, and the autonomy of the mother is frequently as terrifying as it is attractive, for—as Woolf's comments about Charlotte Brontë suggest—it has been won at great cost" (Gilbert and Gubar, *The War of the Words*, p. 195).

52. *Ibid.*, pp. 185–86.

53. Sandra M. Gilbert and Susan Gubar, *Sexchanges*, vol. 2 of *No Man's Land: The Place of the Woman Writer in the Twentieth Century* (New Haven, Conn.: Yale University Press, 1989), p. 221.

54. *Ibid.*, p. 218.

55. See Michael Baker, *Our Three Selves: The Life of Radclyffe Hall* (New York: Morrow, 1985).

56. See Faderman, *Surpassing the Love of Men*; Lillian Faderman and Ann Williams, "Radclyffe Hall and the Lesbian Image," *Conditions* (April 1977), vol. 1; Beverley Brown, " 'A Disgusting Book When Properly Read': The Obscenity Trial," *Hecate* (1984), 10(2):8–19; Gillian Whitlock, " 'Everything Is Out of Place' "; and Newton: The Mythic Mannish Lesbian."

57. DuPlessis, *Writing Beyond the Ending*, p. 60.

58. Benstock, *Women of the Left Bank*, p. 8.

59. *Ibid.*, pp. 333–34.

60. See Barbara Johnson, "Gender Theory and the Yale School," in Elaine Showalter, ed., *Speaking of Gender* (New York: Routledge, 1989), pp. 45–55.

61. Teresa de Lauretis, *Technologies of Gender: Essays on Theory, Film, and Fiction* (Bloomington: Indiana University Press, 1987), p. 2.

62. See Nancy K. Miller, *Subject To Change: Reading Feminist Writing* (New York: Columbia University Press, 1988), especially chapter 3, and Barbara Christian, "The Race for Theory," in Linda Kauffman, ed., *Gender and Theory*, pp. 225–37.

63. Gayatri Spivak, *In Other Worlds: Essays in Cultural Politics* (New York: Methuen, 1987), p. 116.

64. Elizabeth Abel, "Narrative Structure(s) and Female Development," in Elizabeth Abel, Marianne Hirsch, and Elizabeth Langland, eds., *The Voyage In: Fictions of Female Development* (Hanover, N. H.: University Press of New England, 1983), pp. 163, 164.

65. Gertrude Stein, *Everybody's Autobiography*, (New York: Random House, 1973), p. 171.

66. Both feminist and nonfeminist critics have also valorized "silences" as the locations of the most significant meaning, the key to innovative alternative readings. But perhaps (following on from the earlier discussion of problems with the concept of "coding") it could be argued that for historical reasons alone there is a particular distinctive relation between a "text" and its "silences" for lesbian writings?

67. See Lee Edelman, "At Risk in the Sublime: The Politics of Gender and Theory."

68. Elaine Showalter, *Speaking of Gender*, p. 3.

69. This also suggests dubious assumptions about a necessary connection between male homosexuality and gender transgression. For one gay male critic's response to Sedgwick's work, especially *Between Men*, which Showalter suggests has resulted in the formation of a "Sedgwick school, or Ecole d'Eve" (Showalter, *Speaking of Gender*, p. 8), see David Van Leer, "The Beast of the

Closet: Homosociality and the Pathology of Manhood," *Critical Inquiry* (spring 1989), vol. 15.

70. See Louise DeSalvo, "Lighting the Cave: The Relationship Between Vita Sackville-West and Virginia Woolf," *Signs* (1982), 8(2):195–214.

71. Elaine Marks, "Lesbian Intertextuality," in Elaine Marks and George Stambolian, eds., *Homosexualities and French Literature* (Ithaca, N.Y.: Cornell University Press, 1979), pp. 353–77.

72. See Zimmerman, "What Has Never Been"; Whitlock, " 'A Martyr Reluctantly Canonised' "; and Farwell, "Toward a Definition of the Lesbian Literary Imagination."

73. Biddy Martin, "Lesbian Identity and Autobiographical Difference[s]," in Bella Brodzki and Celeste Schenck, *Life/Lines: Theorizing Women's Autobiography* (Ithaca, N.Y.: Cornell University Press, 1988), pp. 78, 79.

74. *Ibid.*, p. 103. For a discussion of issues of identity in gay and lesbian politics see Steven Epstein, "Gay Politics and Ethnic Identity: The Limits of Social Constructionism," *Socialist Review* (May–August 1987), nos. 93–94, pp. 9–54.

75. Djuna Barnes, *Ladies Almanack* (New York: Harper and Row, 1972), p. 34.

76. Teresa de Lauretis, "Sexual Indifference and Lesbian Representation," *Theatre Journal* (May 1988), 40(2):155.

77. Zimmerman, "What Has Never Been," p. 208.

78. See Farwell, "Toward a Definition of the Lesbian Literary Imagination."

79. De Lauretis, *Technologies of Gender*, p. 10.

80. Woolf, *The Diary of Virginia Woolf*, 3:131.

81. Woolf, *Orlando*, p. 113.

82. See Sherron E. Knopp, " 'If I Saw You Would You Kiss Me?': Sapphism and the Subversiveness of Virginia Woolf's *Orlando*," *PMLA* (January 1988), 103(1):24–34.

83. Ellen Bayuk Rosenman, "Sexual Identity and *A Room of One's Own*: 'Secret Economies' in Virginia Woolf's Feminist Discourse," *Signs* (spring 1989), 14 (3):505–634.

84. Rosenman, "Sexual Identity," p. 643.

85. De Lauretis, "Sexual Indifference and Lesbian Representation," p. 159.

# FIVE

## PERSONAL REFLECTIONS

*The political is personal and the personal is political. The writers in this section, either looking back on different political times or reflecting on changes today, assess issues from their own personal perspectives.*

*Robert Rosen questions what it means to be a "radical" teacher while considering the activism of the 1960s and his own teaching experience today. Robert Rich—which, as the writer notes, is a "pseudonym of a teacher at a large western university"—attacks what he sees as repression, cynicism, and paranoia in the academy today. Lillian Robinson, who was one of the original contributors to The Politics of Literature, considers her articles then and now and their respective political atmospheres. Susan O'Malley uses the college experiences of her own daughter as a springboard to discuss her teaching and her students twenty years ago and today. The final essay here is by Louis Kampf who, in a sardonic, fictionalized piece, portrays the machinations of an English department involved in a tenure decision.*

# 13

## Politics and Literature, Then and Now

Robert C. Rosen

A few years ago a student, a serious English major, asked me if I had a copy of the second volume of *The Norton Anthology of English Literature*. I dug up the only copy of this imposing text that I could find, an old one that I had worked my way through during the summer of 1970 in order to prepare myself for graduate school, which I was then about to begin. Upon returning the book the student said, with a meaningful smile, "I found your comments in the margins *very* interesting." That evening, when I had time to flip through the book (which I hadn't opened for at least a decade), I was a bit embarrassed to find that, next to some of the more conservative editorial prefaces and lines of poetry, I had scrawled "elitist pig," "up yours," "off the pig," "fuck you," and the like.

This was not a case of the dignified professor blushingly found out to have once been young and angry—for I'm hardly formal in the classroom. Rather, I was embarrassed for having given vent to feelings that my students today, although themselves young and often angry, would find totally alien, even incomprehensible. Reading my own comments through a student's eyes, I felt like a relic from another era. My students's angers (and enthusiasms) are almost never explicitly political, and certainly don't focus on the politics of literature. Reading my comments, in truth with more amusement than embarrassment, reminded me once again of the differences, in my experience at least, between the late 1960s—the time that gave rise to *The Politics of Literature*—and today. What follows is a brief discussion of my own experiences than and now, which I hope will suggest some of the problems facing literature teachers who were shaped by the 1960s and are teaching in the 1990s.

For me, literature itself as much as the radical politics of the 1960s came as a revelation. From grade school through my junior year at MIT, I had been traveling a very narrow path toward a career as a mathematician. Life as a math (or science, or engineering) student at MIT was, for me and many others, particularly stunting and repressive, immersed as we were in an institutional culture that was intensely competitive, that prized individual performance and efficiency, that distrusted disorder and emotion, that told us there was nothing reason could not do, that encouraged us to view life as a series of discrete problems to be solved one at a time, and that, as I later understood, was shaped by the values of business and the military. Like most others, I had bought into that culture, those values, and suppressed whatever part of myself I had to in order to continue.

But then two things—literature and the student movement—came together for me and changed the way I thought. Literature I'd barely noticed during the first two decades of my life, but in the courses I began to take I suddenly found a serious exploration of human feelings and values, a consideration of more meaningful questions than those on last week's physics homework, and a challenge to the dehumanizing values implicit in what I had been learning and doing. And in the student movement growing around me I discovered an irresistible critique of the alienation and oppression I'd felt as a student, an extension of that critique to society as a whole, and a promise of personal "liberation" and social change.

Those were heady days indeed: demonstrating against MIT war research, challenging racism (and sometimes sexism), "smashing" imperialism, and so on. Words like *Marxism* and *revolution* possessed a magic quality; just speaking them we felt defiant and powerful. Our optimism and what seemed like daring were rooted in part in our privilege. Our elite education ensured that we would land on our feet; but our feelings were genuine, and we did make a difference. For me, literature was central to all this; I was fortunate in my teachers and my courses, and the feelings and the politics came together in what we read and discussed. The political was very personal.

Aglow with enthusiasm, I decided that I would become a literature, not a math, professor. I would teach about people and values, not numbers and functions; I would face my students, not the blackboard; I would serve "the people," not "the military industrial complex." Criticizing in the morning, teaching in the afternoon, demonstrating in the evening, preparing classes after dinner (to mangle Marx)—I would lead a varied yet integrated life. Inspired by teachers like Louis Kampf—although I think he slept late and did criticism at night—I applied to graduate school in English and began with great hope.

Graduate school was a rude awakening (and also a soporific). Revolution gave way to restoration, excitement to boredom. Though Rutgers was more alive than many places, graduate school proved deadly dull; literary study, I learned, was not inherently radical, or even necessarily interesting. The formalist critical approach that reigned at Rutgers allowed me to hide the meagerness of my literary background, but New Criticism also took the life out of literature for me. It isolated literature from history, biography, politics; at times I felt that I might as well have been studying differential equations. Despite the friendship of two or three progressive teachers, I often thought of quitting. But when I finally got the chance to teach, had the freedom to try to work out in class the connections between literature and politics that I had found so clear and compelling as an undergraduate, I knew I would finish.

Now, in 1990, I am beginning my thirteenth year at William Paterson College part of the New Jersey state system. Most of my students live at home, work hard to pay for their education, and have parents who did not go to college; I enjoy their lack of affectation, their irreverent humor, their low tolerance for "bullshit" (including mine), and their real appreciation, and surprise, when a teacher seems to take them seriously and care. Those few students who major in English are often especially interesting; it takes a rebel of sorts to do so in the face of so much pressure to study something more "practical," like marketing or accounting.

But being a "radical teacher" is complicated. Without a student movement outside the classroom to give them life, the issue we talk about in class can easily become abstract, unreal. In discussing a novel or story students may readily acknowledge, or begin to grapple with questions of social injustice (although often not racism), but their interest and understanding quickly dissipate in the absence of any visible movement for social change. In addition, they lack many of the options for personal change that I had as an undergraduate; times are tougher now than in the expanding 1960s; my students' positions in the social hierarchy are very different than mine was; if they take risks, they are not necessarily going to land on their feet. Their need to understand oppression is no doubt greater than mine was because they are oppressed in ways I never was; but they are less able than I was to act on such understanding. Discussing literature may dramatize social problems, raise essential questions, and open up new realms of feeling and thought for a group of students (as it did for me), but once class is over, they are reimmersed, separately, in the ongoing world of family, work, and mass media, and the critical edge of their thinking and feeling is quickly dulled. (Feminist issues are something of an exception, however; the women's movement has had a wide impact, and the possibilities for change on a personal level—say in relationships for change on a personal level—say in relationships or in career choices—are significant.)

My students have a strong sense of social class difference, for example, and discussion—whether of a work of literature, a Studs Terkel interview, or a student paper in a writing class—frequently comes around (with my help) to the question of class mobility. The consensus, by the end, is usually that mobility is limited, that the children of the poor have little chance of becoming rich, that the Dartmouth classmates of mediocre student Nelson Rockefeller were justified in voting him (as I tell the class) "most likely to succeed." Yet almost invariably our next meeting begins with one student insisting (and others quickly agreeing) that anyone who works hard *can* get ahead in the United States, that how far you go in life is entirely up to *you*. This, of course, is the ideology of the American Dream, disseminated endlessly by the media, which are saturated with individual success (not failure) stories. But I think my students' response derives as much from the reality of their lives as from "brainwashing." For them, the alternative to this kind of hope is resignation; looking around, they see no possibility of fundamental social change. They are in college to get ahead (a real possibility, at least), not to change the world.

So I doubt that many of my students are writing "off the pig"— or rather, with the continuing challenges to the literary canon, "right on!"—in the margins of their books. I often wonder how I seem to them—perhaps as a naive idealist, or an amusing oddball, or a 1960s leftover, or just an easy grader. But good things do happen in class; I do see change in how at least some think about themselves and the world. Occasionally a student will even appear at a demonstration, or join the small radical group on campus. Teaching literature and politics isn't exactly what I had envisioned in the exhilarating late 1960s, but it hasn't been bad and it's not over yet.

# 14

## Somewhere Off the Coast of Academia

### Robert Rich

One arrives on campus and feels as though one has wandered onto a set of *Miami Vice*. One acts accordingly: one reminds oneself that one has the right to remain silent, that anything one says may be used against oneself, and that one has the right to counsel. One says this because one is made to feel like an illegal alien, a smuggler, a criminal, a terrorist, an international dealer in contraband by the Crocketts and the Tubbses of the college, the academicians of law and order, the upholders of the unchanging curriculum and the august ideologues of deceit.

The slightest sign of individual difference draws a show of force. One is constantly watched, followed, under surveillance, and the subject of reports. One's clothes are regarded as a text for interpretation, and analysis is directed toward the hat, or the shirt, or the shoes that one wears. A dress code seems to be deeply embedded in the minds of the department members. To violate the code is to invite a citation. One is pulled over in the corridor, stopped and mentally searched.

Briefcase looks suspiciously heavy. Why so many books? Reading Sartre? Isn't he a bit out of date, old chap? And Simone de Beauvoir— surely you're not bothering with that feminist fraud? Saw your review in the paper Sunday. Can't understand where you find the time to dash those things off. You don't really think Paul Bowles is a major figure, do you? By the way, we would all appreciate it if you'd be a tad more discreet. I personally would enjoy reading a *roman à clef* that deconstructs the inner life of the department, but then I've nothing to hide.

Given the level of surveillance, it's no wonder that so many members of the faculty avoid the corridors entirely, remain behind closed doors, hide in their offices, or travel across campus incognito. The job breeds paranoia and duplicity.

To propose a new course to the curriculum committee is like going before the customs authorities. One is taken into a back room and asked to make a declaration, state where one obtained the goods and how they will be used inside academic borders. If rival operatives are already trading in the same or similar texts, one is often denied a permit to import and distribute. If the material is new and has never been brought to the classroom, there is no guarantee of acceptance either. It may be *too* new, the students may not be ready for it, it may not be right for *our* campus. This is what one continually hears, professors who speak in the name of their students, deciding what they should and should not be reading and thinking, what one should and should not be teaching—and this in the most patronizing manner. One is assumed to be guilty until proven otherwise.

Nothing too new ought to be taught. Everything contemporary is superficial, trendy, lacking in seriousness. One doesn't want to pander to current trends, and one doesn't want to be too popular with one's students. It certainly isn't professional. One must watch those reading lists carefully since they may be held against one, especially when one wants tenure, promotion, awards, recognition of services. So one mustn't assign anything feminist unless one has the proper biological credentials. Nothing by an Asian unless one is Asian, because how could one know how an Asian looks at the world. One hears colleagues confess, I could never teach Herman Melville—he's so phallic; I could never teach Emily Dickinson—she's so prissy. Nadine Gordimer in a course on African literature? Why, she's white and Jewish. Chinua Achebe—he's a professional black man, not a writer. Joe Orton. Didn't know you went that way. One's reading list is taken to be a confession of one's inner life. One betrays oneself simply by reading or assigning the wrong books.

The academic world is divided, conquered, ghettoized. One has one's territory. One is given a piece of the turf, and one ought to be grateful, stay within it, exploit its resources to the fullest, and respect boundaries. One ought to be satisfied with one's own intellectual fix. If one wanders into protected zones the law is called. Write an essay in a field that is regarded as foreign to one's own, and one is accused of trespassing, of violating basic trading agreements.

Negotiations are eternal. One goes to a department meeting as though to a gathering of rival Mafiosi. There is always an atmosphere of intrigue and secrecy. The hidden agenda is the order of the day. One never reveals one's hand. Alliances are formed, agreements are reached, and one is bound to say nothing in public, but rather to smile, to shake so and so's hand, to compliment him or her on a brilliant lecture. Flattery and bribery buy space in which to operate one's own syndicate.

Cynicism is endemic to the system. One hears the sound of hopelessness in one's colleagues' voices. There are continual verbal assaults on students. They are stupid, one is told. They have never heard of Virginia Woolf, or James Joyce. They do not know about the war in Vietnam, or the Rosenberg case. And their writing. What an atrocity! They misspell words, make grammatical errors, refuse to have a thesis sentence. But one puts up with them, one tries, one tolerates, one makes sacrifices, one endures. Of course, next semester everything will be different. The department has announced a war on ignorance, and indifference, and sloth. An expert from outside has been hired. The mess will be cleaned up. The problem will be solved. In fact, the report has already been written that describes the actions taken by representatives of the Enforcement Agency. The university is making progress; it is working with industry and serving the community. Learning is going on and the time of troubles is behind us. Fortunately, there are no more experimental courses, and no more deviants. The political contamination has been averted and the area is now sanitized. Teachers and students can return to the work of education, and careers are waiting in the real world.

In this situation one can't help but be a criminal. One likes the adventure and the risk taking. One wants to smuggle ideas and values and books through customs, and under the ever vigilant eyes of Professors Crockett and Tubbs. One enjoys being part of a conspiracy with one's students, who are always eager for subterranean connections. Nothing overt need be said. There is always an underground, always a tacit understanding, a knowing look exchanged by the fugitive members of the group. One knows too that there are allies in the higher echelons. True, one might be set up; one must be on guard against informers, agents, double agents. One learns to recognize opportunists, to detect the careerist who uses the rhetoric of the union, feminism, Marxism, or postmodernism to advance his or her career.

One hones one's skills. One learns to use language in a political context. One understands the need to employ parable, to write a subtext, to insinuate, to wear a mask, to develop a persona, to become

a ventriloquist. In opposition one becomes creative, inventive, inge-
nious. One recapitulates the history of literature, locates the
groundsprings of cultural resistance, and situates oneself in a tradition of rebellion. One realizes that if the university is to renew itself,
to have even the pretense of scholarship, it needs the intellectual
smuggler, the pirate on the high seas of academia. One makes it clear
that one writes one's own dialogue, creates one's own part, that the
series is ongoing, and that the last scenes will unfold spontaneously.
In spite of, or perhaps because of, the level of hypocrisy and cynicism
in the university one works for integrity and a sense of dignity. One
strives to create an atmosphere in which others can express themselves. One aims to undermine the paternalism of the institution, and
to bring individuals out from behind the bureaucratic screen.

The 1980s have been, at least from this perspective, a wonderful
time in which to teach. Resources have been limited, but possibilities
have been tremendous. One has no desire to turn back the clock, to
return to the 1960s or the 1970s, or to any other time or place in the
past. One hopes that the 1990s will not be like the 1960s; one knows
that they will be surprising, and unpredictable, and that is why one
looks forward to the advent of the future. In the repressive atmosphere of the 1980s one has had to learn to be more open, if only for
one's own personal survival. One knows that this is not *the* Age of
Reagan or Bush, that Reagan and Bush have not stamped their like-
nesses on the face of these times, and that the literary and cultural
rhythms of the decade have been laid down by individuals in opposition and dissent.

# 15

## Some Historical Refractions

### Lillian S. Robinson

*How has it come about that I am (arguably) the only food stamp re-cipient anthologized with Wittgenstein?* This is the question, paren-thetical qualification and all, that I attempted to answer in one of the papers I was scheduled to give at a recent MLA meeting. Signif-icantly, it was part of a panel on "the generation gap" in feminist criticism. My other offering that year was a version of the article re-printed earlier in this volume. It is hard to avoid seeing a connection between the two—in my experience, as well as on the MLA meeting program—and to bring both of them to bear on my understanding of what has happened between the last volume entitled *The Politics of Literature* and the present one.

In the fall of 1968 I wrote an essay called "Who's Afraid of *A Room of One's Own?*" whose personal and intellectual context, from the Vietnam War to the nascent women's movement to my dissertation block to the search for my first teaching job is outlined in the intro-duction to my book *Sex, Class, and Culture.* In that introduction I at-tempted, ten years ago, to critique its assumptions and method. What struck me most in looking at "Who's Afraid" from the perspective of the late 1970s was the ease with which, following Woolf herself, I was able to take for granted that social and literary theory were equiva-lent and that, therefore, in building an argument about women and fiction, I would necessarily be saying something not at all fictive about women.

And there, of course, is the answer to my first question. At precisely the moment at which literary feminists were poised to embrace a (sea-changed version of) French theory into their work and, needless to say, their discourse, I was assuming that the first decade of women's studies pointed us to quite different conclusions. My approach was not only materialist rather than idealist, but turned resolutely and overtly away from the new feminist materialism without Marxism and the new literary Marxism without Marx. If I had only followed up on the assumptions of that first essay, I would (again, arguably) not be left in my middle age naked to mine enemies—or at least so firmly and securely out of it all.

Another less solipsistic way of looking at the question is in terms of the political background of my essays for the *Politics of Literature* and this volume as well. From this perspective, the earlier one has an energy, an essential optimism derived from the sense—hell, the untroubled conviction—that it and I were caught up together in the main current of history. "Who's Afraid" comes out of and assumes a movement, one in which the struggle for women's liberation would play an organic and inevitable part. What is more, the university, however sharp my institutional critique and however ambivalent my relationship to it, was clearly a center of the historical forces I believed were in motion.

But "Who's Afraid" is not only or even chiefly a contribution to social analysis. It is a work of feminist literary criticism. Yet, although all three of those words certainly existed in 1968, no one was putting them together to characterize a body of work. As for women's studies, that term would have been equally novel, seen, perhaps, as a crude analogy to (even a parody of) black studies, and set off between quotation marks.

To describe the state of my global political expectations in 1968 is also to imply their defeat; everyone knows it didn't happen as I anticipated, although there are many different interpretations of what did happen and is happening instead. Similarly, any reference to a time when women's studies and feminist criticism were so new as still to be unnamed is freighted with two subsequent decades of intellectual history.

So "Who's Afraid of *A Room of One's Own?*" was written at the height of a radical movment, but in the absence of a tradition or even a concept of feminist criticism, whereas "Canon Fathers and Myth Universe" was written at a time of intense political frustration (look, I crossed out seventeen other nouns before letting that one stand), but in the context of a varied and growing feminist critical experience. The consequences for what I write—what I am *able* to write—are apparent: "Canon Fathers" certainly takes a very wide range of theoretical and social issues as the proper purview of feminist studies in literature, but it does not venture into the even wider realms of social analysis and strategy. On the other hand, it presupposes and indeed could not have been written without the development and achievements of feminist literary criticism.

In 1969, when "Who's Afraid" was accepted for eventual publication in the first *Politics of Literature*, an old-line university press like Columbia's would not have considered such a volume. (At least, it had nothing remotely similar on its list and no series into which it might fit.) In 1990, a commercial publisher like Random House, whose Pantheon division brought out the Kampf-Lauter collection in its "antitexts" series, would not, I suspect, seriously consider its successor. It would be pleasant to think that this was a tradeoff without any particular consequences or implications, but there is a politics as well as a sociology to *this* aspect of literature, too. At best it means that as people like the contributors to these two collections, both in their persons and in their ideas, have ceased to represent a material threat to the academic world, some of them have been granted a more secure foothold within academic institutions—although, as the off-campus world moves further to the right, we have less access to the means of influencing it.

In my own case, however, the person and the ideas are by no means encountering the same fate. Feminist criticism is thriving; it is widely, although by no means universally, regarded as the cutting edge of contemporary literary thought. And my own work, unfashionable though it may be, has a certain place within it. I continue to be solicited for articles, reviews, speaking engagements. My writing gets published and reprinted, and some readers like it. But, without a regular academic position or an independent source of income, I lack the minimal conditions for continued academic production.

So am I really on food stamps? Not at the moment, although I have been in the past. In fact, my teaching and writing are currently supported by an endowed chair, and I am still sufficiently in touch with reality to distinguish between the two conditions. But unemployment is the only condition in which I may be said to have tenure.

Is this confession pertinent to the changes that have occurred on the political scene or in my own work since the first *Politics of Literature* was conceived? I think that it is, not only because of the vulgar materialist issue of who's free to write what about the politics of literature, but because of the larger cultural and social issues my story suggests. Things have changed and not, overall, for the better, yet various versions of radical and feminist criticism are more accepted and more influential than anyone twenty years ago could have imagined—particularly had we also been able to envision this gloomy historical context. It is worth pondering these developments and their possible impact on the *kind* of criticism—even the kind of radical or feminist criticism—we do.

# 16

## What Has Happened to the Seeds of the Flower Children?

**Susan Gushee O'Malley**

Curled up on my daughter's messy bed at Delta Sig, a fraternity at Bowdoin College, the raucous music of the Grateful Dead blasting below, I am amazed at how college has changed in twenty-three years. I have just finished reading the syllabus for her women's history course and have closed the door tightly to my daughter's male roommate's quarters to contemplate the differences between the students of the 1960s (my generation) and those of the 1980s. Obviously, the dormitory rules have changed. And my daughter will be considerably in debt from her undergraduate education, which will influence what she does upon graduation. But I find myself defending this generation against my colleagues' laments that the present generation is apolitical and concerned only with themselves. Granted I am biased, as I have raised two children of this generation (my son won't graduate until the 1990s, so I won't talk about him), but so have many of my radical 1960s friends whose offspring are engaged in political activity at many college campuses.

Perhaps the most startling difference I find between my generation and today's is the absence of rules. In the early 1960s at Smith College men were allowed in our rooms three times a year if we kept the door open and had a collective three feet on the floor. Male roommates and the indescribably filthy bathrooms at Delta Sig were inconceivable. The room inspector fined us weekly if our rooms were not clean; we had to be in our dormitories by 11 P.M. every evening except for weekends, when we were allowed to stay out until midnight on Friday and 1 A.M. on Saturday (I was always having to appear in front of House Council for coming in late); and quiet was to be maintained at all times. Smith undergraduates were also not allowed to spend the night away within a thirty-mile radius of the college, except for Amherst prom weekend. Our reputations were to be maintained.

*In loco parentis* is no longer the role of a college. This turn of events is the result of our protesting in the 1960s. Although the change is a major one, I find it refreshing because students now can control their personal lives. The most difficult part of Smith College for me was adjusting to all of the rules. But if I were an undergraduate today, I'm not sure that I could find the space and calm to study as many hours as we did as undergraduates in the early 1960s. In fact, the *Wall Street Journal* (May 21, 1987) reports that students at SUNY Brockport have asked the administration to provide a traditional dormitory "with required study hours, mandatory visitor sign-in, and no alcohol." Meanwhile, I sleep in my daughter's bed while she spends the night with her boyfriend within a thirty-mile radius of Bowdoin.

In contrast to the absence of parietal rules is the return of more distribution courses. Except for Brown University, where students may take whatever they want, most colleges, influenced by the back-to-basics movement and Allan Bloom's *The Closing of the American Mind*, have started to beef up their requirements. At Smith in the 1960s there were few: one year of calculus (or science), one year of freshman English, one term of French literature, one term of classics, and the rest were mine to choose. Except for calculus, I did not find such courses an interruption to my learning. Of course, I also had to take three terms of physical education, swim across the pool, and pass my posture pictures (these were nude photographs taken of us twice during our college career.)

Today students in most colleges have many more required courses. At best these can expose the student to ideas and disciplines that she has not previously considered; at worst the course becomes a watered-down "gut" course taken only to fulfill the requirement. Core curricula that are being imposed at some of the campuses of the City University of New York can be even more oppressive. Brooklyn College has a required thirty-four-hour core that, with the exception of one course, ignores the history and literature of people of color.

Money is also a factor. Smith College had in the 1960s cost about one-seventh of what college costs today. When my daughter graduates from Bowdoin, she could be over $10,000 in debt to the government and many thousands of dollars in debt to Bowdoin. If she goes to graduate school, her debt will be significantly greater. She will have to start paying back these debts six months after she completes her education. Teaching part time and doing unpaid political work will not be an option for her. Students today increasingly have to consider securing high-paying jobs immediately after their schooling to pay back their loans, unless they come from upper-income families. There is no time to travel, to work in Nicaragua, to spend a year writing a novel, or to attempt being an artist. The writer ends up writing public relations material; the artist lands in advertising.

Also, the student who knows that his parents are paying so much money for his education often becomes intolerant of his professors. "Spending six classes talking about carnival in Brazil was a waste of my time and my parents' money," a Bowdoin student said to me about a required course in interdisciplinary non-Western studies. He was impatient at having been forced to take this "foreign studies" course. Looking at the predominantly white student population at Bowdoin, I applaud the requirement of such a course and the finding of a black feminist to teach it, but I worry about such a vehement response. Students whose parents pay such outrageous tuitions may feel that they can treat their professors as servants. And the faculty teaching the wealthy often resent and put down their students politically without listening first and nurturing the ones with political consciences. My daughter has often expressed dismay at the arrogance of faculty who assume she comes from a wealthy family and has conservative politics.

But I admire my daughter's clear-sightedness and common sense about politics. In her sophomore year she cochaired the Bowdoin Women's Association, helped design the women's studies major and defend it against gender studies, and founded the Nicaragua support group. Outraged, she called me one night to complain that she had to justify to the faculty the legitimacy of women's studies rather than spend her time designing the curriculum. "Isn't that silly?" she said. "They should explain to me why they don't have a women's studies program instead of wasting my time." Another night she called to tell me that she had organized an event at which a lesbian photographer spoke. "The place was mobbed," she told me proudly. "I'm such a good organizer." I resisted the impulse to say, "Of course you are. You are my daughter." Her response to that would have been "Oh, you are such a sixties parent," a type my children and their friends often discuss.

The difference between campus political activities in the 1960s and today was the Vietnam War. Subie, one of my daughter's friends and one of the main organizers of the Left on campus, wistfully told me,

"But you had so much to rebel against: all those rules and the Vietnam War." My daughter feels that the war and those turbulent times gave my generation more of a focus. Her work is more fragmented. She spent more time with women's issues because of the need for and possibility of establishing the women's studies major. Then she would try to keep the Nicaragua Support Group going and attend Struggle and Change meetings. But then what about apartheid? Although Struggle and Change functions as an umbrella organization, the issues for her were not clearly connected. For us the movement was all-encompassing; it was our reason for existence. Today's students seem to have politics more in perspective, which may mean that they will be able to sustain their political activity instead of getting burned out or feeling bitter.

Now there is minimal faculty support for such activity. According to my daughter, faculty brag about not failing anyone in the 1960s, thus keeping male students from getting drafted; but if she were to miss any work for political reasons, she feels that her professors would not support her. Students have to support themselves now. As she put it, the head of Struggle and Change, who lived across the hall from her, would "tuck me in at night and ask me how my organizing had gone during the day."

To compare my students of the 1960s with my students in the 1980s is difficult. In the 1960s I taught at Tulane, a southern, elite, white, male university. In 1966 I started teaching as a graduate assistant at Tulane. Those were heady political days. I took my involvement with the antiwar movement very seriously. We had day-long teach-ins, endless vigils, marches, and guerilla theater happenings disrupting ROTC practices. Richard Schechner, head of the *Tulane Drama Review*, led us in maneuvers against ROTC drills, using his undergraduate ROTC training at Cornell. As I was very round-bellied with my daughter, whose conception has been sped up to keep her father out of the Vietnam War, I was in great demand for peace activities. My students, who were 98 percent male, often wore their ROTC uniforms to class to irritate their earnest young lecturer; intense arguments followed.

In retrospect what felt different in those days was that a political movement existed that influenced what went on in the classroom. In New Orleans there were civil rights issues. We were involved in protesting against teachers who made black students sit in the back rows of some high school classrooms, getting the Justice Department to close restaurants that refused to serve blacks and whites together, reopening integrated swimming pools, electing the first black to the school board, and challenging racist housing practices. There were protests supporting the Chicago Eight after the Democratic convention in 1968; from 1969 onward there was a women's movement that totally encompassed our lives; a free school movement, in which my commune (by this time I was living in a political commune with my two children and husband) started a school; the Black Panther movement, in which our support group—many of whom had been politically involved for years—worked to keep the Panthers from being slaughtered by the local police. All of this could and often was brought into my classroom.

After having taught as a full-time faculty member at Tulane from 1967–1968, I decided to return to part-time teaching to finish my dissertation and to have time for politics and children. Those were the days when faculty gave up jobs because there were plenty available.

Now I teach at Kingsborough Community College in the City University of New York (CUNY) system. I continually bring into the curriculum works by women, people of color, and the working class, and inform everything I teach with an awareness of gender, race, and class. I'm known as a socialist who is ready to encourage political activism and as someone who believes in the possibilities of students organizing to change their lives. This is probably most apparent in my journalism classes and in the two weeks of women's history programs we do each year. Among the faculty, a colleague and I have organized a pedagogy group that has given some professors the courage to change how they teach by paying more attention to the needs of the students in front of them.

My students at Kingsborough are urban and working-class, ranging in age from seventeen to eighty-five. They are black, white, Asian, and Latino, and for the most part highly uneducated. In the 1960s, before open admissions, these students would not have been in college. Even with these differences, I do not sense that students have changed much in twenty years. What has changed is the political climate and the strength of the political movement outside of the classroom. Students are probably less outraged at the lying and corruption of the government than were my students in the 1960s, but part of that is a class difference. The working class is less surprised at corruption of the government than is the upper class. But more to the point, there is no Vietnam War to protest. The mainstream media has been reticent in reporting the horrors of American foreign policy, and there is a desire among Americans to believe in the strength and rightness of the United States. Combined with the struggle of my students to maintain minimum economic security, there is little desire to question the wrongs of the government. We now know that as many as three thousand CUNY students are homeless (*Newsday*, May 23 1986, p. 3), and a large number are single mothers on welfare. For them, the first generation of their families to be college educated, there is much to lose.

But when I compare my political students in the 1990s with those in the 1960s, have they really changed? This year two students, Greg, a black Vietnam veteran from Coney Island, who lectured to my classes on the horrors and contradictions of Vietnam, and Scott, an Italian from Canarsie, who led the defense of the college newspaper against censorship by the administration, gave me sustenance. Last year Margie, in her work with the peace movement and the antiapartheid movement, inspired me. She reminded me of Ann and Jimmy who in 1968 led SDS and the antiwar movement at Tulane, and who Tulane tried to expel (and who I defended as a young faculty member). These students gave and continue to give me hope.

The role of a college may have changed; certainly students are more in debt, and the working class is receiving more education than in the 1960s, but what has changed most is the political movement outside of the academy. My observation is that there is less focus for student activism but much more political activity on campuses than most people realize. Tired of being trashed as the apathetic generation, my daughter and her friends agree.

# 17

# Annals of Academic Life: An Exemplary Tale

**Louis Kampf**

The narrator of the following vignette is not to be mistaken for the author. Although the tale appears to be autobiographical, it must be a fiction. Academic institutions, as we know, are the repositories of rationality. Professors have been bequeathed the patrimony of the Enlightenment. Such evidence indicates that the events described below could not possibly have happened.

The faces are those of ten-year-olds playacting at seriousness. They belong to my colleagues, the tenured members of the English department. Alas, their performance is not staged for the benefit of parents at a grade school's annual Christmas play.

"It's the most agonizing decision I've ever had to make," mumbles Remington. I look for a trace of irony in his face, but find only the grimness of domestic tragedy. He runs his fingers through his neatly trimmed hair, directs the hint of a boyish smile my way, and lets his almost double chin sink onto the knot of his tie. Seated around the oval seminar table, his colleagues nod their heads knowingly. They too are in pain. Their brows are furrowed, their lips tightly shut, their eyes intently fixed on stacks of recommendations ominously marked "confidential."

"I've been up most of the night," Remington continues, "and though I really like Leah, I cannot approve of her scholarly methods. When

Reprinted by permission from *Radical Teacher*, vol. 21.

she quotes from original manuscript sources it's done in the original spelling. This is very misleading for future scholars. She really should modernize the spelling." I'm facing Remington and begin to smile. I'd really like to double over with laughter, but Leah Scott's future is at stake, so I control myself. I glance at my colleagues. Maybe— just maybe—someone will giggle. No. Lips are even more compressed, brows more deeply furrowed. Remington does not respond to my smile. He plays obsessively with the buttons on the vest of his double-knit suit. Leah Scott's many publications—two books, articles, reviews, editions—lie scattered around the table. They draw little attention as this gathering of scholars arduously culls nasty little snippets from the file of confidential recommendations. My colleagues, after six hours of squeezing out scholarly reflections as profound as Remington's, vote to deny Leah Scott tenure.

That morning I had gone through my breakfast ritual of envisioning apocalypse. The newspapers were my book of visions: murder and destruction in El Salvador, the planned deployment of nuclear missiles, starvation in East Timor, a rape in my neighborhood, Reagan's cutback of medical services for old people. Death, destruction, and meanspiritedness on a global scale. Neither my heart nor brain found much room for worries about Leah. After all, nearly everyone (except Leah) had known for at least two years that she would be fired. My colleagues could not officially say that a feminist doing women's studies was not to be taken seriously, but reasons would be found. And we shall sit around a table (do they sit around similar tables in the Pentagon, I wonder) and apply our collective interest to finding them. Six hours that might be spent on halting nuclear madness; on enlightening students; on enjoying oneself; on acts of generosity. As I savor the flavor of a particularly tart grapefruit, I know what the scene will be, and I can barely get myself in motion toward school.

Six hours! I walk into the meeting room beginning to feel ashamed of my revulsion. It's not six hours on an assembly line. It's not six hours correcting compositions. It's not six hours spent preparing lectures about books I do not want to teach. In fact, while several of my friends are unemployed, I have a plush job at an elite institution. I teach what I want to teach. There's an occasional struggle over that, but since I'm tenured I can afford to put up a fight against pesky requests from the curriculum committee, and usually get my way. My hours are not overly long. I have a sense of my own competence as a teacher, and my students, who are mostly intelligent and nice, respond to me in class. I have a good time with them, and some learning does go on. In various pockets around the school there are a few faculty members I respect and have affection for. Working with them enlarges my spirit. They have supported me when I was in trouble, and they will do so again. We have enjoyed each other's company at lunch, across a seminar table, at demonstrations, and in jail. I teach at an elite institution that is involved in the monstrosities I read about at breakfast, yet I enjoy the comfort of doing political work with comrades in the school's socialist group.

But on this particular morning I would rather stay home and vacuum the living room rug.

I creep away from the meeting. My brain, I am convinced, will never again formulate a coherent idea. Clarity is my goddess; at the moment, I cannot envision her. In an hour I shall be teaching "Contemporary Issues in Politics and Ideology" to students who would like to do something decent with their lives. We'll discuss underdevelopment in Central America, and how to support the popular forces in El Salvador. I feel in communion with these young people. Their concern pricks my conscience. Soon their expectant looks will fill me with anxiety: they hope for so much more than the mechanical transfer of knowledge. How can I possibly meet their expectations? Perhaps I can't. But right now anxiety fuels my desire to make the attempt. When I walk into class I shall be a teacher, not an educational bureaucrat; the professor will feel connected to the rest of me. Meanwhile, Leah stays on my mind.

I glance at some lecture notes, but memory interferes and reaches back to the 1960s. Here is what I see:

Remington, a new instructor, has a beard so scraggly it looks like it's been pasted on. Unkempt hair hangs down to his shoulders. His smile hints irony but still tells me he is alive with passion. While he was in graduate school, Remington was arrested twice for participating in sit-ins. Since coming here he has given much of his time to working with antiwar groups. Remington's outrageous sense of humor gives his militance a rare ebullience. He can double me over with laughter while we're trying to dodge a tactical policeman's oversized club. His inventiveness is at the edge of the surreal, spilling out ideas, wisecracks, analyses of Shakespeare or Dylan. His freakiness is tempered by an unfailing rationality.

Where have you gone, Remington? "I do not believe in equal opportunity curricula," he told me a few days ago, when I asked him why there were no women authors in the "Masterpieces of Western

Literature" course. Remington does scholarship so wretchedly conventional, so dull, that it nearly embarrassed the administration into
denying him tenure. As head of the curriculum committee he worries
whether "Popular Narrative" might be used as a catalogue entry for
both "Science Fiction" and "Fantasy Fiction." How does he shut off
his imagination? Why doesn't he explode? No doubt, he has attained
the peace that passeth understanding, since God is a living presence
for those who follow acceptable scholarly procedures. Such peace-
fulness allows him to deny Leah tenure for using early English spelling.

Only half an hour until I am restored by the "Politics and Ideology"
class. But my musings have nearly turned that prospect to ashes. What
am I really doing in that class? Anything more than providing future
Remingtons with a little room to breathe? Right now I do not want
to be here. My institutional life, after all, is composed of more than
the few hours I spend in class. Leah will appeal her firing, and I shall
have to work in her support. More meetings. Political struggles quicken
my pulse, and ordinarily make me feel as if I'm giving history a small
shove. But there is no joy in butting heads with my colleagues; they
simply won't butt. No issue is ever met head on, and I find myself
haggling not over ideas or values, but over formalities. If Leah's head
is to be saved from the chopping block, it will be by the grace of the
good god Procedure. I know: a democracy can work only if consistent
procedures are applied equally to all. And so I'll spar with my colleagues in this ghostly match where all is form and nothing substance; where a real issue—contempt for feminist scholarship—will
have to be ignored; where neither they nor I will say what we think
of each other. Although furious with myself for hiding, I maintain a
politic silence. The faces of nearly all of the men seated around the
table are hidden behind neatly trimmed beards. The features of one
colleague, a woman, are masked by a permanent smile which threatens to crack her jaw; I'm sure it will be there the moment Bush pushes
the atomic button. We are the guardians of the eternal verities, yet
never speak our private truths. I'm part of the act, a performer playing to the demands of institutional life.

I look at my watch. Sixteen minutes until class starts. I try to put
my opening remarks together, but my thoughts fade to Saul Durling,
one of my bearded colleagues with tenure. Saul looks like an obsessed
Hasid lost in the Ivy League. Several years ago, while being interviewed for his job, he sidled up to me, and in a staccato jabber con-
fided that he had been heavily influenced by my writing. What, I

wondered, have I wrought? "Perhaps too heavily," he added mysteriously. Soon after he got hired, he came into my office, closed the door ostentatiously, and urged me to teach black studies. He assured me that I could do it a lot better than any black person the department might hire. "I would be very offended," he explained, "if I were forbidden to teach Milton because I'm Jewish." I began to argue, but stopped in mid-sentence. He knew what I would say; I knew what he would say; we would dance our dance and I would be left in a rage. "Hear me," he nagged, "I often feel that you're not discussing these very serious matters with me. At least (grinning) you should tell me I'm full of shit." I yielded: "All right, you're full of shit."

I look back and wonder about my passivity. I avoided the argument because Durling's intellectual stance, his very personality, offend my sense of what a literary intellectual ought to be. With great hesitation I decided to become a teacher of literature and ideas because I believed that intellectuals spend their time not dancing verbal dances, but moving ideas and history forward. What is the point of one more stupid academic hassle? My inspiration had come from Alexander Herzen's memoirs, from Diderot, from Virginia Woolf's literary essays and reviews. And there I was about to turn an important issue into academic nitpicking with Durling.

I feel depressed. Poor me. I have a nifty little job at a big famous place, but I feel depressed. A contradiction. For years I've written articles telling people that universities are not the guardians of the critical tradition of the Enlightenment, but the ideological servants of ruling elites. So why do I act as if it's news? When I have to deal with this truism in the flesh and bones of my professional life, I nearly boil over with resentment.

I go off to class. Students scramble by me in the halls. One who has the maddened eyes of Alexander Haig tries to stare me down. I wonder how many will comply with the planning of nuclear holocaust or the economic strangulation of millions. How can I, a teacher, hope to change this? What impact can even the best course have? My depression deepens as I walk into class. On this particular day, teaching these very decent students about political possibilities does not brighten my spirit.

I feel cheated. I began teaching this course, which is not part of the English curriculum, during the 1960s. It had been a small part of the challenge to academic dogma initiated by radical students. Here in this class, I said to myself, I am acting out the role of critical intellectual. I am engaged with the world. These ideas will matter in the struggle for social change because they are being carried on the wave of a great social movement. The students and teachers who were trying to invent a more rational curriculum gave me hope for the possibilities of education. This course is one remnant of that hope. So when the small monstrosities of a departmental meeting dampen my pleasure in feeling like a true heir of the Enlightenment, I feel depressed. This, I tell myself, is not the life I wanted to lead. In spite of my pretensions, I am just one more hod-carrying professor.

The class is over. After several minutes of feigned interest in the students' heated discussion, I wander toward my office. I feel separated from everything around me: people pass me like ghosts; the massive stone buildings seem outlines drawn without perspective. The only reality is a bitter memory: the meeting that decided Leah was a malignancy to be removed. Here are the fruits of the Enlightenment: humanity must be protected against the dangers of improper scholarly procedures.

Having felt dangerously exposed in the classroom, I enter my office like a bird returning to its nest. I sit down on my swivel chair, and whirl around to gaze at the books—shelf on shelf of them. Why don't I give them away? What reassurance do they give me? Do they certify me as a man of deep knowledge? My mocking reflections are interrupted by Samuel Smith, who has just wandered in. Smith is handsome; his eyes are frozen in perpetual amusement; he dresses in discreet versions of the latest styles. He is the only black person in the department. He was hired because Andover, Amherst, and Yale had given him the words my colleagues wanted to hear. He saw the film *Platoon* last night, and wants to discuss its structure of images. I observe that *Platoon* is part of a movement to falsify the history of America's war against Vietnam. He listens patiently, then says he's not really interested in such matters. Smith also has an idealized notion of what a literary intellectual ought to be. It's different from mine. He sees himself as a civilized gentleman discussing the arts, frequenting sophisticated bars, leading a life of elegant comfort. He plays this role well, avoiding the appearance of academic seediness. Hassles over departmental policy buffet his image of the academy as a haven for humanistic literary discourse. His experience in the department has led him to conclude that the academic game isn't worth the effort. In the fall he will begin law school: it takes money to be truly civilized. After three years, the living will be easy. I wonder why Smith seeks me out so often. Is it because for me the living is, in fact, easy? In Smith's eyes I do lead a civilized life. My deepest concern does not seem to be whether the introductory course will be structured around genres or historical periods. Who will be the next department chair? I don't give it much thought. I have tenure, travel, discuss the arts with some knowledge. I am, in short, cultured. No wonder I feel depressed. When Smith leaves for law school will Durling once again ask me to teach black studies?

When I get home I head for the kitchen. After taking my first sip of pernod (did Sartre soothe his nerves similarly after a rough day at the École Normale Supérieure?), I begin the intricate task of preparing dinner. Dicing the eggplant for the pasta sauce, my tension recedes as I look forward to the pleasure of my friends and comrades savoring the robust and complex beauty my labor and the tradition of Sicilian cooking have produced.

After dinner, lingering over a glass of wine, we discuss tomorrow's demonstration in support of the Salvadorian rebels. I find that it takes work to convince myself to go. Each demonstration, each meeting, each phone call urging a friend to sign a petition seems like a distinct event. Each demands a new expense of spiritual energy on my part. No compelling historical design urges me to plunge into the next task. Work in school, I reflect, is just one more piece in the political puzzle I can't put together. Nearly every moment I must convince myself that the academic routine is leading somewhere. Am I really pushing the boulder any further up the hill? Will sitting through one more meeting to save Leah's job make the misshapen colossus where I earn my living a more humane workplace? I think so. But then I don't feel sure. Doesn't the battle (grandiose word!) involve a small attempt to control the conditions of my work? It does. But since I teach at an elite institution, there is no union. So the battle over someone's job is carried on in near isolation; it threatens to turn me into a crank. Meanwhile, there is the demonstration I might be working on.

I swallow the last bit of wine. The dishes need to be washed. There is a class to prepare, an essay to be polished, a phone call to be made to a friend about the demonstration. If I do my work with resolution, there might be time to catch a late movie.

# Index